THE POEMS OF
JOHN DRYDEN

THE POEMS OF
JOHN DRYDEN

EDITED BY

JAMES KINSLEY

VOLUME III

OXFORD
AT THE CLARENDON PRESS
1958

Oxford University Press, Amen House, London E.C.4

GLASGOW NEW YORK TORONTO MELBOURNE WELLINGTON
BOMBAY CALCUTTA MADRAS KARACHI KUALA LUMPUR
CAPE TOWN IBADAN NAIROBI ACCRA

PRINTED IN GREAT BRITAIN

CONTENTS

VOLUME III

THE WORKS OF VIRGIL

TO THE MOST HONOURABLE
John, Lord Marquess of *Normanby*,
EARL of *MULGRAVE*, &c. AND Knight of
the *Most Noble Order of the Garter*

A HEROICK Poem, truly such, is undoubtedly the greatest Work which the Soul of Man is capable to perform. The Design of it, is to form the Mind to Heroick Virtue by Example; 'tis convey'd in Verse, that it may delight, while it instructs: The Action of it is always one, entire, and great. The least and most trivial Episodes, or under- 5 Actions, which are interwoven in it, are parts either necessary, or convenient to carry on the main Design. Either so necessary, that without them the Poem must be Imperfect, or so convenient, that no others can be imagin'd more suitable to the place in which they are. There is nothing to be left void in a firm Building; even the Cavities ought not 10 to be fill'd with Rubbish, which is of a perishable kind, destructive to the strength: But with Brick or Stone, though of less pieces, yet of the same Nature, and fitted to the Cranies. Even the least portions of them must be of the Epick kind; all things must be Grave, Majestical, and Sublime: Nothing of a Foreign Nature, like the trifling *Novels*, which 15 *Ariosto* and others have inserted in their Poems. By which the Reader is miss-led into another sort of Pleasure, opposite to that which is design'd in an Epick Poem. One raises the Soul and hardens it to Virtue, the other softens it again and unbends it into Vice. One conduces to the Poet's aim, the compleating of his Work; which he is driving on, 20 labouring and hast'ning in every Line: the other slackens his pace, diverts him from his Way, and locks him up like a Knight Errant in an Enchanted Castle, when he should be pursuing his first Adventure. *Statius*, as *Bossu* has well observ'd, was ambitious of trying his strength with his Master *Virgil*, as *Virgil* had before try'd his with *Homer*. The 25 *Grecian* gave the two *Romans* an Example, in the Games which were Celebrated at the Funerals of *Patroclus*. *Virgil* imitated the Invention of *Homer*, but chang'd the Sports. But both the *Greek* and *Latin* Poet, took their occasions from the Subject; though to confess the Truth, they were both Ornamental, or at best, convenient parts of it, rather than 30 of necessity arising from it. *Statius*, who through his whole Poem, is

To the Most Honourable, &c. 16 *Ariosto Edd.: Aristotle* 97 98

noted for want of Conduct and Judgment; instead of staying, as he might have done, for the Death of *Capaneus, Hippomedon, Tideus,* or some other of his Seven Champions, (who are Heroes all alike) or more properly for the Tragical end of the two Brothers, whose Exequies the 35 next Successor had leisure to perform, when the Siege was rais'd, and in the Interval betwixt the Poets first Action, and his second; went out of his way, as it were on propense Malice to commit a Fault. For he took his opportunity to kill a Royal Infant, by the means of a Serpent, (that Author of all Evil) to make way for those Funeral Honours, which 40 he intended for him. Now if this Innocent had been of any Relation to his *Thebais;* if he had either farther'd or hinder'd the taking of the Town, the Poet might have found some sorry Excuse at least, for detaining the Reader from the promis'd Siege. [I can think of nothing to plead for him, but what I verily believe he thought himself; which was, 45 that as the Funerals of *Anchises* were solemniz'd in *Sicily,* so those of *Archemorus* should be celebrated in *Candy.* For the last was an Island; and a better than the first, because *Jove* was Born there.] On these terms, this *Capaneus* of a Poet ingag'd his two Immortal Predecessours, and his Success was answerable to his Enterprise.   50

If this Oeconomy must be observ'd in the minutest Parts of an Epick Poem, which, to a common Reader, seem to be detach'd from the Body, and almost independent of it; what Soul, tho' sent into the World with great advantages of Nature, cultivated with the liberal Arts and Sciences; conversant with Histories of the Dead, and enrich'd with 55 Observations on the Living, can be sufficient to inform the whole Body of so great a Work? I touch here but transiently, without any strict Method, on some few of those many Rules of imitating Nature, which *Aristotle* drew from *Homer's* Iliads and Odysses, and which he fitted to the *Drama;* furnishing himself also with Observations from the Practice 60 of the Theater, when it flourish'd under *Æschilus, Eurypides,* and *Sophocles.* For the Original of the Stage was from the Epick Poem. Narration, doubtless, preceded Acting, and gave Laws to it: What at first was told Artfully, was, in process of time, represented gracefully to the sight, and hearing. Those Episodes of *Homer,* which were proper 65 for the Stage, the Poets amplify'd each into an Action: Out of his Limbs they form'd their Bodies: What he had Contracted they Enlarg'd: Out of one *Hercules* were made infinite of Pigmies; yet all endued with humane Souls: For from him, their great Creator, they have each of them the *Divinæ particulam Auræ.* They flow'd from him at first, and are 70 at last resolv'd into him. Nor were they only animated by him, but their Measure and Symetry was owing to him. His one, entire, and great Action was Copied by them according to the proportions of the *Drama*: If he finish'd his Orb within the Year, it suffic'd to teach them, that their Action being less, and being also less diversify'd with Inci- 75 dents, their Orb, of consequence, must be circumscrib'd in a less compass, which they reduc'd, within the limits either of a Natural or an Artificial Day. So that as he taught them to amplifie what he had shorten'd, by the same Rule apply'd the contrary way, he taught them to shorten what he had amplifi'd. Tragedy is the minature of Humane 80 Life; an Epick Poem is the draught at length. Here, my Lord, I must contract also, for, before I was aware, I was almost running into a long digression, to prove that there is no such absolute necessity that the time of a Stage-Action shou'd so strictly be confin'd to Twenty Four Hours, as never to exceed them, for which *Aristotle* contends, and the 85 *Grecian* Stage has practis'd. Some longer space, on some occasions, I think may be allow'd, especially for the *English* Theater, which requires more variety of Incidents than the *French*. *Corneille* himself, after long Practice, was inclin'd to think, that the time allotted by the Ancients was too short to raise and finish a great Action: And better a Mechanick 90 Rule were stretch'd or broken, than a great Beauty were omitted. To raise, and afterwards to calm the Passions, to purge the Soul from Pride, by the Examples of Humane Miseries, which befall the greatest; in few words, to expel Arrogance, and introduce Compassion, are the great effects of Tragedy. Great, I must confess, if they were altogether 95 as true as they are pompous. But are Habits to be introduc'd at three Hours warning? Are radical Diseases so suddenly remov'd? A Mountebank may promise such a Cure, but a skilful Physician will not undertake it. An Epick Poem is not in so much haste; it works leisurely; the Changes which it makes are slow; but the Cure is likely to be more 100 perfect. The effects of Tragedy, as I said, are too violent to be lasting. If it be answer'd that for this Reason Tragedies are often to be seen, and the Dose to be repeated; this is tacitely to confess, that there is more Virtue in one Heroick Poem than in many Tragedies. A Man is humbled one Day, and his Pride returns the next. Chymical Medicines 105 are observ'd to Relieve oft'ner than to Cure: For 'tis the nature of Spirits to make swift impressions, but not deep. *Galenical* Decoctions, to which I may properly compare an Epick Poem, have more of Body in them; they work by their substance and their weight. It is one Reason of *Aristotle*'s to prove, that Tragedy is the more Noble, because 110

it turns in a shorter Compass; the whole Action being circumscrib'd
within the space of Four-and-Twenty Hours. He might prove as well
that a Mushroom is to be preferr'd before a Peach, because it shoots up
in the compass of a Night. A Chariot may be driven round the Pillar
in less space than a large Machine, because the Bulk is not so great: Is 115
the *Moon* a more Noble Planet than *Saturn*, because she makes her
Revolution in less than Thirty Days, and He in little less than Thirty
Years? Both their Orbs are in proportion to their several Magnitudes;
and, consequently, the quickness or slowness of their Motion, and the
time of their circumvolutions, is no Argument of the greater or less 120
Perfection. And besides, what Virtue is there in a Tragedy, which is
not contain'd in an Epick Poem? Where Pride is humbled, Vertue
rewarded, and Vice punish'd; and those more amply treated, than the
narrowness of the *Drama* can admit? The shining Quality of an Epick
Heroe, his Magnanimity, his Constancy, his Patience, his Piety, or 125
whatever Characteristical Virtue his Poet gives him, raises first our
Admiration: We are naturally prone to imitate what we admire: And
frequent Acts produce a habit. If the Hero's chief quality be vicious,
as for Example, the Choler and obstinate desire of Vengeance in *Achilles*,
yet the Moral is Instructive: And besides, we are inform'd in the very 130
proposition of the *Iliads*, that this anger was pernicious: That it brought
a thousand ills on the *Grecian* Camp. The Courage of *Achilles* is propos'd
to imitation, not his Pride and Disobedience to his General, nor his
brutal Cruelty to his dead Enemy, nor the selling his Body to his
Father. We abhor these Actions while we read them, and what we 135
abhor we never imitate: The Poet only shews them like Rocks or
Quick-Sands, to be shun'd.

   By this Example the Criticks have concluded that it is not necessary
the Manners of the Heroe should be virtuous. They are Poetically good
if they are of a Piece. Though where a Character of perfect Virtue is set 140
before us, 'tis more lovely: for there the whole Heroe is to be imitated.
This is the *Æneas* of our Author: this is that Idea of perfection in an
Epick Poem, which Painters and Statuaries have only in their minds;
and which no hands are able to express. These are the Beauties of a
God in a Humane Body. When the Picture of *Achilles* is drawn in 145
Tragedy, he is taken with those Warts, and Moles, and hard Features,
by those who represent him on the Stage, or he is no more *Achilles*: for
his Creatour *Homer* has so describ'd him. Yet even thus he appears a
perfect Heroe, though an imperfect Character of Vertue. *Horace* Paints
him after *Homer*, and delivers him to be Copied on the Stage with all 150

those imperfections. Therefore they are either not faults in a Heroick Poem, or faults common to the *Drama*. After all, on the whole merits of the Cause, it must be acknowledg'd that the Epick Poem is more for the Manners, and Tragedy for the Passions. The Passions, as I have said, are violent: and acute Distempers require Medicines of a strong 155 and speedy operation. Ill habits of the Mind are like Chronical Diseases, to be corrected by degrees, and Cur'd by Alteratives: wherein though Purges are sometimes necessary, yet Diet, good Air, and moderate Exercise, have the greatest part. The Matter being thus stated, it will appear that both sorts of Poetry are of use for their proper ends. The 160 Stage is more active, the Epick Poem works at greater leisure, yet is active too, when need requires. For Dialogue is imitated by the *Drama*, from the more active parts of it. One puts off a Fit like the *Quinquina*, and relieves us only for a time; the other roots out the Distemper, and gives a healthful habit. The Sun enlightens and chears us, dispels Fogs, 165 and warms the ground with his daily Beams; but the Corn is sow'd, increases, is ripen'd, and is reap'd for use in process of time, and in its proper Season. I proceed from the greatness of the Action, to the Dignity of the Actours, I mean to the Persons employ'd in both Poems. There likewise Tragedy will be seen to borrow from the *Epopee*; and 170 that which borrows is always of less Dignity, because it has not of its own. A Subject, 'tis true, may lend to his Soveraign, but the act of borrowing makes the King inferiour, because he wants, and the Subject supplies. And suppose the Persons of the *Drama* wholly Fabulous, or of the Poet's Invention, yet Heroick Poetry gave him the Examples of that 175 Invention, because it was first, and *Homer* the common Father of the Stage. I know not of any one advantage, which Tragedy can boast above Heroick Poetry, but that it is represented to the view, as well as read: and instructs in the Closet, as well as on the Theatre. This is an uncontended Excellence, and a chief Branch of its Prerogative; yet I 180 may be allow'd to say without partiality, that herein the Actors share the Poet's praise. Your Lordship knows some Modern Tragedies which are beautiful on the Stage, and yet I am confident you wou'd not read them. *Tryphon* the Stationer complains they are seldom ask'd for in his Shop. The Poet who Flourish'd in the Scene, is damn'd in the *Ruelle*; 185 nay more, he is not esteem'd a good Poet by those who see and hear his Extravagancies with delight. They are a sort of stately Fustian, and lofty Childishness. Nothing but Nature can give a sincere pleasure; where that is not imitated, 'tis Grotesque Painting, the fine Woman ends in a Fishes Tail. 190

I might also add, that many things, which not only please, but are real Beauties in the reading, wou'd appear absurd upon the Stage: and those not only the *Speciosa Miracula*, as *Horace* calls them; of Transformations, of *Scylla*, *Antiphates*, and the *Lestrigons*, which cannot be represented even in Opera's; but the prowess of *Achilles* or *Æneas* wou'd 195 appear ridiculous in our Dwarf-Heroes of the Theatre. We can believe they routed Armies in *Homer* or in *Virgil*, but *ne Hercules contra duos* in the *Drama*. I forbear to instance in many things which the Stage cannot or ought not to represent. For I have said already more than I intended on this Subject, and shou'd fear it might be turn'd against me; that I 200 plead for the pre-eminence of Epick Poetry, because I have taken some pains in translating *Virgil*; if this were the first time that I had deliver'd my Opinion in this Dispute. But I have more than once already maintain'd the Rights of my two Masters against their Rivals of the Scene, even while I wrote Tragedies my self, and had no thoughts of this 205 present Undertaking. I submit my Opinion to your Judgment, who are better qualified than any Man I know to decide this Controversie. You come, my Lord, instructed in the Cause, and needed not that I shou'd open it. Your Essay of Poetry, which was publish'd without a Name, and of which I was not honour'd with the Confidence, I read over and 210 over with much delight, and as much instruction: and, without flattering you, or making my self more Moral than I am, not without some Envy. I was loath to be inform'd how an Epick Poem shou'd be written, or how a Tragedy shou'd be contriv'd and manag'd in better Verse and with more judgment than I cou'd teach others. A Native of *Parnassus*, 215 and bred up in the Studies of its Fundamental Laws, may receive new Lights from his Contemporaries, but 'tis a grudging kind of praise which he gives his Benefactors. He is more oblig'd than he is willing to acknowledge: there is a tincture of Malice in his Commendations. For where I own I am taught, I confess my want of Knowledge. A Judge 220 upon the Bench, may, out of good Nature, or at least interest, encourage the Pleadings of a puny Councellor, but he does not willingly commend his Brother Serjeant at the Bar, especially when he controuls his Law, and exposes that ignorance which is made Sacred by his Place. I gave the unknown Author his due Commendation, I must confess, 225 but who can answer for me, and for the rest of the Poets, who heard me read the Poem, whether we shou'd not have been better pleas'd to have seen our own Names at the bottom of the Title Page? Perhaps we commended it the more, that we might seem to be above the Censure. We are naturally displeas'd with an unknown Critick, as the Ladies are 230 with a Lampooner, because we are bitten in the dark, and know not where to fasten our Revenge. But great Excellencies will work their way through all sorts of opposition. I applauded rather out of decency than Affection; and was Ambitious, as some yet can witness, to be acquainted with a Man, with whom I had the honour to Converse, and 235 that almost daily, for so many years together. Heaven knows if I have heartily forgiven you this deceit. You extorted a Praise whieh I shou'd willingly have given had I known you. Nothing had been more easie than to commend a Patron of a long standing. The World wou'd joyn with me, if the Encomiums were just; and if unjust, wou'd excuse a grateful 240 Flatterer. But to come *Anonymous* upon me, and force me to commend you against my interest, was not altogether so fair, give me leave to say, as it was Politick. For by concealing your Quality, you might clearly understand how your Work succeeded; and that the general approbation was given to your Merit not your Titles. Thus like *Apelles* you 245 stood unseen behind your own *Venus*, and receiv'd the praises of the passing Multitude: the Work was commended, not the Author: And I doubt not this was one of the most pleasing Adventures of your Life.

I have detain'd your Lordship longer than I intended in this Dispute of preference betwixt the Epick Poem, and the *Drama*: and yet have not 250 formally answer'd any of the Arguments which are brought by *Aristotle* on the other side, and set in the fairest light by *Dacier*. But I suppose, without looking on the Book, I may have touch'd on some of the Objections. For in this Address to your Lordship, I design not a Treatise of Heroick Poetry, but write in a loose Epistolary way, some- 255 what tending to that Subject, after the Example of *Horace*, in his First Epistle of the Second Book to *Augustus Cæsar*, and of that to the *Piso's*, which we call his *Art of Poetry*. In both of which he observes no Method that I can trace, whatever *Scaliger* the Father, or *Heinsius* may have seen, or rather think they had seen. I have taken up, laid down, and resum'd 260 as often as I pleas'd the same Subject: and this loose proceeding I shall use thro' all this Prefatory Dedication. Yet all this while I have been Sailing with some side-wind or other toward the Point I propos'd in the beginning; the Greatness and Excellency of an Heroick Poem, with some of the difficulties which attend that work. The Comparison there- 265 fore which I made betwixt the *Epopee* and the Tragedy was not altogether a digression; for 'tis concluded on all hands, that they are both the Master-pieces of Humane Wit.

In the mean time I may be bold to draw this Corollary from what has been already said, That the File of Heroick Poets is very short: all are 270

not such who have assum'd that lofty Title in Ancient or Modern
Ages, or have been so esteem'd by their partial and ignorant Admirers.

There have been but one great *Ilias* and one *Æneis* in so many Ages.
The next, but the next with a long interval betwixt, was the *Jeru-*
salem: I mean not so much in distance of time, as in Excellency. After 275
these three are entred, some Lord Chamberlain should be appointed,
some Critick of Authority shou'd be set before the door, to keep out a
Crowd of little Poets, who press for Admission, and are not of Quality.
Mævius wou'd be deafning your Lordship's Ears with his

       Fortunam Priami, Cantabo, & Nobile Bellum.   280

Meer Fustian, as *Horace* would tell you from behind, without pressing
forward, and more smoak than fire. *Pulci, Boyardo,* and *Ariosto,* wou'd
cry out, make room for the *Italian* Poets, the descendants of *Virgil* in
a right Line. Father *Le Moin* with his Saint *Louis*; and *Scudery* with his
Alaric, for a godly King, and a *Gothick* Conquerour; and *Chapelain* wou'd 285
take it ill that his Maid shou'd be refus'd a place with *Helen* and *Lavinia*.
Spencer has a better plea for his *Fairy-Queen,* had his action been finish'd,
or had been one. And *Milton,* if the Devil had not been his Heroe
instead of *Adam,* if the Gyant had not foil'd the Knight, and driven him
out of his strong hold, to wander through the World with his Lady 290
Errant: and if there had not been more Machining Persons than
Humane, in his Poem. After these, the rest of our *English* Poets shall not
be mention'd. I have that Honour for them which I ought to have: but
if they are Worthies, they are not to be rank'd amongst the three whom
I have nam'd, and who are establish'd in their Reputation.   295

Before I quitted the Comparison betwixt Epick Poetry and Tragedy,
I shou'd have acquainted my Judge with one advantage of the former
over the latter, which I now casually remember out of the Preface of
Segrais before his Translation of the *Æneis*, or out of *Bossu*, no matter
which. The stile of the Heroick Poem is and ought to be more lofty than 300
that of the *Drama.* The Critick is certainly in the right, for the Reason
already urg'd: The work of Tragedy is on the Passions, and in Dialogue;
both of them abhor strong Metaphors, in which the *Epopee* delights. A
Poet cannot speak too plainly on the Stage: for *Volat irrevocabile verbum;*
the sense is lost if it be not taken flying: but what we read alone we 305
have leisure to digest. There an Author may beautifie his Sense by the
boldness of his Expression, which if we understand not fully at the first,
we may dwell upon it, 'till we find the secret force and excellence. That

       302 Dialogue;] Dialogue, *97 98*

which cures the Manners by alterative Physick, as I said before, must proceed by insensible degrees; but that which purges the Passions, must do its business all at once, or wholly fail of its effect, at least in the present Operation, and without repeated Doses. We must beat the Iron while 'tis hot, but we may polish it at leisure. Thus, my Lord, you pay the Fine of my forgetfulness, and yet the merits of both Causes are where they were, and undecided, 'till you declare whether it be more for the benefit of Mankind to have their Manners in general corrected, or their Pride and hard-heartedness remov'd.

I must now come closer to my present business: and not think of making more invasive Wars abroad, when like *Hannibal*, I am call'd back to the defence of my own Country. *Virgil* is attack'd by many Enemies: He has a whole Confederacy against him, and I must endeavour to defend him as well as I am able. But their principal Objections being against his Moral, the duration or length of time taken up in the action of the Poem, and what they have to urge against the Manners of his Hero, I shall omit the rest as meer Cavils of Grammarians: at the worst but casual slips of a Great Man's Pen, or inconsiderable faults of an admirable Poem, which the Author had not leisure to review before his Death. *Macrobius* has answer'd what the Ancients cou'd urge against him: and some things I have lately read in *Tanneguy le Fèvre*, *Valois*, and another whom I name not, which are scarce worth answering. They begin with the Moral of his Poem, which I have elsewhere confess'd, and still must own not to be so Noble as that of *Homer*. But let both be fairly stated, and without contradicting my first Opinion, I can shew that *Virgil*'s was as useful to the *Romans* of his Age, as *Homer*'s was to the *Grecians* of his; in what time soever he may be supposed to have liv'd and flourish'd. *Homer*'s Moral was to urge the necessity of Union, and of a good understanding betwixt Confederate States and Princes engag'd in a War with a Mighty Monarch: as also of Discipline in an Army, and obedience in the several Chiefs, to the Supream Commander of the joynt Forces. To inculcate this, he sets forth the ruinous Effects of Discord in the Camp of those Allies, occasion'd by the quarrel betwixt the General, and one of the next in Office under him. *Agamemnon* gives the provocation, and *Achilles* resents the injury. Both Parties are faulty in the Quarrel, and accordingly they are both punish'd: the Agressor is forc'd to sue for peace to his Inferiour, on dishonourable Conditions; the Deserter refuses the satisfaction offer'd, and his Obstinacy costs him his best Friend. This works the Natural Effect of Choler, and turns his Rage against him, by whom he was last Affronted, and most sensibly. The greater Anger expels the less; but his Character is still preserv'd. In the mean time the *Grecian* 350 Army receives Loss on Loss, and is half destroy'd by a Pestilence into the Bargain.

Quicquid delirant Reges plectuntur Achivi.

As the Poet, in the first part of the Example, had shewn the bad effects of Discord, so after the Reconcilement, he gives the good effects 355 of Unity. For *Hector* is slain, and then *Troy* must fall. By this, 'tis probable, that *Homer* liv'd when the *Median* Monarchy was grown formidable to the *Grecians*: and that the joint Endeavours of his Countrymen, were little enough to preserve their common Freedom, from an encroaching Enemy. Such was his Moral, which all Criticks have 360 allow'd to be more Noble than that of *Virgil*: though not adapted to the times in which the *Roman* Poet liv'd. Had *Virgil* flourish'd in the Age of *Ennius*, and address'd to *Scipio*, he had probably taken the same Moral, or some other not unlike it. For then the *Romans* were in as much danger from the *Carthaginian* Commonwealth, as the *Grecians* were 365 from the *Assyrian*, or *Median* Monarchy. But we are to consider him as writing his Poem in a time when the Old Form of Government was subverted, and a new one just Established by *Octavius Cæsar*: In effect by force of Arms, but seemingly by the Consent of the *Roman* People. The Commonwealth had receiv'd a deadly Wound in the former Civil 370 Wars betwixt *Marius* and *Sylla*. The Commons, while the first prevail'd, had almost shaken off the Yoke of the Nobility; and *Marius* and *Cinna*, like the Captains of the Mobb, under the specious Pretence of the Publick Good, and of doing Justice on the Oppressours of their Liberty, reveng'd themselves, without Form of Law, on their private 375 Enemies. *Sylla*, in his turn, proscrib'd the Heads of the adverse Party: He too had nothing but Liberty and Reformation in his Mouth; (for the Cause of Religion is but a Modern Motive to Rebellion, invented by the Christian Priesthood, refining on the Heathen:) *Sylla*, to be sure, meant no more good to the *Roman* People than *Marius* before him, what- 380 ever he declar'd; but Sacrific'd the Lives, and took the Estates of all his Enemies, to gratifie those who brought him into Power: Such was the Reformation of the Government by both Parties. The Senate and the Commons were the two Bases on which it stood; and the two Champions of either Faction, each destroy'd the Foundations of the other 385 side: So the Fabrique of consequence must fall betwixt them: And

357 *Median* 98: *Persian* 97   366 *Assyrian*, or *Median* 98: *Persian* 97

Tyranny must be built upon their Ruines. This comes of altering
Fundamental Laws and Constitutions. Like him, who being in good
Health, lodg'd himself in a Physician's House, and was over-perswaded
by his Landlord to take Physick, of which he dyed, for the benefit of 390
his Doctor. *Stavo ben* (was written on his Monument) *ma, per star meglio,
sto qui.*

After the Death of those two Usurpers, the Commonwealth seem'd
to recover, and held up its Head for a little time: But it was all the while
in a deep Consumption, which is a flattering Disease. *Pompey, Crassus,* 395
and *Cæsar,* had found the Sweets of Arbitrary Power; and each being a
check to the others growth, struck up a false Friendship amongst themselves; and divided the Government betwixt them, which none of them
was able to assume alone. These were the publick Spirited Men of their
Age, that is, Patriots for their own Interest. The Commonwealth look'd 400
with a florid Countenance in their Management, spread in Bulk, and
all the while was wasting in the Vitals. Not to trouble your Lordship
with the Repetition of what you know: After the death of *Crassus,
Pompey* found himself out-witted by *Cæsar;* broke with him, over-
power'd him in the Senate, and caus'd many unjust Decrees to pass 405
against him: *Cæsar* thus injur'd, and unable to resist the Faction of the
Nobles, which was now uppermost (for he was a *Marian*) had recourse
to Arms; and his Cause was just against *Pompey,* but not against his
Country, whose Constitution ought to have been sacred to him; and
never to have been Violated on the account of any private Wrong. But 410
he prevail'd, and Heav'n declaring for him, he became a Providential
Monarch, under the Title of *Perpetual Dictator.* He being Murther'd by
his own Son, whom I neither dare commend, nor can justly blame
(though *Dante* in his *Inferno,* has put him and *Cassius,* and *Judas Iscariot*
betwixt them, into the great Devil's Mouth) the Commonwealth 415
popp'd up its Head for the third time, under *Brutus* and *Cassius,* and
then sunk for ever.

Thus the *Roman* People were grosly gull'd; twice or thrice over: and
as often enslav'd in one Century, and under the same pretence of
Reformation. At last the two Battles of *Philippi,* gave the decisive stroak 420
against Liberty; and not long after, the Commonwealth was turn'd
into a Monarchy, by the Conduct and good Fortune of *Augustus.* 'Tis
true, that the despotick Power could not have fallen into better Hands,
than those of the first and second *Cæsar.* Your Lordship well knows what
Obligations *Virgil* had to the latter of them: He saw, beside, that the 425

418 gull'd; *98*: gull'd: *97*

Commonwealth was lost without ressource: The Heads of it destroy'd; the Senate new moulded, grown degenerate; and either bought off, or thrusting their own Necks into the Yoke, out of fear of being forc'd. Yet I may safely affirm for our great Author (as Men of good Sense are generally Honest) that he was still of Republican Principles in his 430 Heart.

Secretosque Pios, his dantem jura Catonem.

I think, I need use no other Argument to justify my Opinion, than that of this one Line, taken from the Eighth Book of the *Eneis*. If he had not well studied his Patron's Temper, it might have Ruin'd him with 435 another Prince. But *Augustus* was not discontented, at least that we can find, that *Cato* was plac'd, by his own Poet, in *Elisium*; and there giving Laws to the Holy Souls, who deserv'd to be separated from the Vulgar sort of good Spirits. For his Conscience could not but whisper to the Arbitrary Monarch, that the Kings of *Rome* were at first Elective, and 440 Govern'd not without a Senate: That *Romulus* was no Hereditary Prince, and though, after his Death, he receiv'd Divine Honours, for the good he did on Earth, yet he was but a God of their own making: that the last *Tarquin* was Expell'd justly, for Overt-Acts of Tyranny, and Male-Administration; for such are the Conditions of an Elective King- 445 dom: And I meddle not with others: being, for my own Opinion, of *Montaigns* Principles, that an Honest Man ought to be contented with that Form of Government, and with those Fundamental Constitutions of it, which he receiv'd from his Ancestors, and under which himself was Born: Though at the same time he confess'd freely, that if he could 450 have chosen his Place of Birth, it shou'd have been at *Venice*: Which for many Reasons I dislike, and am better pleas'd to have been born an *English* Man.

But to return from my long rambling: I say that *Virgil* having maturely weigh'd the Condition of the Times in which he liv'd: that 455 an entire Liberty was not to be retriev'd: that the present Settlement had the prospect of a long continuance in the same Family, or those adopted into it: that he held his Paternal Estate from the Bounty of the Conqueror, by whom he was likewise enrich'd, esteem'd and cherish'd: that this Conquerour, though of a bad kind, was the very best of it: 460 that the Arts of Peace flourish'd under him: that all Men might be happy if they would be quiet: that now he was in possession of the whole, yet he shar'd a great part of his Authority with the Senate:

430-1 Republican . . . Heart 97 (*errata*): Republick principles in Heart 97 (*text*)
432 Secretosque Pios] *Secretisque Piis 97 98*

That he would be chosen into the Ancient Offices of the Common- wealth, and Rul'd by the Power which he deriv'd from them; and 465 Prorogu'd his Government from time to time: Still, as it were, threat- ning to dismiss himself from Publick Cares, which he exercis'd more for the common Good, than for any delight he took in greatness: These things, I say, being consider'd by the Poet, he concluded it to be the Interest of his Country to be so Govern'd: To infuse an awful Respect 470 into the People, towards such a Prince: By that respect to confirm their Obedience to him; and by that Obedience to make them Happy. This was the Moral of his Divine Poem: Honest in the Poet: Honourable to the Emperour, whom he derives from a Divine Extraction; and reflect- ing part of that Honour on the *Roman* People, whom he derives also 475 from the *Trojans*; and not only profitable, but necessary to the present Age; and likely to be such to their Posterity. That it was the receiv'd Opinion, that the *Romans* were descended from the *Trojans*, and *Julius Cæsar* from *Julus* the Son of *Æneas*, was enough for *Virgil*; tho' perhaps he thought not so himself: Or that *Æneas* ever was in *Italy*, which 480 *Bochartus* manifestly proves. And *Homer*, where he says that *Jupiter* hated the House of *Priam*, and was resolv'd to transfer the Kingdom to the Family of *Æneas*, yet mentions nothing of his leading a Colony into a Foreign Country, and setling there: But that the *Romans* valued themselves on their *Trojan* Ancestry, is so undoubted a Truth, that I 485 need not prove it. Even the Seals which we have remaining of *Julius Cæsar*, which we know to be Antique, have the Star of *Venus* over them, though they were all graven after his Death, as a Note that he was Deifi'd. I doubt not but it was one Reason, why *Augustus* should be so passionately concern'd for the preservation of the *Æneis*, which its 490 Author had Condemn'd to be Burnt, as an Imperfect Poem, by his last Will and Testament; was, because it did him a real Service as well as an Honour; that a Work should not be lost where his Divine Original was Celebrated in Verse, which had the Character of Immortality stamp'd upon it. 495

Neither were the great *Roman* Families which flourish'd in his time, less oblig'd by him than the Emperour. Your Lordship knows with what Address he makes mention of them, as Captains of Ships, or Leaders in the War; and even some of *Italian* Extraction are not for- gotten. These are the single Stars which are sprinkled through the 500 *Æneis*: But there are whole Constellations of them in the Fifth Book. And I could not but take notice, when I Translated it, of some Favourite Families to which he gives the Victory, and awards the Prizes, in the

Person of his Heroe, at the Funeral Games which were Celebrated in Honour of *Anchises*. I, Insist not on their Names: But am pleas'd to find 505 the *Memmii* amongst them, deriv'd from *Mnestheus*, because *Lucretius* Dedicates to one of that Family, a Branch of which destroy'd *Corinth*. I likewise either found or form'd an Image to my self of the contrary kind; that those who lost the Prizes, were such as had disoblig'd the Poet, or were in disgrace with *Augustus*, or Enemies to *Mecenas*: And 510 this was the Poetical Revenge he took. For *genus irritabile Vatum*, as *Horace* says. When a Poet is throughly provok'd, he will do himself Justice, however dear it cost him, *Animamque, in Vulnere ponit*. I think these are not bare Imaginations of my own, though I find no trace of them in the Commentatours: But one Poet may judge of another by 515 himself. The Vengeance we defer, is not forgotten. I hinted before, that the whole *Roman* People were oblig'd by *Virgil*, in deriving them from *Troy*; an Ancestry which they affected. We, and the *French* are of the same Humour: They would be thought to descend from a Son, I think, of *Hector*: And we wou'd have our *Britain*, both Nam'd and Planted by 520 a descendant of *Æneas*. *Spencer* favours this Opinion what he can. His Prince *Arthur*, or whoever he intends by him, is a *Trojan*. Thus the Heroe of *Homer* was a *Grecian*, of *Virgil* a *Roman*, of *Tasso* an *Italian*.

I have transgress'd my Bounds, and gone farther than the Moral led me. But if your Lordship is not tir'd, I am safe enough. 525

Thus far, I think, my Author is defended. But as *Augustus* is still shadow'd in the Person of *Æneas*, of which I shall say more, when I come to the Manners which the Poet gives his Hero: I must prepare that Subject by shewing how dext'rously he mannag'd both the Prince and People, so as to displease neither, and to do good to both, which is 530 the part of a Wise and an Honest Man: And proves that it is possible for a Courtier not to be a Knave. I shall continue still to speak my Thoughts like a free-born Subject as I am; though such things, perhaps, as no *Dutch* Commentator cou'd, and I am sure no *French*-man durst. I have already told your Lordship my Opinion of *Virgil*; that he 535 was no Arbitrary Man. Oblig'd he was to his Master for his Bounty, and he repays him with good Counsel, how to behave himself in his new Monarchy, so as to gain the Affections of his Subjects, and deserve to be call'd the Father of his Country. From this Consideration it is, that he chose for the ground-work of his Poem, one Empire destroy'd, and 540 another rais'd from the Ruins of it. This was just the Parallel. *Æneas* cou'd not pretend to be *Priam*'s Heir in a Lineal Succession: For

Anchises the Heroe's Father, was only of the second Branch of the Royal
Family: And *Helenus*, a Son of *Priam*, was yet surviving, and might
lawfully claim before him. It may be *Virgil* mentions him on that 545
Account. Neither has he forgotten *Priamus*, in the Fifth of his *Æneis*, the
Son of *Polites*, youngest Son to *Priam*; who was slain by *Pyrrhus*, in the
Second Book. *Æneas* had only Married *Creusa*, *Priam*'s Daughter, and
by her could have no Title, while any of the Male Issue were remaining.
In this case, the Poet gave him the next Title, which is, that of an 550
Elective King. The remaining *Trojans* chose him to lead them forth, and
settle them in some Foreign Country. *Ilioneus* in his Speech to *Dido*,
calls him expresly by the Name of King. Our Poet, who all this while
had *Augustus* in his Eye, had no desire he should seem to succeed by
any right of Inheritance, deriv'd from *Julius Cæsar*; such a Title being 555
but one degree remov'd from Conquest. For what was introduc'd by
force, by force may be remov'd. 'Twas better for the People that they
should give, than he should take. Since that Gift was indeed no more
at bottom than a Trust. *Virgil* gives us an Example of this, in the
Person of *Mezentius*. He Govern'd Arbitrarily, he was expell'd: And 560
came to the deserv'd End of all Tyrants. Our Author shews us another
sort of Kingship in the Person of *Latinus*. He was descended from
Saturn, and as I remember, in the Third Degree. He is describ'd a just
and a gracious Prince; solicitous for the Welfare of his People; always
Consulting with his Senate to promote the common Good. We find 565
him at the head of them, when he enters into the Council-Hall. Speaking first, but still demanding their Advice, and steering by it as far as
the Iniquity of the Times wou'd suffer him. And this is the proper
Character of a King by Inheritance, who is born a Father of his Country.
Æneas, tho' he Married the Heiress of the Crown, yet claim'd no Title 570
to it during the Life of his Father-in-Law. *Pater arma Latinus habeto*, &c.
are *Virgil*'s Words. As for himself, he was contented to take care of his
Country Gods, who were not those of *Latium*. Wherein our Divine
Author seems to relate to the after practice of the *Romans*, which was
to adopt the Gods of those they Conquer'd, or receiv'd as Members of 575
their Commonwealth. Yet withal, he plainly touches at the Office of
the High Priesthood, with which *Augustus* was invested: And which
made his Person more Sacred and inviolable, than even the Tribunitial

546 *Priamus 98: Atis 97. See Commentary*   548 *Second Book.*] *In 97, there follows
a sentence necessarily cancelled in 98 by the correction of* Atis *to* Priamus: *Atis*, then, the
Favourite Companion of *Ascanius*, had a better Right than he; tho' I know he was
introduc'd by *Virgil*, to do Honour to the Family, from which *Julius Cæsar* was
descended by the Mothers side.

Power. It was not therefore for nothing, that the most Judicious of all Poets, made that Office vacant, by the Death of *Panthus*, in the Second 580 Book of the *Æneis*, for his Heroe to succeed in it; and consequently for *Augustus* to enjoy. I know not that any of the Commentatours have taken notice of that passage. If they have not, I am sure they ought: And if they have, I am not indebted to them for the Observation: The words of *Virgil* are very plain.   585

> *Sacra, suosque tibi, commendat Troja Penates.*

As for *Augustus*, or his Uncle *Julius*, claiming by descent from *Æneas*; that Title is already out of doors. *Æneas* succeeded not, but was Elected. *Troy* was fore-doom'd to fall for ever.

> *Postquam res Asiæ, Priamique evertere Regnum,*   590
> *Immeritum, visum superis.* Æneis the 3*d*, line the 1*st*.

Augustus 'tis true, had once resolv'd to re-build that City, and there to make the Seat of Empire: But *Horace* writes an Ode on purpose to deter him from that Thought; declaring the place to be accurs'd, and that the Gods would as often destroy it as it shou'd be rais'd. Hereupon 595 the Emperour laid aside a Project so ungrateful to the *Roman* People: But by this, my Lord, we may conclude that he had still his Pedigree in his Head; and had an Itch of being thought a Divine King, if his Poets had not given him better Counsel.

I will pass by many less material Objections, for want of room to 600 Answer them: What follows next is of great Importance, if the Criticks can make out their Charge; for 'tis levell'd at the Manners which our Poet gives his Heroe; and which are the same which were eminently seen in his *Augustus*. Those Manners were Piety to the Gods, and a dutiful Affection to his Father; Love to his Relations; Care of his 605 People; Courage and Conduct in the Wars; Gratitude to those who had oblig'd him; and Justice in general to Mankind.

Piety, as your Lordship sees, takes place of all, as the chief part of his Character: And the word in Latin is more full than it can possibly be exprest in any Modern Language; for there it comprehends not only 610 Devotion to the Gods, but Filial Love and tender Affection to Relations of all sorts. As instances of this, the Deities of *Troy* and his own *Penates* are made the Companions of his Flight: They appear to him in his Voyage, and advise him; and at last he re-places them in *Italy*, their Native Country. For his Father, he takes him on his Back: He leads his 615

590–1 *Regnum, Immeritum,*] An error for *gentem immeritam*   615 Father, *98*:
Father *97*

little Son, his Wife follows him; but losing his Footsteps through Fear
or Ignorance, he goes back into the midst of his Enemies to find her;
and leaves not his pursute 'till her Ghost appears, to forbid his farther
search. I will say nothing of his Duty to his Father while he liv'd; his
Sorrow for his Death; of the Games instituted in Honour of his 620
Memory; or seeking him, by his Command, even after Death, in the
Elysian Fields. I will not mention his Tenderness for his Son, which
every where is visible; Of his raising a Tomb for *Polydorus*, the Obsequies
for *Misenus*, his pious remembrance of *Deiphobus*: The Funerals of his
Nurse: His Grief for *Pallas*, and his Revenge taken on his Murtherer; 625
whom, otherwise by his Natural Compassion, he had forgiven: And
then the Poem had been left imperfect: For we could have had no certain prospect of his Happiness, while the last Obstacle to it was un-
remov'd. Of the other parts which compose his Character, as a King,
or as a General, I need say nothing: The whole *Æneis* is one continued 630
Instance, of some one or other of them: And where I find any thing of
them tax'd, it shall suffice me, as briefly as I can, to vindicate my
Divine Master to your Lordship, and by you to the Reader. But herein,
Segrais, in his admirable Preface to his Translation of the *Æneis*, as the
Author of the *Dauphin's Virgil* justly calls it, has prevented me. Him I 635
follow; and what I borrow from him, am ready to acknowledge to him.
For, impartially speaking, the *French* are as much better Criticks than
the *English*, as they are worse Poets. Thus we generally allow that they
better understand the management of a War, than our Islanders; but
we know we are superiour to them, in the day of Battel. They value 640
themselves on their Generals; we on our Souldiers. But this is not the
proper place to decide that Question, if they make it one. I shall say
perhaps as much of other Nations, and their Poets, excepting only
Tasso: and hope to make my Assertion good, which is but doing Justice
to my Country. Part of which Honour will reflect on your Lordship, 645
whose Thoughts are always just; your Numbers harmonious; your
Words chosen; your Expressions strong and manly; your Verse flowing,
and your turns as happy as they are easie. If you wou'd set us more
Copies, your Example would make all Precepts needless. In the mean
time, that little you have Written is own'd, and that particularly by 650
the Poets, (who are a Nation not over-lavish of praise to their Contemporaries,) as a principal Ornament of our Language: But the sweetest
Essences are always confin'd in the smallest Glasses.

When I speak of your Lordship, 'tis never a digression, and therefore

635 it, *98*: it; *97*

I need beg no pardon for it; but take up *Segrais* where I left him: And 655
shall use him less often than I have occasion for him. For his Preface is
a perfect piece of Criticism, full and clear, and digested into an exact
Method; mine is loose, and, as I intended it, Epistolary. Yet I dwell on
many things which he durst not touch: For 'tis dangerous to offend an
Arbitrary Master: And every Patron who has the Power of *Augustus*, 660
has not his Clemency. In short, my Lord, I wou'd not Translate him,
because I wou'd bring you somewhat of my own. His Notes and
Observations on every Book, are of the same Excellency; and for the
same Reason I omit the greater part.

He takes notice that *Virgil* is Arraign'd for placing Piety before 665
Valour; and making that Piety the chief Character of his Heroe. I have
said already from *Bossu*, that a Poet is not oblig'd to make his Heroe
a Virtuous Man: Therefore neither *Homer* nor *Tasso* are to be blam'd,
for giving what predominant quality they pleas'd to their first Character. But *Virgil*, who design'd to form a perfect Prince, and would 670
insinuate, that *Augustus*, whom he calls *Æneas* in his Poem, was truly
such, found himself oblig'd to make him without blemish; thoroughly
Virtuous; and a thorough Virtue both begins and ends in Piety. *Tasso*,
without question, observ'd this before me; and therefore split his Heroe
in two. He gave *Godfrey* Piety, and *Rinaldo* Fortitude; for their chief 675
Qualities or Manners. *Homer*, who had chosen another Moral, makes
both *Agamemnon* and *Achilles* vicious: For his design was to instruct in
Virtue, by shewing the deformity of Vice. I avoid repetition of that I
have said above. What follows is Translated literally from *Segrais*.

Virgil had consider'd that the greatest Virtues of *Augustus* consisted 680
in the perfect Art of Governing his People; which caus'd him to Reign
for more than Forty Years in great Felicity. He consider'd that his
Emperour was Valiant, Civil, Popular, Eloquent, Politick, and Religious.
He has given all these Qualities to *Æneas*. But knowing that Piety alone
comprehends the whole Duty of Man towards the Gods, towards his 685
Country, and towards his Relations, he judg'd, that this ought to be
his first Character, whom he would set for a Pattern of Perfection. In
reality, they who believe that the Praises which arise from Valour, are
superiour to those, which proceed from any other Virtues, have not
consider'd (as they ought,) that Valour, destitute of other Virtues, 690
cannot render a Man worthy of any true esteem. That Quality which
signifies no more than an intrepid Courage, may be separated from
many others which are good, and accompany'd with many which are

ill. A Man may be very Valiant, and yet Impious and Vicious. But the
same cannot be said of Piety; which excludes all ill Qualities, and com- 695
prehends even Valour it self, with all other Qualities which are good.
Can we, for example, give the praise of Valour to a Man who shou'd see
his Gods prophan'd, and shou'd want the Courage to defend them? To
a Man who shou'd abandon his Father, or desert his King in his last
Necessity?   700

Thus far *Segrais*, in giving the preference to Piety before Valour. I
will now follow him, where he considers this Valour, or intrepid
Courage, singly in it self; and this also *Virgil* gives to his *Æneas*, and
that in a Heroical Degree.

Having first concluded, that our Poet did for the best in taking the 705
first Character of his Heroe, from that Essential Vertue on which the
rest depend, he proceeds to tell us, that in the Ten Years war of *Troy*,
he was consider'd as the second Champion of his Country; allowing
Hector the first place; and this, even by the Confession of *Homer*, who
took all occasions of setting up his own Countrymen the *Grecians*, and 710
of undervaluing the *Trojan* Chiefs. But *Virgil*, (whom *Segrais* forgot to
cite,) makes *Diomede* give him a higher Character for Strength and
Courage. His Testimony is this, in the Eleventh Book.

> ————————*stetimus tela aspera contra,*
> *Contulimusque manus: experto credite, quantus*   715
> *In clypeum assurgat, quo turbine torqueat hastam.*
> *Si duo præterea tales Idæa tulisset*
> *Terra viros; ultro Inachias venisset ad Urbes*
> *Dardanus, & versis lugeret Græcia fatis.*
> *Quicquid apud duræ cessatum est mœnia Trojæ,*   720
> *Hectoris, Æneæque manu victoria Grajûm*
> *Hæsit; & in decumum vestigia rettulit annum.*
> *Ambo animis, ambo insignes præstantibus armis:*
> *Hic pietate prior.*————————

I give not here my Translation of these Verses; though I think I have 725
not ill succeeded in them; because your Lordship is so great a Master of
the Original, that I have no reason to desire you shou'd see *Virgil* and
me so near together: But you may please, my Lord, to take notice, that
the Latin Author refines upon the Greek; and insinuates, That *Homer*
had done his Heroe Wrong, in giving the advantage of the Duel to 730

his own Country-man: Though *Diomedes* was manifestly the second Champion of the *Grecians*: And *Ulysses* preferr'd him before *Ajax*, when he chose him for the Companion of his Nightly Expedition: For he had a Head-piece of his own; and wanted only the fortitude of another, to bring him off with safety; and that he might compass his Design with 735 Honour.

The *French* Translator thus proceeds: They who accuse *Æneas* for want of Courage, either understand not *Virgil*, or have read him slightly; otherwise they would not raise an Objection so easie to be Answer'd: Hereupon he gives so many instances of the Heroe's Valour, 740 that to repeat them after him would tire your Lordship, and put me to the unnecessary trouble of Transcribing the greatest part of the three last *Æneids*. In short, more could not be expected from an *Amadis*, a Sir *Lancelot*, or the whole round Table, than he performs. *Proxima quæque metit gladio*, is the perfect Account of a Knight Errant. If it be 745 reply'd, continues *Segrais*, that it was not difficult for him to undertake and atchieve such hardy Enterprizes, because he wore Enchanted Arms; that Accusation, in the first place, must fall on *Homer* e're it can reach *Virgil*. *Achilles* was as well provided with them as *Æneas*, though he was invulnerable without them: And, *Ariosto*, the two *Tasso's*, 750 *Bernardo* and *Torquato*, even our own *Spencer*; in a word, all Modern Poets have Copied *Homer* as well as *Virgil*: He is neither the first nor last; but in the midst of them; and therefore is safe if they are so. Who knows, says *Segrais*, but that his fated Armour was only an Allegorical Defence, and signifi'd no more than that he was under the peculiar 755 protection of the Gods; born, as the *Astrologers* will tell us out of *Virgil* (who was well vers'd in the *Chaldæan* Mysteries) under the favourable influence of *Jupiter*, *Venus*, and the *Sun*: But I insist not on this, because I know you believe not there is such an Art: though not only *Horace* and *Persius*, but *Augustus* himself, thought otherwise. But in defence of 760 *Virgil*, I dare positively say, that he has been more cautious in this particular than either his Predecessour, or his Descendants. For *Æneas* was actually wounded, in the Twelfth of the *Æneis*; though he had the same God-Smith to Forge his Arms, as had *Achilles*. It seems he was no War-luck, as the *Scots* commonly call such Men, who they say, are 765 Iron-free, or Lead-free. Yet after this Experiment, that his Arms were not impenetrable, when he was Cur'd indeed by his Mother's help, because he was that day to conclude the War by the death of *Turnus*, the Poet durst not carry the Miracle too far, and restore him wholly to

his former Vigour: He was still too weak to overtake his Enemy; yet 770
we see with what Courage he attacks *Turnus*, when he faces and renews
the Combate. I need say no more, for *Virgil* defends himself, without
needing my assistance; and proves his Heroe truly to deserve that
Name. He was not then a Second-rate Champion, as they would have
him, who think Fortitude the first Vertue in a Heroe. But being beaten 775
from this hold, they will not yet allow him to be Valiant; because he
wept more often, as they think, than well becomes a Man of Courage.

In the first place, if Tears are Arguments of Cowardise, What shall
I say of *Homer*'s Heroe? shall *Achilles* pass for timorous because he wept?
and wept on less occasions than *Æneas*? Herein *Virgil* must be granted 780
to have excell'd his Master. For once both Heroes are describ'd
lamenting their lost Loves: *Briseis* was taken away by force from the
Grecian: *Creusa* was lost for ever to her Husband. But *Achilles* went
roaring along the salt Sea-shore, and like a Booby, was complaining to
his Mother, when he shou'd have reveng'd his Injury by Arms. *Æneas* 785
took a Nobler Course; for having secur'd his Father and his Son, he
repeated all his former Dangers to have found his Wife, if she had been
above ground. And here your Lordship may observe the Address of
Virgil; it was not for nothing, that this Passage was related with all
these tender Circumstances. *Æneas* told it; *Dido* hear'd it: That he had 790
been so affectionate a Husband, was no ill Argument to the coming
Dowager, that he might prove as kind to her. *Virgil* has a thousand
secret Beauties, tho' I have not leisure to remark them.

Segrais on this Subject of a Heroe's shedding Tears, observes that
Historians commend *Alexander* for weeping, when he read the mighty 795
Actions of *Achilles*. And *Julius Cæsar* is likewise prais'd, when out of the
same Noble Envy, he wept at the Victories of *Alexander*. But if we
observe more closely, we shall find, that the tears of *Æneas* were always
on a laudable Occasion. Thus he weeps out of Compassion, and tenderness of Nature, when in the Temple of *Carthage* he beholds the Pictures 800
of his Friends, who Sacrific'd their Lives in Defence of their Country.
He deplores the lamentable End of his Pilot *Palinurus*; the untimely
death of young *Pallas* his Confederate; and the rest, which I omit. Yet
even for these Tears his wretched Criticks dare condemn him. They
make *Æneas* little better than a kind of a St. *Swithen* Heroe, always 805
raining. One of these Censors is bold enough to argue him of Cowardise; when in the beginning of the First Book, he not only weeps, but
trembles at an approaching Storm.

783 *Grecian*] *Grecians* 98

Extemplò Æneæ solvuntur frigore Membra:
Ingemit & duplices tendens ad sydera palmas, &c.   810

But to this I have answer'd formerly; that his fear was not for him-self, but for his People. And who can give a Soveraign a better Com-mendation, or recommend a Heroe more to the affection of the Reader? They were threatned with a Tempest, and he wept; he was promis'd *Italy*, and therefore he pray'd for the accomplishment of that Promise. 815 All this in the beginning of a Storm; therefore he shew'd the more early Piety, and the quicker sense of Compassion. Thus much I have urg'd elsewhere in the defence of *Virgil*; and since I have been inform'd, by Mr. *Moyl*, a young Gentleman, whom I can never sufficiently com-mend, that the Ancients accounted drowning an accursed Death. So 820 that if we grant him to have been afraid, he had just occasion for that fear, both in relation to himself, and to his Subjects. I think our Adver-saries can carry this Argument no farther, unless they tell us that he ought to have had more confidence in the promise of the Gods: But how was he assur'd that he had understood their Oracles aright? 825 *Helenus* might be mistaken, *Phœbus* might speak doubtfully, even his Mother might flatter him, that he might prosecute his Voyage, which if it succeeded happily, he shou'd be the Founder of an Empire. For that she her self was doubtful of his Fortune, is apparent by the Address she made to *Jupiter* on his behalf. To which the God makes answer in 830 these words:

Parce metu, Citherea, manent immota tuorum
Fata tibi, &c.

Notwithstanding which, the Goddess, though comforted, was not assur'd: For even after this, through the course of the whole *Æneis*, 835 she still apprehends the interest which *Juno* might make with *Jupiter* against her Son. For it was a moot Point in Heaven, whether he cou'd alter Fate or not. And indeed, some passages in *Virgil* wou'd make us suspect, that he was of Opinion, *Jupiter* might deferr Fate, though he cou'd not alter it. For in the latter end of the Tenth Book, he introduces 840 *Juno* begging for the Life of *Turnus*, and flattering her Husband with the power of changing Destiny. *Tua qui potes, orsa reflectas.* To which he graciously answers:

Si mora præsentis lethi tempusq; caduco
Oratur Juveni, meq; hoc ita ponere sentis,   845

Tolle fugâ Turnum, atq; instantibus Eripe fatis.
Hactenus indulsisse vacat. Sin altior istis
Sub precibus venia ulla latet, totumq; moveri,
Mutarive putas bellum, spes pascis inaneis.

But that he cou'd not alter those Decrees, the King of Gods himself 850 confesses, in the Book above cited: when he comforts *Hercules,* for the death of *Pallas,* who had invok'd his aid, before he threw his Lance at *Turnus.*

———*Trojæ sub mœnibus altis,*
Tot Nati Cecidere Deûm; quin occidit unâ 855
Sarpedon mea progenies: etiam sua Turnum
Fata manent: metasq; dati pervenit ad ævi.

Where he plainly acknowledges, that he cou'd not save his own Son, or prevent the death which he foresaw. Of his power to deferr the blow, I once occasionally discours'd with that Excellent Person Sir *Robert* 860 *Howard*: who is better conversant than any Man that I know, in the Doctrine of the Stoicks, and he set me right, from the concurrent testimony of Philosophers and Poets, that *Jupiter* cou'd not retard the effects of Fate, even for a moment. For when I cited *Virgil* as favouring the contrary opinion in that Verse, 865

Tolle fugâ Turnum, atq; instantibus eripe fatis.

he reply'd, and I think with an exact Judgment, that when *Jupiter* gave *Juno* leave to withdraw *Turnus* from the present danger, it was because he certainly fore-knew that his Fatal hour was not come: that it was in Destiny for *Juno* at that time to save him; and that he himself obey'd 870 Destiny, in giving her that leave.

I need say no more in justification of our Heroe's Courage, and am much deceiv'd, if he ever be attack'd on this side of his Character again. But he is Arraign'd with more shew of Reason by the Ladies; who will make a numerous Party against him, for being false to Love, in forsaking 875 *Dido.* And I cannot much blame them; for to say the truth, 'tis an ill Precedent for their Gallants to follow. Yet if I can bring him off, with Flying Colours, they may learn experience at her cost; and for her sake, avoid a Cave, as the worst shelter they can chuse from a shower of Rain, especially when they have a Lover in their Company. 880

857 *dati*] *om. 98*   861 Man that I *98*: Man I *97*   862 right, *98*: right; *97*
867 an] *om. 98*   870 he] *om. 98*

In the first place, *Segrais* observes with much acuteness, that they who blame *Æneas* for his insensibility of Love, when he left *Carthage*, contradict their former accusation of him, for being always Crying, Compassionate, and Effeminately sensible of those Misfortunes which befell others. They give him two contrary Characters, but *Virgil* makes 885 him of a piece, always grateful, always tender-hearted. But they are impudent enough to discharge themselves of this blunder, by laying the Contradiction at *Virgil*'s door. He, they say, has shewn his Heroe with these inconsistent Characters: Acknowledging, and Ungrateful, Compassionate, and Hard-harted; but at the bottom, Fickle, and Self- 890 interested. For *Dido* had not only receiv'd his weather-beaten Troops before she saw him, and given them her protection, but had also offer'd them an equal share in her Dominion.

> *Vultis & his mecum pariter considere Regnis?*
> *Urbem quam statuo, vestra est.*——————— 895

This was an obligement never to be forgotten: and the more to be consider'd, because antecedent to her Love. That passion, 'tis true, produc'd the usual effects of Generosity, Gallantry, and care to please, and thither we referr them. But when she had made all these advances, it was still in his power to have refus'd them: After the Intrigue of 900 the Cave, call it Marriage, or Enjoyment only, he was no longer free to take or leave; he had accepted the favour, and was oblig'd to be Constant, if he wou'd be grateful.

My Lord, I have set this Argument in the best light I can, that the Ladies may not think I write booty: and perhaps it may happen to me, 905 as it did to Doctor *Cudworth*, who has rais'd such strong Objections against the being of a God, and Providence, that many think he has not answer'd them. You may please at least to hear the adverse Party. *Segrais* pleads for *Virgil*, that no less than an Absolute Command from *Jupiter*, cou'd excuse this insensibility of the Heroe, and this abrupt 910 departure, which looks so like extream ingratitude. But at the same time, he does wisely to remember you, that *Virgil* had made Piety the first Character of *Æneas*: And this being allow'd, as I am afraid it must, he was oblig'd, antecedent to all other Considerations, to search an *Asylum* for his Gods in *Italy*. For those very Gods, I say, who had 915 promis'd to his Race the Universal Empire. Cou'd a Pious Man dispence with the Commands of *Jupiter* to satisfie his passion; or take it in the strongest sense, to comply with the obligations of his gratitude?

881 acuteness 98: accuteness 97

Religion, 'tis true, must have Moral Honesty for its ground-work, or we shall be apt to suspect its truth; but an immediate Revelation dis- 920 penses with all Duties of Morality. All Casuists agree, that Theft is a breach of the Moral Law: yet if I might presume to mingle Things Sacred with Prophane, the *Israelites* only spoil'd the *Egyptians*, not rob'd them; because the propriety was transferr'd, by a Revelation to their Law-giver. I confess *Dido* was a very Infidel in this Point: for she wou'd 925 not believe, as *Virgil* makes her say, that ever *Jupiter* wou'd send *Mercury* on such an Immoral Errand. But this needs no Answer; at least no more than *Virgil* gives it:

> *Fata obstant, placidasq; viri Deus obstruit aures.*

This notwithstanding, as *Segrais* confesses, he might have shewn a 930 little more sensibility when he left her; for that had been according to his Character.

But let *Virgil* answer for himself; he still lov'd her, and struggled with his inclinations, to obey the Gods.

> ——————*Curam sub Corde premebat,*   935
> *Multa gemens; magnoq; animum labefactus Amore.*

Upon the whole Matter, and humanely speaking, I doubt there was a fault somewhere; and *Jupiter* is better able to bear the blame, than either *Virgil* or *Æneas*. The Poet it seems had found it out, and there-fore brings the deserting Heroe and the forsaken Lady to meet together 940 in the lower Regions; where he excuses himself when 'tis too late, and accordingly she will take no satisfaction, nor so much as hear him. Now *Segrais* is forc'd to abandon his defence, and excuses his Author, by say-ing that the *Æneis* is an imperfect Work, and that Death prevented the Divine Poet from reviewing it; and for that Reason he had condemn'd 945 it to the fire; though at the same time, his two Translators must acknowledge, that the Sixth Book is the most Correct of the whole *Æneis*. Oh, how convenient is a Machine sometimes in a Heroick Poem! This of *Mercury* is plainly one, and *Virgil* was constrain'd to use it here, or the honesty of his Heroe wou'd be ill-defended. And the Fair Sex 950 however, if they had the Desertour in their power, wou'd certainly have shewn him no more mercy, than the *Bacchanals* did *Orpheus*. For if too much Constancy may be a fault sometimes, then want of Constancy, and Ingratitude after the last Favour, is a Crime that never will be for-given. But of Machines, more in their proper place: where I shall shew, 955 with how much judgment they have been us'd by *Virgil*; and in the

924 them; *98*: them, *97*   transferr'd, *98*: transferr'd; *97*

mean time pass to another Article of his defence on the present Subject: where if I cannot clear the Heroe, I hope at least to bring off the Poet; for here I must divide their Causes. Let *Æneas* trust to his Machine, which will only help to break his Fall, but the Address is incomparable. 960 *Plato*, who borrow'd so much from *Homer*, and yet concluded for the Banishment of all Poets, wou'd at least have Rewarded *Virgil*, before he sent him into Exile. But I go farther, and say, that he ought to be acquitted, and deserv'd beside, the Bounty of *Augustus*, and the gratitude of the *Roman* People. If after this, the Ladies will stand out, 965 let them remember, that the Jury is not all agreed; for *Octavia* was of his Party, and was of the first Quality in *Rome*; she was also present at the reading of the Sixth *Æneid*, and we know not that she condemn'd *Æneas*; but we are sure she presented the Poet, for his admirable Elegy on her Son *Marcellus*. 970

But let us consider the secret Reasons which *Virgil* had, for thus framing this Noble Episode, wherein the whole passion of Love is more exactly describ'd than in any other Poet. Love was the Theme of his Fourth Book; and though it is the shortest of the whole *Æneis*, yet there he has given its beginning, its progress, its traverses, and its conclu- 975 sion. And had exhausted so entirely this Subject, that he cou'd resume it but very slightly in the Eight ensuing Books.

She was warm'd with the graceful appearance of the Heroe, she smother'd those Sparkles out of decency, but Conversation blew them up into a Flame. Then she was forc'd to make a Confident of her whom 980 she best might trust, her own Sister, who approves the passion, and thereby augments it, then succeeds her publick owning it; and after that, the consummation. Of *Venus* and *Juno*, *Jupiter* and *Mercury*, I say nothing, for they were all Machining work; but possession having cool'd his Love, as it increas'd hers, she soon perceiv'd the change, or 985 at least grew suspicious of a change; this suspicion soon turn'd to Jealousie, and Jealousie to Rage; then she disdains and threatens, and again is humble, and intreats; and nothing availing, despairs, curses, and at last becomes her own Executioner. See here the whole process of that passion, to which nothing can be added. I dare go no farther, lest 990 I shou'd lose the connection of my Discourse.

To love our Native Country, and to study its Benefit and its Glory, to be interested in its Concerns, is Natural to all Men, and is indeed our common Duty. A Poet makes a farther step; for endeavouring to do

967 was of the first . . . was also present *98*: was also of the first . . . was present *97*
983 *Mercury*, *98*: *Mercury 97*

honour to it, 'tis allowable in him even to be partial in its Cause; for 995
he is not ty'd to truth, or fetter'd by the Laws of History. *Homer* and
Tasso are justly prais'd for chusing their Heroes out of *Greece* and *Italy*;
Virgil indeed made his a *Trojan*, but it was to derive the *Romans*, and
his own *Augustus* from him; but all the three Poets are manifestly
partial to their Heroes, in favour of their Country. For *Dares Phrygius* 1000
reports of *Hector*, that he was slain Cowardly; *Æneas* according to
the best account, slew not *Mezentius*, but was slain by him: and the
Chronicles of *Italy* tell us little of that *Rinaldo d'Estè* who Conquers
Jerusalem in *Tasso*. He might be a Champion of the Church; but we
know not that he was so much as present at the Siege. To apply this 1005
to *Virgil*, he thought himself engag'd in Honour to espouse the Cause
and Quarrel of his Country against *Carthage*. He knew he cou'd not
please the *Romans* better, or oblige them more to Patronize his Poem,
than by disgracing the Foundress of that City. He shews her ungrateful
to the Memory of her first Husband, doting on a Stranger; enjoy'd, 1010
and afterwards forsaken by him. This was the Original, says he, of the
immortal hatred betwixt the two Rival Nations. 'Tis true, he colours
the falsehood of *Æneas* by an express Command from *Jupiter*, to forsake
the Queen, who had oblig'd him: but he knew the *Romans* were to be
his Readers, and them he brib'd, perhaps at the expence of his Heroe's 1015
honesty, but he gain'd his Cause however; as Pleading before Corrupt
Judges. They were content to see their Founder false to Love, for still
he had the advantage of the Amour: It was their Enemy whom he forsook, and she might have forsaken him, if he had not got the start of
her: she had already forgotten her Vows to her *Sichæus*; and *varium & * 1020
mutabile semper femina, is the sharpest Satire in the fewest words that
ever was made on Womankind; for both the Adjectives are Neuter, and
Animal must be understood, to make them Grammar. *Virgil* does well
to put those words into the mouth of *Mercury*. *If a God had not spoken*
them, neither durst he have written them, nor I translated them. Yet the Deity 1025
was forc'd to come twice on the same Errand: and the second time, as
much a Heroe as *Æneas* was, he frighted him. It seems he fear'd not
Jupiter so much as *Dido*. For your Lordship may observe, that as much
intent as he was upon his Voyage, yet he still delay'd it, 'till the
Messenger was oblig'd to tell him plainly, that if he weigh'd not 1030
Anchor in the Night, the Queen wou'd be with him in the Morning.
Notumq; furens quid femina possit; she was Injur'd, she was Revengeful,
she was Powerful. The Poet had likewise before hinted, that her People

1022 ever was *98*: was ever *97*

were naturally perfidious: For he gives their Character in their Queen, and makes a Proverb of *Punica fides*, many Ages before it was invented. 1035

Thus I hope, my Lord, that I have made good my Promise, and justify'd the Poet, whatever becomes of the false Knight. And sure a Poet is as much priviledg'd to lye, as an Ambassador, for the Honour and Interest of his Country; at least as Sir *Henry Wootton* has defin'd.

This naturally leads me to the defence of the Famous *Anachronism*, in 1040 making *Æneas* and *Dido* Contemporaries. For 'tis certain that the Heroe liv'd almost two hundred years before the Building of *Carthage*. One who imitates *Bocaline*, says that *Virgil* was accus'd before *Apollo* for this Error. The God soon found that he was not able to defend his Favourite by Reason, for the Case was clear: he therefore gave this middle Sen- 1045 tence; That any thing might be allow'd to his Son *Virgil* on the account of his other Merits; That being a Monarch he had a dispensing Power, and pardon'd him. But that this special Act of Grace might never be drawn into Example, or pleaded by his puny Successors, in justification of their ignorance; he decreed for the future, No Poet shou'd presume 1050 to make a Lady die for Love two hundred years before her Birth. To Moralize this Story, *Virgil* is the *Apollo*, who has this Dispensing Power. His great Judgment made the Laws of Poetry, but he never made himself a Slave to them: Chronology at best is but a Cobweb-Law, and he broke through it with his weight. They who will imitate 1055 him wisely, must chuse as he did, an obscure and a remote *Æra*, where they may invent at pleasure, and not be easily contradicted. Neither he, nor the *Romans* had ever read the Bible, by which only his false computation of times can be made out against him: this *Segrais* says in his defence, and proves it from his Learned Friend *Bochartus*, whose 1060 Letter on this Subject, he has Printed at the end of the Fourth *Æneid*, to which I referr your Lordship, and the Reader. Yet the Credit of *Virgil* was so great, that he made this Fable of his own Invention pass for an Authentick History, or at least as credible as any thing in *Homer*. *Ovid* takes it up after him, even in the same Age, and makes an ancient 1065 Heroine of *Virgil*'s new-created *Dido*; Dictates a Letter for her just before her death, to the ingrateful Fugitive; and very unluckily for himself, is for measuring a Sword with a Man so much superiour in force to him on the same subject. I think I may be Judge of this, because I have Translated both. The Famous Author of the Art of Love has 1070 nothing of his own, he borrows all from a greater Master in his own profession; and which is worse, improves nothing which he finds.

Nature fails him, and being forc'd to his old shift, he has recourse to Witticism. This passes indeed with his Soft Admirers, and gives him the preference to *Virgil* in their esteem. But let them like for themselves, 1075 and not prescribe to others, for our Author needs not their Admiration.

The Motives that induc'd *Virgil* to Coyn this Fable, I have shew'd already; and have also begun to shew that he might make this *Anacronism*, by superseding the mechanick Rules of Poetry, for the same Reason, that a Monarch may dispense with, or suspend his own Laws, when he 1080 finds it necessary so to do; especially if those Laws are not altogether fundamental. Nothing is to be call'd a fault in Poetry, says *Aristotle*, but what is against the Art; therefore a Man may be an admirable Poet, without being an exact Chronologer. Shall we dare, continues *Segrais*, to condemn *Virgil*, for having made a Fiction against the order of time, 1085 when we commend *Ovid* and other Poets who have made many of their Fictions against the Order of Nature? For what else are the splendid Miracles of the *Metamorphoses*? Yet these are Beautiful as they are related; and have also deep Learning and instructive Mythologies couch'd under them: But to give, as *Virgil* does in this Episode, the 1090 Original Cause of the long Wars betwixt *Rome* and *Carthage*, to draw Truth out of Fiction, after so probable a manner, with so much Beauty, and so much for the Honour of his Country, was proper only to the Divine Wit of *Maro*; and *Tasso* in one of his Discourses, admires him for this particularly. 'Tis not lawful indeed, to contradict a Point of 1095 History, which is known to all the World; as for Example, to make *Hannibal* and *Scipio* Contemporaries with *Alexander*; but in the dark Recesses of Antiquity, a great Poet may and ought to feign such things as he finds not there, if they can be brought to embelish that Subject which he treats. On the other side, the pains and diligence of ill Poets 1100 is but thrown away, when they want the Genius to invent and feign agreeably. But if the Fictions be delightful, which they always are, if they be natural, if they be of a piece; if the beginning, the middle, and the end be in their due places, and artfully united to each other, such Works can never fail of their deserv'd Success. And such is *Virgil*'s 1105 Episode of *Dido* and *Æneas*; where the sourest Critick must acknowledge, that if he had depriv'd his *Æneis* of so great an Ornament, because he found no traces of it in Antiquity, he had avoided their unjust Censure, but had wanted one of the greatest Beauties of his Poem. I shall say more of this, in the next Article of their Charge against him, 1110 which is want of Invention. In the mean time I may affirm in honour of

1087 else are *98*: are else *97*

this Episode, that it is not only now esteem'd the most pleasing entertainment of the *Æneis*, but was so accounted in his own Age; and before
it was mellow'd into that reputation, which time has given it; for which
I need produce no other testimony, than that of *Ovid*, his Contemporary. 1115

> *Nec pars ulla magis legitur de Corpore toto*
> *Quam non legitimo fœdere, junctus Amor.*

Where by the way, you may observe, my Lord, that *Ovid* in those
words, *Non legitimo fœdere junctus Amor*, will by no means allow it to be
a lawful Marriage betwixt *Dido* and *Æneas*. He was in Banishment when 1120
he wrote those Verses, which I cite from his Letter to *Augustus*. You,
Sir, saith he, have sent me into Exile for writing my Art of Love, and
my wanton Elegies; yet your own Poet was happy in your good graces,
though he brought *Dido* and *Æneas* into a Cave, and left them there not
over-honestly together. May I be so bold to ask your Majesty, is it a 1125
greater fault to teach the Art of unlawful Love, than to shew it in the
Action? But was *Ovid* the Court-Poet so bad a Courtier, as to find no
other Plea to excuse himself, than by a plain accusation of his Master?
Virgil confess'd it was a Lawful Marriage betwixt the Lovers; that *Juno*
the Goddess of Matrimony had ratify'd it by her presence, for it was 1130
her business to bring Matters to that issue. That the Ceremonies were
short we may believe, for *Dido* was not only amorous, but a Widow.
Mercury himself, though employ'd on a quite contrary Errand, yet owns
it a Marriage by an *innuendo: pulchramq; Uxorius Urbem Extruis*—He calls
Æneas not only a Husband, but upbraids him for being a fond Husband, 1135
as the word *Uxorius* implies. Now mark a little, if your Lordship pleases,
why *Virgil* is so much concern'd to make this Marriage, (for he seems
to be the Father of the Bride himself, and to give her to the Bridegroom)
it was to make way for the Divorce which he intended afterwards; for
he was a finer Flatterer than *Ovid*: and I more than conjecture that he 1140
had in his eye the Divorce which not long before had pass'd betwixt the
Emperour and *Scribonia*. He drew this dimple in the Cheek of *Æneas*,
to prove *Augustus* of the same Family, by so remarkable a Feature in the
same place. Thus, as we say in our home-spun *English* Proverb, *He
kill'd two Birds with one stone;* pleas'd the Emperour by giving him the 1145
resemblance of his Ancestor; and gave him such a resemblance as was
not scandalous in that Age. For to leave one Wife and take another, was
but a matter of Gallantry at that time of day among the *Romans*. *Neque*

1122 saith *98*: says *97*   1135 for *98*: with *97*   1137 Marriage, *98*: Marriage *97*

hæc in jædera veni, is the very Excuse which *Æneas* makes, when he leaves his Lady. I made no such Bargain with you at our Marriage, to live 1150 always drudging on at *Carthage*; my business was *Italy*, and I never made a secret of it. If I took my pleasure, had not you your share of it? I leave you free at my departure, to comfort your self with the next Stranger who happens to be Shipwreck'd on your Coast. Be as kind an Hostess as you have been to me, and you can never fail of another 1155 Husband. In the mean time, I call the Gods to witness, that I leave your Shore unwillingly; for though *Juno* made the Marriage, yet *Jupiter* Commands me to forsake you. This is the effect of what he saith, when it is dishonour'd out of Latin Verse, into English Prose. If the Poet argued not aright, we must pardon him for a poor blind Heathen, who 1160 knew no better Morals.

I have detain'd your Lordship longer than I intended on this Objection: Which wou'd indeed weigh something in a Spiritual Court; but I am not to defend our Poet there. The next I think is but a Cavil, though the Cry is great against him, and hath continu'd from the time 1165 of *Macrobius* to this present Age. I hinted it before. They lay no less than want of Invention to his Charge. A capital Crime, I must acknowledge. For a Poet is a Maker, as the word signifies: And who cannot make, that is, invent, hath his Name for nothing. That which makes this Accusation look so strange at the first sight, is, That he has 1170 borrow'd so many things from *Homer*, *Apollonius Rhodius*, and others who preceded him. But in the first place, if Invention is to be taken in so strict a sense, that the Matter of a Poem must be wholly new, and that in all its Parts; then *Scaliger* hath made out, saith *Segrais*, that the History of *Troy* was no more the Invention of *Homer*, than of *Virgil*. 1175 There was not an Old Woman, or almost a Child, but had it in their Mouths, before the Greek Poet or his Friends digested it into this admirable order in which we read it. At this rate, as *Solomon* hath told us, there is nothing new beneath the Sun: Who then can pass for an Inventor, if *Homer*, as well as *Virgil* must be depriv'd of that Glory? Is 1180 *Versailles* the less a New Building, because the Architect of that Palace hath imitated others which were built before it? Walls, Doors and Windows, Apartments, Offices, Rooms of convenience and Magnificence, are in all great Houses. So Descriptions, Figures, Fables, and the rest, must be in all Heroick Poems. They are the Common Materials of 1185

1158 saith *98*: says *97*   1165 hath *98*: has *97*   1167 Crime, *98*: Crime *97*
1169 hath *98*: has *97*   1171 *Apollonius 98*: *Appollonius 97*   1174 hath *98*:
has *97*   saith *98*: says *97*   1178 hath *98*: has *97*   1182 hath *98*: has *97*
1184 Descriptions, *98*: Descriptions *97*

Poetry, furnish'd from the Magazine of Nature: Every Poet hath as much right to them, as every Man hath to Air or Water. *Quid prohibetis Aquas? Usus communis aquarum est.* But the Argument of the Work, that is to say, its principal Action, the Oeconomy and Disposition of it; these are the things which distinguish Copies from Originals. The 119 Poet, who borrows nothing from others, is yet to be Born. He and the *Jews* Messias will come together. There are parts of the *Æneis*, which resemble some parts both of the *Ilias* and of the *Odysses*; as for Example, *Æneas* descended into Hell, and *Ulysses* had been there before him: *Æneas* lov'd *Dido,* and *Ulysses* lov'd *Calypso*: In few words, *Virgil* hath 119 imitated *Homer*'s *Odysses* in his first six Books, and in his six last the *Ilias*. But from hence can we infer, that the two Poets write the same History? Is there no invention in some other parts of *Virgil*'s *Æneis*? The disposition of so many various matters, is not that his own? From what Book of *Homer* had *Virgil* his *Episode* of *Nysus* and *Euryalus,* of 120 *Mezentius* and *Lausus*? From whence did he borrow his Design of bring-ing *Æneas* into *Italy,* of Establishing the *Roman* Empire on the Founda-tions of a *Trojan* Colony; to say nothing of the honour he did his Patron, not only in his descent from *Venus,* but in making him so like him in his best Features, that the Goddess might have mistaken *Augustus* for her 120 Son. He had indeed the Story from common Fame, as *Homer* had his from the *Egyptian* Priestess. *Æneadum Genetrix* was no more unknown to *Lucretius* than to him. But *Lucretius* taught him not to form his Heroe; to give him Piety or Valour for his Manners; and both in so eminent a degree, that having done what was possible for Man, to save his King 121 and Country; his Mother was forc'd to appear to him and restrain his Fury, which hurry'd him to death in their Revenge. But the Poet made his Piety more successful; he brought off his Father and his Son; and his Gods witness'd to his Devotion, by putting themselves under his Protection; to be re-plac'd by him in their promis'd *Italy.* Neither the 121 Invention, nor the Conduct of this great Action, were owing to *Homer* or any other Poet. 'Tis one thing to Copy, and another thing to imitate from Nature. The Copyer is that servile Imitator, to whom *Horace* gives no better a Name than that of Animal: He will not so much as allow him to be a Man. *Raphael* imitated Nature: They who Copy one of 122 *Raphael*'s Pieces, imitate but him, for his Work is their Original. They Translate him as I do *Virgil*; and fall as short of him as I of *Virgil*. There is a kind of Invention in the imitation of *Raphael*; for though the thing

1186–7 hath . . . hath *98:* has . . . has *97*   1195 hath *98:* has *97*   1204 like him] like her *98*

was in Nature, yet the Idea of it was his own. *Ulysses* Travell'd, so did
Æneas; but neither of them were the first Travellers; for *Cain* went into 1225
the Land of *Nod*, before they were born: And neither of the Poets ever
heard of such a Man. If *Ulysses* had been kill'd at *Troy*, yet *Æneas* must
have gone to Sea, or he could never have arriv'd in *Italy*. But the
designs of the two Poets were as different as the Courses of their
Heroes; one went Home, and the other sought a Home. To return to 1230
my first similitude: Suppose *Apelles* and *Raphael* had each of them
Painted a burning *Troy*; might not the Modern Painter have succeeded as well as the Ancient, tho' neither of them had seen the Town
on Fire? For the draughts of both were taken from the Idea's which
they had of Nature. Cities had been burnt before either of them 1235
were in Being. But to Close the Simile as I begun it; they wou'd
not have design'd after the same manner. *Apelles* wou'd have distinguish'd *Pyrrhus* from the rest of all the *Grecians*, and shew'd him
forcing his entrance into *Priam*'s Palace; there he had set him in the
fairest Light, and given him the chief place of all his Figures, because 1240
he was a *Grecian*, and he wou'd do Honour to his Country. *Raphael*, who
was an *Italian*, and descended from the *Trojans*, wou'd have made
Æneas the Heroe of his piece: And perhaps not with his Father on his
Back; his Son in one hand, his Bundle of Gods in the other, and his Wife
following; (for an Act of Piety, is not half so graceful in a Picture as an 1245
Act of Courage:) He would rather have drawn him killing *Androgeos*,
or some other, Hand to Hand; and the blaze of the Fires shou'd have
darted full upon his Face, to make him conspicuous amongst his
Trojans. This I think is a just Comparison betwixt the two Poets in the
Conduct of their several designs. *Virgil* cannot be said to copy *Homer*: 1250
The *Grecian* had only the advantage of writing first. If it be urg'd that
I have granted a resemblance in some parts; yet therein *Virgil* has
excell'd him: For what are the Tears of *Calypso* for being left, to the
Fury and Death of *Dido*? Where is there the whole process of her
Passion, and all its violent Effects to be found, in the languishing 1255
Episode of the *Odysses*? If this be to Copy, let the Criticks shew us the
same Disposition, Features, or Colouring in their Original. The like
may be said of the Descent to Hell; which was not of *Homer*'s Invention
neither: He had it from the Story of *Orpheus* and *Eurydice*. But to what
end did *Ulysses* make that Journey? *Æneas* undertook it by the express 1260
Commandment of his Father's Ghost: There he was to shew him all the
succeeding Heroes of his Race; and next to *Romulus*, (mark, if you please,

1237 design'd after] design'd it after *98*

the Address of *Virgil*) his own Patron *Augustus Cæsar*. *Anchises* was likewise to instruct him, how to manage the *Italian* War; and how to conclude it with his Honour. That is, in other words, to lay the Foundations of that Empire which *Augustus* was to Govern. This is the Noble Invention of our Author: But it has been Copyed by so many Signpost Daubers; that now 'tis grown fulsom, rather by their want of Skill, than by the Commonness.

In the last place I may safely grant, that by reading *Homer*, *Virgil* was taught to imitate his Invention: That is, to imitate like him; which is no more, than if a Painter studied *Raphael*, that he might learn to design after his manner. And thus I might imitate *Virgil*, if I were capable of writing an Heroick Poem, and yet the Invention be my own: But I shou'd endeavour to avoid a servile Copying. I would not give the same Story under other Names: With the same Characters, in the same Order, and with the same Sequel: For every common Reader to find me out at the first sight for a Plagiary: And cry, this I read before in *Virgil*, in a better Language, and in better Verse: This is like merry *Andrew* on the low Rope, copying lubberly the same Tricks, which his Master is so dextrously performing on the high.

I will trouble your Lordship but with one Objection more; which I know not whether I found in *Le Fevre* or *Valois*, but I am sure I have read it in another *French* Critick, whom I will not name, because I think it is not much for his Reputation. *Virgil*, in the heat of Action, suppose for Example, in describing the fury of his Heroe in a Battel, when he is endeavouring to raise our concernments to the highest pitch, turns short on the sudden into some similitude, which diverts, say they, your attention from the main Subject, and mispends it on some trivial Image. He pours cold Water into the Caldron when his business is to make it boil.

This Accusation is general against all who wou'd be thought Heroick Poets; but I think it touches *Virgil* less than any. He is too great a Master of his Art, to make a Blott which may so easily be hit. Similitudes, as I have said, are not for Tragedy, which is all violent, and where the Passions are in a perpetual ferment; for there they deaden where they should animate; they are not of the nature of Dialogue, unless in Comedy: A Metaphor is almost all the Stage can suffer, which is a kind of Similitude comprehended in a word. But this Figure has a contrary effect in Heroick Poetry: There 'tis employ'd to raise the Admiration, which is its proper business. And Admiration is not of so

1281 is so dextrously *98*: is dextrously *97*

violent a nature as Fear or Hope, Compassion or Horrour, or any Concernment we can have for such or such a Person on the Stage. Not but
I confess, that Similitudes and Descriptions, when drawn into an un-
reasonable length, must needs nauseate the Reader. Once I remember, 1305
and but once; *Virgil* makes a Similitude of fourteen Lines; and his
description of Fame is about the same number. He is blam'd for both;
and I doubt not but he would have contracted them, had he liv'd to
have review'd his Work: But Faults are no Precedents. This I have
observ'd of his Similitudes in general, that they are not plac'd, as our 1310
unobserving Criticks tell us, in the heat of any Action: But commonly
in its declining: When he has warm'd us in his Description, as much as
possibly he can; then, lest that warmth should languish, he renews it
by some apt Similitude, which illustrates his Subject, and yet palls not
his Audience. I need give your Lordship but one Example of this kind, 1315
and leave the rest to your Observation, when next you review the
whole *Æneis* in the Original unblemish'd by my rude Translation. 'Tis
in the first Book, where the Poet describes *Neptune* composing the
Ocean, on which *Eolus* had rais'd a Tempest, without his permission.
He had already chidden the Rebellious Winds for obeying the Com- 1320
mands of their Usurping Master: He had warn'd them from the Seas:
He had beaten down the Billows with his Mace; dispell'd the Clouds,
restor'd the Sun-shine, while *Triton* and *Cymothoe* were heaving the
Ships from off the Quick-Sands; before the Poet wou'd offer at a
Similitude for illustration.   1325

> *Ac, veluti magno in populo cùm sæpe coorta est*
> *Seditio, sævitque animis ignobile vulgus,*
> *Jamque faces, & saxa volant, furor arma ministrat;*
> *Tum, pietate gravem, ac meritis si forte virum quem*
> *Conspexere, silent, arrectisque auribus adstant:*   1330
> *Ille regit dictis animos, & pectora mulcet:*
> *Sic cunctus pelagi cecidit fragor, æquora postquam*
> *Prospiciens genitor, cæloque invectus aperto*
> *Flectit equos, curruque volans dat lora secundo.*

This is the first Similitude which *Virgil* makes in this Poem: And 1335
one of the longest in the whole; for which Reason I the rather cite it.
While the Storm was in its fury, any Allusion had been improper: For
the Poet cou'd have compar'd it to nothing more impetuous that it
self; consequently he could have made no Illustration. If he cou'd have

1321 Seas: *98*: Seas, *97*

illustrated, it had been an ambitious Ornament out of season, and would 134⟨
have diverted our Concernment: *Nunc, non erat hisce locus;* and therefore
he deferr'd it to its proper place.

These are the Criticisms of most moment which have been made
against the *Æneis*, by the Ancients or Moderns. As for the particular
Exceptions against this or that passage, *Macrobius* and *Pontanus* have 134
answer'd them already. If I desir'd to appear more Learned than I am,
it had been as easie for me to have taken their Objections and Solutions,
as it is for a Country Parson to take the Expositions of the Fathers out
of *Junius* and *Tremellius*: Or not to have nam'd the Authors from whence
I had them: For so *Ruæus*, otherwise a most judicious Commentator on 135
Virgil's Works, has us'd *Pontanus*, his greatest Benefactor; of whom, he
is very silent, and I do not remember that he once cites him.

What follows next, is no Objection; for that implies a Fault: And it
had been none in *Virgil*, if he had extended the time of his Action
beyond a Year. At least *Aristotle* has set no precise limits to it. *Homer's,* 135
we know, was within two Months: *Tasso* I am sure exceeds not a
Summer: And if I examin'd him, perhaps he might be reduc'd into
a much less compass. *Bossu* leaves it doubtful whether *Virgil's* Action
were within the Year, or took up some Months beyond it. Indeed the
whole Dispute is of no more concernment to the common Reader, than 136
it is to a Plough-man, whether *February* this Year had 28 or 29 Days
in it. But for the satisfaction of the more Curious, of which number, I
am sure your Lordship is one; I will Translate what I think convenient
out of *Segrais*, whom perhaps you have not read: For he has made it
highly probable, that the Action of the *Æneis* began in the Spring, and 136
was not extended beyond the Autumn. And we have known Cam-
paigns that have begun sooner, and have ended later.

Ronsard and the rest whom *Segrais* names, who are of Opinion that the
Action of this Poem takes up almost a Year and half; ground their
Calculation thus. *Anchises* dyed in *Sicily* at the end of Winter, or begin- 137
ning of the Spring. *Æneas*, immediately after the Interment of his
Father, puts to Sea for *Italy*: He is surpriz'd by the Tempest describ'd
in the beginning of the first Book; and there it is that the Scene of the
Poem opens; and where the Action must Commence. He is driven
by this Storm on the Coasts of *Affrick*: He stays at *Carthage* all that 137
Summer, and almost all the Winter following: Sets Sail again for *Italy*
just before the beginning of the Spring; meets with contrary Winds,
and makes *Sicily* the second time: This part of the Action compleats the

Year. Then he celebrates the Anniversary of his Father's Funerals, and shortly after arrives at *Cumes*, and from thence his time is taken up in 1380 his first Treaty with *Latinus*; the Overture of the War; the Siege of his Camp by *Turnus*; his going for Succours to relieve it: His return: The raising of the Siege by the first Battel: The twelve days Truce: The second Battel: The Assault of *Laurentum*, and the single Fight with *Turnus*; all which, they say, cannot take up less than four or five Months 1385 more; by which Account we cannot suppose the entire Action to be contain'd in a much less compass than a Year and half.

Segrais reckons another way; and his computation is not condemn'd by the learned *Ruæus*, who compil'd and Publish'd the Commentaries on our Poet, which we call the *Dauphin's Virgil*. 1390

He allows the time of Year when *Anchises* dyed; to be in the latter end of Winter, or the beginning of the Spring; he acknowledges that when *Æneas* is first seen at Sea afterwards, and is driven by the Tempest on the Coast of *Affrick*, is the time when the Action is naturally to begin: He confesses farther, that *Æneas* left *Carthage* in the latter end 1395 of Winter; for *Dido* tells him in express terms, as an Argument for his longer stay,

Quinetiam Hyberno moliris sydere Classem.

But whereas *Ronsard's* Followers suppose that when *Æneas* had buried his Father, he set Sail immediately for *Italy*, (tho' the Tempest drove 1400 him on the Coast of *Carthage*,) *Segrais* will by no means allow that Supposition; but thinks it much more probable that he remain'd in *Sicily* 'till the midst of *July* or the beginning of *August*; at which time he places the first appearance of his Heroe on the Sea; and there opens the Action of the Poem. From which beginning, to the Death of *Turnus*, 1405 which concludes the Action, there need not be suppos'd above ten Months of intermediate time: For arriving at *Carthage* in the latter end of Summer, staying there the Winter following; departing thence in the very beginning of the Spring; making a short abode in *Sicily* the second time, landing in *Italy*, and making the War, may be reasonably judg'd 1410 the business but of ten Months. To this the *Ronsardians* reply, that having been for Seven Years before in quest of *Italy*, and having no more to do in *Sicily*, than to interr his Father; after that Office was perform'd, what remain'd for him, but, without delay, to pursue his first Adventure? To which *Segrais* answers, that the Obsequies of his Father, 1415 according to the Rites of the *Greeks* and *Romans*, would detain him for

many days: That a longer time must be taken up in the refitting of his
Ships, after so tedious a Voyage; and in refreshing his Weather-beaten
Souldiers on a friendly Coast. These indeed are but Suppositions on
both sides, yet those of *Segrais* seem better grounded. For the Feast of 1420
Dido, when she entertain'd *Æneas* first, has the appearance of a Summer's
Night, which seems already almost ended, when he begins his Story:
Therefore the Love was made in Autumn; the Hunting follow'd
properly when the Heats of that scorching Country were declining:
The Winter was pass'd in jollity, as the Season and their Love requir'd; 1425
and he left her in the latter end of Winter, as is already prov'd. This
Opinion is fortify'd by the Arrival of *Æneas* at the Mouth of *Tyber*;
which marks the Season of the Spring, that Season being perfectly
describ'd by the singing of the Birds, saluting the dawn; and by the
Beauty of the place, which the Poet seems to have painted expresly in 1430
the Seventh *Æneid.*

> *Aurora in roseis fulgebat lutea bigis,*
> *Cùm venti posuere; variæ circumque, supraque*
> *Assuetæ ripis volucres, & fluminis alveo,*
> *Æthera mulcebant cantu.*————   1435

The remainder of the Action requir'd but three Months more; for
when *Æneas* went for Succour to the *Tuscans,* he found their Army in a
readiness to march; and wanting only a Commander: So that according
to this Calculation, the *Æneis* takes not up above a Year compleat, and
may be comprehended in less compass.   1440

This, amongst other Circumstances, treated more at large by *Segrais,*
agrees with the rising of *Orion,* which caus'd the Tempest, describ'd
in the beginning of the first Book. By some passages in the Pastorals,
but more particularly in the *Georgicks,* our Poet is found to be an exact
Astronomer, according to the Knowledge of that Age. Now *Ilioneus* 1445
(whom *Virgil* twice employs in Embassies, as the best Speaker of the
Trojans) attributes that Tempest to *Orion* in his Speech to *Dido.*

> *Cum subito, assurgens fluctu nimbosus Orion.*

He must mean either the *Heliacal* or *Achronical* rising of that Sign.
The *Heliacal* rising of a Constellation, is when it comes from under the 1450
Rays of the Sun, and begins to appear before Day-light. The *Achronical*
rising, on the contrary, is when it appears at the close of Day, and in
opposition of the Sun's diurnal Course.

The *Heliacal* rising of *Orion,* is at present computed to be about the

1432 *bigis,* 98: *bigis:* 97

sixth of *July*; and about that time it is, that he either causes, or presages 1455
Tempests on the Seas.

Segrais has observ'd farther, that when *Anna* Counsels *Dido* to stay
Æneas during the Winter; she speaks also of *Orion*;

> *Dum pelago desævit hyems, & aquosus Orion.*

If therefore *Ilioneus*, according to our Supposition, understand the 1460
Heliacal rising of *Orion: Anna* must mean the *Achronical*, which the
different Epithetes given to that Constellation, seem to manifest. *Ilioneus* calls him *nimbosus, Anna aquosus.* He is tempestuous in the Summer when he rises *Heliacally*, and Rainy in the Winter when he rises
Achronically. Your Lordship will pardon me for the frequent repetition 1465
of these cant words; which I cou'd not avoid in this abbreviation
of *Segrais*; who I think deserves no little commendation in this new
Criticism.

I have yet a word or two to say of *Virgil*'s Machines, from my own
observation of them. He has imitated those of *Homer*, but not Copied 1470
them. It was establish'd long before this time, in the *Roman* Religion
as well as in the *Greek*; that there were Gods; and both Nations, for the
most part, worshipp'd the same Deities; as did also the *Trojans*: From
whom the *Romans*, I suppose, wou'd rather be thought to derive the
Rites of their Religion, than from the *Grecians*; because they thought 1475
themselves descended from them. Each of those Gods had his proper
Office, and the chief of them their particular Attendants. Thus *Jupiter*
had in propriety, *Ganimede* and *Mercury*; and *Juno* had *Iris*. It was not
then for *Virgil* to create new Ministers; he must take what he found in
his Religion. It cannot therefore be said that he borrow'd them from 1480
Homer, any more than *Apollo, Diana*, and the rest, whom he uses as he
finds occasion for them, as the *Grecian* Poet did: But he invents the
occasions for which he uses them. *Venus*, after the destruction of *Troy*,
had gain'd *Neptune* entirely to her Party; therefore we find him busie in
the beginning of the *Æneis*, to calm the Tempest rais'd by *Æolus*, and 1485
afterwards conducting the *Trojan* Fleet to *Cumes* in safety, with the loss
only of their Pilot; for whom he Bargains. I name those two Examples
amongst a hundred which I omit; to prove that *Virgil*, generally speaking, employ'd his Machines in performing those things, which might
possibly have been done without them. What more frequent then a 1490
Storm at Sea, upon the rising of *Orion*? What wonder, if amongst so
many Ships there shou'd one be overset, which was commanded by

1469 *Editor's paragraph*   1479 then for *Virgil*] for *Virgil* then 98   1481 than
Apollo] than from *Apollo* 98

Orontes; though half the Winds had not been there, which *Æolus* employ'd? Might not *Palinurus*, without a Miracle, fall asleep, and drop into the Sea, having been over-wearied with watching, and secure of 1495 a quiet passage, by his observation of the Skies? At least *Æneas*, who knew nothing of the Machine of *Somnus*, takes it plainly in this Sense.

> *O nimium Cælo & Pelago confise sereno,*
> *Nudus in ignotâ Palinure jacebis arenâ.*

But Machines sometimes are specious things to amuse the Reader, 1500 and give a colour of probability to things otherwise incredible. And besides, it sooth'd the vanity of the *Romans*, to find the Gods so visibly concern'd in all the Actions of their Predecessors. We who are better taught by our Religion, yet own every wonderful Accident which befalls us for the best, to be brought to pass by some special Providence 1505 of Almighty God; and by the care of guardian Angels: And from hence I might infer, that no Heroick Poem can be writ on the *Epicuræan* Principles. Which I cou'd easily demonstrate, if there were need to prove it, or I had leisure.

When *Venus* opens the Eyes of her Son *Æneas*, to behold the Gods who 1510 Combated against *Troy*, in that fatal Night when it was surpriz'd; we share the pleasure of that glorious Vision, (which *Tasso* has not ill Copied in the sacking of *Jerusalem*.) But the *Greeks* had done their business; though neither *Neptune*, *Juno*, or *Pallas*, had given them their Divine assistance. The most crude Machine which *Virgil* uses, is in the 1515 *Episode* of *Camilla*, where *Opis* by the command of her Mistress, kills *Aruns*. The next is in the Twelfth *Æneid*, where *Venus* cures her Son *Æneas*. But in the last of these, the Poet was driven to a necessity; for *Turnus* was to be slain that very day: And *Æneas*, wounded as he was, cou'd not have Engag'd him in single Combat, unless his Hurt had 1520 been miraculously heal'd. And the Poet had consider'd that the *Dittany* which she brought from *Crete*, cou'd not have wrought so speedy an effect, without the Juice of *Ambrosia*, which she mingled with it. After all, that his Machine might not seem too violent, we see the Heroe limping after *Turnus*. The Wound was skin'd; but the strength of his 1525 Thigh was not restor'd. But what Reason had our Author to wound *Æneas* at so critical a time? And how came the Cuisses to be worse temper'd than the rest of his Armour, which was all wrought by *Vulcan* and his Journey-men? These difficulties are not easily to be solv'd, without confessing that *Virgil* had not life enough to correct his Work: 1530

1498 *confise* 97 (*errata*): *contise* 97 (*text*)

Tho' he had review'd it, and found those Errours which he resolv'd to mend: But being prevented by Death, and not willing to leave an imperfect work behind him, he ordain'd, by his last Testament, that his *Æneis* should be burn'd. As for the death of *Aruns*, who was shot by a Goddess, the Machine was not altogether so outragious, as the wound- 1535 ing *Mars* and *Venus* by the Sword of *Diomede*. Two Divinities, one wou'd have thought, might have pleaded their Prerogative of Impassibility, or, at least not to have been wounded by any mortal Hand. Beside that the ἰχώρ which they shed, was so very like our common Blood, that it was not to be distinguish'd from it, but only by the Name and Colour. 1540 As for what *Horace* says in his Art of Poetry; that no Machines are to be us'd, unless on some extraordinary occasion,

Nec Deus intersit, nisi dignus vindice nodus:

That Rule is to be apply'd to the Theatre, of which he is then speaking, and means no more than this, that when the Knot of the Play is to be 1545 unty'd, and no other way is left, for making the discovery; then and not otherwise, let a God descend upon a Rope, and clear the Business to the Audience: But this has no relation to the Machines which are us'd in an Epick Poem.

In the last place, for the *Dira*, or Flying-Pest, which flapping on the 1550 Shield of *Turnus*, and fluttering about his Head, dishearten'd him in the Duel, and presag'd to him his approaching Death, I might have plac'd it more properly amongst the Objections. For the Criticks, who lay want of Courage to the Charge of *Virgil*'s Heroe; quote this Passage as a main proof of their Assertion. They say our Author had not only 1555 secur'd him before the Duel, but also in the beginning of it, had given him the advantage in impenetrable Arms, and in his Sword: (for that of *Turnus* was not his own, which was forg'd by *Vulcan* for his Father, but a Weapon which he had snatch'd in haste, and by mistake, belonging to his Charioteer *Metiscus*.) That after all this, *Jupiter*, who was 1560 partial to the *Trojan*, and distrustful of the Event, though he had hung the Ballance, and given it a jog of his hand to weigh down *Turnus*, thought convenient to give the Fates a collateral Security, by sending the Screech-Owl to discourage him. For which they quote these words of *Virgil*, 1565

————————*Non me tua turbida virtus*
Terret, ait; Dii me terrent, & Jupiter Hostis.

1538 to] *om.* 98   1539 ἰχώρ] εἰκωρ 97: εἴχωρ 98   1543 *nodus:*] *nodus.* 97 98
1558–60 Father, . . . *Metiscus.*)] Father) . . . *Metiscus.* 97 98   1563 collateral 98:
collatteral 97   1565 *Virgil,* 98: *Virgil.* 07   1566 *virtus* 98: *virtus,* 97
1567 *Terret,* 98: *Terret* 97

In answer to which, I say, that this Machine is one of those which the Poet uses only for Ornament, and not out of Necessity. Nothing can be more Beautiful, or more Poetical than his description of the three 157 *Diræ*, or the setting of the Balance, which our *Milton* has borrow'd from him, but employ'd to a different end: For first he makes God Almighty set the Scales for St. *Gabriel* and *Sathan*, when he knew no Combat was to follow; then he makes the good Angel's Scale descend, and the Devils mount; quite contrary to *Virgil*, if I have Translated the three Verses, 157 according to my Author's Sense.

> *Jupiter ipse duas, æquato Examine lances*
> *Sustinet; & fata imponit diversa duorum:*
> *Quem damnet labor, & quo vergat pondere lethum.*

For I have taken these words *Quem damnet labor*, in the Sense which 158 *Virgil* gives them in another place; *Damnabis tu quoque votis;* to signifie a prosperous Event. Yet I dare not condemn so great a Genius as *Milton:* For I am much mistaken if he alludes not to the Text in *Daniel*, where *Belshazzar* was put into the Balance, and found too light. This is digression, and I return to my Subject. I said above, that these two 158 Machines of the Balance, and the *Dira*, were only Ornamental, and that the success of the Duel had been the same without them. For when *Æneas* and *Turnus* stood fronting each other before the Altar, *Turnus* look'd dejected, and his Colour faded in his Face, as if he desponded of the Victory before the Fight; and not only he, but all his Party, when 159 the strength of the two Champions was judg'd by the proportion of their Limbs, concluded it was *impar pugna*, and that their Chief was over-match'd: Whereupon *Juturna* (who was of the same Opinion) took this opportunity to break the Treaty and renew the War. *Juno* her self had plainly told the Nymph beforehand, that her Brother was to Fight 159

> *Imparibus fatis; nec Diis, nec viribus æquis;*

So that there was no need of an Apparition to fright *Turnus*. He had the presage within himself of his impending Destiny. The *Dira* only serv'd to confirm him in his first Opinion, that it was his Destiny to die in the ensuing Combat. And in this sense are those words of *Virgil* to 160 be taken;

> ————*Non me tua turbida virtus*
> *Terret, ait; Dii me terrent, & Jupiter Hostis.*

I doubt not but the Adverb (*solùm*) is to be understood; 'tis not your

Valour only that gives me this concernment; but I find also, by this 1605
portent, that *Jupiter* is my Enemy. For *Turnus* fled before, when his
first Sword was broken, 'till his Sister supply'd him with a better;
which indeed he cou'd not use; because *Æneas* kept him at a distance
with his Spear. I wonder *Ruæus* saw not this, where he charges his
Author so unjustly, for giving *Turnus* a second Sword, to no purpose. 1610
How cou'd he fasten a blow, or make a thrust, when he was not suffer'd
to approach? Besides, the chief Errand of the *Dira*, was to warn *Juturna*
from the Field, for she cou'd have brought the Chariot again, when she
saw her Brother worsted in the Duel. I might farther add, that *Æneas*
was so eager of the Fight, that he left the City, now almost in his 1615
Possession, to decide his quarrel with *Turnus* by the Sword: Whereas
Turnus had manifestly declin'd the Combate, and suffer'd his Sister to convey him as far from the reach of his Enemy as she cou'd. I say not only
suffer'd her, but consented to it; for 'tis plain, he knew her by these words;

> *O soror, & dudum agnovi, cùm prima per artem,*   1620
> *Fœdera turbasti, teque hæc in bella dedisti;*
> *Et nunc nequicquam fallis Dea.————*

I have dwelt so long on this Subject, that I must contract what I
have to say, in reference to my Translation: Unless I wou'd swell my
Preface into a Volume, and make it formidable to your Lordship, when 1625
you see so many Pages yet behind. And indeed what I have already
written either in justification or praise of *Virgil*, is against my self; for
presuming to Copy, in my course English, the Thoughts and Beautiful
Expressions of this inimitable Poet: Who flourish'd in an Age when his
Language was brought to its last perfection, for which it was particu- 1630
larly owing to him and *Horace*. I will give your Lordship my Opinion,
that those two Friends had consulted each others Judgment, wherein
they should endeavour to excel; and they seem to have pitch'd on
Propriety of Thought, Elegance of Words, and Harmony of Numbers.
According to this Model, *Horace* writ his *Odes* and *Epods*: For his *Satires* 1635
and *Epistles*, being intended wholly for instruction, requir'd another Style:

> *Ornari res ipsa negat, contenta doceri:*

And therefore as he himself professes, are *Sermoni propiora*, nearer Prose
than Verse. But *Virgil*, who never attempted the Lyrick Verse, is every
where Elegant, sweet and flowing in his *Hexameters*. His words are not 1640
only chosen, but the places in which he ranks them for the sound; he
who removes them from the Station wherein their Master sets them,

spoils the Harmony. What he says of the *Sybill*'s Prophecies, may be
as properly apply'd to every word of his: They must be read, in order
as they lie; the least breath discomposes them, and somewhat of their 164
Divinity is lost. I cannot boast that I have been thus exact in my Verses,
but I have endeavour'd to follow the Example of my Master: And am
the first *Englishman*, perhaps, who made it his design to copy him in his
Numbers, his choice of Words, and his placing them for the sweetness
of the sound. On this last Consideration, I have shun'd the *Cæsura* as 165
much as possibly I cou'd. For wherever that is us'd, it gives a roughness
to the Verse, of which we can have little need, in a Language which
is over-stock'd with Consonants. Such is not the Latine, where the
Vowels and Consonants are mix'd in proportion to each other: yet
Virgil judg'd the Vowels to have somewhat of an over-balance, and 165
therefore tempers their sweetness with *Cæsuras*. Such difference there is
in Tongues, that the same Figure which roughens one, gives Majesty to
another: and that was it which *Virgil* studied in his Verses. *Ovid* uses it but
rarely; and hence it is that his Versification cannot so properly be call'd
sweet, as luscious. The *Italians* are forc'd upon it, once or twice in every 166
line, because they have a redundancy of Vowels in their Language.
Their Metal is so soft, that it will not Coyn without Alloy to harden
it. On the other side, for the Reason already nam'd, 'tis all we can do
to give sufficient sweetness to our Language: We must not only chuse
our words for Elegance, but for sound. To perform which, a Mastery in 166
the Language is requir'd; the Poet must have a Magazine of Words, and
have the Art to mannage his few Vowels to the best advantage, that they
may go the farther. He must also know the nature of the Vowels, which
are more sonorous, and which more soft and sweet; and so dispose
them as his present occasions require: All which, and a thousand secrets 167
of Versification beside, he may learn from *Virgil*, if he will take him for
his Guide. If he be above *Virgil*, and is resolv'd to follow his own *Verve*
(as the *French* call it,) the Proverb will fall heavily upon him; *Who
teaches himself, has a Fool for his Master.*

   Virgil employ'd Eleven Years upon his *Æneis*, yet he left it as he 167
thought himself imperfect. Which when I seriously consider, I wish,
that instead of three years which I have spent in the Translation of his
Works, I had four years more allow'd me to correct my Errours, that
I might make my Version somewhat more tolerable than it is. For a
Poet cannot have too great a reverence for his Readers, if he expects 168
his Labours shou'd survive him. Yet I will neither plead my Age nor
Sickness in excuse of the faults which I have made: That I wanted time

is all I have to say. For some of my Subscribers grew so clamorous, that I cou'd no longer deferr the Publication. I hope from the Candour of your Lordship, and your often experienc'd goodness to me, that if the 1685 faults are not too many, you will make allowances with *Horace*.

> *Si plura nitent in Carmine, non ego paucis*
> *Offendar maculis, quas aut incuria fudit,*
> *Aut humana parùm cavit Natura.*

You may please also to observe, that there is not, to the best of my 1690 remembrance, one Vowel gaping on another for want of a *Cæsura*, in this whole Poem. But where a Vowel ends a word, the next begins either with a Consonant, or what is its equivalent; for our *W* and *H* aspirate, and our Diphthongues are plainly such: The greatest latitude I take, is in the Letter *Υ*, when it concludes a word, and the first 1695 Syllable of the next begins with a Vowel. Neither need I have call'd this a latitude, which is only an explanation of this general Rule: That no Vowel can be cut off before another, when we cannot sink the Pronunciation of it: As *He, She, Me, I,* &c. *Virgil* thinks it sometimes a Beauty, to imitate the License of the *Greeks*, and leave two Vowels 1700 opening on each other, as in that Verse of the Third Pastoral,

> *Et succus pecori & lac subducitur Agnis.*

But *nobis non licet, esse tam disertis.* At least, if we study to refine our Numbers. I have long had by me the Materials of an English *Prosodia*, containing all the Mechanical Rules of Versification, wherein I have 1705 treated with some exactness of the Feet, the Quantities, and the Pauses. The *French* and *Italians* know nothing of the two first; at least their best Poets have not practis'd them. As for the Pauses, *Malherb* first brought them into *France*, within this last Century: And we see how they adorn their *Alexandrins.* But as *Virgil* propounds a Riddle which he leaves 1710 unsolv'd:

> *Dic quibus in terris, inscripti nomina Regum*
> *Nascantur flores, & Phyllida solus habeto.*

So I will give your Lordship another, and leave the Exposition of it to your acute Judgment. I am sure there are few who make Verses, have 1715 observ'd the sweetness of these two Lines in *Coopers Hill,*

> *Tho' deep, yet clear; though gentle, yet not dull;*
> *Strong without rage, without o'reflowing, full.*

1694 Diphthongues 98: Dipthongues 97   1697 Rule: 98: Rule. 97   1703
least, 98: least 97   1716 Hill, 98: Hill. 97

And there are yet fewer who can find the Reason of that sweetness. I
have given it to some of my Friends in Conversation, and they have   172
allow'd the Criticism to be just. But since the evil of false quantities
is difficult to be cur'd in any Modern Language; since the *French* and
the *Italians* as well as we, are yet ignorant what feet are to be us'd in
Heroick Poetry; since I have not strictly observ'd those Rules my self,
which I can teach others; since I pretend to no Dictatorship among my   172
Fellow-Poets; since if I shou'd instruct some of them to make well-
running Verses, they want Genius to give them strength as well as
sweetness; and above all, since your Lordship has advis'd me not to
publish that little which I know, I look on your Counsel as your Command, which I shall observe inviolably, 'till you shall please to revoke   173
it, and leave me at liberty to make my thoughts publick. In the mean
time, that I may arrogate nothing to my self, I must acknowledge that
Virgil in Latine, and *Spencer* in English, have been my Masters. *Spencer*
has also given me the boldness to make use sometimes of his *Alexandrin*
Line, which we call, though improperly, the *Pindarick*; because Mr.   173
Cowley has often employ'd it in his *Odes*. It adds a certain Majesty to the
Verse, when 'tis us'd with Judgment, and stops the sense from over-
flowing into another Line. Formerly the *French*, like us, and the *Italians*,
had but five Feet, or ten Syllables in their Heroick Verse: but since
Ronsard's time, as I suppose, they found their Tongue too weak to   174
support their Epick Poetry, without the addition of another Foot. That
indeed has given it somewhat of the run, and measure of a *Trimeter*; but
it runs with more activity than strength: Their Language is not strung
with Sinews like our English. It has the nimbleness of a Greyhound,
but not the bulk and body of a Mastiff. Our Men and our Verses over-   174
bear them by their weight; and *Pondere non Numero*, is the *British* Motto.
The *French* have set up Purity for the Standard of their Language; and
a Masculine Vigour is that of ours. Like their Tongue is the Genius of
their Poets, light and trifling in comparison of the English; more proper
for Sonnets, Madrigals, and Elegies, than Heroick Poetry. The turn on   175
Thoughts and Words is their chief Talent, but the Epick Poem is too
stately to receive those little Ornaments. The Painters draw their
Nymphs in thin and airy Habits, but the weight of Gold and of Em-
broideries is reserv'd for Queens and Goddesses. *Virgil* is never frequent
in those Turns, like *Ovid*, but much more sparing of them in his *Æneis*,   175
than in his *Pastorals* and *Georgicks*.

Ignoscenda quidem, scirent si ignoscere Manes.

That turn is Beautiful indeed; but he employs it in the Story of *Orpheus* and *Eurydice*, not in his great Poem. I have us'd that License in his *Æneis* sometimes: but I own it as my fault. 'Twas given to those 1760 who understand no better. 'Tis like *Ovid*'s

> *Semivirumq; bovem, semibovemq; virum.*

The Poet found it before his Criticks, but it was a darling Sin which he wou'd not be perswaded to reform. The want of Genius, of which I have accus'd the *French*, is laid to their Charge by one of their own great 1765 Authors, though I have forgotten his Name, and where I read it. If Rewards cou'd make good Poets, their great Master has not been wanting on his part in his bountiful Encouragements: For he is wise enough to imitate *Augustus*, if he had a *Maro*. The *Triumvir* and *Proscriber* had descended to us in a more hideous form than they now 1770 appear, if the Emperour had not taken care to make Friends of him and *Horace*. I confess the Banishment of *Ovid* was a Blot in his Escutcheon, yet he was only Banish'd, and who knows but his Crime was Capital, and then his Exile was a Favour? *Ariosto*, who with all his faults, must be acknowledg'd a great Poet, has put these words into the 1775 mouth of an Evangelist, but whether they will pass for Gospel now, I cannot tell.

> *Non fu si santo ni benigno Augusto,*
> *Come la tuba di Virgilio suona;*
> *L'haver havuto, in poesia buon gusto* 1780
> *La proscrittione, iniqua gli perdona.*

But Heroick Poetry is not of the growth of *France*, as it might be of *England*, if it were Cultivated. *Spencer* wanted only to have read the Rules of *Bossu*: for no Man was ever Born with a greater Genius, or had more Knowledge to support it. But the performance of the *French* is 1785 not equal to their Skill; and hitherto we have wanted Skill to perform better. *Segrais*, whose Preface is so wonderfully good, yet is wholly destitute of Elevation; though his Version is much better than that of the two Brothers, or any of the rest who have attempted *Virgil*. *Hannibal Caro* is a great Name amongst the *Italians*, yet his Transla- 1790 tion of the *Æneis* is most scandalously mean, though he has taken the advantage of writing in Blank Verse, and freed himself from the shackles of modern Rhime: (if it be modern, for *Le Clerc* has told us lately, and I believe has made it out, that *David*'s Psalms were written in as errant Rhime as they are Translated.) Now if a Muse cannot run 1795 when she is unfetter'd, 'tis a sign she has but little speed. I will not make a digression here, though I am strangely tempted to it; but will only say, that he who can write well in Rhime, may write better in Blank Verse. Rhime is certainly a constraint even to the best Poets, and those who make it with most ease; though perhaps I have as little reason to complain of that hardship as any Man, excepting *Quarles*, and *Withers*. What it adds to sweetness, it takes away from sense; and he who loses the least by it, may be call'd a gainer: it often makes us swerve from an Author's meaning. As if a Mark be set up for an Archer at a great distance, let him aim as exactly as he can, the least wind will take his Arrow, and divert it from the White. I return to our *Italian* Translatour of the *Æneis*: He is a Foot-Poet, he Lacquies by the side of *Virgil* at the best, but never mounts behind him. Doctor *Morelli*, who is no mean Critick in our Poetry, and therefore may be presum'd to be a better in his own Language, has confirm'd me in this Opinion by his Judgment, and thinks withall, that he has often mistaken his Master's Sense. I wou'd say so, if I durst, but I am afraid I have committed the same fault more often, and more grosly: For I have forsaken *Ruæus*, (whom generally I follow) in many places, and made Expositions of my own in some, quite contrary to him. Of which I will give but two Examples, because they are so near each other in the Tenth *Æneid*.

———————*Sorti Pater æquus utrique.*

Pallas says it to *Turnus* just before they Fight. *Ruæus* thinks that the word *Pater* is to be referr'd to *Evander* the Father of *Pallas*. But how cou'd he imagine that it was the same thing to *Evander*, if his Son were slain, or if he overcame. The Poet certainly intended *Jupiter* the common Father of Mankind; who, as *Pallas* hop'd, wou'd stand an impartial Spectatour of the Combat, and not be more favourable to *Turnus*, than to him. The Second is not long after it, and both before the Duel is begun. They are the words of *Jupiter*, who comforts *Hercules* for the death of *Pallas*, which was immediately to ensue, and which *Hercules* cou'd not hinder (though the young Heroe had address'd his Prayers to him for his assistance:) Because the Gods cannot controul Destiny— The Verse follows.

Sic ait; atq; oculos Rutulorum rejicit arvis.

Which the same *Ruæus* thus construes. *Jupiter* after he had said this, immediately turns his eyes to the *Rutulian* Fields, and beholds the Duel. I have given this place another Exposition, that he turn'd his Eyes from the Field of Combat, that he might not behold a sight so unpleasing to him. The word *Rejicit* I know will admit of both senses; but *Jupiter* having confess'd that he could not alter Fate, and being griev'd he cou'd not, in consideration of *Hercules*, it seems to me that he shou'd avert his Eyes, rather than take pleasure in the Spectacle. But of this I am not so confident as the other, though I think I have follow'd 1840 *Virgil*'s sense.

What I have said, though it has the face of arrogance, yet is intended for the honour of my Country; and therefore I will boldly own, that this *English* Translation has more of *Virgil*'s Spirit in it, than either the *French*, or the *Italian*. Some of our Country-men have translated 1845 Episodes, and other parts of *Virgil*, with great Success. As particularly your Lordship, whose Version of *Orpheus* and *Eurydice*, is eminently good. Amongst the dead Authors, the *Silenus* of my Lord *Roscommon* cannot be too much commended. I say nothing of Sir *John Denham*, Mr. *Waller*, and Mr. *Cowley*; 'tis the utmost of my Ambition to be thought 1850 their Equal, or not to be much inferiour to them, and some others of the Living. But 'tis one thing to take pains on a Fragment, and Translate it perfectly; and another thing to have the weight of a whole Author on my shoulders. They who believe the burthen light, let them attempt the Fourth, Sixth or Eighth *Pastoral*, the First or Fourth 1855 *Georgick*; and amongst the *Æneids*, the Fourth, the Fifth, the Seventh, the Ninth, the Tenth, the Eleventh, or the Twelfth; for in these I think I have succeeded best.

Long before I undertook this Work, I was no stranger to the Original. I had also studied *Virgil*'s Design, his disposition of it, his Manners, his 1860 judicious management of the Figures, the sober retrenchments of his Sense, which always leaves somewhat to gratifie our imagination, on which it may enlarge at pleasure; but above all, the Elegance of his Expressions, and the harmony of his Numbers. For, as I have said in a former Dissertation, the words are in Poetry, what the Colours are in 1865 Painting. If the Design be good, and the Draught be true, the Colouring is the first Beauty that strikes the Eye. *Spencer* and *Milton* are the nearest in English to *Virgil* and *Horace* in the Latine; and I have endeavour'd to form my Stile by imitating their Masters. I will farther own to you, my Lord, that my chief Ambition is to please those Readers, who have 1870 discernment enough to prefer *Virgil* before any other Poet in the Latine Tongue. Such Spirits as he desir'd to please, such wou'd I chuse for my Judges, and wou'd stand or fall by them alone. *Segrais* has distinguish'd the Readers of Poetry, according to their capacity of judging,

1868 I] *om.* 97 98

into three Classes: (He might have said the same of Writers too if he 187
had pleas'd.) In the lowest Form he places those whom he calls *Les
Petits Esprits*: such things as are our Upper-Gallery Audience in a Play-
House; who like nothing but the Husk and Rhind of Wit; preferr a
Quibble, a Conceit, an Epigram, before solid Sense, and Elegant Ex-
pression: These are Mobb-Readers: If *Virgil* and *Martial* stood for 188
Parliament-Men, we know already who wou'd carry it. But though
they make the greatest appearance in the Field, and cry the loudest,
the best on't is, they are but a sort of *French Hugonots*, or *Dutch Boors*,
brought over in Herds, but not Naturaliz'd: who have not Land of two
Pounds *per Annum* in *Parnassus*, and therefore are not priviledg'd to Poll. 188
Their Authors are of the same level; fit to represent them on a Mountebank's-Stage, or to be Masters of the Ceremonies in a Bear-Garden.
Yet these are they who have the most Admirers. But it often happens,
to their mortification, that as their Readers improve their Stock of
Sense, (as they may by reading better Books, and by Conversation with 189
Men of Judgment,) they soon forsake them: And when the Torrent
from the Mountains falls no more, the swelling Writer is reduc'd into
his shallow Bed, like the *Mançanares* at *Madrid*, with scarce water to
moisten his own Pebbles. There are a middle sort of Readers (as we
hold there is a middle state of Souls) such as have a farther insight than 189
the former; yet have not the capacity of judging right; (for I speak
not of those who are brib'd by a Party, and know better if they were not
corrupted;) but I mean a Company of warm young Men, who are not
yet arriv'd so far as to discern the difference betwixt Fustian, or ostenta-
tious Sentences, and the true sublime. These are above liking *Martial*, 190
or *Owen*'s Epigrams, but they wou'd certainly set *Virgil* below *Statius*,
or *Lucan*. I need not say their Poets are of the same Paste with their
Admirers. They affect greatness in all they write, but 'tis a bladder'd
greatness, like that of the vain Man whom *Seneca* describes: An ill habit
of Body, full of Humours, and swell'd with Dropsie. Even these too 190
desert their Authors, as their Judgment ripens. The young Gentlemen
themselves are commonly miss-led by their *Pedagogue* at School, their
Tutor at the University, or their Governour in their Travels. And many
of those three sorts are the most positive Blockheads in the World.
How many of those flatulent Writers have I known, who have sunk in 191
their Reputation, after Seven or Eight Editions of their Works? for
indeed they are Poets only for young Men. They had great success at
their first appearance; but not being of God, as a Wit said formerly,
they cou'd not stand.

I have already nam'd two sorts of Judges, but *Virgil* wrote for neither 1915
of them: and by his Example, I am not ambitious of pleasing the lowest,
or the middle form of Readers.

He chose to please the most Judicious: Souls of the highest Rank,
and truest Understanding. These are few in number; but whoever is
so happy as to gain their approbation, can never lose it, because they 1920
never give it blindly. Then they have a certain *Magnetism* in their
Judgment, which attracts others to their Sense. Every day they gain
some new Proselyte, and in time become the Church. For this Reason,
a well-weigh'd Judicious Poem, which at its first appearance gains no
more upon the World than to be just receiv'd, and rather not blam'd, 1925
than much applauded, insinuates it self by insensible degrees into the
liking of the Reader: The more he studies it, the more it grows upon
him; every time he takes it up, he discovers some new Graces in it. And
whereas Poems which are produc'd by the vigour of Imagination only,
have a gloss upon them at the first, which Time wears off; the Works 1930
of Judgment, are like the Diamond, the more they are polish'd, the
more lustre they receive. Such is the difference betwixt *Virgil's Æneis*,
and *Marini's Adone*. And if I may be allow'd to change the Metaphor,
I wou'd say, that *Virgil* is like the Fame which he describes;

Mobilitate viget, viresq; acquirit eundo. 1935

Such a sort of Reputation is my aim, though in a far inferiour degree,
according to my Motto in the Title Page: *Sequiturq; Patrem, non passibus
æquis;* and therefore I appeal to the Highest Court of Judicature, like
that of the Peers, of which your Lordship is so great an Ornament.

Without this Ambition which I own, of desiring to please the *Judices* 1940
Natos, I cou'd never have been able to have done any thing at this Age,
when the fire of Poetry is commonly extinguish'd in other Men. Yet
Virgil has given me the Example of *Entellus* for my Encouragement:
When he was well heated, the younger Champion cou'd not stand
before him. And we find the Elder contended not for the Gift, but for 1945
the Honour; *Nec dona moror.* For *Dampier* has inform'd us, in his Voyages,
that the Air of the Country which produces Gold, is never wholsom.

I had long since consider'd, that the way to please the best Judges,
is not to Translate a Poet literally; and *Virgil* least of any other. For
his peculiar Beauty lying in his choice of Words, I am excluded from it 1950
by the narrow compass of our Heroick Verse, unless I wou'd make use
of Monosyllables only, and those clog'd with Consonants, which are
the dead weight of our Mother-Tongue. 'Tis possible, I confess, though

it rarely happens, that a Verse of Monosyllables may sound har-
moniously; and some Examples of it I have seen. My first Line of the
Æneis is not harsh:

> *Arms, and the Man I Sing, who forc'd by Fate,* &c.

But a much better instance may be given from the last Line of
Manilius, made English by our Learned and Judicious Mr. *Creech*:

> *Nor could the World have born so fierce a Flame.*

Where the many Liquid Consonants are plac'd so Artfully, that they
give a pleasing sound to the Words, though they are all of one Syllable.

'Tis true, I have been sometimes forc'd upon it in other places of this
Work, but I never did it out of choice: I was either in haste, or *Virgil*
gave me no occasion for the Ornament of Words; for it seldom happens
but a Monosyllable Line turns Verse to Prose, and even that Prose is
rugged, and unharmonious. *Philarchus*, I remember, taxes *Balzac* for
placing Twenty Monosyllables in file, without one dissyllable betwixt
them. The way I have taken, is not so streight as Metaphrase, nor so
loose as Paraphrase: Some things too I have omitted, and sometimes
have added of my own. Yet the omissions I hope, are but of Circumstances, and such as wou'd have no grace in English; and the Additions,
I also hope, are easily deduc'd from *Virgil*'s Sense. They will seem (at
least I have the Vanity to think so,) not stuck into him, but growing
out of him. He studies brevity more than any other Poet, but he had
the advantage of a Language wherein much may be comprehended in
a little space. We, and all the Modern Tongues, have more Articles and
Pronouns, besides signs of Tenses and Cases, and other Barbarities on
which our Speech is built by the faults of our Forefathers. The *Romans*
founded theirs upon the *Greek*: And the *Greeks*, we know, were labouring
many hundred years upon their Language, before they brought it to
perfection. They rejected all those Signs, and cut off as many Articles
as they cou'd spare; comprehending in one word, what we are constrain'd to express in two; which is one Reason why we cannot write
so concisely as they have done. The word *Pater*, for Example, signifies
not only a Father, but your Father, my Father, his or her Father, all
included in a word.

This inconvenience is common to all Modern Tongues, and this alone
constrains us to employ more words than the Ancients needed. But
having before observ'd, that *Virgil* endeavours to be short, and at the
same time Elegant, I pursue the Excellence, and forsake the Brevity.

For there he is like Ambergreace, a Rich Perfume, but of so close and glutinous a Body, that it must be open'd with inferiour scents of Musk or Civet, or the sweetness will not be drawn out into another Language.

On the whole Matter, I thought fit to steer betwixt the two Extreams, 1995 of Paraphrase, and literal Translation: To keep as near my Author as I cou'd, without losing all his Graces, the most Eminent of which, are in the Beauty of his words: And those words, I must add, are always Figurative. Such of these as wou'd retain their Elegance in our Tongue, I have endeavour'd to graff on it; but most of them are of necessity to 2000 be lost, because they will not shine in any but their own. *Virgil* has sometimes two of them in a Line; but the scantiness of our Heroick Verse, is not capable of receiving more than one: And that too must expiate for many others which have none. Such is the difference of the Languages, or such my want of skill in chusing words. Yet I may 2005 presume to say, and I hope with as much reason as the *French* Translator, that taking all the Materials of this divine Author, I have endeavour'd to make *Virgil* speak such *English*, as he wou'd himself have spoken, if he had been born in *England*, and in this present Age. I acknowledge, with *Segrais*, that I have not succeeded in this attempt, according to my 2010 desire: yet I shall not be wholly without praise, if in some sort I may be allow'd to have copied the Clearness, the Purity, the Easiness and the Magnificence of his Stile. But I shall have occasion to speak farther on this Subject, before I end the Preface.

When I mention'd the Pindarick Line, I should have added, that I 2015 take another License in my Verses: For I frequently make use of Triplet Rhymes, and for the same Reason: Because they bound the Sense. And therefore I generally join these two Licenses together: And make the last Verse of the Triplet a Pindarique: For besides the Majesty which it gives, it confines the sense within the barriers of three Lines, which 2020 wou'd languish if it were lengthen'd into four. *Spencer* is my Example for both these priviledges of *English* Verses. And *Chapman* has follow'd him in his Translation of *Homer*. Mr. *Cowley* has given in to them after both: And all succeeding Writers after him. I regard them now as the *Magna Charta* of Heroick Poetry; and am too much an *English*-man to 2025 lose what my Ancestors have gain'd for me. Let the *French* and *Italians* value themselves on their Regularity: Strength and Elevation are our Standard. I said before, and I repeat it, that the affected purity of the *French*, has unsinew'd their Heroick Verse. The Language of an Epick Poem is almost wholly figurative: Yet they are so fearful of a Metaphor, 2030

2019 besides] besides, *97 98*

that no Example of *Virgil* can encourage them to be bold with safety.
Sure they might warm themselves by that sprightly Blaze, without
approaching it so close as to singe their Wings; they may come as near
it as their Master. Not that I wou'd discourage that purity of diction,
in which he excels all other Poets. But he knows how far to extend 20
his Franchises: And advances to the verge, without venturing a Foot
beyond it. On the other side, without being injurious to the Memory of
our *English Pindar*, I will presume to say, that his Metaphors are sometimes too violent, and his Language is not always pure. But at the same
time, I must excuse him. For through the Iniquity of the times, he was 26
forc'd to Travel, at an Age, when, instead of Learning Foreign Languages, he shou'd have studied the Beauties of his Mother Tongue:
Which like all other Speeches, is to be cultivated early, or we shall never
Write it with any kind of Elegance. Thus by gaining abroad he lost
at home: Like the Painter in the *Arcadia*, who going to see a Skirmish, 20
had his Arms lop'd off: and return'd, says Sir *Philip Sydney*, well instructed how to draw a Battel, but without a Hand to perform his
Work.

There is another thing in which I have presum'd to deviate from him
and *Spencer*. They both make Hemysticks (or half Verses) breaking off 26
in the middle of a Line. I confess there are not many such in the *Fairy
Queen*: And even those few might be occasion'd by his unhappy choice
of so long a Stanza. Mr. *Cowley* had found out, that no kind of Staff is
proper for an Heroick Poem; as being all too Lyrical: Yet though he
wrote in Couplets, where Rhyme is freer from constraint, he frequently 20
affects half Verses: of which we find not one in *Homer*, and I think not
in any of the *Greek* Poets, or the *Latin*, excepting only *Virgil*; and there
is no question but he thought, he had *Virgil's* Authority for that
License. But I am confident, our Poet never meant to leave him or any
other such a Precedent. And I ground my Opinion on these two 26
Reasons. First, we find no Example of a Hemystick in any of his
Pastorals or *Georgicks*. For he had given the last finishing Strokes to both
these Poems: But his *Æneis* he left so uncorrect, at least so short of that
perfection at which he aim'd, that we know how hard a Sentence He
pass'd upon it: And in the second place, I reasonably presume, that he 26
intended to have fill'd up all those *Hemysticks*, because in one of them
we find the sense imperfect:

> *Quem tibi jam Trojâ——————*

Which some foolish Gramarian, has ended for him, with a half Line of
Nonsense; 2070

—————Peperit fumante Crëusa.

For *Ascanius* must have been born some Years before the burning of that
City; which I need not prove. On the other side we find also, that he
himself fill'd up one Line in the sixth *Æneid,* the Enthusiasm seizing
him, while he was reading to *Augustus.* 2075

> *Misenum Æolidem, quo non præstantior alter*
> *Ære, ciere viros.—————*

To which he added in that transport, *Martemque accendere Cantu.* And
never was any Line more nobly finish'd; for the reasons which I have
given in the Book of Painting. On these Considerations I have shun'd 2080
Hemysticks: Not being willing to imitate *Virgil* to a Fault; like *Alexander*'s
Courtiers, who affected to hold their Necks awry, because he cou'd not
help it: I am confident your Lordship is by this time of my Opinion;
and that you will look on those half lines hereafter, as the imperfect
products of a hasty Muse: Like the Frogs and Serpents in the *Nile*; part 2085
of them kindled into Life; and part a lump of unform'd unanimated
Mudd.

I am sensible that many of my whole Verses, are as imperfect as those
halves; for want of time to digest them better: But give me leave to
make the Excuse of *Boccace*: Who when he was upbraided, that some 2090
of his Novels had not the Spirit of the rest, return'd this Answer; that
Charlemain who made the *Paladins,* was never able to raise an Army of
them. The Leaders may be Heroes, but the multitude must consist of
Common Men.

I am also bound to tell your Lordship, in my own defence: That from 2095
the beginning of the first *Georgick* to the end of the last *Æneid*; I found
the difficulty of Translation growing on me in every succeeding Book.
For *Virgil*, above all Poets, had a stock, which I may call almost inexhaustible, of figurative, Elegant, and sounding Words. I who inherit
but a small portion of his Genius, and write in a Language so much 2100
inferiour to the Latin, have found it very painful to vary Phrases, when
the same sense returns upon me. Even he himself, whether out of
necessity or choice, has often express'd the same thing in the same

---

2070 Nonsense; *98*: Nonsense. *97*　　2078 transport, *98*: transport. *97*　　2091
Answer; *98*: Answer, *97*　　2092 *Paladins, 98*: *Paladins; 97*　　2098-9 inexhaustible, *98*: inexhaustible *97*

words; and often repeated two or three whole Verses, which he had us'd before. Words are not so easily Coyn'd as Money: And yet we see that the Credit not only of Banks, but of Exchequers cracks, when little comes in, and much goes out. *Virgil* call'd upon me in every line for some new word: And I paid so long, that I was almost Banckrupt. So that the latter end must needs be more burdensom than the beginning or the middle. And consequently the Twelfth *Æneid* cost me double the time of the first and second. What had become of me, if *Virgil* had tax'd me with another Book? I had certainly been reduc'd to pay the Publick in hammer'd Money for want of Mill'd; that is in the same old Words which I had us'd before: And the Receivers must have been forc'd to have taken any thing, where there was so little to be had.

Besides this difficulty (with which I have strugled, and made a shift to pass it over) there is one remaining, which is insuperable to all Translators. We are bound to our Author's Sense, though with the latitudes already mention'd (for I think it not so sacred, as that one Iota must not be added or diminish'd on pain of an *Anathema*.) But Slaves we are; and labour on another Man's Plantation; we dress the Vine-yard, but the Wine is the Owners: If the Soil be sometimes Barren, then we are sure of being scourg'd: If it be fruitful, and our Care succeeds, we are not thank'd; for the proud Reader will only say, the poor drudge has done his duty. But this is nothing to what follows; for being oblig'd to make his Sense intelligible, we are forc'd to untune our own Verses, that we may give his meaning to the Reader. He who Invents is Master of his Thoughts and Words: He can turn and vary them as he pleases, 'till he renders them harmonious. But the wretched Translator has no such priviledge: For being ty'd to the Thoughts, he must make what Musick he can in the Expression. And for this reason it cannot always be so sweet as that of the Original. There is a beauty of Sound, as *Segrais* has observ'd, in some Latin Words, which is wholly lost in any Modern Language. He instances in that *Mollis Amaracus*, on which *Venus* lays *Cupid* in the First *Æneid*. If I should Translate it Sweet Marjoram, as the word signifies; the Reader would think I had mistaken *Virgil*: For those Village-words, as I may call them, give us a mean Idea of the thing; but the Sound of the Latin is so much more pleasing, by the just mixture of the Vowels with the Consonants, that it raises our Fancies, to conceive somewhat more Noble than a common Herb; and to spread Roses under him, and strew Lillies over him; a Bed not unworthy the Grandson of the Goddess.

If I cannot Copy his Harmonious Numbers, how shall I imitate his

noble Flights; where his Thoughts and Words are equally sublime?
Quem   2145

> —*quisquis studet æmulari,*
> —*Cæratis ope Dædaleâ*
> *Nititur pennis, vitreo daturus*
> *Nomina Ponto.*

What Modern Language, or what Poet can express the Majestick 2150
Beauty of this one Verse amongst a thousand others!

> *Aude Hospes contemnere opes, & te quoque dignum*
> *Finge Deo.——————*

For my part I am lost in the admiration of it: I contemn the World,
when I think on it, and my self when I Translate it.   2155

Lay by *Virgil*, I beseech your Lordship, and all my better sort of
Judges, when you take up my Version, and it will appear a passable
Beauty, when the Original Muse is absent: But like *Spencer*'s false
Florimel made of Snow, it melts and vanishes, when the true one comes
in sight. I will not excuse but justifie my self for one pretended Crime, 2160
with which I am liable to be charg'd by false Criticks, not only in this
Translation, but in many of my Original Poems; that I latinize too
much. 'Tis true, that when I find an *English* word, significant and sounding, I neither borrow from the *Latin* or any other Language: But when
I want at home, I must seek abroad.   2165

If sounding Words are not of our growth and Manufacture, who shall
hinder me to Import them from a Foreign Country? I carry not out the
Treasure of the Nation, which is never to return: but what I bring
from *Italy*, I spend in *England*: Here it remains, and here it circulates;
for if the Coyn be good, it will pass from one hand to another. I Trade 2170
both with the Living and the Dead, for the enrichment of our Native
Language. We have enough in *England* to supply our necessity; but if
we will have things of Magnificence and Splendour, we must get them
by Commerce. Poetry requires Ornament, and that is not to be had
from our Old *Teuton* Monosyllables; therefore if I find any Elegant 2175
Word in a Classick Author, I propose it to be Naturaliz'd, by using it
my self: and if the Publick approves of it, the Bill passes. But every Man
cannot distinguish betwixt Pedantry and Poetry: Every Man therefore
is not fit to innovate. Upon the whole matter, a Poet must first be
certain that the Word he wou'd Introduce is Beautiful in the *Latin*; and 2180

2145 *Quem*] *printed as part of the first Latin verse in* 97 98   2147 *Dædaleâ*] *Dedalæâ* 97:
Dedaleâ 98

is to consider, in the next place, whether it will agree with the *English*
Idiom: After this, he ought to take the Opinion of judicious Friends,
such as are Learned in both Languages: And lastly, since no Man is
infallible, let him use this License very sparingly; for if too many
Foreign Words are pour'd in upon us, it looks as if they were design'd 2185
not to assist the Natives, but to Conquer them.

I am now drawing towards a Conclusion, and suspect your Lordship
is very glad of it. But permit me first, to own what Helps I have had in
this Undertaking. The late Earl of *Lauderdail*, sent me over his new
Translation of the *Æneis*; which he had ended before I ingag'd in the 2190
same Design. Neither did I then intend it: But some Proposals being
afterwards made me by my Bookseller, I desir'd his Lordship's leave,
that I might accept them, which he freely granted; and I have his Letter
yet to shew, for that permission. He resolv'd to have Printed his Work;
which he might have done two Years before I cou'd Publish mine: and 2195
had perform'd it, if Death had not prevented him. But having his
Manuscript in my hands, I consulted it as often as I doubted of my
Author's sense. For no Man understood *Virgil* better than that Learned
Noble Man. His Friends, I hear, have yet another, and more Correct
Copy of that Translation by them: which had they pleas'd to have 2200
given the Publick, the Judges must have been convinc'd, that I have
not flatter'd him. Besides this help, which was not inconsiderable,
Mr. *Congreve* has done me the Favour to review the *Æneis*; and compare
my Version with the Original. I shall never be asham'd to own, that
this Excellent Young Man, has shew'd me many Faults, which I have 2205
endeavour'd to Correct. 'Tis true, he might have easily found more,
and then my Translation had been more Perfect.

Two other Worthy Friends of mine, who desire to have their Names
conceal'd, seeing me straitned in my time, took Pity on me, and gave
me the Life of *Virgil*, the two Prefaces to the Pastorals, and the *Georgics*, 2210
and all the Arguments in Prose to the whole Translation. Which perhaps, has caus'd a Report that the two First Poems are not mine. If it
had been true, that I had taken their Verses for my own, I might have
glory'd in their Aid; and like *Terence*, have farther'd the Opinion, that
Scipio and *Lælius* join'd with me. But the same Style being continu'd 2215
thro' the whole, and the same Laws of Versification observ'd, are proofs
sufficient, that this is one Man's Work: And your Lordship is too well
acquainted with my manner, to doubt that any part of it is anothers.

That your Lordship may see I was in earnest, when I promis'd to

2212 caus'd *98*: occasion'd *97*

hasten to an end, I will not give the Reasons, why I Writ not always in 2220
the proper terms of Navigation, Land-Service, or in the Cant of any
Profession. I will only say, that *Virgil* has avoided those proprieties,
because he Writ not to Mariners, Souldiers, Astronomers, Gardners,
Peasants, &c. but to all in general, and in particular to Men and
Ladies of the first Quality: who have been better Bred than to be too 2225
nicely knowing in the Terms. In such cases, 'tis enough for a Poet to
write so plainly, that he may be understood by his Readers: To avoid
impropriety, and not affect to be thought Learn'd in all things.

I have omitted the Four Preliminary Lines of the First *Æneid*: Because
I think them inferiour to any Four others, in the whole Poem: and con- 2230
sequently, believe they are not *Virgil*'s. There is too great a gap betwixt
the Adjective *vicina* in the Second Line, and the Substantive *Arva* in
the latter end of the Third, which keeps his meaning in obscurity too
long: And is contrary to the clearness of his Style.

Ut quamvis avido   2235

Is too ambitious an Ornament to be his, and

Gratum opus Agricolis,

Are all words unnecessary, and Independent of what he had said before.

————————*Horrentia Martis*

Arma,   2240

Is worse than any of the rest. *Horrentia* is such a flat Epithete, as *Tully*
wou'd have given us in his Verses. 'Tis a meer filler; to stop a vacancy
in the Hexameter, and connect the Preface to the Work of *Virgil*. Our
Author seems to sound a Charge, and begins like the clangour of a
Trumpet.   2245

Arma, virumque cano; Trojæ qui primus ab oris.

Scarce a word without an *R*, and the Vowels for the greater part
sonorous. The Prefacer began with *Ille ego*, which He was constrain'd
to patch up in the Fourth line with *At nunc*, to make the Sense cohere.
And if both those words are not notorious botches, I am much deceiv'd, 2250
though the *French* Translator thinks otherwise. For my own part, I am
rather of the Opinion, that they were added by *Tucca* and *Varius*, than
Retrench'd.

I know it may be answer'd by such as think *Virgil* the Author of the

---

2235 avido] avidis 97 98   2239-40 Horrentia Martis Arma,] printed as one line in
97 98   2247 R, 98: R. 97   2252 of the Opinion 98: of Opinion 97

four Lines; that he asserts his Title to the *Æneis*, in the beginning of 225
this Work, as he did to the two former, in the last lines of the fourth
Georgic. I will not reply otherwise to this, than by desiring them to
compare these four Lines with the four others; which we know are his,
because no Poet but he alone could write them. If they cannot distinguish Creeping from Flying, let them lay down *Virgil*, and take up 2260
Ovid de Ponto in his stead. My Master needed not the assistance of
that Preliminary Poet to prove his Claim. His own Majestick Meen
discovers him to be the King, amidst a Thousand Courtiers. It was a
superfluous Office, and therefore I wou'd not set those Verses in the
Front of *Virgil*; but have rejected them to my own Preface.   2265

> *I, who before, with Shepherds in the Groves,*
> *Sung to my Oaten Pipe, their Rural Loves,*
> *And issuing thence, compell'd the Neighb'ring Field*
> *A plenteous Crop of rising Corn to yield,*
> *Manur'd the Glebe, and stock'd the fruitful Plain,*   2270
> (*A Poem grateful to the greedy Swain.*) &c.

If there be not a tolerable Line in all these six, the Prefacer gave me
no occasion to write better. This is a just Apology in this place. But I
have done great Wrong to *Virgil* in the whole Translation: Want of
Time, the Inferiority of our Language, the inconvenience of Rhyme, 2275
and all the other Excuses I have made, may alleviate my Fault, but
cannot justifie the boldness of my Undertaking. What avails it me to
acknowledge freely, that I have not been able to do him right in any
line? For even my own Confession makes against me; and it will always
be return'd upon me, Why then did you attempt it? To which, no other 2280
Answer can be made, than that I have done him less Injury than any
of his former Libellers.

What they call'd his Picture, had been drawn at length, so many
times, by the Daubers of almost all Nations, and still so unlike him,
that I snatch'd up the Pencil with disdain: being satisfi'd before hand, 2285
that I cou'd make some small resemblance of him, though I must be
content with a worse likeness. A Sixth Pastoral, a *Pharmaceutria*, a single
Orpheus, and some other Features, have been exactly taken: But those
Holiday Authors writ for Pleasure; and only shew'd us what they cou'd
have done, if they wou'd have taken pains, to perform the whole.   2290

2265 *Virgil*; but *98*: *Virgil*. But *97*   2272 Prefacer *98*: Prefacer *97*   2275 Language, *98*: Language; *97*

Be pleas'd, My Lord, to accept, with your wonted goodness, this unworthy Present, which I make you. I have taken off one trouble from you, of defending it, by acknowledging its Imperfections: And though some part of them are cover'd in the Verse; (as *Erichthonius* rode always in a Chariot, to hide his lameness:) Such of them as cannot be con- 2295 ceal'd, you will please to connive at, though in the strictness of your Judgment, you cannot Pardon. If *Homer* was allow'd to nod sometimes, in so long a Work, it will be no wonder if I often fall asleep. You took my *Aureng-zeb* into your Protection, with all his faults: And I hope here cannot be so many, because I Translate an Author, who gives me such 2300 Examples of Correctness. What my Jury may be, I know not; but 'tis good for a Criminal to plead before a favourable Judge: If I had said Partial, wou'd your Lordship have forgiven me? Or will you give me leave to acquaint the World, that I have many times been oblig'd to your Bounty since the Revolution. Though I never was reduc'd to beg 2305 a Charity, nor ever had the Impudence to ask one, either of your Lord-ship, or your Noble Kinsman the Earl of *Dorset*, much less of any other, yet when I least expected it, you have both remember'd me. So inherent it is in your Family not to forget an Old Servant. It looks rather like Ingratitude on my part, that where I have been so often oblig'd, I have 2310 appear'd so seldom to return my thanks: and where I was also so sure of being well receiv'd. Somewhat of Laziness was in the case; and some-what too of Modesty: But nothing of Disrespect, or of Unthankfulness. I will not say that your Lordship has encourag'd me to this Presump-tion, lest if my Labours meet with no success in Publick, I may expose 2315 your Judgment to be Censur'd. As for my own Enemies I shall never think them worth an Answer; and if your Lordship has any, they will not dare to Arraign you for want of Knowledge in this Art, till they can produce somewhat better of their own, than your *Essay* on Poetry. 'Twas on this Consideration, that I have drawn out my Preface to so 2320 great a length. Had I not address'd to a Poet, and a Critick of the first Magnitude, I had my self been tax'd for want of Judgment, and sham'd my Patron for want of Understanding. But neither will you, My Lord, so soon be tir'd as any other, because the Discourse is on your Art; Neither will the Learned Reader think it tedious, because it is *ad* 2325 *Clerum*. At least, when he begins to be weary, the Church Doors are open. That I may pursue the Allegory with a short Prayer, after a long Sermon:

May you Live happily and long, for the Service of your Country, the

2295 lameness:] lameness. *97 98*   2318 for want *98*: for your want *97*

Encouragement of good Letters and the Ornament of Poetry; which 233
cannot be wish'd more earnestly by any Man, than by

Your Lordships, most Humble,

Most Oblig'd, and most Obedient Servant.

John Dryden.

VIRGIL'S ÆNEIS

THE FIRST BOOK OF THE ÆNEIS

THE ARGUMENT

The Trojans, *after a seven Years Voyage, set sail for* Italy, *but are overtaken by a dreadful Storm, which* Æolus *raises at* Juno's *Request. The Tempest sinks one, and scatters the rest:* Neptune *drives off the Winds and calms the Sea.* Æneas *with his own Ship, and six more, arrives safe at an* Affrican *Port.* Venus *complains to* Jupiter *of her Son's Misfortunes.* Jupiter *comforts her,* 5 *and sends* Mercury *to procure him a kind Reception among the* Cartha- *ginians.* Æneas *going out to discover the Country, meets his Mother in the Shape of an Huntress, who conveys him in a Cloud to* Carthage; *where he sees his Friends whom he thought lost, and receives a kind Entertainment from the Queen.* Dido *by a device of* Venus *begins to have a Passion for him, and after* 10 *some Discourse with him, desires the History of his Adventures since the Siege of* Troy, *which is the Subject of the two following Books.*

A RMS, and the Man I sing, who, forc'd by Fate,
  And haughty *Juno's* unrelenting Hate;
Expell'd and exil'd, left the *Trojan* Shoar:
Long Labours, both by Sea and Land he bore;
And in the doubtful War, before he won   5
The *Latian* Realm, and built the destin'd Town:
His banish'd Gods restor'd to Rites Divine,
And setl'd sure Succession in his Line:
From whence the Race of *Alban* Fathers come,
And the long Glories of Majestick *Rome.*   10
  O Muse! the Causes and the Crimes relate,
What Goddess was provok'd, and whence her hate:
For what Offence the Queen of Heav'n began
To persecute so brave, so just a Man!

Involv'd his anxious Life in endless Cares,   15
Expos'd to Wants, and hurry'd into Wars!
Can Heav'nly Minds such high resentment show;
Or exercise their Spight in Human Woe?
    Against the *Tiber*'s Mouth, but far away,
An ancient Town was seated on the Sea: 20
A *Tyrian* Colony; the People made
Stout for the War, and studious of their Trade.
Carthage the Name, belov'd by *Juno* more
Than her own *Argos*, or the *Samian* Shoar.
Here stood her Chariot, here, if Heav'n were kind,   25
The Seat of awful Empire she design'd.
Yet she had heard an ancient Rumour fly,
(Long cited by the People of the Sky;)
That times to come shou'd see the *Trojan* Race
Her *Carthage* ruin, and her Tow'rs deface: 30
Nor thus confin'd, the Yoke of Sov'raign Sway,
Should on the Necks of all the Nations lay.
She ponder'd this, and fear'd it was in Fate;
Nor cou'd forget the War she wag'd of late,
For conq'ring *Greece* against the *Trojan* State.   35
Besides long Causes working in her Mind,
And secret Seeds of Envy lay behind.
Deep graven in her Heart, the Doom remain'd
Of partial *Paris*, and her Form disdain'd:
The Grace bestow'd on ravish'd *Ganimed*,   40
Electra's Glories, and her injur'd Bed.
Each was a Cause alone, and all combin'd
To kindle Vengeance in her haughty Mind.
For this, far distant from the *Latian* Coast,
She drove the Remnants of the *Trojan* Hoast: 45
And sev'n long Years th' unhappy wand'ring Train,
Were toss'd by Storms, and scatter'd through the Main.
Such Time, such Toil requir'd the *Roman* Name,
Such length of Labour for so vast a Frame.
    Now scarce the *Trojan* Fleet with Sails and Oars,   50
Had left behind the Fair *Sicilian* Shoars:
Ent'ring with chearful Shouts the wat'ry Reign,
And ploughing frothy Furrows in the Main:
When lab'ring still, with endless discontent,

The Queen of Heav'n did thus her Fury vent.   55
 Then am I vanquish'd, must I yield, said she,
And must the *Trojans* reign in *Italy*?
So Fate will have it, and *Jove* adds his Force;
Nor can my Pow'r divert their happy Course.
Cou'd angry *Pallas*, with revengeful Spleen,   60
The *Grecian* Navy burn, and drown the Men?
She for the Fault of one offending Foe,
The Bolts of *Jove* himself presum'd to throw:
With Whirlwinds from beneath she toss'd the Ship,
And bare expos'd the Bosom of the deep: 65
Then, as an Eagle gripes the trembling Game,
The Wretch yet hissing with her Father's Flame,
She strongly seiz'd, and with a burning Wound,
Transfix'd and naked, on a Rock she bound.
But I, who walk in awful State above,   70
The Majesty of Heav'n, the Sister-wife of *Jove*;
For length of Years, my fruitless Force employ
Against the thin remains of ruin'd *Troy*.
What Nations now to *Juno*'s Pow'r will pray,
Or Off'rings on my slighted Altars lay?   75
 Thus rag'd the Goddess, and with Fury fraught,
The restless Regions of the Storms she sought.
Where in a spacious Cave of living Stone,
The Tyrant *Eolus* from his Airy Throne,
With Pow'r Imperial curbs the strugling Winds,   80
And sounding Tempests in dark Prisons binds.
This Way, and that, th' impatient Captives tend,
And pressing for Release, the Mountains rend;
High in his Hall, th' undaunted Monarch stands,
And shakes his Scepter, and their Rage commands: 85
Which did he not, their unresisted Sway
Wou'd sweep the World before them, in their Way:
Earth, Air, and Seas through empty Space wou'd rowl,
And Heav'n would fly before the driving Soul.
In fear of this, the Father of the Gods   90
Confin'd their Fury to those dark Abodes,
And lock'd 'em safe within, oppress'd with Mountain loads:
Impos'd a King, with arbitrary Sway,

The First Book. 79 Eolus 97 (errata): E'lus 97 (text)

To loose their Fetters, or their Force allay.
To whom the suppliant Queen her Pray'rs addrest,   95
And thus the tenour of her Suit express'd.
  O *Eolus*! for to thee the King of Heav'n
The Pow'r of Tempests, and of Winds has giv'n:
Thy Force alone their Fury can restrain,
And smooth the Waves, or swell the troubl'd Main.   100
A race of wand'ring Slaves, abhorr'd by me,
With prosp'rous Passage cut the *Thuscan* Sea:
To fruitful *Italy* their Course they steer,
And for their vanquish'd Gods design new Temples there.
Raise all thy Winds, with Night involve the Skies;   105
Sink, or disperse my fatal Enemies.
Twice sev'n, the charming Daughters of the Main,
Around my Person wait, and bear my Train:
Succeed my Wish, and second my Design,
The fairest, *Deiopeia*, shall be thine;   ⎫ 110
And make thee Father of a happy Line.   ⎭
   To this the God—'Tis yours, O Queen! to will
The Work, which Duty binds me to fulfil.
These airy Kingdoms, and this wide Command,
Are all the Presents of your bounteous Hand: 115
Yours is my Sov'raign's Grace, and, as your Guest,
I sit with Gods at their Cœlestial Feast.
Raise Tempests at your Pleasure, or subdue;
Dispose of Empire, which I hold from you.
He said, and hurld against the Mountain side,   120
His quiv'ring Spear; and all, the God apply'd.
The raging Winds rush through the hollow Wound,
And dance aloft in Air, and skim along the Ground:
Then setling on the Sea, the Surges sweep;
Raise liquid Mountains, and disclose the deep.   125
South, East, and West, with mix'd Confusion roar,
And rowl the foaming Billows to the Shoar.
The Cables crack, the Sailors fearful Cries   ⎫
Ascend; and sable Night involves the Skies;   ⎬
And Heav'n it self is ravish'd from their Eyes.   ⎭ 130
Loud Peals of Thunder from the Poles ensue,
Then flashing Fires the transient Light renew:

97 *Eolus* 97 (*errata*): *E'lus* 97 (*text*)   121 Spear;] Spear, *97 98*

The Face of things a frightful Image bears,
And present Death in various Forms appears.
Struck with unusual Fright, the *Trojan* Chief,   13
With lifted Hands and Eyes, invokes Relief.
And thrice, and four times happy those, he cry'd,
That under *Ilian* Walls before their Parents dy'd.
Tydides, bravest of the *Grecian* Train,
Why cou'd not I by that strong Arm be slain,   14
And lye by noble *Hector* on the Plain,
Or great *Sarpedon*, in those bloody Fields,
Where *Simois* rouls the Bodies, and the Shields
Of Heroes, whose dismember'd Hands yet bear
The Dart aloft, and clench the pointed Spear?   14
Thus while the Pious Prince his Fate bewails,
Fierce *Boreas* drove against his flying Sails,
And rent the Sheets: The raging Billows rise,
And mount the tossing Vessel to the Skies:
Nor can the shiv'ring Oars sustain the Blow;   15
The Galley gives her side, and turns her Prow:
While those astern descending down the Steep,
Thro' gaping Waves behold the boiling deep.
Three Ships were hurry'd by the Southern Blast,
And on the secret Shelves with Fury cast.   15
Those hidden Rocks, th' *Ausonian* Sailors knew,
They call'd them Altars, when they rose in view,
And show'd their spacious Backs above the Flood.
Three more, fierce *Eurus* in his angry Mood,
Dash'd on the Shallows of the moving Sand,   16
And in mid Ocean left them moor'd a-land.
Orontes Barque that bore the *Lycian* Crew,
(A horrid Sight) ev'n in the Hero's view,
From Stem to Stern, by Waves was overborn:
The trembling Pilot, from his Rudder torn,   16
Was headlong hurl'd; thrice round, the Ship was tost,
Then bulg'd at once, and in the deep was lost.
And here and there above the Waves were seen
Arms, Pictures, precious Goods, and floating Men.
The stoutest Vessel to the Storm gave way,   17
And suck'd through loosen'd Planks the rushing Sea.
Ilioneus was her Chief: *Alethes* old,

Achates faithful, *Abas* young and bold
Endur'd not less: their Ships, with gaping Seams,
Admit the Deluge of the briny Streams.   175
   Mean time Imperial *Neptune* heard the Sound
Of raging Billows breaking on the Ground:
Displeas'd, and fearing for his Wat'ry Reign,
He reard his awful Head above the Main:
Serene in Majesty, then rowl'd his Eyes   180
Around the Space of Earth, and Seas, and Skies.
He saw the *Trojan* Fleet dispers'd, distress'd
By stormy Winds and wintry Heav'n oppress'd.
Full well the God his Sister's envy knew,
And what her Aims, and what her Arts pursue: 185
He summon'd *Eurus* and the western Blast,
And first an angry glance on both he cast:
Then thus rebuk'd; Audacious Winds! from whence
This bold Attempt, this Rebel Insolence?
Is it for you to ravage Seas and Land,   190
Unauthoriz'd by my supream Command?
To raise such Mountains on the troubl'd Main?
Whom I—But first 'tis fit, the Billows to restrain,
And then you shall be taught obedience to my Reign.
Hence, to your Lord my Royal Mandate bear,   195
The Realms of Ocean and the Fields of Air
Are mine, not his; by fatal Lot to me
The liquid Empire fell, and Trident of the Sea.
His Pow'r to hollow Caverns is confin'd,
There let him reign, the Jailor of the Wind: 200
With hoarse Commands his breathing Subjects call,
And boast and bluster in his empty Hall.
He spoke: And while he spoke, he smooth'd the Sea,
Dispell'd the Darkness, and restor'd the Day:
Cymothoe, Triton, and the Sea-green Train   205
Of beauteous Nymphs, the Daughters of the Main,
Clear from the Rocks the Vessels with their hands;
The God himself with ready Trident stands,
And opes the Deep, and spreads the moving sands;
Then heaves them off the sholes: where e're he guides   210
His finny Coursers, and in Triumph rides,
The Waves unruffle and the Sea subsides.

As when in Tumults rise th' ignoble Crowd,
Mad are their Motions, and their Tongues are loud;
And Stones and Brands in ratling Vollies fly,
And all the Rustick Arms that Fury can supply:
If then some grave and Pious Man appear,
They hush their Noise, and lend a list'ning Ear;
He sooths with sober Words their angry Mood,
And quenches their innate Desire of Blood:
So when the Father of the Flood appears,
And o're the Seas his Sov'raign Trident rears,
Their Fury falls: He skims the liquid Plains,
High on his Chariot, and with loosen'd Reins,
Majestick moves along, and awful Peace maintains.
The weary *Trojans* ply their shatter'd Oars,
To nearest Land, and make the *Lybian* Shoars.

Within a long Recess there lies a Bay,
An Island shades it from the rowling Sea,
And forms a Port secure for Ships to ride,
Broke by the jutting Land on either side:
In double Streams the briny Waters glide.
Betwixt two rows of Rocks, a Sylvan Scene
Appears above, and Groves for ever green:
A Grott is form'd beneath, with Mossy Seats,
To rest the *Nereids*, and exclude the Heats.
Down thro' the Cranies of the living Walls
The Crystal Streams descend in murm'ring Falls.
No Haulsers need to bind the Vessels here,
Nor bearded Anchors, for no Storms they fear.
Sev'n Ships within this happy Harbour meet,
The thin Remainders of the scatter'd Fleet.
The *Trojans*, worn with Toils, and spent with Woes,
Leap on the welcome Land, and seek their wish'd Repose.
First, good *Achates*, with repeated stroaks
Of clashing Flints, their hidden Fire provokes;
Short Flame succeeds, a Bed of wither'd Leaves
The dying Sparkles in their Fall receives:
Caught into Life, in fiery Fumes they rise,
And, fed with stronger Food, invade the Skies.
The *Trojans*, dropping wet, or stand around

220 Blood: *98*: Blood. *97*   249 fiery *98*: smoaking *97*

The chearful blaze, or lye along the Ground:
Some dry their Corn infected with the Brine,
Then grind with Marbles, and prepare to dine.
Æneas climbs the Mountain's airy Brow,　　　255
And takes a Prospect of the Seas below:
If *Capys* thence, or *Antheus* he cou'd spy;
Or see the Streamers of *Caicus* fly.
No Vessels were in view: But, on the Plain,
Three beamy Stags command a Lordly Train　　　260
Of branching Heads; the more ignoble Throng
Attend their stately Steps, and slowly graze along.
He stood; and while secure they fed below,
He took the Quiver, and the trusty Bow
Achates us'd to bear; the Leaders first　　　265
He laid along, and then the Vulgar pierc'd:
Nor ceas'd his Arrows, 'till the shady Plain
Sev'n mighty Bodies, with their Blood distain.
For the sev'n Ships he made an equal Share,
And to the Port return'd, Triumphant from the War.　　　270
The Jarrs of gen'rous Wine, (*Acestes* Gift,
When his *Trinacrian* Shoars the Navy left)
He set abroach, and for the Feast prepar'd;
In equal Portions, with the Ven'son shar'd.
Thus while he dealt it round, the pious Chief,　　　275
With chearful Words, allay'd the common Grief:
Endure, and conquer; *Jove* will soon dispose
To future Good, our past and present Woes.
With me, the Rocks of *Scylla* you have try'd;
Th' inhuman *Cyclops*, and his Den defy'd.　　　280
What greater Ills hereafter can you bear?
Resume your Courage, and dismiss your Care.
An Hour will come, with Pleasure to relate
Your Sorrows past, as Benefits of Fate.
Through various Hazards, and Events we move　　　285
To *Latium*, and the Realms foredoom'd by *Jove*.
Call'd to the Seat, (the Promise of the Skies,)
Where *Trojan* Kingdoms once again may rise.
Endure the Hardships of your present State,
Live, and reserve your selves for better Fate.　　　290
　These Words he spoke; but spoke not from his Heart;

His outward Smiles conceal'd his inward Smart.
The jolly Crew, unmindful of the past,
The Quarry share, their plenteous Dinner haste:
Some strip the Skin, some portion out the Spoil;　　　　2
The Limbs yet trembling, in the Cauldrons boyl:
Some on the Fire the reeking Entrails broil.
Stretch'd on the grassy Turf, at ease they dine;
Restore their Strength with Meat, and chear their Souls with Wine.
Their Hunger thus appeas'd, their Care attends,　　　　3
The doubtful Fortune of their absent Friends:
Alternate Hopes and Fears, their Minds possess,
Whether to deem 'em dead, or in Distress.
Above the rest, *Æneas* mourns the Fate
Of brave *Orontes*, and th' uncertain State　　　　3
Of *Gyas*, *Lycus*, and of *Amycus*:
The Day, but not their Sorrows, ended thus.

　　When, from aloft, Almighty *Jove* surveys
Earth, Air, and Shoars, and navigable Seas,
At length on *Lybian* Realms he fix'd his Eyes:　　　　3
Whom, pond'ring thus on Human Miseries,
When *Venus* saw, she with a lowly Look,
Not free from Tears, her Heav'nly Sire bespoke.

　　O King of Gods and Men, whose awful Hand,
Disperses Thunder on the Seas and Land;　　　　3
Disposing all with absolute Command:
How cou'd my Pious Son thy Pow'r incense,
Or what, alas! is vanish'd *Troy*'s Offence?
Our hope of *Italy* not only lost,
On various Seas, by various Tempests tost,　　　　3
But shut from ev'ry Shoar, and barr'd from ev'ry Coast.
You promis'd once, a Progeny Divine,
Of *Romans*, rising from the *Trojan* Line,
In after-times shou'd hold the World in awe,
And to the Land and Ocean give the Law.　　　　3
How is your Doom revers'd, which eas'd my Care;
When *Troy* was ruin'd in that cruel War?
Then Fates to Fates I cou'd oppose; but now,
When Fortune still pursues her former Blow,
What can I hope? What worse can still succeed?　　　　3

What end of Labours has your Will decreed?
Antenor, from the midst of *Grecian* Hosts,
Could pass secure, and pierce th' *Illyrian* Coasts:
Where rowling down the Steep, *Timavus* raves,
And through nine Channels disembogues his Waves. 335
At length he founded *Padua*'s happy Seat,
And gave his *Trojans* a secure Retreat:
There fix'd their Arms, and there renew'd their Name,
And there in Quiet rules, and crown'd with Fame.
But we, descended from your sacred Line, 340
Entitled to your Heav'n, and Rites Divine,
Are banish'd Earth, and, for the Wrath of one,
Remov'd from *Latium*, and the promis'd Throne.
Are these our Scepters? These our due Rewards?
And is it thus that *Jove* his plighted Faith regards? 345
   To whom, the Father of th' immortal Race,
Smiling with that serene indulgent Face,
With which he drives the Clouds, and clears the Skies:
First gave a holy Kiss, then thus replies.
   Daughter, dismiss thy Fears: To thy desire 350
The Fates of thine are fix'd, and stand entire.
Thou shalt behold thy wish'd *Lavinian* Walls,
And, ripe for Heav'n, when Fate *Æneas* calls,
Then shalt thou bear him up, sublime, to me;
No Councils have revers'd my firm Decree. 355
And lest new Fears disturb thy happy State,
Know, I have search'd the Mystick Rolls of Fate:
Thy Son (nor is th' appointed Season far)
In *Italy* shall wage successful War:
Shall tame fierce Nations in the bloody Field, 360
And Sov'raign Laws impose, and Cities build.
'Till, after ev'ry Foe subdu'd, the Sun
Thrice through the Signs his Annual Race shall run:
This is his time prefix'd. *Ascanius* then,
Now called *Julus*, shall begin his Reign. 365
He thirty rowling Years the Crown shall wear:
Then from *Lavinium* shall the Seat transfer;
And, with hard Labour, *Alba-longa* build:
The Throne with his Succession shall be fill'd,

Three hundred Circuits more: then shall be seen,
Ilia the fair, a Priestess and a Queen.
Who full of *Mars*, in time, with kindly Throws,
Shall at a Birth two goodly Boys disclose.
The Royal Babes a tawny Wolf shall drain,
Then *Romulus* his Grandsire's Throne shall gain,
Of Martial Tow'rs the Founder shall become,
The People *Romans* call, the City *Rome*.
To them, no Bounds of Empire I assign;
Nor term of Years to their immortal Line.
Ev'n haughty *Juno*, who, with endless Broils,
Earth, Seas, and Heav'n, and *Jove* himself turmoils;
At length atton'd, her friendly Pow'r shall joyn,
To cherish and advance the *Trojan* Line.
The subject World shall *Rome*'s Dominion own,
And, prostrate, shall adore the Nation of the Gown.
An Age is ripening in revolving Fate,
When *Troy* shall overturn the *Grecian* State:
And sweet Revenge her conqu'ring Sons shall call,
To crush the People that conspir'd her Fall.
Then *Cæsar* from the *Julian* Stock shall rise,
Whose Empire Ocean, and whose Fame the Skies
Alone shall bound. Whom, fraught with *Eastern* Spoils,
Our Heav'n, the just Reward of Human Toyls,
Securely shall repay with Rites Divine;
And Incense shall ascend before his sacred Shrine.
Then dire Debate, and impious War shall cease,
And the stern Age be softned into Peace:
Then banish'd Faith shall once again return,
And Vestal Fires in hallow'd Temples burn;
And *Remus* with *Quirinus* shall sustain
The righteous Laws, and Fraud and Force restrain.
Janus himself before his Fane shall wait,
And keep the dreadful issues of his Gate,
With Bolts and Iron Bars: within remains
Imprison'd Fury, bound in brazen Chains:
High on a Trophie rais'd, of useless Arms,
He sits, and threats the World with vain Alarms.
    He said, and sent *Cyllenius* with Command

370

375

380

385

390

395

400

405

394 repay *98*: reward *97*   400 sustain] sustain, *97 98*

To free the Ports, and ope the *Punique* Land
To *Trojan* Guests; lest ignorant of Fate, 410
The Queen might force them from her Town and State.
Down from the Steep of Heav'n *Cyllenius* flies,
And cleaves with all his Wings the yielding Skies.
Soon on the *Lybian* Shoar descends the God;
Performs his Message, and displays his Rod: 415
The surly Murmurs of the People cease,
And, as the Fates requir'd, they give the Peace.
The Queen her self suspends the rigid Laws,
The *Trojans* pities, and protects their Cause.

   Mean time, in Shades of Night *Æneas* lies; 420
Care seiz'd his Soul, and Sleep forsook his Eyes.
But when the Sun restor'd the chearful Day,
He rose, the Coast and Country to survey,
Anxious and eager to discover more:
It look'd a wild uncultivated Shoar: 425
But whether Human Kind, or Beasts alone
Possess'd the new-found Region, was unknown.
Beneath a ledge of Rocks his Fleet he hides;
Tall Trees surround the Mountains shady sides:
The bending Brow above, a safe Retreat provides. 430
Arm'd with two pointed Darts, he leaves his Friends,
And true *Achates* on his steps attends.
Loe, in the deep Recesses of the Wood,
Before his Eyes his Goddess Mother stood:
A Huntress in her Habit and her Meen; 435
Her dress a Maid, her Air confess'd a Queen.
Bare were her Knees, and knots her Garments bind;
Loose was her Hair, and wanton'd in the Wind;
Her Hand sustain'd a Bow, her Quiver hung behind.
She seem'd a Virgin of the *Spartan* Blood: 440
With such Array *Harpalice* bestrode
Her *Thracian* Courser, and outstrip'd the rapid Flood.
Ho! Strangers! have you lately seen, she said,
One of my Sisters, like my self array'd;
Who crost the Lawn, or in the Forest stray'd? 445

428 ledge of Rocks *98*: hollow Rock *97*

A Painted Quiver at her Back she bore;
Vary'd with Spots, a *Linx*'s Hide she wore:
And at full Cry pursu'd the tusky Boar?
Thus *Venus*: Thus her Son reply'd agen;
None of your Sisters have we heard or seen,
O virgin! or what other Name you bear
Above that stile; O more than mortal fair!
Your Voice and Meen Cœlestial Birth betray!
If, as you seem, the Sister of the Day;
Or one at least of Chast *Diana*'s Train,
Let not an humble Suppliant sue in vain:
But tell a Stranger, long in Tempests tost,
What Earth we tread, and who commands the Coast?
Then on your Name shall wretched Mortals call;
And offer'd Victims at your Altars fall.
I dare not, she reply'd, assume the Name
Of Goddess, or Cœlestial Honours claim:
For *Tyrian* Virgins Bows and Quivers bear,
And Purple Buskins o're their Ankles wear.
Know, gentle Youth, in *Lybian* Lands you are:
A People rude in Peace, and rough in War.
The rising City, which from far you see,
Is *Carthage*; and a *Tyrian* Colony.
Phenician Dido rules the growing State,
Who fled from *Tyre*, to shun her Brother's hate:
Great were her wrongs, her Story full of Fate;
Which I will sum in short. *Sicheus* known
For wealth, and Brother to the *Punic* Throne,
Possess'd fair *Dido*'s Bed: And either heart
At once was wounded with an equal Dart.
Her Father gave her, yet a spotless Maid;
Pigmalion then the *Tyrian* Scepter sway'd:
One who contemn'd Divine and Humane Laws:
Then Strife ensu'd, and cursed Gold the Cause.
The Monarch, blinded with desire of Wealth,
With Steel invades his Brother's life by stealth;
Before the sacred Altar made him bleed,
And long from her conceal'd the cruel deed.
Some Tale, some new Pretence, he daily coin'd,

4

4.

4●

4●

4●

4●

4●

4●

480 Wealth,] Wealth; *97 98*

To sooth his Sister, and delude her Mind.   485
At length, in dead of Night, the Ghost appears
Of her unhappy Lord: the Spectre stares,
And with erected Eyes his bloody Bosom bares.
The cruel Altars, and his Fate he tells,
And the dire Secret of his House reveals.   490
Then warns the Widdow, with her household Gods,
To seek a Refuge in remote abodes.
Last, to support her, in so long a way,
He shows her where his hidden Treasure lay.
Admonish'd thus, and seiz'd with mortal fright,   495
The Queen provides Companions of her flight:
They meet; and all combine to leave the State,
Who hate the Tyrant, or who fear his hate.
They seize a Fleet, which ready rigg'd they find:
Nor is *Pigmalion*'s Treasure left behind.   500
The Vessels, heavy laden, put to Sea
With prosprous winds; a Woman leads the way.
I know not, if by stress of Weather driv'n,
Or was their fatal Course dispos'd by Heav'n;
At last they landed, where from far your Eyes   505
May view the Turrets of new *Carthage* rise:
There bought a space of Ground, which *Byrsa* call'd
From the Bulls hide, they first inclos'd, and wall'd.
But whence are you, what Country claims your Birth?
What seek you, Strangers, on our *Lybian* Earth?   510
    To whom, with sorrow streaming from his Eyes,
And deeply sighing, thus her Son replyes:
Cou'd you with Patience hear, or I relate,
O Nymph! the tedious Annals of our Fate!
Thro' such a train of Woes if I shou'd run,   515
The day wou'd sooner than the Tale be done!
From ancient *Troy*, by Force expell'd, we came,
If you by chance have heard the *Trojan* Name:
On various Seas by various Tempests tost,
At length we landed on your *Lybian* Coast.   520
The Good *Æneas* am I call'd, a Name,
While Fortune favour'd, not unknown to Fame:
My houshold Gods, Companions of my Woes,
With pious Care I rescu'd from our Foes.

To fruitful *Italy* my Course was bent, 52
And from the King of Heav'n is my Descent.
With twice ten Sail I crost the *Phrygian* Sea;
Fate, and my Mother Goddess, led my Way.
Scarce sev'n, the thin Remainders of my Fleet,
From Storms preserv'd, within your Harbour meet: 53
My self distress'd, an Exile, and unknown,
Debarr'd from *Europe*, and from *Asia* thrown,
In *Lybian* Desarts wander thus alone.

   His tender Parent could no longer bear;
But, interposing, sought to sooth his Care. 53
Who e're you are, not unbelov'd by Heav'n,
Since on our friendly Shoar your Ships are driv'n:
Have Courage: To the Gods permit the rest,
And to the Queen expose your just Request.
Now take this earnest of Success, for more: 54
Your scatter'd Fleet is join'd upon the Shoar;
The Winds are chang'd, your Friends from danger free,
Or I renounce my Skill in Augury.
Twelve Swans behold, in beauteous order move,
And stoop with closing Pinions from above: 54
Whom late the Bird of *Jove* had driv'n along,
And through the Clouds pursu'd the scatt'ring Throng:
Now all united in a goodly Team,
They skim the Ground, and seek the quiet Stream.
As they, with Joy returning, clap their Wings, 550
And ride the Circuit of the Skies in Rings:
Not otherwise your Ships, and ev'ry Friend,
Already hold the Port, or with swift Sails descend.
No more Advice is needful, but pursue
The Path before you, and the Town in view. 555
Thus having said, she turn'd, and made appear
Her Neck refulgent, and dishevel'd Hair;
Which flowing from her Shoulders, reach'd the Ground,
And widely spread Ambrosial Scents around:
In length of Train descends her sweeping Gown, 560
And by her graceful Walk, the Queen of Love is known.
The Prince pursu'd the parting Deity,
With Words like these: Ah! whither do you fly?
Unkind and cruel, to deceive your Son

In borrow'd Shapes, and his Embrace to shun: 565
Never to bless my Sight, but thus unknown;
And still to speak in Accents not your own.
Against the Goddess these Complaints he made;
But took the Path, and her Commands obey'd.
They march obscure, for *Venus* kindly shrouds,   570
With Mists, their Persons, and involves in Clouds:
That, thus unseen, their Passage none might stay,
Or force to tell the Causes of their Way.
This part perform'd, the Goddess flies sublime,
To visit *Paphos*; and her native Clime: 575
Where Garlands ever green, and ever fair,
With Vows are offer'd, and with solemn Pray'r:
A hundred Altars in her Temple Smoke,
A thousand bleeding Hearts her Pow'r invoke.

    They climb the next Ascent, and, looking down,   580
Now at a nearer Distance view the Town:
The Prince, with Wonder, sees the stately Tow'rs,
Which late were Huts, and Shepherds homely Bow'rs;
The Gates and Streets; and hears, from ev'ry part,
The Noise, and buisy Concourse of the Mart.   585
The toiling *Tyrians* on each other call,
To ply their Labour: Some extend the Wall,
Some build the Citadel; the brawny Throng,
Or dig, or push unweildy Stones along.
Some for their Dwellings chuse a Spot of Ground,   590
Which, first design'd, with Ditches they surround.
Some Laws ordain, and some attend the Choice
Of holy Senates, and elect by Voice.
Here some design a Mole, while others there
Lay deep Foundations for a Theatre: 595
From Marble Quarries mighty Columns hew,
For Ornaments of Scenes, and future view.
Such is their Toyl, and such their buisy Pains,
As exercise the Bees in flow'ry Plains;
When Winter past, and Summer scarce begun,   600
Invites them forth to labour in the Sun:
Some lead their Youth abroad, while some condense
Their liquid Store, and some in Cells dispence.

   583 Shepherds] Shepherd's *97 98*   Bow'rs;] Bow'rs. *97 98*

Some at the Gate stand ready to receive
The Golden Burthen, and their Friends relieve.   60
All, with united Force, combine to drive
The lazy Drones from the laborious Hive;
With Envy stung, they view each others Deeds;
The fragrant Work with Diligence proceeds.
Thrice happy you, whose Walls already rise;   61
Æneas said; and view'd, with lifted Eyes,
Their lofty Tow'rs; then ent'ring at the Gate,
Conceal'd in Clouds, (prodigious to relate)
He mix'd, unmark'd, among the buisy Throng,
Born by the Tide, and pass'd unseen along.   61
   Full in the Centre of the Town there stood,
Thick set with Trees, a venerable Wood:
The *Tyrians* landing near this holy Ground,
And digging here, a prosp'rous Omen found:
From under Earth a Courser's Head they drew,   62
Their Growth and future Fortune to foreshew:
This fated Sign their Foundress *Juno* gave,
Of a Soil fruitful, and a People brave.
Sidonian Dido here with solemn State
Did *Juno*'s Temple build, and consecrate: 62
Enrich'd with Gifts, and with a Golden Shrine;
But more the Goddess made the Place Divine.
On Brazen Steps the Marble Threshold rose,
And brazen Plates the Cedar Beams inclose:
The Rafters are with brazen Cov'rings crown'd,   63
The lofty Doors on brazen Hinges sound.
What first *Æneas* in this place beheld,
Reviv'd his Courage, and his Fear expel'd.
For while, expecting there the Queen, he rais'd
His wond'ring Eyes, and round the Temple gaz'd;   63
Admir'd the Fortune of the rising Town,
The striving Artists, and their Arts renown.
He saw in order painted on the Wall,
Whatever did unhappy *Troy* befall:
The Wars that Fame around the World had blown,   64
All to the Life, and ev'ry Leader known.
There *Agamemnon*, *Priam* here he spies,

622 fated *98*: fatal *97*   640 Fame *97* (*errata*): Fate *97* (*text*)

And fierce *Achilles* who both Kings defies.
He stop'd, and weeping said, O Friend! ev'n here
The Monuments of *Trojan* Woes appear!   645
Our known Disasters fill ev'n foreign Lands:
See there, where old unhappy *Priam* stands!
Ev'n the Mute Walls relate the Warrior's Fame,
And *Trojan* Griefs the *Tyrians* Pity claim.
He said, his Tears a ready Passage find,   650
Devouring what he saw so well design'd;
And with an empty Picture fed his Mind.
For there he saw the fainting *Grecians* yield,
And here the trembling *Trojans* quit the Field,
Pursu'd by fierce *Achilles* through the Plain,   655
On his high Chariot driving o're the Slain.
The Tents of *Rhesus* next, his Grief renew,
By their white Sails betray'd to nightly view.
And wakeful *Diomede*, whose cruel Sword
The Centries slew; nor spar'd their slumb'ring Lord.   660
Then took the fiery Steeds, e're yet the Food
Of *Troy* they taste, or drink the *Xanthian* Flood.
Elsewhere he saw where *Troilus* defy'd
Achilles, and unequal Combat try'd.
Then, where the Boy disarm'd with loosen'd Reins,   665
Was by his Horses hurry'd o're the Plains:
Hung by the Neck and Hair, and drag'd around,
The hostile Spear yet sticking in his Wound;
With tracks of Blood inscrib'd the dusty Ground.
   Mean time the *Trojan* Dames oppress'd with Woe,   670
To *Pallas* Fane in long Procession goe,
In hopes to reconcile their Heav'nly Foe:
They weep, they beat their Breasts, they rend their Hair,
And rich embroider'd Vests for Presents bear:
But the stern Goddess stands unmov'd with Pray'r.   675
Thrice round the *Trojan* Walls *Achilles* drew
The Corps of *Hector*, whom in Fight he slew.
Here *Priam* sues, and there, for Sums of Gold,
The lifeless Body of his Son is sold.
So sad an Object, and so well express'd,   680
Drew Sighs and Groans from the griev'd Heroes Breast:

671 Procession *98*: Precession *97*

To see the Figure of his lifeless Friend,
And his old Sire his helpless Hand extend.
Himself he saw amidst the *Grecian* Train,
Mix'd in the bloody Battel on the Plain.
And swarthy *Memnon* in his Arms he knew,
His pompous Ensigns, and his *Indian* Crew.
Penthisilea there, with haughty Grace,
Leads to the Wars an *Amazonian* Race:
In their right Hands a pointed Dart they wield;
The left, for Ward, sustains the Lunar Shield.
Athwart her Breast a Golden Belt she throws,
Amidst the Press alone provokes a thousand Foes:
And dares her Maiden Arms to Manly Force oppose.

   Thus, while the *Trojan* Prince employs his Eyes,
Fix'd on the Walls with wonder and surprise;
The Beauteous *Dido*, with a num'rous Train,
And pomp of Guards, ascends the sacred Fane.
Such on *Eurotas* Banks, or *Cynthus* hight,
Diana seems; and so she charms the sight,
When in the Dance the graceful Goddess leads
The Quire of Nymphs, and overtops their Heads.
Known by her Quiver, and her lofty Meen,
She walks Majestick, and she looks their Queen:
Latona sees her shine above the rest,
And feeds with secret Joy her silent Breast.
Such *Dido* was; with such becoming State,
Amidst the Crowd, she walks serenely great.
Their Labour to her future Sway she speeds,
And passing with a gracious Glance proceeds:
Then mounts the Throne, high plac'd before the Shrine;
In Crowds around the swarming People joyn.
She takes Petitions, and dispenses Laws,
Hears, and determines ev'ry Private Cause.
Their Tasks in equal Portions she divides,
And where unequal, there by Lots decides.
Another Way by chance *Æneas* bends
His Eyes, and unexpected sees his Friends:
Antheus, Sergestus grave, *Cloanthus* strong,

686 knew,] knew *97 98*   695 *Editor's paragraph*   699 *Eurotas* . . . *Cynthus*]
                                Eurota's . . . *Cynthus's 97 98*

And at their Backs a mighty *Trojan* Throng: 720
Whom late the Tempest on the Billows tost,
And widely scatter'd on another Coast.
The Prince, unseen, surpriz'd with Wonder stands,
And longs, with joyful haste to join their Hands:
But doubtful of the wish'd Event, he stays,   725
And from the hollow Cloud his Friends surveys:
Impatient 'till they told their present State,
And where they left their Ships, and what their Fate;
And why they came, and what was their Request:
For these were sent commission'd by the rest,   730
To sue for leave to land their sickly Men,
And gain Admission to the Gracious Queen.
Ent'ring, with Cries they fill'd the holy Fane;
Then thus, with lowly Voice, *Ilioneus* began.

   O Queen! indulg'd by Favour of the Gods,   735
To found an Empire in these new Abodes;
To build a Town, with Statutes to restrain
The wild Inhabitants beneath thy Reign:
We wretched *Trojans* tost on ev'ry Shore,
From Sea to Sea, thy Clemency implore: 740
Forbid the Fires our Shipping to deface,
Receive th' unhappy Fugitives to Grace,
And spare the remnant of a Pious Race.
We come not with design of wastful Prey,
To drive the Country, force the Swains away: 745
Nor such our Strength, nor such is our Desire,
The vanquish'd dare not to such Thoughts aspire.
A Land there is, *Hesperia* nam'd of old,
The Soil is fruitful, and the Men are bold:
Th' *Oenotrians* held it once, by common Fame,   750
Now call'd *Italia*, from the Leaders Name.
To that sweet Region was our Voyage bent,
When Winds, and ev'ry warring Element,
Disturb'd our Course, and far from sight of Land,
Cast our torn Vessels on the moving Sand: 755
The Sea came on; the South with mighty Roar,
Dispers'd and dash'd the rest upon the Rocky Shoar.
Those few you see escap'd the Storm, and fear,

   734 lowly *98*: humble *97*   735 *Editor's paragraph*

Unless you interpose, a Shipwreck here:
What Men, what Monsters, what inhuman Race,
What Laws, what barb'rous Customs of the Place,
Shut up a desart Shoar to drowning Men,
And drive us to the cruel Seas agen!
If our hard Fortune no Compassion draws,
Nor hospitable Rights, nor human Laws,
The Gods are just, and will revenge our Cause.
Æneas was our Prince, a juster Lord,
Or nobler Warriour, never drew a Sword:
Observant of the Right, religious of his Word.
If yet he lives, and draws this vital Air:
Nor we his Friends of Safety shall despair;
Nor you, great Queen, these Offices repent,
Which he will equal, and perhaps augment.
We want not Cities, nor *Sicilian* Coasts,
Where King *Acestes Trojan* Lineage boasts.
Permit our Ships a Shelter on your Shoars,
Refitted from your Woods with Planks and Oars;
That if our Prince be safe, we may renew
Our destin'd Course, and *Italy* pursue.
But if, O best of Men! the Fates ordain
That thou art swallow'd in the *Lybian* Main:
And if our young *Iulus* be no more,
Dismiss our Navy from your friendly Shoar.
That we to good *Acestes* may return,
And with our Friends our common Losses mourn.
Thus spoke *Ilioneus*; the *Trojan* Crew
With Cries and Clamours his Request renew.
The modest Queen a while, with down-cast Eyes,
Ponder'd the Speech; then briefly thus replies.

   Trojans dismiss your Fears: my cruel Fate,
And doubts attending an unsetled State,
Force me to guard my Coast, from Foreign Foes.
Who has not heard the story of your Woes?
The Name and Fortune of your Native Place,
The Fame and Valour of the *Phrygian* Race?
We *Tyrians* are not so devoid of Sense,
Nor so remote from *Phœbus* influence.

763 drive *98*: drives *97*   773 augment *98*: prevent *97*

Whether to *Latian* Shores your Course is bent,
Or driv'n by Tempests from your first intent,
You seek the good *Acestes* Government;   800
Your Men shall be receiv'd, your Fleet repair'd,
And sail, with Ships of Convoy for your guard:
Or, wou'd you stay, and joyn your friendly Pow'rs,
To raise and to defend the *Tyrian* Tow'rs;
My Wealth, my City, and my Self are yours.   805
And wou'd to Heav'n the Storm, you felt, wou'd bring
On *Carthaginian* Coasts your wand'ring King.
My People shall, by my Command, explore
The Ports and Creeks of ev'ry winding shore;
And Towns, and Wilds, and shady Woods, in quest   810
Of so renown'd and so desir'd a Guest.
Rais'd in his Mind the *Trojan* Heroe stood,
And long'd to break from out his Ambient Cloud;
Achates found it; and thus urg'd his way;
From whence, O Goddess born, this long delay?   815
What more can you desire, your Welcome sure,
Your Fleet in safety, and your Friends secure?
One only wants; and him we saw in vain
Oppose the Storm, and swallow'd in the Main.
Orontes in his Fate our Forfeit paid,   820
The rest agrees with what your Mother said.
Scarce had he spoken, when the Cloud gave way,
The Mists flew upward, and dissolv'd in day.
The *Trojan* Chief appear'd in open sight,
August in Visage, and serenely bright.   825
His Mother Goddess, with her hands Divine,
Had form'd his Curling Locks, and made his Temples shine:
And giv'n his rowling Eyes a sparkling grace;
And breath'd a youthful vigour on his Face:
Like polish'd Iv'ry, beauteous to behold,   830
Or *Parian* Marble, when enchas'd in Gold:
Thus radiant from the circling Cloud he broke;
And thus with manly modesty he spoke.
   He whom you seek am I: by Tempests tost,
And sav'd from Shipwreck on your *Lybian* Coast: 835
Presenting, gracious Queen, before your Throne,

799 Tempests *98*: Tempest's *97*   802 guard:] guard; *97 98*

A Prince that ows his Life to you alone.
Fair Majesty, the Refuge and Redresss
Of those whom Fate pursues, and Wants oppress.
You, who your pious Offices employ   84
To save the Reliques of abandon'd *Troy*;
Receive the Shipwreck'd on your friendly Shore,
With hospitable Rites relieve the Poor:
Associate in your Town a wandring Train,
And Strangers in your Palace entertain.   84
What thanks can wretched Fugitives return,
Who scatter'd thro' the World in exile mourn?
The Gods, (if Gods to Goodness are inclin'd,)
If Acts of mercy touch their Heav'nly Mind;
And more than all the Gods, your gen'rous heart,   85
Conscious of worth, requite its own desert!
In you this Age is happy, and this Earth:
And Parents more than Mortal gave you birth.
While rowling Rivers into Seas shall run,
And round the space of Heav'n the radiant Sun;   85
While Trees the Mountain tops with Shades supply,
Your Honour, Name, and Praise shall never dye.
What e're abode my Fortune has assign'd,
Your Image shall be present in my Mind.
Thus having said; he turn'd with pious hast,   86
And joyful his expecting Friends embrac'd:
With his right hand *Ilioneus* was grac'd,
Serestus with his left; then to his breast
Cloanthus and the Noble *Gyas* prest;
And so by turns descended to the rest.   86

   The *Tyrian* Queen stood fix'd upon his Face,
Pleas'd with his motions, ravish'd with his grace:
Admir'd his Fortunes, more admir'd the Man;
Then recollected stood; and thus began.
   What Fate, O Goddess born, what angry Pow'rs   87
Have cast you shipwrack'd on our barren Shores?
Are you the great *Æneas*, known to Fame,
Who from Cœlestial Seed your Lineage claim!
The same *Æneas* whom fair *Venus* bore
To fam'd *Anchises* on th' *Idæan* Shore?   87
It calls into my mind, tho' then a Child,

When *Teucer* came from *Salamis* exil'd;
And sought my Father's aid, to be restor'd:
My Father *Belus* then with Fire and Sword
Invaded *Cyprus*, made the Region bare,   880
And, Conqu'ring, finish'd the successful War.
From him the *Trojan* Siege I understood,
The *Grecian* Chiefs, and your Illustrious Blood.
Your Foe himself the *Dardan* Valour prais'd,
And his own Ancestry from *Trojans* rais'd.   885
Enter, my Noble Guest; and you shall find,
If not a costly welcome, yet a kind.
For I my self, like you, have been distress'd;
Till Heav'n afforded me this place of rest.
Like you an Alien in a Land unknown;   890
I learn to pity Woes, so like my own.
She said, and to the Palace led her Guest,
Then offer'd Incense, and proclaim'd a Feast.
Nor yet less careful for her absent Friends,
Twice ten fat Oxen to the Ships she sends: 895
Besides a hundred Boars, a hundred Lambs,
With bleating cries, attend their Milky Dams.
And Jars of gen'rous Wine, and spacious Bowls,
She gives to chear the Sailors drooping Souls.
Now Purple Hangings cloath the Palace Walls,   900
And sumptuous Feasts are made in splendid Halls:
On *Tyrian* Carpets, richly wrought, they dine;
With loads of Massy Plate the Side-boards shine.
And Antique Vases all of Gold Emboss'd;
(The Gold it self inferiour to the Cost:)   905
Of curious Work, where on the sides were seen
The Fights and Figures of Illustrious Men;
From their first Founder to the present Queen.
   The Good *Æneas*, whose Paternal Care
Iulus absence could no longer bear,   910
Dispatch'd *Achates* to the Ships in hast,
To give a glad Relation of the past;
And, fraught with precious Gifts, to bring the Boy
Snatch'd from the Ruins of unhappy *Troy*:
A Robe of Tissue, stiff with golden Wire;   915
An upper Vest, once *Hellen*'s rich Attire;

From *Argos* by the fam'd Adultress brought,
With Golden flow'rs and winding foliage wrought;
Her Mother *Læda*'s Present, when she came
To ruin *Troy*, and set the World on flame: 920
The Scepter *Priam*'s eldest Daughter bore,
Her orient Necklace, and the Crown she wore;
Of double texture, glorious to behold;
One order set with Gems, and one with Gold.
Instructed thus, the wise *Achates* goes: 925
And in his diligence his duty shows.
    But *Venus*, anxious for her Son's Affairs,
New Councils tryes; and new Designs prepares:
That *Cupid* should assume the Shape and Face
Of sweet *Ascanius*, and the sprightly grace: 930
Shou'd bring the Presents, in her Nephews stead,
And in *Eliza*'s Veins the gentle Poison shed.
For much she fear'd the *Tyrians*, double tongu'd,
And knew the Town to *Juno*'s care belong'd.
These thoughts by Night her Golden Slumbers broke;   935
And thus alarm'd, to winged Love she spoke.
My Son, my strength, whose mighty Pow'r alone
Controuls the Thund'rer, on his awful Throne;
To thee thy much afflicted Mother flies,
And on thy Succour, and thy Faith relies.   940
Thou know'st, my Son, how *Jove*'s revengeful Wife,
By force and Fraud, attempts thy Brother's life.
And often hast thou mourn'd with me his Pains:
Him *Dido* now with Blandishment detains;
But I suspect the Town where *Juno* reigns.   94
For this, 'tis needful to prevent her Art,
And fire with Love the proud *Phœnician*'s heart.
A Love so violent, so strong, so sure,
As neither Age can change, nor Art can cure.
How this may be perform'd, now take my mind: 95
Ascanius, by his Father is design'd
To come, with Presents, laden from the Port,
To gratifie the Queen, and gain the Court.
I mean to plunge the Boy in pleasing Sleep,
And, ravish'd, in *Idalian* Bow'rs to keep;   95

Or high *Cythæra*: That the sweet Deceipt
May pass unseen, and none prevent the Cheat,
Take thou his Form and Shape. I beg the Grace
But only for a Night's revolving Space;
Thy self a Boy, assume a Boy's dissembled Face.   960
That when amidst the fervour of the Feast,
The *Tyrian* hugs, and fonds thee on her Breast,
And with sweet Kisses in her Arms constrains,
Thou may'st infuse thy Venom in her Veins.
The God of Love obeys, and sets aside   965
His Bow, and Quiver, and his plumy Pride:
He walks *Iulus* in his Mother's Sight,
And in the sweet Resemblance takes Delight.
    The Goddess then to young *Ascanius* flies,
And in a pleasing Slumber seals his Eyes;   970
Lull'd in her Lap, amidst a Train of Loves,
She gently bears him to her blissful Groves:
Then with a Wreath of Myrtle crowns his Head,
And softly lays him on a flow'ry Bed.
Cupid mean time assum'd his Form and Face,   975
Foll'wing *Achates* with a shorter Pace;
And brought the Gifts. The Queen, already sate
Amidst the *Trojan* Lords, in shining State,
High on a Golden Bed: Her Princely Guest
Was next her side, in order sate the rest.   980
Then Canisters with Bread are heap'd on high;
Th' Attendants Water for their Hands supply;
And having wash'd, with silken Towels dry.
Next fifty Handmaids in long order bore
The Censers, and with Fumes the Gods adore.   985
Then Youths, and Virgins twice as many, join
To place the Dishes, and to serve the Wine.
The *Tyrian* Train, admitted to the Feast,
Approach, and on the painted Couches rest.
All on the *Trojan* Gifts, with Wonder gaze;   990
But view the beauteous Boy with more amaze.
His Rosy-colour'd Cheeks, his radiant Eyes,
His Motions, Voice, and Shape, and all the God's disguise.
Nor pass unprais'd the Vest and Veil Divine,
Which wand'ring Foliage and rich Flow'rs entwine.   995

But far above the rest, the Royal Dame,
(Already doom'd to Love's disastrous Flame;)
With Eyes insatiate, and tumultuous Joy,
Beholds the Presents, and admires the Boy.
The guileful God, about the Heroe long,
With Children's play, and false Embraces hung;
Then sought the Queen: She took him to her Arms,
With greedy Pleasure, and devour'd his Charms.
Unhappy *Dido* little thought what Guest,
How dire a God she drew so near her Breast.
But he, not mindless of his Mother's Pray'r,
Works in the pliant Bosom of the Fair;
And moulds her Heart anew, and blots her former Care.
The dead is to the living Love resign'd,
And all *Æneas* enters in her Mind.

 Now, when the Rage of Hunger was appeas'd,
The Meat remov'd, and ev'ry Guest was pleas'd;
The Golden Bowls with sparkling Wine are crown'd,
And through the Palace chearful Cries resound.
From gilded Roofs depending Lamps display
Nocturnal Beams, that emulate the Day.
A Golden Bowl, that shone with Gems Divine,
The Queen commanded to be crown'd with Wine;
The Bowl that *Belus* us'd, and all the *Tyrian* Line.
Then, Silence through the Hall proclaim'd, she spoke:
O hospitable *Jove*! we thus invoke,
With solemn Rites, thy sacred Name and Pow'r!
Bless to both Nations this auspicious Hour.
So may the *Trojan* and the *Tyrian* Line,
In lasting Concord, from this Day combine.
Thou, *Bacchus*, God of Joys and friendly Cheer,
And gracious *Juno*, both be present here:
And you, my Lords of *Tyre*, your Vows address
To Heav'n with mine, to ratifie the Peace.
The Goblet then she took, with *Nectar* crown'd,
(Sprinkling the first Libations on the Ground,)
And rais'd it to her Mouth with sober Grace,
Then sipping, offer'd to the next in place.
'Twas *Bitias* whom she call'd, a thirsty Soul,

He took the Challenge, and embrac'd the Bowl: 1035
With Pleasure swill'd the Gold, nor ceas'd to draw,
'Till he the bottom of the Brimmer saw.
The Goblet goes around: *Iopas* brought
His Golden Lyre, and sung what ancient *Atlas* taught.
The various Labours of the wand'ring Moon, 1040
And whence proceed th' Eclipses of the Sun.
Th' Original of Men, and Beasts; and whence
The Rains arise, and Fires their Warmth dispence; }
And fix'd, and erring Stars, dispose their Influence.
What shakes the solid Earth, what Cause delays 1045
The Summer Nights, and shortens Winter Days.
With Peals of Shouts the *Tyrians* praise the Song;
Those Peals are echo'd by the *Trojan* Throng.
Th' unhappy Queen with Talk prolong'd the Night,
And drank large Draughts of Love with vast Delight. 1050
Of *Priam* much enquir'd, of *Hector* more;
Then ask'd what Arms the swarthy *Memnon* wore; }
What Troops he landed on the *Trojan* Shore.
The Steeds of *Diomede* vary'd the Discourse,
And fierce *Achilles*, with his matchless Force. 1055
At length, as Fate and her ill Stars requir'd,
To hear the Series of the War desir'd.
Relate at large, my God-like Guest, she said,
The *Grecian* Stratagems, the Town betray'd;
The fatal Issue of so long a War, 1060
Your Flight, your Wand'rings, and your Woes declare.
For since on ev'ry Sea, on ev'ry Coast,
Your Men have been distress'd, your Navy tost,
Sev'n times the Sun has either Tropick view'd,
The Winter banish'd, and the Spring renew'd. 1065

THE SECOND BOOK OF THE ÆNEIS

THE ARGUMENT

Æneas relates how the City of Troy *was taken, after a Ten Years Siege, by the Treachery of* Sinon, *and the Stratagem of a wooden Horse. He declares the fixt Resolution he had taken not to survive the Ruins of his Country, and the*

1054 *Diomede 97 (errata):* Di'mede *97 (text)*

various Adventures he met with in the Defence of it: at last having been before
advis'd by Hector's *Ghost, and now by the Appearance of his Mother* Venus, 5
he is prevail'd upon to leave the Town, and settle his Houshold-Gods in another
Country. In order to this, he carries off his Father on his Shoulders, and leads
his little Son by the Hand, his Wife following him behind. When he comes to
the Place appointed for the general Rendezvouze, he finds a great Confluence
of People, but misses his Wife, whose Ghost afterwards appears to him, and tells 10
him the Land which was design'd for him.

A<small>LL</small> were attentive to the God-like Man;
  When from his lofty Couch he thus began.
Great Queen, what you command me to relate,
Renews the sad remembrance of our Fate.
An Empire from its old Foundations rent,   5
And ev'ry Woe the *Trojans* underwent:
A Peopl'd City made a Desart Place;
All that I saw, and part of which I was:
Not ev'n the hardest of our Foes cou'd hear,
Nor stern *Ulysses* tell without a Tear.   10
And now the latter Watch of wasting Night,
And setting Stars to kindly Rest invite.
But since you take such Int'rest in our Woe,
And *Troy*'s disast'rous end desire to know:
I will restrain my Tears, and briefly tell   15
What in our last and fatal Night befel.
  By Destiny compell'd, and in Despair,
The *Greeks* grew weary of the tedious War:
And by *Minerva*'s Aid a Fabrick rear'd,
Which like a Steed of monstrous height appear'd;   20
The Sides were planck'd with Pine, they feign'd it made
For their Return, and this the Vow they paid.
Thus they pretend, but in the hollow Side,
Selected Numbers of their Souldiers hide:
With inward Arms the dire Machine they load,   25
And Iron Bowels stuff the dark Abode.
In sight of *Troy* lies *Tenedos*, an Isle,
(While Fortune did on *Priam*'s Empire smile)
Renown'd for Wealth, but since a faithless Bay,
Where Ships expos'd to Wind and Weather lay.   30

The Second Book. Argument. 9 *Rendezvouze* 98: *Rendevouze* 97   2 his 97 (*errata*):
the 97 (*text*)   26 And 98: With 97

There was their Fleet conceal'd: We thought for *Greece*
Their Sails were hoisted, and our Fears release.
The *Trojans* coop'd within their Walls so long,
Unbar their Gates, and issue in a Throng,
Like swarming Bees, and with Delight survey   35
The Camp deserted, where the *Grecians* lay:
The Quarters of the sev'ral Chiefs they show'd,
Here *Phœnix*, here *Achilles* made abode,
Here join'd the Battels, there the Navy rode.
Part on the Pile their wond'ring Eyes employ,   40
(The Pile by *Pallas* rais'd to ruin *Troy*.)
Thymœtes first ('tis doubtful whether hir'd,
Or so the *Trojan* Destiny requir'd)
Mov'd that the Ramparts might be broken down,
To lodge the Monster Fabrique in the Town.   45
But *Capys*, and the rest of sounder Mind,
The fatal Present to the Flames design'd;
Or to the watry deep: At least to bore
The hollow sides, and hidden Frauds explore:
The giddy Vulgar, as their Fancies guide,   50
With Noise say nothing, and in parts divide.
Laocoon, follow'd by a num'rous Crowd,
Ran from the Fort; and cry'd, from far, aloud;
O wretch'd Country-men! what Fury reigns?
What more than Madness has possess'd your Brains?   55
Think you the *Grecians* from your Coasts are gone,
And are *Ulysses* Arts no better known?
This hollow Fabrick either must inclose,
Within its blind Recess, our secret Foes;
Or 'tis an Engine rais'd above the Town,   60
T' o'relook the Walls, and then to batter down.
Somewhat is sure design'd; by Fraud or Force;
Trust not their Presents, nor admit the Horse.
Thus having said, against the Steed he threw
His forceful Spear, which, hissing as it flew,   65
Pierc'd through the yielding Planks of jointed Wood,
And trembling in the hollow Belly stood.
The sides transpierc'd, return a ratling Sound,
And Groans of *Greeks* inclos'd come issuing through the Wound.

45 Monster Fabrique *98*: fatal Engine *97*

And had not Heav'n the fall of *Troy* design'd,
Or had not Men been fated to be blind,
Enough was said and done, t' inspire a better Mind:
Then had our Lances pierc'd the treach'rous Wood,
And *Ilian* Tow'rs, and *Priam*'s Empire stood.

Mean time, with Shouts, the *Trojan* Shepherds bring
A captive *Greek* in Bands, before the King:
Taken, to take; who made himself their Prey,
T' impose on their Belief, and *Troy* betray.
Fix'd on his Aim, and obstinately bent
To die undaunted, or to circumvent.

About the Captive, tides of *Trojans* flow;
All press to see, and some insult the Foe.
Now hear how well the *Greeks* their Wiles disguis'd,
Behold a Nation in a Man compris'd.

Trembling the Miscreant stood, unarm'd and bound;
He star'd, and rowl'd his hagger'd Eyes around:
Then said, Alas! what Earth remains, what Sea
Is open to receive unhappy me!
What Fate a wretched Fugitive attends,
Scorn'd by my Foes, abandon'd by my Friends.

He said, and sigh'd, and cast a ruful Eye:
Our Pity kindles, and our Passions dye.
We chear the Youth to make his own Defence,
And freely tell us what he was, and whence:
What News he cou'd impart, we long to know,
And what to credit from a captive Foe.

His fear at length dismiss'd, he said, what e're
My Fate ordains, my Words shall be sincere:
I neither can, nor dare my Birth disclaim,
Greece is my Country, *Sinon* is my Name:
Though plung'd by Fortune's Pow'r in Misery,
'Tis not in Fortune's Pow'r to make me lye.
If any chance has hither brought the Name
Of *Palamedes*, not unknown to Fame,
Who suffer'd from the Malice of the times;
Accus'd and sentenc'd for pretended Crimes:
Because these fatal Wars he would prevent;
Whose Death the wretched *Greeks* too late lament;

Me, then a Boy, my Father, poor and bare
Of other Means, committed to his Care: 110
His Kinsman and Companion in the War.
While Fortune favour'd, while his Arms support
The Cause, and rul'd the Counsels of the Court,
I made some figure there; nor was my Name
Obscure, nor I without my share of Fame.   115
But when *Ulysses*, with fallacious Arts,
Had made Impression in the Peoples Hearts;
And forg'd a Treason in my Patron's Name,
(I speak of things too far divulg'd by Fame)
My Kinsman fell; then I, without support,   120
In private mourn'd his Loss, and left the Court.
Mad as I was, I could not bear his Fate
With silent Grief, but loudly blam'd the State:
And curs'd the direful Author of my Woes.
'Twas told again, and hence my Ruin rose.   125
I threatn'd, if indulgent Heav'n once more
Wou'd land me safely on my Native Shore,
His Death with double Vengeance to restore.
This mov'd the Murderer's Hate, and soon ensu'd
Th' Effects of Malice from a Man so proud.   130
Ambiguous Rumors thro the Camp he spread,
And sought, by Treason, my devoted Head:
New Crimes invented, left unturn'd no Stone,
To make my Guilt appear, and hide his own.
'Till *Calchas* was by Force and Threatning wrought: 135
But why—Why dwell I on that anxious Thought?
If on my Nation just Revenge you seek,
And 'tis t' appear a Foe, t' appear a *Greek*;
Already you my Name and Country know,
Asswage your thirst of Blood, and strike the Blow: 140
My Death will both the Kingly Brothers please,
And set insatiate *Ithacus* at ease.
This fair unfinish'd Tale, these broken starts,
Rais'd expectations in our longing Hearts;
Unknowing as we were in *Grecian* Arts.   145
His former trembling once again renew'd,
With acted Fear, the Villain thus pursu'd.
    Long had the *Grecians* (tir'd with fruitless Care,

And weary'd with an unsuccessful War,)
Resolv'd to raise the Siege, and leave the Town;
And had the Gods permitted, they had gone.
But oft the Wintry Seas, and Southern Winds,
Withstood their passage home, and chang'd their Minds.
Portents and Prodigies their Souls amaz'd;
But most, when this stupendous Pile was rais'd.
Then flaming Meteors, hung in Air, were seen,
And Thunders ratled through a Skie serene:
Dismay'd, and fearful of some dire Event,
Eurypylus, t' enquire their Fate, was sent;
He from the Gods this dreadful Answer brought;
O *Grecians*, when the *Trojan* Shores you sought,
Your Passage with a Virgin's Blood was bought:
So must your safe Return be bought again;
And *Grecian* Blood, once more attone the Main.
The spreading Rumour round the People ran;
All fear'd, and each believ'd himself the Man.
Ulysses took th' advantage of their fright;
Call'd *Calchas*, and produc'd in open sight:
Then bade him name the Wretch, ordain'd by Fate,
The Publick Victim, to redeem the State.
Already some presag'd the dire Event,
And saw what Sacrifice *Ulysses* meant.
For twice five days the good old Seer withstood
Th' intended Treason, and was dumb to Blood.
Till Tir'd with endless Clamours, and pursute
Of *Ithacus*, he stood no longer Mute:
But, as it was agreed, pronounc'd, that I
Was destin'd by the wrathful Gods to die.
All prais'd the Sentence, pleas'd the storm should fall
On one alone, whose Fury threatn'd all.
The dismal day was come, the Priests prepare
Their leaven'd Cakes; and Fillets for my Hair.
I follow'd Natur's Laws, and must avow
I broke my Bonds, and fled the fatal blow.
Hid in a weedy Lake all Night I lay,
Secure of Safety when they sail'd away.
But now what further Hopes for me remain,

169 Then] Than *97 98*

To see my Friends or Native Soil again?
My tender Infants, or my careful Sire;
Whom they returning will to Death require? 190
Will perpetrate on them their first Design,
And take the forfeit of their heads for mine?
Which, O if Pity mortal Minds can move!
If there be Faith below, or Gods above!
If Innocence and Truth can claim desert, 195
Ye *Trojans* from an injur'd Wretch avert.
　　False Tears true Pity move: the King Commands
To loose his Fetters, and unbind his hands:
Then adds these friendly words; dismiss thy Fears,
Forget the *Greeks*, be mine as thou wert theirs. 200
But truly tell, was it for Force or Guile,
Or some Religious End, you rais'd the Pile?
Thus said the King. He full of fraudful Arts,
This well invented Tale for Truth imparts.
Ye Lamps of Heav'n! he said, and lifted high 205
His hands now free, thou venerable Sky,
Inviolable Pow'rs, ador'd with dread,
Ye fatal Fillets, that once bound this head,
Ye sacred Altars, from whose flames I fled!
Be all of you adjur'd; and grant I may, 210
Without a Crime, th' ungrateful *Greeks* betray!
Reveal the Secrets of the guilty State,
And justly punish whom I justly hate!
But you, O King, preserve the Faith you gave,
If I to save my self your Empire save. 215
The *Grecian* Hopes, and all th' Attempts they made,
Were only founded on *Minerva*'s Aid.
But from the time when impious *Diomede*,
And false *Ulysses*, that inventive Head,
Her fatal Image from the Temple drew, 220
The sleeping Guardians of the Castle slew,
Her Virgin Statue with their bloody Hands
Polluted, and prophan'd her holy Bands:
From thence the Tide of Fortune left their Shore,
And ebb'd much faster than it flow'd before: 225
Their Courage languish'd, as their Hopes decay'd,

　　197 *Editor's paragraph*　　210 adjur'd] abjur'd *98*

And *Pallas*, now averse, refus'd her Aid.
Nor did the Goddess doubtfully declare
Her alter'd Mind, and alienated Care:
When first her fatal Image touch'd the Ground,   23
She sternly cast her glaring Eyes around;
That sparkl'd as they rowl'd, and seem'd to threat:
Her Heav'nly Limbs distill'd a briny Sweat.
Thrice from the Ground she leap'd, was seen to wield
Her brandish'd Lance, and shake her horrid Shield.   23
Then *Calchas* bad our Host for flight prepare,
And hope no Conquest from the tedious War:
'Till first they sail'd for *Greece*; with Pray'rs besought
Her injur'd Pow'r, and better Omens brought.
And now their Navy ploughs the wat'ry Main,   ⎫
Yet, soon expect it on your Shoars again,   ⎬ 24
With *Pallas* pleas'd; as *Calchas* did ordain.   ⎭
But first, to reconcile the blue-ey'd Maid,
For her stoln Statue, and her Tow'r betray'd;
Warn'd by the Seer, to her offended Name   24
We rais'd, and dedicate this wond'rous Frame:
So lofty, lest through your forbidden Gates
It pass, and intercept our better Fates.
For, once admitted there, our hopes are lost;
And *Troy* may then a new *Palladium* boast.   25
For so Religion and the Gods ordain;
That if you violate with Hands prophane
Minerva's Gift, your Town in Flames shall burn,
(Which Omen, O ye Gods, on *Grecia* turn!)
But if it climb, with your assisting Hands,   25
The *Trojan* Walls, and in the City stands;
Then *Troy* shall *Argos* and *Mycenæ* burn,
And the reverse of Fate on us return.

   With such Deceits he gain'd their easie Hearts,
Too prone to credit his perfidious Arts.   26
What *Diomede*, nor *Thetis* greater Son,   ⎫
A thousand Ships, nor ten years Siege had done: ⎬
False Tears and fawning Words the City won.   ⎭
A greater Omen, and of worse portent,   ⎫
Did our unwary Minds with fear torment: ⎬ 26
Concurring to produce the dire Event.   ⎭

Laocoon, Neptune's Priest by Lot that Year,
With solemn pomp then sacrific'd a Steer.
When, dreadful to behold, from Sea we spy'd
Two Serpents rank'd abreast, the Seas divide,   } 270
And smoothly sweep along the swelling Tide.
Their flaming Crests above the Waves they show,
Their Bellies seem to burn the Seas below:
Their speckled Tails advance to steer their Course,
And on the sounding Shoar the flying Billows force.   275
And now the Strand, and now the Plain they held,
Their ardent Eyes with bloody streaks were fill'd:
Their nimble Tongues they brandish'd as they came,
And lick'd their hissing Jaws, that sputter'd Flame.
We fled amaz'd; their destin'd Way they take,   280
And to *Laocoon* and his Children make:
And first around the tender Boys they wind,
Then with their sharpen'd Fangs their Limbs and Bodies grind.
The wretched Father, running to their Aid
With pious Haste, but vain, they next invade: 285
Twice round his waste their winding Volumes rowl'd,
And twice about his gasping Throat they fold.
The Priest, thus doubly choak'd, their Crests divide,
And tow'ring o're his Head, in Triumph ride.
With both his Hands he labours at the Knots,   290
His Holy Fillets the blue Venom blots:
His roaring fills the flitting Air around.
Thus, when an Oxe receives a glancing Wound,
He breaks his Bands, the fatal Altar flies,
And with loud Bellowings breaks the yielding Skies.   295
Their Tasks perform'd, the Serpents quit their prey,
And to the Tow'r of *Pallas* make their way:
Couch'd at her Feet, they lie protected there,
By her large Buckler, and protended Spear.
Amazement seizes all; the gen'ral Cry   300
Proclaims *Laocoon* justly doom'd to die,
Whose hand the Will of *Pallas* had withstood,
And dar'd to violate the Sacred Wood.
All vote t' admit the Steed, that Vows be paid,
And Incense offer'd to th' offended Maid.   305

301 die,] die. *97 98*

A spacious Breach is made, the Town lies bare,
Some hoisting Leavers, some the Wheels prepare,
And fasten to the Horses Feet: the rest
With Cables haul along th' unweildy Beast.
Each on his Fellow for Assistance calls: 3*
At length the fatal Fabrick mounts the Walls,
Big with Destruction. Boys with Chaplets crown'd,
And Quires of Virgins sing, and dance around.
Thus rais'd aloft, and then descending down,
It enters o're our Heads, and threats the Town.   3*
O sacred City! built by Hands Divine!
O valiant Heroes of the *Trojan* Line!
Four times he struck; as oft the clashing sound
Of Arms was heard, and inward Groans rebound.
Yet mad with Zeal, and blinded with our Fate,   3*
We hawl along the Horse, in solemn state;
Then place the dire Portent within the Tow'r.
Cassandra cry'd, and curs'd th' unhappy Hour;
Foretold our Fate; but by the Gods decree
All heard, and none believ'd the Prophecy.   3*
With Branches we the Fanes adorn, and wast
In jollity, the Day ordain'd to be the last.
Mean time the rapid Heav'ns rowl'd down the Light,
And on the shaded Ocean rush'd the Night:
Our Men secure, nor Guards nor Centries held,   3*
But easie Sleep their weary Limbs compell'd.
The *Grecians* had embark'd their Naval Pow'rs
From *Tenedos*, and sought our well known Shoars;
Safe under Covert of the silent Night,
And guided by th' Imperial Galley's light: 3
When *Sinon*, favour'd by the Partial Gods,
Unlock'd the Horse, and op'd his dark abodes:
Restor'd to vital Air our hidden Foes,
Who joyful from their long Confinement rose.
Tysander bold, and *Sthenelus* their Guide,   3
And dire *Ulysses* down the Cable slide:
Then *Thoas*, *Athamas*, and *Pyrrhus* hast;
Nor was the *Podalyrian* Heroe last:

312 crown'd, *98*: crown'd; *97*   333 Shoars;] Shoars: *97 98*   335 light:]
light. *97 98*

Nor injur'd *Menelaus*, nor the fam'd
Epeus, who the fatal Engine fram'd.   345
A nameless Crowd succeed; their Forces join
T' invade the Town, oppress'd with Sleep and Wine.
Those few they find awake, first meet their Fate,
Then to their Fellows they unbar the Gate.
'Twas in the dead of Night, when Sleep repairs   350
Our Bodies worn with Toils, our Minds with Cares,
When *Hector*'s Ghost before my sight appears:
A bloody Shrowd he seem'd, and bath'd in Tears.
Such as he was, when, by *Pelides* slain,
Thessalian Coursers drag'd him o're the Plain.   355
Swoln were his Feet, as when the Thongs were thrust
Through the bor'd holes, his Body black with dust.
Unlike that *Hector*, who return'd from toils
Of War Triumphant, in *Æacian* Spoils:
Or him, who made the fainting *Greeks* retire,   360
And lanch'd against their Navy *Phrygian* Fire.
His Hair and Beard stood stiffen'd with his gore;
And all the Wounds he for his Country bore,
Now stream'd afresh, and with new Purple ran:
I wept to see the visionary Man: } 365
And while my Trance continu'd, thus began.
O Light of *Trojans*, and Support of *Troy*,
Thy Father's Champion, and thy Country's Joy!
O, long expected by thy Friends! from whence
Art thou so late return'd for our Defence?   370
Do we behold thee, weary'd as we are,
With length of Labours, and with Toils of War?
After so many Fun'rals of thy own,
Art thou restor'd to thy declining Town?
But say, what Wounds are these? What new Disgrace   375
Deforms the Manly Features of thy Face?
To this the Spectre no Reply did frame;
But answer'd to the Cause for which he came:
And, groaning from the bottom of his Breast,
This Warning, in these mournful Words express'd.   380
O Goddess-born! escape, by timely flight,
The Flames, and Horrors of this fatal Night.

350 *Editor's paragraph*   354 *Pelides 98*: foul Treason *97*

The Foes already have possess'd the Wall,
Troy nods from high, and totters to her Fall.
Enough is paid to *Priam*'s Royal Name,   3
More than enough to Duty and to Fame.
If by a Mortal Hand my Father's Throne
Cou'd be defended, 'twas by mine alone:
Now *Troy* to thee commends her future State,
And gives her Gods Companions of thy Fate: 3
From their assistance happyer Walls expect,
Which, wand'ring long, at last thou shalt erect.
He said, and brought me, from their blest abodes,
The venerable Statues of the Gods:
With ancient *Vesta* from the sacred Quire,   3
The Wreaths and Relicks of th' Immortal Fire.
   Now peals of Shouts come thund'ring from afar,
Cries, Threats, and loud Laments, and mingl'd War:
The Noise approaches, though our Palace stood
Aloof from Streets, encompass'd with a Wood.   4
Louder, and yet more loud, I hear th' Allarms
Of Human Cries distinct, and clashing Arms:
Fear broke my Slumbers; I no longer stay,   ⎫
But mount the Terrass, thence the Town survey,   ⎬
And hearken what the frightful Sounds convey.   ⎭   4
Thus when a flood of Fire by Wind is born,
Crackling it rowls, and mows the standing Corn:
Or Deluges, descending on the Plains,   ⎫
Sweep o're the yellow Year, destroy the pains   ⎬
Of lab'ring Oxen, and the Peasant's gains: ⎭   4
Unroot the Forrest Oaks, and bear away
Flocks, Folds, and Trees, an undistinguish'd Prey.
The Shepherd climbs the Cliff, and sees from far,
The wastful Ravage of the wat'ry War.
Then *Hector*'s Faith was manifestly clear'd;   4
And *Grecian* Frauds in open light appear'd.
The Palace of *Deiphobus* ascends
In smoaky Flames, and catches on his Friends.
Ucalegon burns next; the Seas are bright
With splendor, not their own; and shine with *Trojan* light.   4
New Clamours, and new Clangors now arise,

The sound of Trumpets mix'd with fighting cries.
With frenzy seiz'd, I run to meet th' Alarms,
Resolv'd on death, resolv'd to die in Arms.
But first to gather Friends, with them t' oppose,   425
If Fortune favour'd, and repel the Foes.
Spurr'd by my Courage, by my Country fir'd;
With sense of Honour, and Revenge inspir'd.
   Pantheus, *Apollo*'s Priest, a sacred Name,
Had scap'd the *Grecian* Swords, and pass'd the Flame;   430
With Reliques loaden, to my Doors he fled,
And by the hand his tender Grand-son led.
What hope, O *Pantheus*! whither can we run?
Where make a stand? and what may yet be done?
Scarce had I said, when *Pantheus*, with a groan,   435
Troy is no more, and *Ilium* was a Town!
The fatal Day, th' appointed Hour is come,
When wrathful *Jove*'s irrevocable doom
Transfers the *Trojan* State to *Grecian* hands.
The Fire consumes the Town, the Foe commands: 440
And armed Hosts, an unexpected Force,
Break from the Bowels of the Fatal Horse.
Within the Gates, proud *Sinon* throws about
The flames, and Foes for entrance press without.
With thousand others, whom I fear to name,   445
More than from *Argos*, or *Mycenæ* came.
To sev'ral Posts their Parties they divide;
Some block the narrow Streets, some scour the wide.
The bold they kill, th' unwary they surprise;
Who fights finds Death, and Death finds him who flies.   450
The Warders of the Gate but scarce maintain
Th' unequal Combat, and resist in vain.
I Heard; and Heav'n, that well-born Souls inspires,
Prompts me, thro' lifted Swords, and rising Fires
To run, where clashing Arms and Clamour calls,   455
And rush undaunted to defend the Walls.
Ripheus and *Iph'itus* by my side engage,
For Valour one Renown'd, and one for Age.
Dymas and *Hypanis* by Moonlight knew
My motions, and my Meen, and to my Party drew;   460
With young *Choræbus*, who by Love was led

To win Renown, and fair *Cassandra*'s Bed;
And lately brought his Troops to *Priam*'s aid:
Forewarn'd in vain, by the Prophetic Maid.
Whom, when I saw, resolv'd in Arms to fall,
And that one Spirit animated all;
Brave Souls, said I, but Brave, alas! in vain:
Come, finish what our Cruel Fates ordain.
You see the desp'rate state of our Affairs;
And Heav'ns protecting Pow'rs are deaf to Pray'rs.
The passive Gods behold the *Greeks* defile
Their Temples, and abandon to the Spoil
Their own Abodes: we, feeble few, conspire
To save a sinking Town, involv'd in Fire.
Then let us fall, but fall amidst our Foes,
Despair of Life, the Means of Living shows.
So bold a Speech incourag'd their desire
Of Death, and added fuel to their fire.

As hungry Wolves, with raging appetite,
Scour thro' the fields, nor fear the stormy Night;
Their Whelps at home expect the promis'd Food,
And long to temper their dry Chaps in Blood:
So rush'd we forth at once, resolv'd to die,
Resolv'd in Death the last Extreams to try.
We leave the narrow Lanes behind, and dare
Th' unequal Combat in the publick Square:
Night was our Friend, our Leader was Despair.
What Tongue can tell the Slaughter of that Night?
What Eyes can weep the Sorrows and Affright!
An ancient and imperial City falls,
The Streets are fill'd with frequent Funerals:
Houses and Holy Temples float in Blood,
And hostile Nations make a common Flood.
Not only *Trojans* fall, but in their turn,
The vanquish'd Triumph, and the Victors mourn.
Ours take new Courage from Despair and Night;
Confus'd the Fortune is, confus'd the Fight.
All parts resound with Tumults, Plaints, and Fears,
And grisly Death in sundry shapes appears.
Androgeos fell among us, with his Band,

Who thought us *Grecians* newly come to Land:
From whence, said he, my Friends this long delay?
You loiter, while the Spoils are born away:
Our Ships are laden with the *Trojan* Store,
And you like Truants come too late ashore.   505
He said, but soon corrected his Mistake,
Found, by the doubtful Answers which we make:
Amaz'd, he wou'd have shun'd th' unequal Fight,
But we, more num'rous, intercept his flight.
As when some Peasant in a bushy Brake,   510
Has with unwary Footing press'd a Snake;
He starts aside, astonish'd, when he spies
His rising Crest, blue Neck, and rowling Eyes;
So from our Arms, surpriz'd *Androgeos* flies.
In vain; for him and his we compass'd round,   515
Possess'd with Fear, unknowing of the Ground;
And of their Lives an easy Conquest found.
Thus Fortune on our first Endeavour smil'd:
Chorœbus then, with youthful Hopes beguil'd,
Swoln with Success, and of a daring Mind,   520
This new Invention fatally design'd.
My Friends, said he, since Fortune shows the way,
'Tis fit we shou'd th' auspicious Guide obey.
For what has she these *Grecian* Arms bestow'd,
But their Destruction, and the *Trojans* good?   525
Then change we Shields, and their Devices bear,
Let Fraud supply the want of Force in War.
They find us Arms; this said, himself he dress'd
In dead *Androgeos* Spoils, his upper Vest,
His painted Buckler, and his plumy Crest.   530
Thus *Ripheus*, *Dymas*, all the *Trojan* Train
Lay down their own Attire, and strip the slain.
Mix'd with the *Greeks*, we go with ill Presage,
Flatter'd with hopes to glut our greedy Rage:
Unknown, assaulting whom we blindly meet,   535
And strew, with *Grecian* Carcasses, the Street.
Thus while their stragling Parties we defeat,
Some to the Shoar and safer Ships retreat:
And some oppress'd with more ignoble Fear,

529 *Androgeos*] *Androgeos*'s 97 98

Remount the hollow Horse, and pant in secret there.   5
   But ah! what use of Valour can be made,
When Heav'ns propitious Pow'rs refuse their Aid!
Behold the royal Prophetess, the Fair
Cassandra, drag'd by her dishevel'd Hair;
Whom not *Minerva*'s Shrine, nor sacred Bands,   5
In safety cou'd protect from sacrilegious Hands:
On Heav'n she cast her Eyes, she sigh'd, she cry'd,
('Twas all she cou'd) her tender Arms were ty'd.
So sad a Sight *Chorœbus* cou'd not bear;
But fir'd with Rage, distracted with Despair,   5
Amid the barb'rous Ravishers he flew:
Our Leader's rash Example we pursue.
But storms of Stones, from the proud Temple's height,
Pour down, and on our batter'd Helms alight.
We from our Friends receiv'd this fatal Blow,   5
Who thought us *Grecians*, as we seem'd in show.
They aim at the mistaken Crests, from high,
And ours beneath the pond'rous Ruin lie.
Then, mov'd with Anger and Disdain, to see
Their Troops dispers'd, the Royal Virgin free: 5
The *Grecians* rally, and their Pow'rs unite;
With Fury charge us, and renew the Fight.
The Brother-Kings with *Ajax* join their force,
And the whole Squadron of *Thessalian* Horse.
   Thus, when the Rival Winds their Quarrel try,   5
Contending for the Kingdom of the Skie;
South, East, and West, on airy Coursers born,
The Whirlwind gathers, and the Woods are torn:
Then *Nereus* strikes the deep, the Billows rise,
And, mix'd with Ooze and Sand, pollute the Skies.   5
The Troops we squander'd first, again appear
From sev'ral Quarters, and enclose the Rear.
They first observe, and to the rest betray
Our diff'rent Speech; our borrow'd Arms survey.
Oppress'd with odds, we fall; *Chorœbus* first,   5
At *Pallas* Altar, by *Peneleus* pierc'd.
Then *Ripheus* follow'd, in th' unequal Fight;

---

549 bear;] bear, *97 98*   550 Despair,] Despair; *97 98*   576 *Pallas*] *Pallas*'s
97 98

Just of his Word, observant of the right;
Heav'n thought not so: *Dymas* their Fate attends,
With *Hypanis*, mistaken by their Friends.   580
Nor *Pantheus*, thee, thy Mitre nor the Bands
Of awful *Phœbus*, sav'd from impious Hands.
Ye *Trojan* Flames your Testimony bear,
What I perform'd, and what I suffer'd there:
No Sword avoiding in the fatal Strife,   585
Expos'd to Death, and prodigal of Life.
Witness, ye Heav'ns! I live not by my Fault,
I strove to have deserv'd the Death I sought.
But when I cou'd not fight, and wou'd have dy'd,
Born off to distance by the growing Tide,   590
Old *Iphitus* and I were hurry'd thence,
With *Pelias* wounded, and without Defence.
New Clamors from th' invested Palace ring;
We run to die, or disengage the King.
So hot th' Assault, so high the Tumult rose,   595
While ours defend, and while the *Greeks* oppose;
As all the *Dardan* and *Argolick* Race
Had been contracted in that narrow Space:
Or as all *Ilium* else were void of Fear,
And Tumult, War, and Slaughter only there.   600
Their Targets in a Tortoise cast, the Foes
Secure advancing, to the Turrets rose:
Some mount the scaling Ladders, some more bold
Swerve upwards, and by Posts and Pillars hold:
Their left hand gripes their Bucklers, in th' ascent,   605
While with the right they seise the Battlement.
From their demolish'd Tow'rs the *Trojans* throw
Huge heaps of Stones, that falling, crush the Foe:
And heavy Beams, and Rafters from the sides,
(Such Arms their last necessity provides:)   610
And gilded Roofs come tumbling from on high,
The marks of State, and ancient Royalty.
The Guards below, fix'd in the Pass, attend
The Charge undaunted, and the Gate defend.
Renew'd in Courage with recover'd Breath,   615
A second time we ran to tempt our Death:
To clear the Palace from the Foe, succeed

The weary living, and revenge the dead.
A Postern-door, yet unobserv'd and free,
Join'd by the length of a blind Gallery,   6
To the King's Closet led; a way well known
To *Hector*'s Wife, while *Priam* held the Throne:
Through which she brought *Astyanax*, unseen,
To chear his Grandsire, and his Grandsire's Queen.
Through this we pass, and mount the Tow'r, from whence 6
With unavailing Arms the *Trojans* make defence.
From this the trembling King had oft descry'd
The *Grecian* Camp, and saw their Navy ride.
Beams from its lofty height with Swords we hew;
Then wrenching with our hands, th' Assault renew.   6
And where the Rafters on the Columns meet,
We push them headlong with our Arms and Feet:
The Lightning flies not swifter than the Fall;
Nor Thunder louder than the ruin'd Wall:
Down goes the top at once; the *Greeks* beneath   6
Are piecemeal torn, or pounded into Death.
Yet more succeed, and more to death are sent;
We cease not from above, nor they below relent.

  Before the Gate stood *Pyrrhus*, threat'ning loud,
With glitt'ring Arms conspicuous in the Crowd.   6
So shines, renew'd in Youth, the crested Snake,
Who slept the Winter in a thorny Brake:
And casting off his Slough, when Spring returns,
Now looks aloft, and with new Glory burns:
Restor'd with pois'nous Herbs, his ardent sides   6
Reflect the Sun, and rais'd on Spires he rides:
High o're the Grass, hissing he rowls along,
And brandishes by fits his forky Tongue.
Proud *Periphas*, and fierce *Automedon*,
His Father's Charioteer, together run   6
To force the Gate: The *Scyrian* Infantry
Rush on in Crowds, and the barr'd Passage free.
Ent'ring the Court, with Shouts the Skies they rend,
And flaming Firebrands to the Roofs ascend.
Himself, among the foremost, deals his Blows,   6
And with his Axe repeated Stroaks bestows

On the strong Doors: then all their Shoulders ply,
'Till from the Posts the brazen Hinges fly.
He hews apace, the double Bars at length
Yield to his Ax, and unresisted Strength.   660
A mighty Breach is made; the Rooms conceal'd
Appear, and all the Palace is reveal'd.
The Halls of Audience, and of publick State,
And where the lonely Queen in secret sate.
Arm'd Souldiers now by trembling Maids are seen,   665
With not a Door, and scarce a Space between.
The House is fill'd with loud Laments and Cries,
And Shrieks of Women rend the vaulted Skies.
The fearful Matrons run from place to place,
And kiss the Thresholds, and the Posts embrace.   670
The fatal work inhuman *Pyrrhus* plies,
And all his Father sparkles in his Eyes.
Nor Bars, nor fighting Guards his force sustain;
The Bars are broken, and the Guards are slain.
In rush the *Greeks*, and all the Apartments fill;   675
Those few Defendants whom they find, they kill.
Not with so fierce a Rage, the foaming Flood
Roars, when he finds his rapid Course withstood:
Bears down the Dams with unresisted sway,
And sweeps the Cattle and the Cots away.   680
These Eyes beheld him, when he march'd between
The Brother-Kings: I saw th' unhappy Queen,
The hundred Wives, and where old *Priam* stood,
To stain his hallow'd Altar with his Blood.
The fifty Nuptial Beds: (such Hopes had he,   685
So large a Promise of a Progeny.)
The Posts of plated Gold, and hung with Spoils,
Fell the Reward of the proud Victor's Toils.
Where e're the raging Fire had left a space,
The *Grecians* enter, and possess the Place.   690
    Perhaps you may of *Priam*'s Fate enquire.
He, when he saw his Regal Town on fire,
His ruin'd Palace, and his ent'ring Foes,
On ev'ry side inevitable woes;
In Arms, disus'd, invests his Limbs decay'd   695

691 *Editor's paragraph*

Like them, with Age; a late and useless aid.
His feeble shoulders scarce the weight sustain:
Loaded, not arm'd, he creeps along, with pain;
Despairing of Success; ambitious to be slain!
Uncover'd but by Heav'n, there stood in view   700
An Altar; near the hearth a Lawrel grew;
Dodder'd with Age, whose Boughs encompass round
The Household Gods, and shade the holy Ground.
Here *Hecuba*, with all her helpless Train
Of Dames, for shelter sought, but sought in vain.   705
Driv'n like a Flock of Doves along the skie,
Their Images they hugg, and to their Altars fly.
The Queen, when she beheld her trembling Lord,
And hanging by his side a heavy Sword,
What Rage, she cry'd, has seiz'd my Husband's mind;   710
What Arms are these, and to what use design'd?
These times want other aids: were *Hector* here,
Ev'n *Hector* now in vain, like *Priam* wou'd appear.
With us, one common shelter thou shalt find,
Or in one common Fate with us be join'd.   715
She said, and with a last Salute embrac'd
The poor old Man, and by the Lawrel plac'd.
Behold *Polites*, one of *Priam*'s Sons,
Pursu'd by *Pyrrhus*, there for safety runs.
Thro Swords, and Foes, amaz'd and hurt, he flies   720
Through empty Courts, and open Galleries:
Him *Pyrrhus*, urging with his Lance, pursues;
And often reaches, and his thrusts renews.
The Youth transfix'd, with lamentable Cries
Expires, before his wretched Parent's Eyes.   725
Whom, gasping at his feet, when *Priam* saw,
The Fear of Death gave place to Nature's Law.
And shaking more with Anger, than with Age,
The Gods, said He, requite thy brutal Rage:
As sure they will, Barbarian, sure they must,   730
If there be Gods in Heav'n, and Gods be just:
Who tak'st in Wrongs an insolent delight;
With a Son's death t' infect a Father's sight.
Not He, whom thou and lying Fame conspire
To call thee his; Not He, thy vaunted Sire,   735

Thus us'd my wretched Age: The Gods he fear'd,
The Laws of Nature and of Nations heard.
He chear'd my Sorrows, and for Sums of Gold
The bloodless Carcass of my *Hector* sold.
Pity'd the Woes a Parent underwent,　　　740
And sent me back in safety from his Tent.
　　This said, his feeble hand a Javelin threw,
Which flutt'ring, seem'd to loiter as it flew:
Just, and but barely, to the Mark it held,
And faintly tinckl'd on the Brazen Shield.　　　745
　　Then *Pyrrhus* thus: go thou from me to Fate;
And to my Father my foul deeds relate.
Now dye: with that he dragg'd the trembling Sire,
Slidd'ring through clotter'd Blood, and holy Mire,
(The mingl'd Paste his murder'd Son had made,)　　　750
Haul'd from beneath the violated Shade;
And on the Sacred Pile, the Royal Victim laid.
His right Hand held his bloody Fauchion bare;
His left he twisted in his hoary Hair:
Then, with a speeding Thrust, his Heart he found:　　　755
The lukewarm Blood came rushing through the wound,
And sanguine Streams distain'd the sacred Ground.
Thus *Priam* fell: and shar'd one common Fate
With *Troy* in Ashes, and his ruin'd State:
He, who the Scepter of all *Asia* sway'd,　　　760
Whom Monarchs like domestick Slaves obey'd.
On the bleak Shoar now lies th' abandon'd King,
*A headless Carcass, and a nameless thing.
　　Then, not before, I felt my crudled Blood
Congeal with Fear; my Hair with horror stood:　　　765
My Father's Image fill'd my pious Mind;
Lest equal Years might equal Fortune find.
Again I thought on my forsaken Wife;
And trembl'd for my Son's abandon'd Life.
I look'd about; but found my self alone:　　　770
Deserted at my need, my Friends were gone.
Some spent with Toil, some with Despair oppress'd,

　　　This whole line is taken from Sir John Denham.

761 obey'd.] obey'd, *97 98*　　　763 *footnote* Denham] Derhan *97 98*

Leap'd headlong from the Heights; the Flames consum'd the rest.
Thus, wand'ring in my way, without a Guide,
The graceless *Helen* in the Porch I spy'd   77
Of *Vesta*'s Temple: there she lurk'd alone;
Muffled she sate, and what she cou'd, unknown:
But, by the Flames, that cast their Blaze around,
That common Bane of *Greece* and *Troy*, I found.
For *Ilium* burnt, she dreads the *Trojan* Sword;   ⎫
More dreads the Vengeance of her injur'd Lord;   ⎬ 78
Ev'n by those Gods, who refug'd her, abhorr'd.   ⎭
Trembling with Rage, the Strumpet I regard;
Resolv'd to give her Guilt the due reward.
Shall she triumphant sail before the Wind,   78
And leave in Flames, unhappy *Troy* behind?
Shall she, her Kingdom and her Friends review,
In State attended with a Captive Crew;
While unreveng'd the good old *Priam* falls,
And *Grecian* Fires consume the *Trojan* Walls?   79
For this the *Phrygian* Fields, and *Xanthian* Flood
Were swell'd with Bodies, and were drunk with Blood?
'Tis true a Souldier can small Honour gain,
And boast no Conquest from a Woman slain:
Yet shall the Fact not pass without Applause,   79
Of Vengeance taken in so just a Cause.
The punish'd Crime shall set my Soul at ease:
And murm'ring Manes of my Friends appease.
Thus while I rave, a gleam of pleasing Light   ⎫
Spread o're the Place, and shining Heav'nly bright,   ⎬ 80
My Mother stood reveal'd before my Sight.   ⎭
Never so radiant did her Eyes appear;
Not her own Star confess'd a Light so clear.
Great in her Charms, as when on Gods above
She looks, and breaths her self into their Love.   80
She held my hand, the destin'd Blow to break:
Then from her rosie Lips began to speak.
My Son, from whence this Madness, this neglect
Of my Commands, and those whom I protect?
Why this unmanly Rage? Recall to mind   81
Whom you forsake, what Pledges leave behind.
Look if your helpless Father yet survive;

Or if *Ascanius*, or *Creusa* live.
Around your House the greedy *Grecians* err;
And these had perish'd in the nightly War,　815
But for my Presence and protecting Care.
Not *Helen*'s Face, nor *Paris* was in fault;
But by the Gods was this Destruction brought.
Now cast your Eyes around; while I dissolve
The Mists and Films that mortal Eyes involve:　820
Purge from your sight the Dross, and make you see
The Shape of each avenging Deity.
Enlighten'd thus, my just Commands fulfill;
Nor fear Obedience to your Mother's Will.
Where yon disorder'd heap of Ruin lies,　825
Stones rent from Stones, where Clouds of dust arise,
Amid that smother, *Neptune* holds his place:
Below the Wall's foundation drives his Mace:
And heaves the Building from the solid Base.
Look where, in Arms, Imperial *Juno* stands,　830
Full in the *Scæan* Gate, with loud Commands;
Urging on Shore the tardy *Grecian* Bands.
See *Pallas*, of her snaky Buckler proud,
Bestrides the Tow'r, refulgent through the Cloud:
See *Jove* new Courage to the Foe supplies,　835
And arms against the Town, the partial Deities.
Haste hence, my Son; this fruitless Labour end:
Haste where your trembling Spouse, and Sire attend:
Haste, and a Mother's Care your Passage shall befriend.
She said: and swiftly vanish'd from my Sight,　840
Obscure in Clouds, and gloomy Shades of Night.
I look'd, I listen'd; dreadful Sounds I hear;
And the dire Forms of hostile Gods appear.
Troy sunk in Flames I saw, nor could prevent;
And *Ilium* from its old Foundations rent.　845
Rent like a Mountain Ash, which dar'd the Winds;
And stood the sturdy Stroaks of lab'ring Hinds:
About the Roots the cruel Ax resounds,
The Stumps are pierc'd, with oft repeated Wounds.
The War is felt on high, the nodding Crown　850
Now threats a Fall, and throws the leafy Honours down.
To their united Force it yields, though late;

And mourns with mortal Groans th' approaching Fate:
The Roots no more their upper load sustain;
But down she falls, and spreads a ruin thro' the Plain.   8
   Descending thence, I scape through Foes, and Fire:
Before the Goddess, Foes and Flames retire.
Arriv'd at home, he for whose only sake,
Or most for his, such Toils I undertake,
The good *Anchises*, whom, by timely Flight,   8
I purpos'd to secure on *Ida*'s height,
Refus'd the Journey: Resolute to die,
And add his Fun'rals to the fate of *Troy*:
Rather than Exile and old Age sustain.
Go you, whose Blood runs warm in ev'ry Vein: 8
Had Heav'n decreed that I shou'd Life enjoy,
Heav'n had decreed to save unhappy *Troy*.
'Tis sure enough, if not too much for one;
Twice to have seen our *Ilium* overthrown.
Make haste to save the poor remaining Crew;   8
And give this useless Corps a long Adieu.
These weak old Hands suffice to stop my Breath:
At least the pitying Foes will aid my Death,
To take my Spoils: and leave my Body bare:
As for my Sepulchre let Heav'n take Care.   8
'Tis long since I, for my Cœlestial Wife,
Loath'd by the Gods, have drag'd a ling'ring Life:
Since ev'ry Hour and Moment I expire,
Blasted from Heav'n by *Jove*'s avenging Fire.
This oft repeated, he stood fix'd to die: ⎫ 88
My self, my Wife, my Son, my Family,   ⎬
Intreat, pray, beg, and raise a doleful Cry.   ⎭
What, will he still persist, on Death resolve,
And in his Ruin all his House involve!
He still persists, his reasons to maintain;   88
Our Pray'rs, our Tears, our loud Laments are vain.
   Urg'd by Despair, again I go to try
The fate of Arms, resolv'd in Fight to die.
What hope remains, but what my Death must give?
Can I without so dear a Father live?   89
You term it Prudence, what I Baseness call:
Cou'd such a Word from such a Parent fall?

If Fortune please, and so the Gods ordain,
That nothing shou'd of ruin'd *Troy* remain:
And you conspire with Fortune, to be slain;   895
The way to Death is wide, th' Approaches near:
For soon relentless *Pyrrhus* will appear,
Reeking with *Priam*'s Blood: The wretch who slew
The Son (inhuman) in the Father's view,
And then the Sire himself, to the dire Altar drew.   900

O Goddess Mother, give me back to fate;
Your Gift was undesir'd, and came too late.
Did you for this, unhappy me convey
Through Foes and Fires to see my House a Prey?
Shall I, my Father, Wife, and Son, behold   905
Welt'ring in Blood, each others Arms infold?
Haste, gird my Sword, tho' spent, and overcome:
'Tis the last Summons to receive our Doom.
I hear thee, Fate, and I obey thy Call:
Not unreveng'd the Foe shall see my Fall.   910
Restore me to the yet unfinish'd Fight:
My Death is wanting to conclude the Night.
Arm'd once again, my glitt'ring Sword I wield,
While th' other hand sustains my weighty Shield:
And forth I rush to seek th' abandon'd Field.   915
I went; but sad *Creusa* stop'd my way,
And cross the Threshold in my Passage lay;
Embrac'd my Knees; and when I wou'd have gone
Shew'd me my feeble Sire, and tender Son.
If Death be your Design, at least, said she,   920
Take us along, to share your Destiny.
If any farther hopes in Arms remain,
This Place, these Pledges of your Love, maintain.
To whom do you expose your Father's Life,
Your Son's, and mine, your now forgotten Wife!   925
While thus she fills the House with clam'rous Cries,
Our Hearing is diverted by our Eyes.
For while I held my Son, in the short space,
Betwixt our Kisses and our last Embrace;

Strange to relate, from young *Iulus* Head
A lambent Flame arose, which gently spread
Around his Brows, and on his Temples fed.
Amaz'd, with running Water we prepare
To quench the sacred Fire, and shake his Hair;
But old *Anchises*, vers'd in Omens, rear'd
His hands to Heav'n, and this request preferr'd.
If any Vows, Almighty *Jove*, can bend
Thy Will, if Piety can Pray'rs commend,
Confirm the glad Presage which thou art pleas'd to send.
Scarce had he said, when, on our left, we hear
A peal of ratling Thunder rowl in Air:
There shot a streaming Lamp along the Sky,
Which on the winged Lightning seem'd to fly;
From o're the Roof the blaze began to move;
And trailing vanish'd in th' *Idean* Grove.
It swept a path in Heav'n, and shone a Guide;
Then in a steaming stench of Sulphur dy'd.
    The good old Man with suppliant hands implor'd
The Gods protection, and their Star ador'd.
Now, now, said he, my Son, no more delay,
I yield, I follow where Heav'n shews the way.
Keep (O my Country Gods) our dwelling Place,
And guard this Relick of the *Trojan* Race:
This tender Child; these Omens are your own;
And you can yet restore the ruin'd Town.
At least accomplish what your Signs foreshow:
I stand resign'd, and am prepar'd to go.
    He said; the crackling Flames appear on high,
And driving Sparkles dance along the Sky.
With *Vulcan*'s rage the rising Winds conspire;
And near our Palace rowl the flood of Fire.
Haste, my dear Father, ('tis no time to wait,)
And load my Shoulders with a willing Fraight.
What e're befalls, your Life shall be my care,
One Death, or one Deliv'rance we will share.
My hand shall lead our little Son; and you
My faithful Consort, shall our Steps pursue.
Next, you my Servants, heed my strict Commands:

Without the Walls a ruin'd Temple stands,
To *Ceres* hallow'd once; a Cypress nigh 970
Shoots up her venerable Head on high;
By long Religion kept: there bend your Feet;
And in divided Parties let us meet.
Our Country Gods, the Relicks, and the Bands,
Hold you, my Father, in your guiltless Hands: 975
In me 'tis impious holy things to bear,
Red as I am with Slaughter, new from War:
'Till in some living Stream I cleanse the Guilt
Of dire Debate, and Blood in Battel spilt.
Thus, ord'ring all that Prudence cou'd provide, 980
I cloath my Shoulders with a Lion's Hide;
And yellow Spoils: Then, on my bending Back,
The welcome load of my dear Father take.
While on my better Hand *Ascanius* hung,
And with unequal Paces tript along. 985
Creusa kept behind: by choice we stray
Through ev'ry dark and ev'ry devious Way.
I, who so bold and dauntless just before,
The *Grecian* Darts and shock of Lances bore,
At ev'ry Shadow now am seiz'd with Fear: 990
Not for my self, but for the Charge I bear.
Till near the ruin'd Gate arriv'd at last,
Secure, and deeming all the Danger past;
A frightful noise of trampling Feet we hear;
My Father looking through the Shades, with fear, 995
Cry'd out, haste, haste my Son, the Foes are nigh;
Their Swords, and shining Armour I descry.
Some hostile God, for some unknown Offence,
Had sure bereft my Mind of better Sence:
For while through winding Ways I took my Flight; 1000
And sought the shelter of the gloomy Night;
Alas! I lost *Creusa*: hard to tell
If by her fatal Destiny she fell,
Or weary sate, or wander'd with affright;
But she was lost for ever to my sight. 1005
I knew not, or reflected, 'till I meet
My Friends, at *Ceres* now deserted Seat:

970 hallow'd *98*: hollow'd *97*

We met: not one was wanting, only she
Deceiv'd her Friends, her Son, and wretched me.
What mad expressions did my Tongue refuse!
Whom did I not of Gods or Men accuse!
This was the fatal Blow, that pain'd me more
Than all I felt from ruin'd *Troy* before.
Stung with my Loss, and raving with Despair,
Abandoning my now forgotten Care,
Of Counsel, Comfort, and of Hope bereft,
My Sire, my Son, my Country Gods, I left.
In shining Armour once again I sheath
My Limbs, not feeling Wounds, nor fearing Death.
Then headlong to the burning Walls I run,
And seek the Danger I was forc'd to shun.
I tread my former Tracks: through Night explore
Each Passage, ev'ry Street I cross'd before.
All things were full of Horrour and Affright,
And dreadful ev'n the silence of the Night.
Then, to my Father's House I make repair,
With some small Glimps of hope to find her there:
Instead of her the cruel *Greeks* I met;
The house was fill'd with Foes, with Flames beset.
Driv'n on the wings of Winds, whole sheets of Fire,
Through Air transported, to the Roofs aspire.
From thence to *Priam*'s Palace I resort;
And search the Citadel, and desart Court.
Then, unobserv'd, I pass by *Juno*'s Church;
A guard of *Grecians* had possess'd the Porch:
There *Phœnix* and *Ulysses* watch the Prey:
And thither all the Wealth of *Troy* convey.
The Spoils which they from ransack'd Houses brought;
And golden Bowls from burning Altars caught.
The Tables of the Gods, the Purple Vests;
The People's Treasure, and the Pomp of Priests.
A ranck of wretched Youths, with pinion'd Hands,
And captive Matrons in long Order stands.
Then, with ungovern'd Madness, I proclaim,
Through all the silent Streets, *Creusa*'s Name.
Creusa still I call: At length she hears;
And suddain, through the Shades of Night appears.

Appears, no more *Creusa*, nor my Wife:
But a pale Spectre, larger than the Life.
Aghast, astonish'd, and struck dumb with Fear, 1050
I stood; like Bristles rose my stiffen'd Hair.
Then thus the Ghost began to sooth my Grief:
Nor Tears, nor Cries can give the dead Relief;
Desist, my much lov'd Lord, t' indulge your Pain:
You bear no more than what the Gods ordain. 1055
My Fates permit me not from hence to fly;
Nor he, the great Comptroller of the Sky.
Long wandring Ways for you the Pow'rs decree:
On Land hard Labors, and a length of Sea.
Then, after many painful Years are past, 1060
On *Latium*'s happy Shore you shall be cast:
Where gentle *Tiber* from his Bed beholds
The flow'ry Meadows, and the feeding Folds.
There end your Toils: And there your Fates provide
A quiet Kingdom, and a Royal Bride: 1065
There Fortune shall the *Trojan* Line restore;
And you for lost *Creusa* weep no more.
Fear not that I shall watch with servile Shame,
Th' imperious Looks of some proud *Grecian* Dame:
Or, stooping to the Victor's Lust, disgrace 1070
My Goddess Mother, or my Royal Race.
And now, farewell: the Parent of the Gods
Restrains my fleeting Soul in her Abodes:
I trust our common Issue to your Care.
She said: And gliding pass'd unseen in Air. 1075
I strove to speak, but Horror ty'd my Tongue;
And thrice about her Neck my Arms I flung;
And thrice deceiv'd, on vain Embraces hung.
Light as an empty Dream at break of Day,
Or as a blast of Wind, she rush'd away. 1080
    Thus, having pass'd the Night in fruitless Pain,
I, to my longing Friends, return again.
Amaz'd th' augmented Number to behold,
Of Men, and Matrons mix'd, of young and old:
A wretched Exil'd Crew together brought, 1085
With Arms appointed, and with Treasure fraught.
Resolv'd, and willing under my Command,

To run all hazards both of Sea and Land.
The Morn began, from *Ida*, to display
Her rosy Cheeks, and *Phosphor* led the day;
Before the Gates the *Grecians* took their Post:
And all pretence of late Relief was lost.
I yield to Fate, unwillingly retire;
And loaded, up the Hill convey my Sire.

THE THIRD BOOK OF THE ÆNEIS

THE ARGUMENT

Æneas proceeds in his Relation: He gives an Account of the Fleet with which he sail'd, and the Success of his first Voyage to Thrace; *from thence he directs his Course to* Delos, *and asks the Oracle what place the Gods had appointed for his Habitation? By a mistake of the Oracle's Answer, he settles in* Crete; *his household Gods give him the true sense of the Oracle, in a Dream. He follows their advice, and makes the best of his way for* Italy: *He is cast on several Shores, and meets with very surprising Adventures, 'till at length he lands on* Sicily: *where his Father* Anchises *dies. This is the place which he was sailing from when the Tempest rose and threw him upon the* Carthaginian Coast.*

WHEN Heav'n had overturn'd the *Trojan* State,
And *Priam*'s Throne, by too severe a Fate:
When ruin'd *Troy* became the *Grecians* Prey,
And *Ilium*'s lofty Tow'rs in Ashes lay:
Warn'd by Cœlestial Omens, we retreat,
To seek in foreign Lands a happier Seat.
Near old *Antandros*, and at *Ida*'s foot,
The Timber of the sacred Groves we cut:
And build our Fleet; uncertain yet to find
What place the Gods for our Repose assign'd.
Friends daily flock; and scarce the kindly Spring
Began to cloath the Ground, and Birds to sing;
When old *Anchises* summon'd all to Sea:
The Crew, my Father and the Fates obey.
With Sighs and Tears I leave my native Shore,
And empty Fields, where *Ilium* stood before.

My Sire, my Son, our less, and greater Gods,
All sail at once; and cleave the briny Floods.

    Against our Coast appears a spacious Land,
Which once the fierce *Lycurgus* did command: 20
Thracia the Name; the People bold in War;
Vast are their Fields, and Tillage is their Care.
A hospitable Realm while Fate was kind;
With *Troy* in friendship and Religion join'd.
I land; with luckless Omens, then adore 25
Their Gods, and draw a Line along the Shore:
I lay the deep Foundations of a Wall;
And *Enos*, nam'd from me, the City call.
To *Dionæan Venus* Vows are paid,
And all the Pow'rs that rising Labours aid; } 30
A Bull on *Jove's* Imperial Altar laid.
Not far, a rising Hillock stood in view;
Sharp Myrtles, on the sides, and Cornels grew.
There, while I went to crop the Silvan Scenes,
And shade our Altar with their leafy Greens; 35
I pull'd a Plant; with horror I relate
A Prodigy so strange, and full of Fate.
The rooted Fibers rose; and from the Wound,
Black bloody Drops distill'd upon the Ground.
Mute, and amaz'd, my Hair with Terrour stood; 40
Fear shrunk my Sinews, and congeal'd my Blood.
Man'd once again, another Plant I try;
That other gush'd with the same sanguine Dye.
Then, fearing Guilt, for some Offence unknown,
With Pray'rs and Vows the *Driads* I attone: 45
With all the Sisters of the Woods, and most
The God of Arms, who rules the *Thracian* Coast:
That they, or he, these Omens wou'd avert;
Release our Fears, and better signs impart.
Clear'd, as I thought, and fully fix'd at length 50
To learn the Cause, I tug'd with all my Strength;
I bent my knees against the Ground; once more
The violated Myrtle ran with Gore.
Scarce dare I tell the Sequel: From the Womb

The Third Book. 18 cleave *98*: tempt *97*   40 Terrour *97* (*errata*): Horror *97*
(*text*)   53 with Gore *98*: with purple Gore *97*

Of wounded Earth, and Caverns of the Tomb,
A Groan, as of a troubled Ghost, renew'd
My Fright, and then these dreadful Words ensu'd.
Why dost thou thus my bury'd Body rend?
O spare the Corps of thy unhappy Friend!
Spare to pollute thy pious Hands with Blood:
The Tears distil not from the wounded Wood;
But ev'ry drop this living Tree contains,
Is kindred Blood, and ran in *Trojan* Veins:
O fly from this unhospitable Shore,
Warn'd by my Fate; for I am *Polydore*!
Here loads of Lances, in my Blood embru'd,
Again shoot upward, by my Blood renew'd.

My faultring Tongue, and shiv'ring Limbs declare
My Horror, and in Bristles rose my Hair.
When *Troy* with *Grecian* Arms was closely pent,
Old *Priam*, fearful of the Wars Event,
This hapless *Polydore* to *Thracia* sent.
Loaded with Gold, he sent his Darling, far
From Noise and Tumults, and destructive War:
Committed to the faithless Tyrant's Care.
Who, when he saw the Pow'r of *Troy* decline,
Forsook the weaker, with the strong to join.
Broke ev'ry Bond of Nature, and of Truth;
And murder'd, for his Wealth, the Royal Youth.
O sacred Hunger of pernicious Gold,
What bands of Faith can impious Lucre hold!
Now, when my Soul had shaken off her Fears,
I call my Father, and the *Trojan* Peers:
Relate the Prodigies of Heav'n; require
What he commands, and their Advice desire.
All vote to leave that execrable Shore,
Polluted with the Blood of *Polydore*.
But e're we sail, his Fun'ral Rites prepare;
Then, to his Ghost, a Tomb and Altars rear.
In mournful Pomp the Matrons walk the round:
With baleful Cypress, and blue Fillets crown'd;
With Eyes dejected, and with Hair unbound.
Then Bowls of tepid Milk and Blood we pour,

And thrice invoke the Soul of *Polydore*.
　Now when the raging Storms no longer reign;　　　95
But Southern Gales invite us to the Main;
We launch our Vessels, with a prosp'rous Wind;
And leave the Cities and the Shores behind.
　An Island in th' *Ægean* Main appears:
Neptune and wat'ry *Doris* claim it theirs.　　　100
It floated once, till *Phœbus* fix'd the sides
To rooted Earth, and now it braves the Tides.
Here, born by friendly Winds, we come ashore;
With needful ease our weary Limbs restore;
And the Sun's Temple, and his Town adore.　　　105
　Anius the Priest, and King, with Lawrel crown'd,
His hoary Locks with purple Fillets bound,
Who saw my Sire the *Delian* Shore ascend,
Came forth with eager haste to meet his Friend.
Invites him to his Palace; and in sign　　　110
Of ancient Love, their plighted Hands they join.
Then to the Temple of the God I went;
And thus, before the Shrine, my Vows present.
Give, O *Thymbræus*, give a resting place,
To the sad Relicks of the *Trojan* Race:　　　115
A Seat secure, a Region of their own,
A lasting Empire, and a happier Town.
Where shall we fix, where shall our Labours end,
Whom shall we follow, and what Fate attend?
Let not my Pray'rs a doubtful Answer find,　　　120
But in clear Auguries unveil thy Mind.
Scarce had I said, He shook the holy Ground;
The Lawrels, and the lofty Hills around:
And from the *Tripos* rush'd a bellowing sound.
Prostrate we fell; confess'd the present God,　　　125
Who gave this Answer from his dark Abode.
Undaunted Youths, go seek that Mother Earth
From which your Ancestors derive their Birth.
The Soil that sent you forth, her Ancient Race,
In her old Bosom, shall again embrace.　　　130
Through the wide World th' *Æneian* House shall reign,
And Childrens Children shall the Crown sustain.

103 ashore;] ashore *97 98*　　　**122** Ground;] Ground: *97 98*

Thus *Phœbus* did our future Fates disclose;
A mighty Tumult, mix'd with Joy, arose.
    All are concern'd to know what place the God   13
Assign'd, and where determind our abode.
My Father, long revolving in His Mind,
The Race and Lineage of the *Trojan* Kind,
Thus answer'd their demands: Ye Princes, hear
Your pleasing Fortune; and dispel your fear.   14
The fruitful Isle of *Crete* well known to Fame,
Sacred of old to *Jove*'s Imperial Name,
In the mid Ocean lies, with large Command;
And on its Plains a hundred Cities stand.
Another *Ida* rises there; and we   14
From thence derive our *Trojan* Ancestry.
From thence, as 'tis divulg'd by certain Fame,
To the *Rhœtean* Shores old *Teucrus* came.
There fix'd, and there the Seat of Empire chose,
E're *Ilium* and the *Trojan* Tow'rs arose.   15
In humble Vales they built their soft abodes:
Till *Cybele*, the Mother of the Gods,
With tinckling Cymbals charm'd th' *Idean* Woods.
She, secret Rites and Ceremonies taught,
And to the Yoke, the salvage Lions brought.   15
Let us the Land, which Heav'n appoints, explore;
Appease the Winds, and seek the *Gnossian* Shore.
If *Jove* assists the passage of our Fleet,
The third propitious dawn discovers *Creet*.
Thus having said, the Sacrifices laid   16
On smoking Altars, to the Gods He paid.
A Bull, to *Neptune* an Oblation due,
Another Bull to bright *Apollo* slew:
A milk white Ewe the Western Winds to please;
And one cole black to calm the stormy Seas.   16
E're this, a flying Rumour had been spred,
That fierce *Idomeneus* from *Crete* was fled;
Expell'd and exil'd; that the Coast was free
From Foreign or Domestick Enemy:
We leave the *Delian* Ports, and put to Sea: 17
By *Naxos*, fam'd for Vintage, make our way:

Then green *Donysa* pass; and Sail in sight
Of *Paros* Isle, with Marble Quarries white.
We pass the scatter'd Isles of *Cyclades*;
That, scarce distinguish'd, seem to stud the Seas.   175
The shouts of Saylors double near the shores;
They stretch their Canvass, and they ply their Oars.
All hands aloft, for *Creet* for *Creet* they cry,
And swiftly through the foamy Billows fly.
Full on the promis'd Land at length we bore,   180
With Joy descending on the *Cretan* Shore.
With eager haste a rising Town I frame,
Which from the *Trojan Pergamus* I name:
The Name it self was grateful; I exhort
To found their Houses, and erect a Fort.   185
Our Ships are haul'd upon the yellow strand,
The Youth begin to till the labour'd Land.
And I my self new Marriages promote,
Give Laws: and Dwellings I divide by Lot.
When rising Vapours choak the wholesom Air,   190
And blasts of noisom Winds corrupt the Year:
The Trees, devouring Caterpillers burn:
Parch'd was the Grass, and blited was the Corn.
Nor scape the Beasts: for *Syrius* from on high,
With pestilential Heat infects the Sky: } 195
My Men, some fall, the rest in Feavers fry.
Again my Father bids me seek the Shore
Of sacred *Delos*; and the God implore:
To learn what end of Woes we might expect,
And to what Clime, our weary Course direct.   200
   'Twas Night, when ev'ry Creature, void of Cares,
The common gift of balmy Slumber shares:
The Statues of my Gods, (for such they seem'd)
Those Gods whom I from flaming *Troy* redeem'd,
Before me stood; Majestically bright,   205
Full in the Beams of *Phœbe*'s entring light.
Then thus they spoke; and eas'd my troubled Mind:
What from the *Delian* God thou go'st to find,
He tells thee here; and sends us to relate:
Those Pow'rs are we, Companions of thy Fate,   210
Who from the burning Town by thee were brought;

Thy Fortune follow'd, and thy safety wrought.
Through Seas and Lands, as we thy Steps attend,
So shall our Care thy Glorious Race befriend.
An ample Realm for thee thy Fates ordain;   21
A Town, that o're the conquer'd World shall reign.
Thou, mighty Walls for mighty Nations build;
Nor let thy weary Mind to Labours yield:
But change thy Seat; for not the *Delian* God,
Nor we, have giv'n thee *Crete* for our Abode.   22
A Land there is, *Hesperia* call'd of old,
The Soil is fruitful, and the Natives bold.
Th' *Oenotrians* held it once; by later Fame,
Now call'd *Italia* from the Leader's Name.
Jasius there, and *Dardanus* were born: 22
From thence we came, and thither must return.
Rise, and thy Sire with these glad Tidings greet;
Search *Italy*, for *Jove* denies thee *Creet*.

  Astonish'd at their Voices, and their sight,
(Nor were they Dreams, but Visions of the Night;   23
I saw, I knew their Faces, and descry'd
In perfect View, their Hair with Fillets ty'd:)
I started from my Couch, a clammy Sweat
On all my Limbs, and shiv'ring Body sate.
To Heav'n I lift my Hands with pious haste,   23
And sacred Incense in the Flames I cast.
Thus to the Gods their perfect Honours done,
More chearful to my good old Sire I run:
And tell the pleasing News; in little space
He found his Error, of the double Race.   24
Not, as before he deem'd, deriv'd from *Creet*;
No more deluded by the doubtful Seat.
Then said, O Son, turmoil'd in *Trojan* Fate,
Such things as these *Cassandra* did relate.
This Day revives within my Mind, what she   24
Foretold of *Troy* renew'd in *Italy*;
And *Latian* Lands: but who cou'd then have thought, ⎫
That *Phrygian* Gods to *Latium* should be brought; ⎬
Or who believ'd what mad *Cassandra* taught?   ⎭
Now let us go, where *Phœbus* leads the way: 25

    229 Editor's paragraph   243 Fate,] Fate; 97 98

He said, and we with glad Consent obey.
Forsake the Seat; and leaving few behind,
We spread our sails before the willing Wind.
Now from the sight of Land, our Gallies move,
With only Seas around, and Skies above.   255
When o're our Heads, descends a burst of Rain;
And Night, with sable Clouds involves the Main:
The ruffling Winds the foamy Billows raise:
The scatter'd Fleet is forc'd to sev'ral Ways:
The face of Heav'n is ravish'd from our Eyes,   260
And in redoubl'd Peals the roaring Thunder flys.
Cast from our Course, we wander in the Dark;
No Stars to guide, no point of Land to mark.
Ev'n *Palinurus* no distinction found
Betwixt the Night and Day; such Darkness reign'd around. 265
Three starless Nights the doubtful Navy strays
Without Distinction, and three Sunless Days.
The fourth renews the Light, and from our Shrowds
We view a rising Land like distant Clouds:
The Mountain tops confirm the pleasing Sight;   270
And curling Smoke ascending from their Height.
The Canvas falls; their Oars the Sailors ply;
From the rude strokes the whirling Waters fly.
At length I land upon the *Strophades*;
Safe from the danger of the stormy Seas: 275
Those Isles are compass'd by th' *Ionian* Main;
The dire Abode where the foul *Harpies* reign:
Forc'd by the winged Warriors to repair
To their old Homes, and leave their costly Fare.
Monsters more fierce, offended Heav'n ne're sent   280
From Hell's Abyss, for Human Punishment.
With Virgin-faces, but with Wombs obscene,
Foul Paunches, and with Ordure still unclean:
With Claws for Hands, and Looks for ever lean.

   We landed at the Port; and soon beheld   285
Fat Herds of Oxen graze the flowry Field:
And wanton Goats without a Keeper stray'd:
With Weapons we the welcome Prey invade.
Then call the Gods, for Partners of our Feast:
And *Jove* himself the chief invited Guest.   290

We spread the Tables, on the greensword Ground:
We feed with Hunger, and the Bowls go round.
When from the Mountain tops, with hideous Cry,
And clatt'ring Wings, the hungry Harpies fly:
They snatch the Meat; defiling all they find: 295
And parting leave a loathsom Stench behind.
Close by a hollow Rock, again we sit;
New dress the Dinner, and the Beds refit:
Secure from Sight, beneath a pleasing Shade;
Where tufted Trees a native Arbour made.   300
Again the Holy Fires on Altars burn:
And once again the rav'nous Birds return:
Or from the dark Recesses where they ly,
Or from another Quarter of the Sky.
With filthy Claws their odious Meal repeat,   305
And mix their loathsom Ordures with their Meat.
I bid my Friends for Vengeance then prepare;
And with the Hellish Nation wage the War.
They, as commanded, for the Fight provide,
And in the Grass their glitt'ring Weapons hide: 310
Then, when along the crooked Shoar we hear
Their clatt'ring Wings, and saw the Foes appear;
Misenus sounds a charge: We take th' Alarm;
And our strong hands with Swords and Bucklers arm.
In this new kind of Combat, all employ   31C
Their utmost Force, the Monsters to destroy.
In vain; the fated Skin is proof to Wounds:
And from their Plumes the shining Sword rebounds.
At length rebuff'd, they leave their mangled Prey,
And their stretch'd Pinions to the Skies display.   32C
Yet one remain'd, the Messenger of Fate;
High on a craggy Cliff *Celæno* sate,
And thus her dismal Errand did relate.
What, not contented with our Oxen slain,
Dare you with Heav'n an impious War maintain,   32
And drive the Harpies from their Native Reign?
Heed therefore what I say; and keep in mind
What *Jove* decrees, what *Phœbus* has design'd:
And I, the Fury's Queen, from both relate:
You seek th' *Italian* Shores, foredoom'd by Fate: 33C

Th' *Italian* Shores are granted you to find:
And a safe Passage to the Port assign'd.
But know, that e're your promis'd Walls you build,
My Curses shall severely be fulfill'd.
Fierce Famine is your Lot, for this Misdeed,   335
Reduc'd to grind the Plates on which you feed.
She said; and to the neighb'ring Forest flew:
Our Courage fails us, and our Fears renew.
Hopeless to win by War, to Pray'rs we fall:
And on th' offended Harpies humbly call.   340
And whether Gods, or Birds obscene they were,
Our Vows for Pardon, and for Peace prefer.
But old *Anchises*, off'ring Sacrifice,
And lifting up to Heav'n his Hands, and Eyes;
Ador'd the greater Gods: Avert, said he,   } 345
These Omens, render vain this Prophecy: }
And from th' impending Curse, a Pious People free.   }
Thus having said, he bids us put to Sea;   }
We loose from Shore our Haulsers, and obey: }
And soon with swelling Sails, pursue the wat'ry Way.   } 350
    Amidst our course *Zacynthian* Woods appear;
And next by rocky *Neritos* we steer:
We fly from *Ithaca*'s detested Shore,
And curse the Land which dire *Ulysses* bore.
At length *Leucates* cloudy top appears;   355
And the Sun's Temple, which the Sailor fears.
Resolv'd to breath a while from Labour past,   }
Our crooked Anchors from the Prow we cast;   }
And joyful to the little City haste.   }
Here safe beyond our Hopes, our Vows we pay   360
To *Jove*, the Guide and Patron of our way.
The Customs of our Country we pursue;
And *Trojan* Games on *Actian* Shores renew.
Our Youth, their naked Limbs besmear with Oyl;
And exercise the Wrastlers noble Toil.   365
Pleas'd to have sail'd so long before the Wind;
And left so many *Grecian* Towns behind.
The Sun had now fulfill'd his Annual Course,
And *Boreas* on the Seas display'd his Force:

351 *Editor's paragraph*   356 the Sun's *98: Phœbus 97*

I fix'd upon the Temples lofty Door,　　　　　　　3
The brazen Shield which vanquish'd *Abas* bore:
The Verse beneath, my Name and Action speaks,
These Arms, *Æneas* took from Conqu'ring *Greeks*.
Then I command to weigh; the Seamen ply
Their sweeping Oars, the smokeing Billows fly.　　3
The sight of high *Phæacia* soon we lost:
And skim'd along *Epirus* rocky Coast.
Then to *Chaonia*'s Port our Course we bend,
And landed, to *Buthrotus* heights ascend.
Here wond'rous things were loudly blaz'd by Fame;　3
How *Helenus* reviv'd the *Trojan* Name;
And raign'd in *Greece*: That *Priam*'s captive Son
Succeeded *Pyrrhus* in his Bed and Throne.
And fair *Andromache*, restor'd by Fate,
Once more was happy in a *Trojan* Mate.　　　　3
I leave my Gallies riding in the Port;
And long to see the new *Dardanian* Court.
By chance, the mournful Queen, before the Gate,
Then solemniz'd her former Husbands Fate.
Green Altars rais'd of Turf, with Gifts she Crown'd;　⎫
And sacred Priests in order stand around;　　　　⎬ 39
And thrice the Name of hapless *Hector* sound.　　⎭
The Grove it self resembles *Ida*'s Wood;
And *Simois* seem'd the well dissembl'd Flood.
But when, at nearer distance, she beheld　　　　39
My shining Armour, and my *Trojan* Shield;
Astonish'd at the sight, the vital Heat
Forsakes her Limbs, her Veins no longer beat:
She faints, she falls, and scarce recov'ring strength,
Thus, with a falt'ring Tongue, she speaks at length.　40
　Are you alive, O Goddess born! she said,
Or if a Ghost, then where is *Hector*'s Shade?
At this, she cast a loud and frightful Cry:
With broken words, I made this brief Reply.
All of me that remains, appears in sight,　　　　40
I live; if living be to loath the Light.
No Phantome; but I drag a wretched life;
My Fate resembling that of *Hector*'s Wife.
What have you suffer'd since you lost your Lord,

By what strange blessing are you now restor'd! 410
Still are you *Hector*'s, or is *Hector* fled,
And his Remembrance lost in *Pyrrhus* Bed?
With Eyes dejected, in a lowly tone,
After a modest pause, she thus begun.

    Oh only happy Maid of *Priam*'s Race, 415
Whom Death deliver'd from the Foes embrace!
Commanded on *Achilles* Tomb to die,
Not forc'd, like us, to hard Captivity:
Or in a haughty Master's Arms to lie.
In *Grecian* Ships unhappy we were born: 420
Endur'd the Victor's Lust, sustain'd the Scorn:
Thus I submitted to the lawless pride
Of *Pyrrhus*, more a Handmaid than a Bride.
Cloy'd with Possession, He forsook my Bed,
And *Helen*'s lovely Daughter sought to wed. 425
Then me, to *Trojan Helenus* resign'd:
And his two Slaves in equal Marriage join'd.
Till young *Orestes*, pierc'd with deep despair,
And longing to redeem the promis'd Fair,
Before *Apollo*'s Altar slew the Ravisher. 430
By *Pyrrhus* death the Kingdom we regain'd:
At least one half with *Helenus* remain'd;
Our part, from *Chaon*, He *Chaonia* calls:
And names, from *Pergamus*, his rising Walls.
But you, what Fates have landed on our Coast, 435
What Gods have sent you, or what Storms have tost?
Does young *Ascanius* life and health enjoy,
Sav'd from the Ruins of unhappy *Troy*!
O tell me how his Mothers loss he bears,
What hopes are promis'd from his blooming years, 440
How much of *Hector* in his Face appears?
She spoke: and mix'd her Speech with mournful Cries:
And fruitless Tears came trickling from her Eyes.

    At length her Lord descends upon the Plain;
In pomp, attended with a num'rous Train: 445
Receives his Friends, and to the City leads;
And Tears of Joy amidst his Welcome sheds.
Proceeding on, another *Troy* I see;

444 Editor's paragraph

Or, in less compass, *Troy*'s Epitome.
A Riv'let by the name of *Xanthus* ran:
And I embrace the *Scæan* Gate again.
My Friends in Portico's were entertain'd;
And Feasts and Pleasures through the City reign'd.
The Tables fill'd the spacious Hall around:
And Golden Bowls with sparkling Wine were crown'd.
Two days we pass'd in mirth, till friendly Gales,
Blown from the South, supply'd our swelling Sails.
Then to the Royal Seer I thus began:
O thou who know'st beyond the reach of Man,
The Laws of Heav'n, and what the Stars decree,
Whom *Phœbus* taught unerring Prophecy,
From his own Tripod, and his holy Tree:
Skill'd in the wing'd Inhabitants of Air,
What Auspices their notes, and flights declare:
O say; for all Religious Rites portend
A happy Voyage, and a prosp'rous End:
And ev'ry Pow'r and Omen of the Sky,
Direct my Course for destin'd *Italy*:
But only dire *Celæno*, from the Gods,
A dismal Famine fatally fore-bodes:
O say what Dangers I am first to shun:
What Toils to vanquish, and what Course to run.

 The Prophet first with Sacrifice adores
The greater Gods; their Pardon then implores:
Unbinds the Fillet from his holy Head;
To *Phœbus* next, my trembling Steps he led:
Full of religious Doubts, and awful dread.
Then with his God possess'd, before the Shrine,
These words proceeded from his Mouth Divine.
O Goddess-born, (for Heav'n's appointed Will,
With greater Auspices of good than ill,
Fore-shows thy Voyage, and thy Course directs;
Thy Fates conspire, and *Jove* himself protects:)
Of many things, some few I shall explain,
Teach thee to shun the dangers of the Main,
And how at length the promis'd Shore to gain.
The rest the Fates from *Helenus* conceal;
And *Juno*'s angry Pow'r forbids to tell.

First then, that happy Shore, that seems so nigh,
Will far from your deluded Wishes fly:
Long tracts of Seas divide your hopes from *Italy*.   490
For you must cruise along *Sicilian* Shoars;
And stem the Currents with your struggling Oars:
Then round th' *Italian* Coast your Navy steer;
And after this to *Circe*'s Island veer.   495
And last, before your new Foundations rise,
Must pass the *Stygian* Lake, and view the neather Skies.
Now mark the Signs of future Ease and Rest;
And bear them safely treasur'd in thy Breast.
When in the shady Shelter of a Wood,   500
And near the Margin of a gentle Flood,
Thou shalt behold a Sow upon the Ground,
With thirty sucking young encompass'd round;
The Dam and Off-spring white as falling Snow:
These on thy City shall their Name bestow: 505
And there shall end thy Labours and thy Woe.
Nor let the threatned Famine fright thy Mind,
For *Phœbus* will assist; and Fate the way will find.
Let not thy Course to that ill Coast be bent,
Which fronts from far th' *Epirian* Continent;   510
Those parts are all by *Grecian* Foes possess'd:
The salvage *Locrians* here the Shores infest:
There fierce *Idomeneus* his City builds,
And guards with Arms the *Salentinian* Fields.
And on the Mountains brow *Petilia* stands,   515
Which *Philoctetes* with his Troops commands.
Ev'n when thy Fleet is landed on the Shore,
And Priests with holy Vows the Gods adore;
Then with a Purple Veil involve your Eyes,
Lest hostile Faces blast the Sacrifice.   520
These Rites and Customs to the Rest commend;
That to your Pious Race they may descend.
   When parted hence, the Wind that ready waits
For *Sicily*, shall bear you to the Streights:
Where proud *Pelorus* opes a wider way,   525
Tack to the Larboord, and stand off to Sea:
Veer Star-board Sea and Land. Th' *Italian* Shore,
And fair *Sicilia*'s Coast were one, before

An Earthquake caus'd the Flaw, the roaring Tides
The Passage broke, that Land from Land divides:
And where the Lands retir'd, the rushing Ocean rides.
Distinguish'd by the Streights, on either hand,
Now rising Cities in long order stand;
And fruitful Fields: So much can Time invade
The mouldring Work, that beauteous Nature made.
Far on the right, her Dogs foul *Scylla* hides:
Charibdis roaring on the left presides;
And in her greedy Whirl-pool sucks the Tides:
Then Spouts them from below; with Fury driv'n,
The Waves mount up, and wash the face of Heav'n.
But *Scylla* from her Den, with open Jaws,
The sinking Vessel in her Eddy draws;
Then dashes on the Rocks: A Human Face,
And Virgin Bosom, hides her Tails disgrace.
Her Parts obscene below the Waves descend,
With Dogs inclos'd; and in a Dolphin end.
'Tis safer, then, to bear aloof to Sea,
And coast *Pachynus*, though with more delay;
Than once to view mishapen *Scylla* near,
And the loud yell of watry Wolves to hear.

Besides, if Faith to *Helenus* be due,
And if Prophetick *Phœbus* tell me true;
Do not this Precept of your Friend forget;
Which therefore more than once I must repeat.
Above the rest, great *Juno's* Name adore:
Pay Vows to *Juno*; *Juno's* Aid implore.
Let Gifts be to the mighty Queen design'd;
And mollify with Pray'rs her haughty Mind.
Thus, at the length, your Passage shall be free,
And you shall safe descend on *Italy*.
Arriv'd at *Cumæ*, when you view the Flood
Of black *Avernus*, and the sounding Wood,
The mad prophetick *Sybil* you shall find,
Dark in a Cave, and on a Rock reclin'd.
She sings the Fates, and in her frantick Fitts,
The Notes and Names inscrib'd, to Leafs commits.
What she commits to Leafs, in order laid,

534-5 So . . . made.] (So . . . made.) *98*

Before the Caverns Entrance are display'd:
Unmov'd they lie, but if a Blast of Wind
Without, or Vapours issue from behind,   570
The Leafs are born aloft in liquid Air,
And she resumes no more her Museful Care:
Nor gathers from the Rocks her scatter'd Verse;
Nor sets in order what the Winds disperse.
Thus, many not succeeding, most upbraid   575
The Madness of the visionary Maid;
And with loud Curses leave the mystick Shade.
   Think it not loss of time a while to stay;
Though thy Companions chide thy long delay:
Tho' summon'd to the Seas, tho' pleasing Gales   580
Invite thy Course, and stretch thy swelling Sails.
But beg the sacred Priestess to relate
With willing Words, and not to write thy Fate.
The fierce *Italian* People she will show;
And all thy Wars, and all thy Future Woe;   585
And what thou may'st avoid, and what must undergo.
She shall direct thy Course, instruct thy Mind;
And teach thee how the happy Shores to find.
This is what Heav'n allows me to relate:
Now part in Peace; pursue thy better Fate,   590
And raise, by strength of Arms, the *Trojan* State.
   This, when the Priest with friendly Voice declar'd,
He gave me Licence, and rich Gifts prepar'd:
Bounteous of Treasure, he supply'd my want
With heavy Gold, and polish'd Elephant.   595
Then *Dodonæan* Caldrons put on Bord,
And ev'ry Ship with Sums of Silver stor'd.
A trusty Coat of Mail to me he sent,
Thrice chain'd with Gold, for Use and Ornament:
The Helm of *Pyrrhus* added to the rest,   600
That flourish'd with a Plume and waving Crest.
Nor was my Sire forgotten, nor my Friends:
And large Recruits he to my Navy sends;
Men, Horses, Captains, Arms, and warlick Stores:
Supplies new Pilots, and new sweeping Oars.   605
Mean time, my Sire commands to hoist our Sails;
Lest we shou'd lose the first auspicious Gales.

The Prophet bless'd the parting Crew: and last,
With Words like these, his ancient Friend embrac'd.
Old happy Man, the Care of Gods above,
Whom Heav'nly *Venus* honour'd with her Love,
And twice preserv'd thy Life, when *Troy* was lost;
Behold from far the wish'd *Ausonian* Coast:
There land; but take a larger Compass round;
For that before is all forbidden Ground.
The Shore that *Phœbus* has design'd for you,
At farther distance lies, conceal'd from view.
Go happy hence, and seek your new Abodes;
Bless'd in a Son, and favour'd by the Gods:
For I with useless words prolong your stay;
When Southern Gales have summon'd you away.

    Nor less the Queen our parting thence deplor'd;
Nor was less bounteous than her *Trojan* Lord.
A noble Present to my Son she brought,
A Robe with Flow'rs on Golden Tissue wrought;
A *Phrygian* Vest; and loads, with Gifts beside
Of precious Texture, and of *Asian* Pride.
Accept, she said, these Monuments of Love;
Which in my Youth with happier Hands I wove:
Regard these Trifles for the Giver's sake;
Tis the last Present *Hector*'s Wife can make.
Thou call'st my lost *Astyanax* to mind:
In thee his Features, and his Form I find.
His Eyes so sparkled with a lively Flame;
Such were his Motions, such was all his Frame;
And ah! had Heav'n so pleas'd, his Years had been the same. }

    With Tears I took my last adieu, and said,
Your Fortune, happy pair, already made,
Leaves you no farther Wish: My diff'rent state,
Avoiding one, incurs another Fate.
To you a quiet Seat the Gods allow,
You have no Shores to search, no Seas to plow,
Nor Fields of flying *Italy* to chase:
(Deluding Visions, and a vain Embrace!)
You see another *Simois*, and enjoy
The labour of your Hands, another *Troy*;
With better Auspice than her ancient Tow'rs:

And less obnoxious to the *Grecian* Pow'rs.
If e're the Gods, whom I with Vows adore,
Conduct my Steps to *Tiber*'s happy Shore: 650
If ever I ascend the *Latian* Throne,
And build a City I may call my own,
As both of us our Birth from *Troy* derive,
So let our Kindred Lines in Concord live:
And both in Acts of equal Friendship strive. 655
Our Fortunes, good or bad, shall be the same,
The double *Troy* shall differ but in Name:
That what we now begin, may never end;
But long, to late Posterity descend.

Near the *Ceraunean* Rocks our Course we bore: 660
(The shortest passage to th' *Italian* shore:)
Now had the Sun withdrawn his radiant Light,
And Hills were hid in dusky Shades of Night:
We land; and on the bosom of the Ground
A safe Retreat, and a bare *Lodging* found; 665
Close by the Shore we lay; the Sailors keep
Their watches, and the rest securely sleep.
The Night proceeding on with silent pace,
Stood in her noon; and view'd with equal Face,
Her steepy rise, and her declining Race. 670
Then wakeful *Palinurus* rose, to spie
The face of Heav'n, and the Nocturnal Skie;
And listen'd ev'ry breath of Air to try:
Observes the Stars, and notes their sliding Course,
The *Pleiads*, *Hyads*, and their wat'ry force; 675
And both the Bears is careful to behold;
And bright *Orion* arm'd with burnish'd Gold.
Then when he saw no threat'ning Tempest Nigh,
But a sure promise of a settled Skie;
He gave the Sign to weigh; we break our sleep; 680
Forsake the pleasing Shore, and plow the deep.
And now the rising Morn, with rosie light
Adorns the Skies, and puts the Stars to flight:
When we from far, like bluish Mists, descry
The Hills, and then the Plains of *Italy*. 685
Achates first pronounc'd the Joyful sound;
Then *Italy* the chearful Crew rebound.

My Sire *Anchises* crown'd a Cup with Wine:
And off'ring, thus implor'd the Pow'rs Divine.
Ye Gods, presiding over Lands and Seas,   690
And you who raging Winds and Waves appease,
Breath on our swelling Sails a prosp'rous Wind:
And smooth our Passage to the Port assign'd.
The gentle Gales their flagging force renew;
And now the happy Harbour is in view.   695
Minerva's Temple then salutes our sight;
Plac'd, as a Land-mark, on the Mountains height:
We furl our Sails, and turn the Prows to shore;
The curling Waters round the Galleys roar:
The Land lies open to the raging East,   700
Then, bending like a Bow, with Rocks compress'd,
Shuts out the Storms; the Winds and Waves complain,
And vent their malice on the Cliffs in vain.
The Port lies hid within; on either side
Two Tow'ring Rocks the narrow mouth divide.   705
The Temple, which aloft we view'd before,
To distance flies, and seems to shun the Shore.
Scarce landed, the first Omens I beheld
Were four white Steeds that crop'd the flow'ry Field.
War, War is threaten'd from this Forreign Ground,   710
(My Father cry'd) where warlike Steeds are found.
Yet, since reclaim'd to Chariots they submit,
And bend to stubborn Yokes, and champ the Bitt,
Peace may succeed to Warr. Our way we bend
To *Pallas*, and the sacred Hill ascend.   715
There, prostrate to the fierce *Virago* pray;
Whose Temple was the Land-Mark of our way.
Each with a *Phrygian* Mantle veil'd his Head;
And all Commands of *Helenus* obey'd;
And pious Rites to *Grecian Juno* paid.   720
      These dues perform'd, we stretch our Sails, and **stand**
To Sea, forsaking that suspected Land.
From hence *Tarentum*'s Bay appears in view;
For *Hercules* renown'd, if Fame be true.
Just opposite, *Lacinian Juno* stands;   725
Caulonian Tow'rs and *Scylacæan* Strands,

For Shipwrecks fear'd: Mount *Etna* thence we spy,
Known by the smoaky Flames which Cloud the Skie.
Far off we hear the Waves, with surly sound
Invade the Rocks, the Rocks their groans rebound.   730
The Billows break upon the sounding Strand;
And roul the rising Tide, impure with Sand.
Then thus *Anchises*, in Experience old,
'Tis that *Charibdis* which the Seer foretold:
And those the promis'd Rocks; bear off to Sea: 735
With haste the frighted Mariners obey.
First *Palinurus* to the Larboor'd veer'd;
Then all the Fleet by his Example steer'd.
To Heav'n aloft on ridgy Waves we ride;
Then down to Hell descend, when they divide.   740
And thrice our Gallies knock'd the stony ground,
And thrice the hollow Rocks return'd the sound,
And thrice we saw the Stars, that stood with dews around.
The flagging Winds forsook us, with the Sun;
And weary'd, on *Cyclopean* Shores we run.   745
The Port capacious, and secure from Wind,
Is to the foot of thundring *Etna* joyn'd.
By turns a pitchy Cloud she rowls on high;
By turns hot Embers from her entrails fly;
And flakes of mounting Flames, that lick the Skie.   750
Oft from her Bowels massy Rocks are thrown,
And shiver'd by the force come piece-meal down.
Oft liquid Lakes of burning Sulphur flow,
Fed from the fiery Springs that boil below.
Enceladus they say, transfix'd by *Jove*,   755
With blasted Limbs came tumbling from above:
And, where he fell, th' Avenging Father drew
This flaming Hill, and on his Body threw:
As often as he turns his weary sides,
He shakes the solid Isle, and smoke the Heavens hides.   760
In shady Woods we pass the tedious Night,
Where bellowing Sounds and Groans our Souls affright,
Of which no Cause is offer'd to the sight.
For not one Star was kindled in the Skie;
Nor cou'd the Moon her borrow'd Light supply: 765

762 affright,] affright. *97 98*

For misty Clouds involv'd the Firmament;
The Stars were muffled, and the Moon was pent.
  Scarce had the rising Sun the day reveal'd;
Scarce had his heat the pearly dews dispell'd;
When from the Woods there bolts, before our sight,   77
Somewhat, betwixt a Mortal and a Spright.
So thin, so ghastly meagre, and so wan,
So bare of flesh, he scarce resembled Man.
This thing, all tatter'd, seem'd from far t' implore
Our pious aid, and pointed to the Shore.   77
We look behind; then view his shaggy Beard;
His Cloaths were tagg'd with Thorns, and Filth his Limbs besmear'd:
The rest, in Meen, in habit, and in Face,
Appear'd a *Greek*; and such indeed he was.
He cast on us, from far, a frightful view,   78
Whom soon for *Trojans* and for Foes he knew:
Stood still, and paus'd; then all at once began
To stretch his Limbs, and trembled as he ran.
Soon as approach'd, upon his Knees he falls,
And thus with Tears and Sighs for pity calls.   78
Now by the Pow'rs above, and what we share
From Nature's common Gift, this vital Air,
O *Trojans* take me hence: I beg no more,
But bear me far from this unhappy Shore.
'Tis true I am a *Greek*, and farther own,   79
Among your Foes besieg'd th' Imperial Town;
For such Demerits if my death be due,
No more for this abandon'd life I sue:
This only Favour let my Tears obtain,
To throw me headlong in the rapid Main: 79
Since nothing more than Death my Crime demands,
I dye content, to dye by human Hands.
He said, and on his Knees my Knees embrac'd,
I bad him boldly tell his Fortune past;
His present State, his Lineage and his Name;   80
Th' occasion of his Fears, and whence he came.
The good *Anchises* rais'd him with his Hand;
Who, thus encourag'd, answer'd our Demand:
From *Ithaca* my native Soil I came

768 *Editor's paragraph*   787 From *98*: As *97*

To *Troy*, and *Achæmenides* my Name.   805
Me, my poor Father, with *Ulysses* sent;
(Oh had I stay'd, with Poverty content!)
But fearful for themselves, my Country-men
Left me forsaken in the *Cyclops* Den.
The Cave, though large, was dark, the dismal Flore   810
Was pav'd with mangled Limbs and putrid Gore.
Our monstrous Host, of more than Human Size,
Erects his Head, and stares within the Skies.
Bellowing his Voice, and horrid is his Hue.
Ye Gods, remove this Plague from Mortal View!   815
The Joints of slaughter'd Wretches are his Food:
And for his Wine he quaffs the streaming Blood.
These Eyes beheld, when with his spacious Hand
He seiz'd two Captives of our *Grecian* Band;
Stretch'd on his Back, he dash'd against the Stones 820
Their broken Bodies, and their crackling Bones:
With spouting Blood the Purple Pavement swims,
While the dire Glutton grinds the trembling Limbs.
    Not unreveng'd, *Ulysses* bore their Fate,
Nor thoughtless of his own unhappy State: 825
For, gorg'd with Flesh, and drunk with Human Wine,
While fast asleep the Gyant lay supine;
Snoaring aloud, and belching from his Maw
His indigested Foam, and Morsels raw:
We pray, we cast the Lots, and then surround   830
The monstrous Body, stretch'd along the Ground:
Each, as he cou'd approach him, lends a hand
To bore his Eyeball with a flaming Brand.
Beneath his frowning Forehead lay his Eye,
(For onely one did the vast Frame supply;)   835
But that a Globe so large, his Front it fill'd,
Like the Sun's disk, or like a *Grecian* Shield.
The Stroke succeeds; and down the Pupil bends;
This Vengeance follow'd for our slaughter'd Friends.
But haste, unhappy Wretches, haste to fly;   840
Your Cables cut, and on your Oars rely.
Such, and so vast as *Polypheme* appears,
A hundred more this hated Island bears:

809 *Cyclops*] *Cyclop's* 97 98

Like him in Caves they shut their woolly Sheep,
Like him, their Herds on tops of Mountains keep;   845
Like him, with mighty Strides, they stalk from Steep to Steep.
And now three Moons their sharpen'd Horns renew,
Since thus in Woods and Wilds, obscure from view,
I drag my loathsom Days with mortal Fright;
And in deserted Caverns lodge by Night.   850
Oft from the Rocks a dreadful Prospect see,
Of the huge *Cyclops*, like a walking Tree:
From far I hear his thund'ring Voice resound;
And trampling Feet that shake the solid Ground.
Cornels, and salvage Berries of the Wood,   855
And Roots and Herbs have been my meagre Food.
　　While all around my longing Eyes I cast,
I saw your happy Ships appear at last.
On those I fix'd my hopes, to these I run,
'Tis all I ask this cruel Race to shun: 860
What other Death you please your selves, bestow.
Scarce had he said, when on the Mountain's brow,
We saw the Gyant-Shepherd stalk before
His following Flock, and leading to the Shore.
A monstrous Bulk, deform'd, depriv'd of Sight,   865
His Staff a trunk of Pine, to guide his steps aright.
His pondrous Whistle from his Neck descends;
His woolly Care their pensive Lord attends:
This onely Solace his hard Fortune sends.
Soon as he reach'd the Shore, and touch'd the Waves,   870
From his bor'd Eye the gutt'ring Blood he laves:
He gnash'd his Teeth and groan'd; thro' Seas he strides,
And scarce the topmost Billows touch'd his sides.
　　Seiz'd with a sudden Fear, we run to Sea,
The Cables cut, and silent haste away: 875
The well deserving Stranger entertain;
Then, buckling to the Work, our Oars divide the Main.
The Gyant harken'd to the dashing Sound:
But when our Vessels out of reach he found,
He strided onward; and in vain essay'd   880
Th' *Ionian* Deep, and durst no farther wade.

With that he roar'd aloud; the dreadful Cry
Shakes Earth, and Air, and Seas; the Billows fly
Before the bellowing Noise, to distant *Italy.*
The neighb'ring *Ætna* trembled all around;   885
The winding Caverns echo to the sound.
His brother *Cyclops* hear the yelling Roar;
And, rushing down the Mountains, crowd the Shoar:
We saw their stern distorted looks, from far,
And one ey'd Glance, that vainly threatned War.   890
A dreadful Council, with their heads on high;
The misty Clouds about their Foreheads fly:
Not yielding to the tow'ring Tree of *Jove*;
Or tallest Cypress of *Diana*'s Grove.
New Pangs of mortal Fear our Minds assail,   895
We tug at ev'ry Oar, and hoist up ev'ry Sail;
And take th' Advantage of the friendly Gale.
Forewarn'd by *Helenus*, we strive to shun
Charibdis Gulph, nor dare to *Scylla* run.
An equal Fate on either side appears;   900
We, tacking to the left, are free from Fears.
For from *Pelorus* Point, the North arose,
And drove us back where swift *Pantagias* flows.
His Rocky Mouth we pass; and make our Way
By *Thapsus*, and *Megara*'s winding Bay;   905
This Passage *Achæmenides* had shown,
Tracing the Course which he before had run.
    Right o're-against *Plemmyrium*'s watry Strand,
There lies an Isle once call'd th' *Ortygian* Land:
Alpheus, as Old Fame reports, has found   910
From *Greece* a secret Passage under-ground:
By Love to beauteous *Arethusa* led;
And mingling here, they rowl in the same Sacred Bed.
As *Helenus* enjoyn'd, we next adore
Diana's Name, Protectress of the Shore.   915
With prosp'rous Gales we pass the quiet Sounds
Of still *Elorus* and his fruitful Bounds.
Then doubling Cape *Pachynus*, we survey
The rocky Shore extended to the Sea.
The Town of *Camarine* from far we see;   920

885 trembled] trembling *98*   912 led;] led, *97 98*

And fenny Lake undrain'd by Fates decree.
In sight of the *Geloan* Fields we pass,
And the large Walls, where mighty *Gela* was:
Then *Agragas* with lofty Summets crown'd;
Long for the Race of warlike Steeds renown'd: 925
We pass'd *Selinus*, and the Palmy Land,
And widely shun the *Lilybæan* Strand,
Unsafe, for secret Rocks, and moving Sand.
At length on Shore the weary Fleet arriv'd;
Which *Drepanum*'s unhappy Port receiv'd.   930
Here, after endless Labours, often tost
By raging Storms, and driv'n on ev'ry Coast,
My dear, dear Father, spent with Age, I lost.
Ease of my Cares, and Solace of my Pain,
Sav'd through a thousand Toils, but sav'd in vain: 935
The Prophet, who my future Woes reveal'd,
Yet this, the greatest and the worst, conceal'd.
And dire *Celæno*, whose foreboding Skill
Denounc'd all else, was silent of this Ill:
This my last Labour was. Some friendly God,   940
From thence convey'd us to your blest Abode.

     Thus to the listning Queen, the Royal Guest
His wand'ring Course, and all his Toils express'd;
And here concluding, he retir'd to rest.

THE FOURTH BOOK OF THE ÆNEIS

THE ARGUMENT

Dido *discovers to her Sister her Passion for* Æneas, *and her thoughts of marrying him. She prepares a Hunting-Match for his Entertainment.* Juno *by* Venus's *consent raises a Storm, which separates the Hunters, and drives* Æneas *and* Dido *into the same Cave, where their Marriage is suppos'd to be compleated.* Jupiter *dispatches* Mercury *to* Æneas, *to warn him from* Carthage;   5 Æneas *secretly prepares for his Voyage:* Dido *finds out his Design, and to put a stop to it, makes use of her own, and her Sister's Entreaties, and discovers all the variety of Passions that are incident to a neglected Lover: When nothing wou'd prevail upon him, she contrives her own Death, with which this Book concludes.*   10

BUT anxious Cares already seiz'd the Queen:
She fed within her Veins a Flame unseen:
The Heroe's Valour, Acts, and Birth inspire
Her Soul with Love, and fann the secret Fire.
His Words, his Looks imprinted in her Heart,   5
Improve the Passion, and increase the Smart.
Now, when the Purple Morn had chas'd away
The dewy Shadows, and restor'd the Day;
Her Sister first, with early Care she sought,
And thus in mournful Accents eas'd her Thought. 10
My dearest *Anna*, what new Dreams affright
My lab'ring Soul; what Visions of the Night
Disturb my Quiet, and distract my Breast,
With strange Ideas of our *Trojan* Guest?
His Worth, his Actions, and Majestick Air,   15
A Man descended from the Gods declare:
Fear ever argues a degenerate kind,
His Birth is well asserted by his Mind.
Then, what he suffer'd, when by Fate betray'd,
What brave Attempts for falling *Troy* he made! 20
Such were his Looks, so gracefully he spoke,
That were I not resolv'd against the Yoke
Of hapless Marriage; never to be curs'd
With second Love, so fatal was my first;
To this one Error I might yield again: 25
For since *Sichæus* was untimely slain,
This onely Man, is able to subvert
The fix'd Foundations of my stubborn Heart.
And to confess my Frailty, to my shame,
Somewhat I find within, if not the same,   } 30
Too like the Sparkles of my former Flame.
 But first let yawning Earth a Passage rend;
And let me through the dark Abyss descend;
First let avenging *Jove*, with Flames from high,
Drive down this Body, to the neather Sky,   } 35
Condemn'd with Ghosts in endless Night to lye;

The Fourth Book. 17–18 Fear . . . Mind. 98: 97 *has*

   Fear never harbours in a Noble Mind,
   But Modesty, with just Assurance join'd.

Before I break the plighted Faith I gave;
No; he who had my Vows, shall ever have;
For whom I lov'd on Earth, I worship in the Grave. }

    She said; the Tears ran gushing from her Eyes,
And stop'd her Speech: her Sister thus replies.
O dearer than the vital Air I breath,
Will you to Grief your blooming Years bequeath?
Condemn'd to wast in Woes, your lonely Life,
Without the Joys of Mother, or of Wife.
Think you these Tears, this pompous Train of Woe,
Are known, or valu'd by the Ghosts below?
I grant, that while your Sorrows yet were green,
It well became a Woman, and a Queen,
The Vows of *Tyrian* Princes to neglect,
To scorn *Hyarbas*, and his Love reject,
With all the *Lybian* Lords of mighty Name;
But will you fight against a pleasing Flame!
This little Spot of Land, which Heav'n bestows,
On ev'ry side is hemm'd with warlike Foes:
Getulian Cities here are spread around;
And fierce *Numidians* there your Frontiers bound;
Here lies a barren Wast of thirsty Land,
And there the *Syrtes* raise the moving Sand:
Barcæan Troops besiege the narrow Shore;
And from the Sea *Pigmalion* threatens more.
Propitious Heav'n, and gracious *Juno*, lead
This wand'ring Navy to your needful Aid:
How will your Empire spread, your City rise
From such an Union, and with such Allies!
Implore the Favour of the Pow'rs above;
And leave the Conduct of the rest to Love.
Continue still your hospitable way,
And still invent occasions of their Stay;
'Till Storms, and winter Winds, shall cease to threat,
And Plancks and Oars, repair their shatter'd Fleet.

    These Words, which from a Friend, and Sister came,
With Ease resolv'd the Scruples of her Fame;
And added Fury to the kindled Flame. }

44 Condemn'd 98: Condem'd 97   51 reject,] reject; 97 98   52 Name;]
Name, 97 98

Inspir'd with Hope, the Project they pursue;   75
On ev'ry Altar Sacrifice renew;
A chosen Ewe of two Years old they pay
To *Ceres*, *Bacchus*, and the God of Day:
Preferring *Juno*'s Pow'r: For *Juno* ties
The Nuptial Knot, and makes the Marriage Joys.   80
The beauteous Queen before her Altar stands,
And holds the Golden Goblet in her Hands:
A milk-white Heifar she with Flow'rs adorns,
And pours the ruddy Wine betwixt her Horns;
And while the Priests with Pray'r the Gods invoke,   85
She feeds their Altars with *Sabæan* Smoke.
With hourly Care the Sacrifice renews,
And anxiously the panting Entrails Views.
What Priestly Rites, alas! what Pious Art,
What Vows avail to cure a bleeding Heart!   90
A gentle Fire she feeds within her Veins;
Where the soft God secure in silence reigns.
   Sick with desire, and seeking him she loves,
From Street to Street, the raving *Dido* roves.
So when the watchful Shepherd, from the Blind,   95
Wounds with a random Shaft the careless Hind;
Distracted with her pain she flies the Woods,
Bounds o're the Lawn, and seeks the silent Floods;
With fruitless Care; for still the fatal Dart
Sticks in her side; and ranckles in her Heart.   100
And now she leads the *Trojan* Chief, along
The lofty Walls, amidst the buisie Throng;
Displays her *Tyrian* Wealth, and rising Town,
Which Love, without his Labour, makes his own.
This Pomp she shows to tempt her wand'ring Guest;   105
Her falt'ring Tongue forbids to speak the rest.
When Day declines, and Feasts renew the Night,
Still on his Face she feeds her famish'd sight;
She longs again to hear the Prince relate
His own Adventures, and the *Trojan* Fate: 110
He tells it o're and o're; but still in vain;
For still she begs to hear it, once again.
The Hearer on the Speaker's Mouth depends;

105 wand'ring 98: wond'ring 97

And thus the Tragick Story never ends.
    Then, when they part, when *Phœbe's* paler Light
Withdraws, and falling Stars to Sleep invite,
She last remains, when ev'ry Guest is gone,
Sits on the Bed he press'd, and sighs alone;
Absent, her absent Heroe sees and hears;
Or in her Bosom young *Ascanius* bears:
And seeks the Father's Image in the Child,
If Love by Likeness might be so beguil'd.
    Mean time the rising Tow'rs are at a stand:
No Labours exercise the youthful Band:
Nor use of Arts, nor Toils of Arms they know;
The Mole is left unfinish'd to the Foe.
The Mounds, the Works, the Walls, neglected lye,
Short of their promis'd height that seem'd to threat the Sky.
    But when Imperial *Juno*, from above,
Saw *Dido* fetter'd in the Chains of Love;
Hot with the Venom, which her Veins inflam'd,
And by no sense of Shame to be reclaim'd:
With soothing Words to *Venus* she begun.
High Praises, endless Honours you have won,
And mighty Trophees with your worthy Son:
Two Gods a silly Woman have undone.
Nor am I ignorant, you both suspect
This rising City, which my Hands erect:
But shall Cœlestial Discord never cease?
'Tis better ended in a lasting Peace.
You stand possess'd of all your Soul desir'd;
Poor *Dido* with consuming Love is fir'd:
Your *Trojan* with my *Tyrian* let us join,
So *Dido* shall be yours, *Æneas* mine:
One common Kingdom, one united Line.
Elisa shall a *Dardan* Lord obey,
And lofty *Carthage* for a Dow'r convey.
Then *Venus*, who her hidden Fraud descry'd,
(Which wou'd the Scepter of the World, misguide
To *Lybian* Shores,) thus artfully reply'd,
Who but a Fool, wou'd Wars with *Juno* chuse,
And such Alliance, and such Gifts refuse?

    128 Short . . . Sky. *98*: And, left unbuilt, are shorter of the Sky. *97*

If Fortune with our joint Desires comply:
The Doubt is all from *Jove*, and Destiny:
Lest he forbid, with absolute Command,   155
To mix the People in one common Land.
Or will the *Trojan*, and the *Tyrian* Line,
In lasting Leagues, and sure Succession join?
But you, the Partner of his Bed and Throne,
May move his Mind; my Wishes are your own.   160
   Mine, said Imperial *Juno*, be the Care;
Time urges, now, to perfect this Affair:
Attend my Counsel, and the Secret share.
When next the Sun his rising Light displays,
And guilds the World below, with Purple Rays;   165
The Queen, *Æneas*, and the *Tyrian* Court,
Shall to the shady Woods, for Silvan Game, resort.
There, while the Huntsmen pitch their Toils around,
And chearful Horns, from Side to Side, resound;
A Pitchy Cloud shall cover all the Plain   170
With Hail, and Thunder, and tempestuous Rain:
The fearful Train shall take their speedy Flight,
Dispers'd, and all involv'd in gloomy Night:
One Cave a grateful Shelter shall afford
To the fair Princess, and the *Trojan* Lord.   175
I will my self, the bridal Bed prepare,
If you, to bless the Nuptials, will be there:
So shall their Loves be crown'd with due Delights,
And *Hymen* shall be present at the Rites.
The Queen of Love consents, and closely smiles   180
At her vain Project, and discover'd Wiles.
   The rosy Morn was risen from the Main,
And Horns and Hounds awake the Princely Train:
They issue early through the City Gate,
Where the more wakeful Huntsmen ready wait,   185
With Nets, and Toils, and Darts, beside the force
Of *Spartan* Dogs, and swift *Massylian* Horse.
The *Tyrian* Peers, and Officers of State,
For the slow Queen, in Anti-Chambers wait:
Her lofty Courser, in the Court below,   190
(Who his Majestick Rider seems to know,)

154 Destiny:] Destiny. 97 98

Proud of his Purple Trappings, paws the Ground;
And champs the Golden Bitt; and spreads the Foam around.
The Queen at length appears: On either Hand
The brawny Guards in Martial Order stand.
A flow'rd Cymarr, with Golden Fringe, she wore;
And at her Back a Golden Quiver bore:
Her flowing Hair, a Golden Caul restrains;
A golden Clasp, the *Tyrian* Robe sustains.
Then young *Ascanius*, with a sprightly Grace,
Leads on the *Trojan* Youth to view the Chace.
But far above the rest in beauty shines
The great *Æneas*, when the Troop he joins:
Like fair *Apollo*, when he leaves the frost
Of wintry *Xanthus*, and the *Lycian* Coast;
When to his Native *Delos* he resorts,
Ordains the Dances, and renews the Sports:
Where painted *Scythians*, mix'd with *Cretan* Bands,
Before the joyful Altars join their Hands.
Himself, on *Cynthus* walking, sees below
The merry Madness of the sacred Show.
Green Wreaths of Bays his length of Hair inclose,
A Golden Fillet binds his awful Brows:
His Quiver sounds: Not less the Prince is seen
In manly Presence, or in lofty Meen.
   Now had they reach'd the Hills, and storm'd the Seat
Of salvage Beasts, in Dens, their last Retreat;
The Cry pursues the Mountain-Goats; they bound
From Rock to Rock, and keep the craggy Ground:
Quite otherwise the Stags, a trembling Train,
In Herds unsingl'd, scour the dusty Plain;
And a long Chace, in open view, maintain.
The glad *Ascanius*, as his Courser guides,
Spurs through the Vale; and these and those outrides.
His Horses flanks and sides are forc'd to feel
The clanking lash, and goring of the Steel.
Impatiently he views the feeble Prey,
Wishing some Nobler Beast to cross his way.
And rather wou'd the tusky Boar attend,
Or see the tawny Lyon downward bend.

230 tawny Lyon downward bend. *98*: Lyon from the Hills descend. *97*

Mean time, the gath'ring Clouds obscure the Skies;
From Pole to Pole the forky Lightning flies;
The ratling Thunders rowl; and *Juno* pours
A wintry Deluge down; and sounding Show'rs.
The Company dispers'd, to Coverts ride,   235
And seek the homely Cotts, or Mountains hollow side.
The rapid Rains, descending from the Hills,
To rowling Torrents raise the creeping Rills.
The Queen and Prince, as Love or Fortune guides,
One common Cavern in her Bosom hides.   240
Then first the trembling Earth the signal gave;
And flashing Fires enlighten all the Cave:
Hell from below, and *Juno* from above,
And howling Nymphs, were conscious to their Love.
From this ill Omend Hour, in Time arose   245
Debate and Death, and all succeeding woes.
    The Queen whom sense of Honour cou'd not move
No longer made a Secret of her Love;
But call'd it Marriage, by that specious Name,
To veil the Crime and sanctifie the Shame.   250
    The loud Report through *Lybian* Cities goes;
Fame, the great Ill, from small beginnings grows.
Swift from the first; and ev'ry Moment brings
New Vigour to her flights, new Pinions to her wings.
Soon grows the Pygmee to Gygantic size;   255
Her Feet on Earth, her Forehead in the Skies:
Inrag'd against the Gods, revengeful Earth
Produc'd her last of the *Titanian* birth.
Swift is her walk, more swift her winged hast:
A monstrous Fantom, horrible and vast;   260
As many Plumes as raise her lofty flight,
So many piercing Eyes inlarge her sight:
Millions of opening Mouths to Fame belong;
And ev'ry Mouth is furnish'd with a Tongue:
And round with listning Ears the flying Plague is hung.   265
She fills the peaceful Universe with Cries;
No Slumbers ever close her wakeful Eyes.
By Day from lofty Tow'rs her Head she shews;
And spreads through trembling Crowds disastrous News.
With Court Informers haunts, and Royal Spies,   270

Things done relates, not done she feigns; and mingles Truth with Lyes.
Talk is her business; and her chief delight
To tell of Prodigies, and cause affright.
She fills the Peoples Ears with *Dido*'s Name;
Who, lost to Honour, and the sense of Shame,   2
Admits into her Throne and Nuptial Bed
A wandring Guest, who from his Country fled:
Whole days with him she passes in delights;
And wasts in Luxury long Winter Nights.
Forgetful of her Fame, and Royal Trust;   2
Dissolv'd in Ease, abandon'd to her Lust.

    The Goddess widely spread the loud Report;
And flies at length to King *Hyarba*'s Court.
When first possess'd with this unwelcome News,
Whom did he not of Men and Gods accuse!   2
This Prince, from ravish'd *Garamantis* born,
A hundred Temples did with Spoils adorn,
In *Ammon*'s Honour, his Cœlestial Sire;
A hundred Altars fed, with wakeful Fire:
And through his vast Dominions, Priests ordain'd,   2
Whose watchful Care these holy Rites maintain'd.
The Gates and Columns were with Garlands crown'd,
And Blood of Victim Beasts enrich the Ground.

    He, when he heard a Fugitive cou'd move
The *Tyrian* Princess, who disdain'd his Love,   2
His Breast with Fury burn'd, his Eyes with Fire;
Mad with Despair, impatient with Desire.
Then on the Sacred Altars pouring Wine,
He thus with Pray'rs implor'd his Sire divine.

    Great *Jove*, propitious to the *Moorish* Race,   3
Who feast on painted Beds, with Off'rings grace
Thy Temples, and adore thy Pow'r Divine
With Blood of Victims, and with sparkling Wine:
Seest thou not this? or do we fear in vain
Thy boasted Thunder, and thy thoughtless Reign?   3
Do thy broad Hands the forky Lightnings lance,
Thine are the Bolts, or the blind work of Chance?
A wandring Woman builds, within our State,
A little Town, bought at an easie Rate;

She pays me Homage, and my Grants allow, 310
A narrow space of *Lybian* Lands to plough.
Yet scorning me, by Passion blindly led,
Admits a banish'd *Trojan* to her Bed:
And now this other *Paris*, with his Train
Of conquer'd Cowards, must in *Affrick* reign! 315
(Whom, what they are, their Looks and Garb confess;
Their Locks with Oil perfum'd, their *Lydian* dress:)
He takes the Spoil, enjoys the Princely Dame;
And I, rejected I, adore an empty Name.

His Vows, in haughty Terms, he thus preferr'd, 320
And held his Altar's Horns; the mighty Thund'rer heard,
Then cast his Eyes on *Carthage*, where he found
The lustful Pair, in lawless pleasure drown'd.
Lost in their Loves, insensible of Shame;
And both forgetful of their better Fame. 325
He calls *Cyllenius*; and the God attends;
By whom his menacing Command he sends.
Go, mount the Western Winds, and cleave the Skie;
Then, with a swift descent, to *Carthage* fly:
There find the *Trojan* Chief, who wastes his Days 330
In sloathful Riot, and inglorious Ease,
Nor minds the future City, giv'n by Fate;
To him this Message from my Mouth relate.
Not so, fair *Venus* hop'd, when twice she won
Thy Life with Pray'rs; nor promis'd such a Son. 335
Hers was a Heroe, destin'd to command
A Martial Race; and rule the *Latian* Land.
Who shou'd his ancient Line from *Teucer* draw;
And, on the conquer'd World, impose the Law.
If Glory cannot move a Mind so mean, 340
Nor future Praise, from fading Pleasure wean,
Yet why shou'd he defraud his Son of Fame;
And grudge the *Romans* their Immortal Name!
What are his vain Designs! what hopes he more,
From his long ling'ring on a hostile Shore? 345
Regardless to redeem his Honour lost,
And for his Race to gain th' *Ausonian* Coast!
Bid him with Speed the *Tyrian* Court forsake;

331 Ease,] Ease. *97 98*

With this Command the slumb'ring Warrior wake.
  Hermes obeys; with Golden Pinions binds   35
His flying Feet, and mounts the Western Winds:
And whether o're the Seas or Earth he flies,
With rapid Force, they bear him down the Skies.
But first he grasps within his awful Hand,
The mark of Sov'raign Pow'r, his Magick Wand: 35
With this, he draws the Ghosts from hollow Graves,
With this he drives them down the *Stygian* Waves;
With this he seals in Sleep, the wakeful sight;
And Eyes, though clos'd in Death restores to Light.
Thus arm'd, the God begins his Airy Race;   36
And drives the racking Clouds along the liquid Space.
Now sees the Tops of *Atlas*, as he flies;
Whose brawny Back supports the starry Skies:
Atlas, whose Head with Piny Forests crown'd,
Is beaten by the Winds; with foggy Vapours bound.   36
Snows hide his Shoulders; from beneath his Chin
The Founts of rolling Streams their Race begin:
A beard of Yce on his large Breast depends:
Here pois'd upon his Wings, the God descends.
Then, rested thus, he from the tow'ring height   37
Plung'd downward, with precipitated Flight:
Lights on the Seas, and skims along the Flood:
As Water-fowl, who seek their fishy Food,
Less, and yet less, to distant Prospect show,
By turns they dance aloft, and dive below: 37
Like these, the steerage of his Wings he plies;
And near the surface of the Water flies.
'Till having pass'd the Seas, and cross'd the Sands,
He clos'd his Wings, and stoop'd on *Lybian* Lands:
Where Shepherds once were hous'd in homely Sheds,   38
Now Tow'rs within the Clouds, advance their Heads.
Arriving there, he found the *Trojan* Prince,
New Ramparts raising for the Town's defence:
A Purple Scarf, with Gold embroider'd o're,
(Queen *Dido*'s Gift) about his Waste he wore;   38
A Sword with glitt'ring Gems diversify'd,
For Ornament, not use, hung idly by his side.
Then thus, with winged Words, the God began;

(Resuming his own Shape) degenerate Man,
Thou Woman's Property, what mak'st thou here,
These foreign Walls, and *Tyrian* Tow'rs to rear? 390
Forgetful of thy own? All pow'rful *Jove*,
Who sways the World below, and Heav'n above,
Has sent me down, with this severe Command:
What means thy ling'ring in the *Lybian* Land? 395
If Glory cannot move a Mind so mean,
Nor future Praise, from flitting Pleasure wean,
Regard the Fortunes of thy rising Heir;
The promis'd Crown let young *Ascanius* wear.
To whom th' *Ausonian* Scepter, and the State 400
Of *Rome*'s Imperial Name, is ow'd by Fate.
So spoke the God; and speaking took his flight,
Involv'd in Clouds; and vanish'd out of sight.

The Pious Prince was seiz'd with sudden Fear;
Mute was his Tongue, and upright stood his Hair: 405
Revolving in his Mind the stern Command,
He longs to fly, and loaths the charming Land.
What shou'd he say, or how shou'd he begin,
What Course, alas! remains, to steer between
Th' offended Lover, and the Pow'rful Queen! 410
This way, and that, he turns his anxious Mind,
And all Expedients tries, and none can find:
Fix'd on the Deed, but doubtful of the Means;
After long Thought to this Advice he leans.
Three Chiefs he calls, commands them to repair 415
The Fleet, and ship their Men with silent Care:
Some plausible Pretence he bids them find,
To colour what in secret he design'd.
Himself, mean time, the softest Hours wou'd chuse,
Before the Love-sick Lady heard the News; 420
And move her tender Mind, by slow degrees,
To suffer what the Sov'raign Pow'r decrees:
Jove will inspire him, when, and what to say:
They hear with Pleasure, and with haste obey.

But soon the Queen perceives the thin Disguise; 425
(What Arts can blind a jealous Woman's Eyes!)
She was the first to find the secret Fraud,

420 News;] News. *97 98*

Before the fatal News was blaz'd abroad.
Love, the first Motions of the Lover hears,
Quick to presage, and ev'n in Safety fears.   430
Nor impious Fame was wanting to report
The Ships repair'd; the *Trojans* thick Resort,   }
And purpose to forsake the *Tyrian* Court.
Frantick with Fear, impatient of the Wound,
And impotent of Mind, she roves the City round.   435
Less wild the *Bacchanalian* Dames appear,   }
When, from afar, their nightly God they hear,
And houl about the Hills, and shake the wreathy Spear. }
At length she finds the dear perfidious Man;
Prevents his form'd Excuse, and thus began.   440
Base and ungrateful, cou'd you hope to fly,
And undiscover'd scape a Lover's Eye!
Nor cou'd my Kindness your Compassion move,
Nor plighted Vows, nor dearer bands of Love!
Or is the Death of a despairing Queen   445
Not worth preventing, though too well foreseen?
Ev'n when the Wint'ry Winds command your stay,
You dare the Tempests, and defie the Sea.
False, as you are, suppose you were not bound
To Lands unknown, and foreign Coasts to sound;   450
Were *Troy* restor'd, and *Priam*'s happy Reign,
Now durst you tempt for *Troy*, the raging Main?
See, whom you fly; am I the Foe you shun?
Now by those holy Vows, so late begun,
By this right Hand, (since I have nothing more   455
To challenge, but the Faith you gave before;)
I beg you by these Tears too truly shed,
By the new Pleasures of our Nuptial Bed;
If ever *Dido*, when you most were kind,
Were pleasing in your Eyes, or touch'd your Mind;   460
By these my Pray'rs, if Pray'rs may yet have Place,
Pity the Fortunes of a falling Race.
For you I have provok'd a Tyrant's Hate,
Incens'd the *Lybian*, and the *Tyrian* State;
For you alone I suffer in my Fame;   465
Bereft of Honour, and expos'd to Shame:

447 Ev'n *98*: Even *97*

Whom have I now to trust, (ungrateful Guest,)
That only Name remains of all the rest!
What have I left, or whither can I fly;
Must I attend *Pygmalion*'s Cruelty! 470
Or till *Hyarba* shall in Triumph lead
A Queen, that proudly scorn'd his proffer'd Bed!
Had you deferr'd, at least, your hasty Flight,
And left behind some Pledge of our delight,
Some Babe to bless the Mother's mournful sight; 475
Some young *Æneas*, to supply your place;
Whose Features might express his Father's Face;
I should not then complain to live bereft
Of all my Husband, or be wholly left.

   Here paus'd the Queen; unmov'd he holds his Eyes, 480
By *Jove*'s Command; nor suffer'd Love to rise,
Tho' heaving in his Heart; and thus at length, replies.
Fair Queen, you never can enough repeat
Your boundless Favours, or I own my Debt;
Nor can my Mind forget *Eliza*'s Name, 485
While vital Breath inspires this Mortal Frame.
This, only let me speak in my Defence,
I never hop'd a secret Flight from hence:
Much less pretended to the Lawful Claim
Of Sacred Nuptials, or, a Husband's Name. 490
For if indulgent Heav'n would leave me free,
And not submit my Life to Fate's Decree,
My Choice would lead me to the *Trojan* Shore,
Those Reliques to review, their Dust adore;
And *Priam*'s ruin'd Palace to restore. 495
But now the *Delphian Oracle* Commands,
And Fate invites me to the *Latian* Lands.
That is the promis'd Place to which I steer,
And all my Vows are terminated there.
If you, a *Tyrian*, and a Stranger born, 500
With Walls and Tow'rs a *Lybian* Town adorn;
Why may not we, like you, a Foreign Race,
Like you seek shelter in a Foreign Place?
As often as the Night obscures the Skies
With humid Shades, or twinkling Stars arise, 505
Anchises angry Ghost in Dreams appears;

Chides my delay, and fills my Soul with fears:
And young *Ascanius* justly may complain,
Of his defrauded Fate, and destin'd Reign.
Ev'n now the Herald of the Gods appear'd,   51
Waking I saw him, and his Message heard.
From *Jove* he came commission'd, Heav'nly bright
With Radiant Beams, and manifest to Sight.
The Sender and the Sent, I both attest,
These Walls he enter'd, and those Words express'd.   51
Fair Queen, oppose not what the Gods command;
Forc'd by my Fate, I leave your happy Land.

Thus, while he spoke, already She began,
With sparkling Eyes, to view the guilty Man:
From Head to Foot survey'd his Person o're,   52
Nor longer these outrageous Threats forbore.
False as thou art, and more than false, forsworn;
Not sprung from Noble Blood, nor Goddess-born,
But hewn from hardned Entrails of a Rock;
And rough *Hyrcanian* Tygers gave thee suck.   52
Why shou'd I fawn, what have I worse to fear?
Did he once look, or lent a list'ning Ear;
Sigh'd when I sob'd, or shed one kindly Tear?
All Symptoms of a base Ungrateful Mind,
So foul, that which is worse, 'tis hard to find.   530
Of Man's Injustice, why shou'd I complain?
The Gods, and *Jove* himself behold in vain
Triumphant Treason, yet no Thunder flyes:
Nor *Juno* views my Wrongs with equal Eyes;
Faithless is Earth, and Faithless are the Skies!   535
Justice is fled, and Truth is now no more;
I sav'd the Shipwrack'd Exile on my Shore:
With needful Food his hungry *Trojans* fed;
I took the Traytor to my Throne and Bed:
Fool that I was—'tis little to repeat   540
The rest, I stor'd and Rigg'd his ruin'd Fleet.
I rave, I rave: A God's Command he pleads,
And makes Heav'n accessary to his Deeds.
Now *Lycian* Lotts, and now the *Delian* God;
Now *Hermes* is employ'd from *Jove's* abode,   545
To warn him hence; as if the peaceful State

Of Heav'nly Pow'rs were touch'd with Humane Fate!
But go; thy flight no longer I detain;
Go seek thy promis'd Kingdom through the Main:
Yet if the Heav'ns will hear my Pious Vow,   550
The faithless Waves, not half so false as thou,
Or secret Sands, shall Sepulchers afford
To thy proud Vessels, and their perjur'd Lord.
Then shalt thou call on injur'd *Dido*'s Name;
Dido shall come, in a black Sulph'ry flame;   555
When death has once dissolv'd her Mortal frame.
Shall smile to see the Traitor vainly weep,
Her angry Ghost arising from the Deep,
Shall haunt thee waking, and disturb thy Sleep.
At least my Shade thy Punishment shall know;   560
And Fame shall spread the pleasing News below.
   Abruptly here she stops: Then turns away
Her loathing Eyes, and shuns the sight of Day.
Amaz'd he stood, revolving in his Mind
What Speech to frame, and what Excuse to find.   565
Her fearful Maids their fainting Mistress led;
And softly laid her on her Iv'ry Bed.
   But good *Æneas*, tho' he much desir'd
To give that Pity, which her Grief requir'd,
Tho' much he mourn'd, and labour'd with his Love,   570
Resolv'd at length, obeys the Will of *Jove*:
Reviews his Forces; they with early Care
Unmoor their Vessels, and for Sea prepare.
The Fleet is soon afloat, in all its Pride:
And well calk'd Gallies in the Harbour ride.   575
Then Oaks for Oars they fell'd; or as they stood,
Of its green Arms despoil'd the growing Wood,
Studious of Flight: The Beach is cover'd o're
With *Trojan* Bands that blacken all the Shore:
On ev'ry side are seen, descending down,   580
Thick swarms of Souldiers loaden from the Town.
Thus, in Battalia, march embody'd Ants,
Fearful of Winter, and of future Wants,
T' invade the Corn, and to their Cells convey
The plunder'd Forrage of their yellow Prey.   585

    551 thou,] thou; *97 98*   577 Wood,] Wood. *97 98*

The sable Troops, along the narrow Tracks,
Scarce bear the weighty Burthen on their Backs:
Some set their Shoulders to the pond'rous Grain;
Some guard the Spoil, some lash the lagging Train;
All ply their sev'ral Tasks, and equal Toil sustain.   590

What Pangs the tender Breast of *Dido* tore,
When, from the Tow'r, she saw the cover'd Shore,
And heard the Shouts of Sailors from afar,
Mix'd with the Murmurs of the wat'ry War?
All pow'rful Love, what Changes canst thou cause   595
In Human Hearts, subjected to thy Laws!
Once more her haughty Soul the Tyrant bends;
To Pray'rs and mean Submissions she descends.
No female Arts or Aids she left untry'd,
Nor Counsels unexplor'd, before she dy'd.   600
Look, *Anna*, look; the *Trojans* crowd to Sea,
They spread their Canvass, and their Anchors weigh.
The shouting Crew, their Ships with Garlands bind;
Invoke the Sea-Gods, and invite the Wind.
Cou'd I have thought this threatning Blow so near,   605
My tender Soul had been forewarn'd to bear.
But do not you my last Request deny,
With yon perfidious Man your Int'rest try;
And bring me News, if I must live or dye.
You are his Fav'rite, you alone can find   610
The dark recesses of his inmost Mind:
In all his trusted Secrets you have part,
And know the soft Approaches to his Heart.
Haste then, and humbly seek my haughty Foe;
Tell him, I did not with the *Grecians* goe;   615
Nor did my Fleet against his Friends employ,
Nor swore the Ruin of unhappy *Troy*.
Nor mov'd with Hands prophane his Father's Dust;
Why shou'd he then reject a suit so just!
Whom does he shun, and whither would he fly;   620
Can he this last, this only Pray'r deny!
Let him at least his dang'rous Flight delay,
Wait better Winds, and hope a calmer Sea.
The Nuptials he disclaims I urge no more;

591 *Editor's paragraph*   603 bind *98*: binds *97*   604 Wind *98*: Winds *97*

Let him pursue the promis'd *Latian* Shore.   625
A short delay is all I ask him now,
A pause of Grief; an interval from Woe:
'Till my soft Soul be temper'd to sustain
Accustom'd Sorrows, and inur'd to Pain.
If you in Pity grant this one Request,   630
My Death shall glut the Hatred of his Brest.
This mournful message, Pious *Anna* bears,
And seconds, with her own, her Sister's Tears:
But all her Arts are still employ'd in vain;
Again she comes, and is refus'd again.   635
His harden'd Heart nor Pray'rs nor Threatnings move;
Fate, and the God, had stop'd his Ears to Love.

   As when the Winds their airy Quarrel try;
Justling from ev'ry quarter of the Sky;
This way and that, the Mountain Oak they bend,   640
His Boughs they shatter, and his Branches rend;
With Leaves, and falling Mast, they spread the Ground,
The hollow Vallies echo to the Sound:
Unmov'd, the Royal Plant their Fury mocks;
Or shaken, clings more closely to the Rocks: 645
Far as he shoots his tow'ring Head on high,
So deep in Earth his fix'd Foundations lye.
No less a Storm the *Trojan* Heroe bears;
Thick Messages and loud Complaints he hears;
And bandy'd Words, still beating on his Ears.   650
Sighs, Groans and Tears, proclaim his inward Pains,
But the firm purpose of his Heart remains.

   The wretched Queen, pursu'd by cruel Fate,
Begins at length the light of Heav'n to hate:
And loaths to live: Then dire Portents she sees,   655
To hasten on the Death her Soul decrees.
Strange to relate: for when before the Shrine
She pours, in Sacrifice, the Purple Wine,
The Purple Wine is turn'd to putrid Blood:
And the white offer'd Milk, converts to Mud.   660
This dire Presage, to her alone reveal'd,
From all, and ev'n her Sister, she conceal'd.

---

631 glut the Hatred of his Brest. *98:* leave you of my Crown possess'd. *97. See Commentary*

A Marble Temple stood within the Grove,
Sacred to Death, and to her murther'd Love;
That honour'd Chappel she had hung around
With snowy Fleeces, and with Garlands crown'd:
Oft, when she visited this lonely Dome,
Strange Voices issu'd from her Husband's Tomb:
She thought she heard him summon her away;
Invite her to his Grave; and chide her stay.
Hourly 'tis heard, when with a bodeing Note
The solitary Screech-Owl strains her Throat:
And on a Chimney's top, or Turret's hight,
With Songs obscene, disturbs the Silence of the Night.
Besides, old Prophesies augment her Fears;
And stern *Æneas* in her Dreams appears,
Disdainful as by Day: She seems alone,
To wander in her Sleep, thro ways unknown,
Guidless and dark: or, in a Desart Plain,
To seek her Subjects, and to seek in vain.
Like *Pentheus*, when distracted with his Fear,
He saw two Suns, and double *Thebes* appear:
Or mad *Orestes*, when his Mother's Ghost
Full in his Face, infernal Torches tost;
And shook her snaky locks: He shuns the sight,
Flies o're the Stage, surpris'd with mortal fright;
The Furies guard the Door; and intercept his flight.
    Now, sinking underneath a load of Grief,
From Death alone, she seeks her last Relief:
The Time and Means, resolv'd within her Breast,
She to her mournful Sister, thus address'd.
(Dissembling hope, her cloudy front she clears,
And a false Vigour in her Eyes appears.)
Rejoice she said, instructed from above,
My Lover I shall gain, or lose my Love.
Nigh rising *Atlas*, next the falling Sun,
Long tracts of *Ethiopian* Clymates run:
There, a *Massylian* Priestess I have found,
Honour'd for Age; for Magick Arts renown'd:
Th' *Hesperian* Temple was her trusted Care;
'Twas she supply'd the wakeful Dragons Fare.
She Poppy-Seeds in Honey taught to steep;

Reclaim'd his Rage; and sooth'd him into sleep.
She watch'd the Golden Fruit; her Charms unbind
The Chains of Love; or fix them on the Mind.   705
She stops the Torrents, leaves the Channel dry;
Repels the Stars; and backward bears the Sky.
The yawning Earth rebellows to her Call;
Pale Ghosts ascend; and Mountain Ashes fall.
Witness, ye Gods, and thou my better part,   710
How loth I am to try this impious Art!
Within the secret Court, with silent Care,
Erect a lofty Pile, expos'd in Air:
Hang on the topmost part, the *Trojan* Vest;
Spoils, Arms, and Presents of my faithless Guest.   715
Next, under these, the bridal Bed be plac'd,
Where I my Ruin in his Arms embrac'd:
All Relicks of the Wretch are doom'd to Fire;
For so the Priestess, and her Charms require.
Thus far she said, and farther Speech forbears: 720
A Mortal Paleness in her Face appears:
Yet, the mistrustless *Anna*, could not find   ⎫
The secret Fun'ral, in these Rites design'd;   ⎬
Nor thought so dire a Rage possess'd her Mind. ⎭
Unknowing of a Train conceal'd so well,   725
She fear'd no worse than when *Sichæus* fell:
Therefore obeys. The fatal Pile they rear,
Within the secret Court, expos'd in Air.
The cloven Holms and Pines are heap'd on high;
And Garlands on the hollow Spaces lye.   730
Sad Cypress, Vervain, Eugh, compose the Wreath;
And ev'ry baleful green denoting Death.
The Queen, determin'd to the fatal Deed,   ⎫
The Spoils and Sword he left, in order spread: ⎬ 735
And the Man's Image on the Nuptial Bed.   ⎭
   And now (the sacred Altars plac'd around)   ⎫
The Priestess enters, with her Hair unbound,   ⎬
And thrice invokes the Pow'rs below the Ground. ⎭
Night, *Erebus*, and *Chaos* she proclaims,
And threefold *Hecat*, with her hundred Names,   740
And three *Diana's*: next she sprinkles round,
With feign'd *Avernian* Drops, the hallow'd ground;

Culls hoary Simples, found by *Phœbe*'s Light,
With brazen Sickles reap'd at Noon of Night.
Then mixes baleful Juices in the Bowl: 74
And cuts the Forehead of a new-born Fole;
Robbing the Mother's love. The destin'd Queen
Observes, assisting at the Rites obscene:
A leaven'd Cake in her devoted Hands
She holds, and next the highest Altar stands: 7
One tender Foot was shod, her other bare;
Girt was her gather'd Gown, and loose her Hair.
Thus dress'd, she summon'd with her dying Breath,
The Heav'ns and Planets conscious of her Death:
And ev'ry Pow'r, if any rules above,   7
Who minds, or who revenges injur'd Love.

'Twas dead of Night, when weary Bodies close
Their Eyes in balmy Sleep, and soft Repose:
The Winds no longer whisper through the Woods,
Nor murm'ring Tides disturb the gentle Floods.   7
The Stars in silent order mov'd around,
And Peace, with downy wings, was brooding on the ground.
The Flocks and Herds, and parti-colour'd Fowl,
Which haunt the Woods, or swim the weedy Pool;
Stretch'd on the quiet Earth securely lay,   7
Forgetting the past Labours of the day.
All else of Nature's common Gift partake;
Unhappy *Dido* was alone awake.
Nor Sleep nor Ease the Furious Queen can find,
Sleep fled her Eyes, as Quiet fled her mind.   7
Despair, and Rage, and Love, divide her heart;
Despair and Rage had some, but Love the greater part.

Then thus she said within her secret Mind:
What shall I do, what Succour can I find!
Become a Supplyant to *Hyarba*'s Pride,   7
And take my turn, to Court and be deny'd!
Shall I with this ungrateful *Trojan* go,
Forsake an Empire, and attend a Foe?
Himself I refug'd, and his Train reliev'd;
Tis true; but am I sure to be receiv'd?   7
Can Gratitude in *Trojan* Souls have place!

After 780 97 has An Exile follows whom a Queen reliev'd!*: om. 98*

Laomedon still lives in all his Race!
Then, shall I seek alone the Churlish Crew,
Or with my Fleet their flying Sails pursue?
What force have I but those, whom scarce before   785
I drew reluctant from their Native Shore?
Will they again Embark at my desire,
Once more sustain the Seas, and quit their second *Tyre*?
Rather with Steel thy guilty Breast invade,
And take the Fortune thou thy self hast made.   790
Your pity, Sister, first seduc'd my Mind;
Or seconded too well, what I design'd.
These dear-bought Pleasures had I never known,
Had I continu'd free, and still my own;
Avoiding Love; I had not found Despair: 795
But shar'd with Salvage Beasts the Common Air.
Like them a lonely life I might have led,
Not mourn'd the Living, nor disturb'd the Dead.
These Thoughts she brooded in her anxious Breast;
On Boord, the *Trojan* found more easie rest.   800
Resolv'd to sail, in Sleep he pass'd the Night;
And order'd all things for his early flight.

    To whom once more the winged God appears;
His former Youthful Meen and Shape he wears,
And with this new alarm invades his Ears.   805
Sleep'st thou, O Goddess born! and can'st thou drown
Thy needful Cares, so near a Hostile Town?
Beset with Foes; nor hear'st the Western Gales
Invite thy passage, and Inspire thy sails?
She harbours in her Heart a furious hate;   810
And thou shalt find the dire Effects too late;
Fix'd on Revenge, and Obstinate to die:
Haste swiftly hence, while thou hast pow'r to fly.
The Sea with Ships will soon be cover'd o're,
And blazing Firebrands kindle all the Shore.   815
Prevent her rage, while Night obscures the Skies;
And sail before the purple Morn arise.
Who knows what Hazards thy Delay may bring?
Woman's a various and a changeful Thing.
Thus *Hermes* in the Dream; then took his flight,   820
Aloft in Air unseen; and mix'd with Night.

Twice warn'd by the Cœlestial Messenger,
The pious Prince arose with hasty fear:
Then rowz'd his drowsie Train without delay,
Haste to your banks; your crooked Anchors weigh;
And spread your flying Sails, and stand to Sea.
A God commands; he stood before my sight;
And urg'd us once again to speedy flight.
O sacred Pow'r, what Pow'r so e're thou art,
To thy bless'd Orders I resign my heart:
Lead thou the way; protect thy *Trojan* Bands;
And prosper the Design thy Will Commands.
He said, and drawing forth his flaming Sword,
His thund'ring Arm divides the many twisted Cord:
An emulating Zeal inspires his Train;
They run, they snatch; they rush into the main.
With headlong haste they leave the desert Shores,
And brush the liquid Seas with lab'ring Oars.
   Aurora now had left her Saffron Bed,
And beams of early Light the Heav'ns o'respread,
When from a Tow'r the Queen, with wakeful Eyes,
Saw Day point upward from the rosie Skies:
She look'd to Seaward, but the Sea was void,
And scarce in ken the sailing Ships descry'd:
Stung with despight, and furious with despair,
She struck her trembling Breast, and tore her Hair.
And shall th' ungrateful Traytor go, she said,
My Land forsaken, and my Love betray'd?
Shall we not Arm, not rush from ev'ry Street,
To follow, sink, and burn his perjur'd Fleet?
Haste, haul my Gallies out, pursue the Foe:
Bring flaming Brands, set sail, and swiftly row.
What have I said? where am I? Fury turns
My Brain; and my distemper'd Bosom burns.
Then, when I gave my Person and my Throne,
This Hate, this Rage, had been more timely shown.
See now the promis'd Faith, the vaunted Name,
The Pious Man, who, rushing through the Flame,
Preserv'd his Gods; and to the *Phrygian* Shore
The Burthen of his feeble Father bore!

I shou'd have torn him piecemeal; strow'd in Floods
His scatter'd Limbs, or left expos'd in Woods:
Destroy'd his Friends and Son; and from the Fire
Have set the reeking Boy before the Sire.
Events are doubtful, which on Battels wait;   865
Yet where 's the doubt, to Souls secure of Fate!
My *Tyrians*, at their injur'd Queen's Command,
Had toss'd their Fires amid the *Trojan* Band:
At once extinguish'd all the faithless Name;
And I my self, in vengeance of my Shame,   870
Had fall'n upon the Pile to mend the Fun'ral Flame.
Thou Sun, who view'st at once the World below,
Thou *Juno*, Guardian of the Nuptial Vow,
Thou *Hecat*, hearken from thy dark abodes;
Ye Furies, Fiends, and violated Gods,   875
All Pow'rs invok'd with *Dido*'s dying breath,
Attend her Curses, and avenge her death.
If so the Fates ordain, and *Jove* commands,
Th' ungrateful Wretch should find the *Latian* Lands,
Yet let a Race untam'd, and haughty Foes,   880
His peaceful Entrance with dire Arms oppose;
Oppress'd with Numbers in th' unequal Field,
His Men discourag'd, and himself expell'd,
Let him for Succour sue from place to place,
Torn from his Subjects, and his Son's embrace: 885
First let him see his Friends in Battel slain;
And their untimely Fate lament in vain:
And when, at length, the cruell War shall cease;
On hard Conditions may he buy his Peace.
Nor let him then enjoy supreme Command;   890
But fall untimely, by some hostile Hand:
And lye unbury'd on the barren Sand.
These are my Pray'rs, and this my dying Will:
And you my *Tyrians* ev'ry Curse fulfill.
Perpetual Hate, and mortal Wars proclaim,   895
Against the Prince, the People, and the Name.
These grateful Off'rings on my Grave bestow;
Nor League, nor Love, the Hostile Nations know:
Now, and from hence in ev'ry future Age,

898 Hostile *98*: jarring *97*

When Rage excites your Arms, and Strength supplies the Rage: 90
Rise some Avenger of our *Lybian* Blood,
With Fire and Sword pursue the perjur'd Brood:
Our Arms, our Seas, our Shores, oppos'd to theirs,
And the same hate descend on all our Heirs.

This said, within her anxious Mind she weighs 90
The Means of cutting short her odious Days.
Then to *Sicheus* Nurse, she briefly said,
(For when she left her Country, hers was dead)
Go *Barcè*, call my Sister; let her Care
The solemn Rites of Sacrifice prepare: 9
The Sheep, and all th' attoneing Off'rings bring;
Sprinkling her Body from the Crystal Spring
With living Drops: then let her come, and thou
With sacred Fillets, bind thy hoary Brow.
Thus will I pay my Vows, to *Stygian Jove*; 9
And end the Cares of my disastrous Love.
Then cast the *Trojan* Image on the Fire;
And as that burns, my Passion shall expire.

The Nurse moves onward, with officious Care,
And all the speed her aged Limbs can bear. 9
But furious *Dido*, with dark Thoughts involv'd,
Shook at the mighty Mischief she resolv'd.
With livid Spots distinguish'd was her Face,
Red were her rowling Eyes, and discompos'd her Pace:
Ghastly she gaz'd, with Pain she drew her Breath, 9
And Nature shiver'd at approaching Death.

Then swiftly to the fatal place she pass'd;
And mounts the Fun'ral Pile, with furious haste.
Unsheaths the Sword the *Trojan* left behind,
(Not for so dire an Enterprise design'd,) 9
But when she view'd the Garments loosely spred,
Which once he wore, and saw the conscious Bed,
She paus'd, and, with a Sigh, the Robes embrac'd;
Then on the Couch her trembling Body cast,
Repress'd the ready Tears, and spoke her last. 9
Dear Pledges of my Love, while Heav'n so pleas'd,
Receive a Soul, of Mortal Anguish eas'd:
My fatal Course is finish'd; and I go

907 *Sicheus*] *Sicheus's* 97 98

A glorious Name, among the Ghosts below.
A lofty City by my Hands is rais'd;   940
Pygmalion punish'd, and my Lord appeas'd.
What cou'd my Fortune have afforded more,
Had the false *Trojan* never touch'd my Shore!
Then kiss'd the Couch; and must I die, she said;
And unreveng'd; 'tis doubly to be dead!   945
Yet ev'n this Death with Pleasure I receive;
On any Terms, 'tis better than to live.
These Flames, from far, may the false *Trojan* view;
These boding Omens his base flight pursue.
She said, and struck: Deep enter'd in her side   950
The piercing Steel, with reeking Purple dy'd:
Clog'd in the Wound the cruel Weapon stands;
The spouting Blood came streaming on her Hands.
Her sad Attendants saw the deadly Stroke,
And with loud Cries the sounding Palace shook.   955
Distracted from the fatal sight they fled;
And thro the Town the dismal Rumor spread.
First from the frighted Court, the Yell began,
Redoubled thence from House to House it ran:
The groans of Men, with Shrieks, Laments, and Cries   960
Of mixing Women, mount the vaulted Skies.
Not less the Clamour, than if ancient *Tyre*,
Or the new *Carthage*, set by Foes on Fire,
The rowling Ruin, with their lov'd Abodes,
Involv'd the blazing Temples of their Gods.   965
Her Sister hears, and, furious with Despair,
She beats her Breast, and rends her yellow Hair:
And calling on *Eliza*'s Name aloud,
Runs breathless to the Place, and breaks the Crowd.
Was all that Pomp of Woe for this prepar'd,   970
These Fires, this Fun'ral Pile, these Altars rear'd;
Was all this Train of Plots contriv'd, said she,
All only to deceive unhappy me?
Which is the worst, didst thou in Death pretend
To scorn thy Sister, or delude thy Friend!   975
Thy summon'd Sister, and thy Friend had come:
One Sword had serv'd us both, one common Tomb.
Was I to raise the Pile, the Pow'rs invoke,

Not to be present at the fatal Stroke?
At once thou hast destroy'd thy self and me;　　9⸱
Thy Town, thy Senate, and thy Colony!
Bring Water, bathe the Wound; while I in death
Lay close my Lips to hers; and catch the flying Breath.
This said, she mounts the Pile with eager haste;
And in her Arms the gasping Queen embrac'd:　　9⸱
Her Temples chaf'd; and her own Garments tore
To stanch the streaming Blood, and cleanse the Gore.
Thrice *Dido* try'd to raise her drooping Head,
And fainting thrice, fell grov'ling on the Bed.
Thrice op'd her heavy Eyes, and sought the Light, ⎫
But having found it, sicken'd at the sight; 　　⎬ 9⸱
And clos'd her Lids at last, in endless Night. 　⎭

　　Then *Juno*, grieving that she shou'd sustain
A Death so ling'ring, and so full of Pain;
Sent *Iris* down, to free her from the Strife　　9⸱
Of lab'ring Nature, and dissolve her Life.
For since she dy'd, not doom'd by Heav'ns Decree,
Or her own Crime; but Human Casualty;
And rage of Love, that plung'd her in Despair;
The Sisters had not cut the topmost Hair;　　1⸱
Which *Proserpine*, and they can only know;
Nor made her sacred to the Shades below.
Downward the various Goddess took her flight;
And drew a thousand Colours from the Light:
Then stood above the dying Lover's Head,　　1⸱
And said, I thus devote thee to the dead.
This Off'ring to th' Infernal Gods I bear: 　　⎫
Thus while she spoke, she cut the fatal Hair; 　⎬
The strugling Soul was loos'd; and Life dissolv'd in Air. ⎭

THE FIFTH BOOK OF THE ÆNEIS

THE ARGUMENT

Æneas setting sail from Africk, *is driven by a Storm on the Coasts of* Sicily:
Where he is hospitably receiv'd by his friend Acestes, *King of part of the*

Island, and born of Trojan *Parentage. He applies himself to celebrate the*
Memory of his Father with Divine Honours: And accordingly institutes
Funeral Games, and appoints Prizes for those who shou'd conquer in them. 5
While the Ceremonies were performing, Juno *sends* Iris *to perswade the* Trojan
Women to burn the Ships, who upon her instigation set fire to them, which
burnt four, and would have consum'd the rest, had not Jupiter *by a miraculous*
Shower extinguish'd it. Upon this Æneas *by the advice of one of his Generals,*
and a Vision of his Father, builds a City for the Women, Old Men, and others, 10
who were either unfit for War, or weary of the Voyage, and sails for Italy:
Venus *procures of* Neptune *a safe Voyage for him and all his Men, excepting*
only his Pilot Palinurus, *who is unfortunately lost.*

M EAN TIME the *Trojan* cuts his wat'ry way,
　　Fix'd on his Voyage, thro' the curling Sea:
Then, casting back his Eyes, with dire Amaze,
Sees on the *Punic* Shore the mounting Blaze.
The Cause unknown; yet his presaging Mind,　　　　　　　5
The Fate of *Dido* from the Fire divin'd:
He knew the stormy Souls of Woman-kind:
What secret Springs their eager Passions move,
How capable of Death for injur'd Love.
Dire Auguries from hence the *Trojans* draw;　　　　　　10
'Till neither Fires, nor shining Shores they saw.
Now Seas and Skies, their Prospect only bound;
An empty space above, a floating Field around.
But soon the Heav'ns with shadows were o'respread;
A swelling Cloud hung hov'ring o're their Head:　　　　15
Livid it look'd, (the threatning of a Storm;)
Then Night and Horror Ocean's Face deform.
The Pilot, *Palinurus*, cry'd aloud,
What Gusts of Weather from that gath'ring Cloud
My Thoughts presage; e're yet the Tempest roars,　　　20
Stand to your Tackle, Mates, and stretch your Oars;
Contract your swelling Sails, and luff to Wind:
The frighted Crew perform the Task assign'd.
Then, to his fearless Chief, not Heav'n, said he,
Tho *Jove* himself shou'd promise *Italy*,　　　　　　　25
Can stem the Torrent of this raging Sea.

The Fifth Book. The Argument. 13 *is 98: was 97*

Mark how the shifting Winds from West arise,
And what collected Night involves the Skies!
Nor can our shaken Vessels live at Sea,
Much less against the Tempest force their way;   } 30
'Tis Fate diverts our Course; and Fate we must obey.
Not far from hence, if I observ'd aright
The southing of the Stars, and Polar Light,
Sicilia lies; whose hospitable Shores
In safety we may reach with strugling Oars.   35
Æneas then reply'd, too sure I find,
We strive in vain against the Seas, and Wind:
Now shift your Sails: What place can please me more
Than what you promise, the *Sicilian* Shore;
Whose hallow'd Earth *Anchises* Bones contains,   40
And where a Prince of *Trojan* Lineage reigns?
The Course resolv'd, before the Western Wind
They scud amain; and make the Port assign'd.

   Mean time *Acestes*, from a lofty Stand,
Beheld the Fleet descending on the Land;   45
And not unmindful of his ancient Race,
Down from the Cliff he ran with eager Pace;   }
And held the Heroe in a strict Embrace.
Of a rough *Lybian* Bear the Spoils he wore;
And either Hand a pointed Jav'lin bore.   50
His Mother was a Dame of *Dardan* Blood;
His Sire *Crinisus*, a *Sicilian* Flood;
He welcomes his returning Friends ashore
With plenteous Country Cates; and homely Store.

   Now, when the following Morn had chas'd away   55
The flying Stars, and light restor'd the Day,
Æneas call'd the *Trojan* Troops around;
And thus bespoke them from a rising Ground.
Off-spring of Heav'n, Divine *Dardanian* Race,
The Sun revolving thro' th' Etherial Space,   60
The shining Circle of the Year has fill'd,
Since first this Isle my Father's Ashes held:
And now the rising Day renews the Year,
(A Day for ever sad, for ever dear,)
This wou'd I celebrate with Annual Games,   65
With Gifts on Altars pil'd, and holy Flames,

Tho banish'd to *Getulia*'s barren Sands,
Caught on the *Grecian* Seas, or hostile Lands:
But since this happy Storm our Fleet has driv'n,
(Not, as I deem, without the Will of Heav'n,)   70
Upon these friendly Shores, and flow'ry Plains,
Which hide *Anchises*, and his blest Remains;
Let us with Joy perform his Honours due;
And pray for prosp'rous Winds, our Voyage to renew.
Pray, that in Towns, and Temples of our own,   75
The Name of great *Anchises* may be known;
And yearly Games may spread the Gods renown.
Our Sports, *Acestes* of the *Trojan* Race,
With royal Gifts, ordain'd, is pleas'd to grace:
Two Steers on ev'ry Ship the King bestows;   80
His Gods and ours, shall share your equal Vows.
Besides, if nine days hence, the rosy Morn
Shall with unclouded Light the Skies adorn,
That Day with solemn Sports I mean to grace;
Light Gallies on the Seas, shall run a wat'ry Race.   85
Some shall in Swiftness for the Goal contend,
And others try the twanging Bow to bend:
The strong with Iron Gauntlets arm'd shall stand,
Oppos'd in Combat on the yellow Sand.
Let all be present at the Games prepar'd;   90
And joyful Victors wait the Just Reward.
But now assist the Rites, with Garlands crown'd;
He said, and first his Brows with Myrtle bound.
Then *Helymus*, by his Example led,
And old *Acestes*, each adorn'd his Head;   95
Thus, young *Ascanius*, with a sprightly Grace,
His Temples ty'd, and all the *Trojan* Race.
    Æneas then advanc'd amidst the Train,
By thousands follow'd thro' the flowry Plain,
To great *Anchises* Tomb: Which when he found,   100
He pour'd to *Bacchus*, on the hallow'd Ground,
Two Bowls of sparkling Wine, of Milk two more,
And two from offer'd Bulls of Purple Gore.
With Roses then the Sepulchre he strow'd;
And thus, his Father's Ghost bespoke aloud.   105

99 flowry 9 8: fruitful 97

Hail, O ye Holy Manes; hail again
Paternal Ashes, now review'd in vain!
The Gods permitted not, that you, with me,
Shou'd reach the promis'd Shores of *Italy*;
Or *Tiber's* Flood, what Flood so e're it be.   ⎫ 11
Scarce had he finish'd, when, with speckled Pride,
A Serpent from the Tomb began to glide;
His hugy Bulk on sev'n high Volumes roll'd;
Blue was his breadth of Back, but streak'd with scaly Gold:
Thus riding on his Curls, he seem'd to pass   11
A rowling Fire along; and singe the Grass.
More various Colours thro' his Body run,
Than *Iris* when her Bow imbibes the Sun;
Betwixt the rising Altars, and around,
The sacred Monster shot along the Ground;   12
With harmless play amidst the Bowls he pass'd;
And with his lolling Tongue assay'd the Taste:
Thus fed with Holy Food, the wond'rous Guest
Within the hollow Tomb retir'd to rest.
The Pious Prince, surpris'd at what he view'd,   12
The Fun'ral Honours with more Zeal renew'd:
Doubtful if this the Place's Genius were,
Or Guardian of his Father's Sepulchre.
Five Sheep, according to the Rites, he slew;
As many Swine, and Steers of sable Hue;   130
New gen'rous Wine he from the Goblets pour'd,
And call'd his Fathers Ghost, from Hell restor'd.
The glad Attendants in long Order come,
Off'ring their Gifts at great *Anchises* Tomb:
Some add more Oxen, some divide the Spoil,   ⎫ 13
Some place the Chargers on the grassy Soil;   ⎬
Some blow the Fires and offer'd Entrails broil.   ⎭
    Now came the Day desir'd; the Skies were bright
With rosy Lustre of the rising Light:
The bord'ring People, rowz'd by sounding Fame   140
Of *Trojan* Feasts, and great *Acestes* Name;
The crowded Shore with Acclamations fill,
Part to behold, and part to prove their Skill.
And first the Gifts in Publick view they place,
Green Lawrel Wreaths, and Palm, (the Victors grace:) 145

Within the Circle, Arms and Tripods lye; ⎫
Ingotts of Gold, and Silver, heap'd on high; ⎬
And Vests embroider'd of the *Tyrian* dye. ⎭
The Trumpet's clangor then the Feast proclaims;
And all prepare for their appointed Games.   150
Four Gallies first, which equal Rowers bear,
Advancing, in the wat'ry Lists appear.
The speedy *Dolphin*, that out-strips the Wind,
Bore *Mnestheus*, Author of the *Memmian* kind:
Gyas, the vast *Chymæra*'s Bulk commands,   155
Which rising like a tow'ring City stands:
Three *Trojans* tug at ev'ry lab'ring Oar; ⎫
Three Banks in three degrees the Sailors bore; ⎬
Beneath their sturdy Stroaks the Billows roar. ⎭
Sergesthus, who began the *Sergian* Race,   160
In the great *Centaur* took the leading Place:
Cloanthus on the Sea-green *Scylla* stood;
From whom *Cluentius* draws his *Trojan* Blood.
    Far in the Sea, against the foaming Shoar,
There stands a Rock; the raging Billows roar   165
Above his Head in Storms; but when 'tis clear,
Uncurl their ridgy Backs, and at his Foot appear.
In Peace below the gentle Waters run;
The Cormorants above, lye basking in the Sun.
On this the Heroe fix'd an Oak in sight,   170
The mark to guide the Mariners aright.
To bear with this, the Seamen stretch their Oars;
Then round the Rock they steer, and seek the former Shoars.
The Lots decide their place; above the rest,
Each Leader shining in his *Tyrian* Vest: 175
The common Crew, with Wreaths of Poplar Boughs,
Their Temples crown, and shade their sweaty Brows.
Besmear'd with Oil, their naked Shoulders shine;
All take their Seats, and wait the sounding sign.
They gripe their Oars, and ev'ry panting Breast   180
Is rais'd by turns with Hope, by turns with Fear depress'd.
The clangor of the Trumpet gives the Sign;
At once they start, advancing in a Line:

153 et passim *Dolphin*] Dolphin *97 98*

With shouts the Sailors rend the starry Skys,
Lash'd with their Oars, the smoaky Billows rise;   18
Sparkles the briny Main, and the vex'd Ocean fries.

Exact in time, with equal Strokes they row;
At once the brushing Oars, and brazen prow
Dash up the sandy Waves, and ope the Depths below.

Not fiery Coursers, in a Chariot Race,   19
Invade the Field with half so swift a Pace.

Not the fierce Driver with more Fury lends
The sounding Lash; and, e're the Stroke descends,
Low to the Wheels his pliant Body bends.

The partial Crowd their Hopes and Fears divide;   19
And aid, with eager shouts, the favour'd Side.

Cries, Murmurs, Clamours, with a mixing Sound,
From Woods to Woods, from Hills to Hills rebound.

   Amidst the loud Applauses of the Shore,
Gyas outstrip'd the rest, and sprung before;
Cloanthus, better mann'd, pursu'd him fast;   20
But his o're-masted Gally check'd his Haste.

The *Centaur*, and the *Dolphin*, brush the brine
With equal Oars, advancing in a Line:
And now the mighty *Centaur* seems to lead,   20
And now the speedy *Dolphin* gets a head:
Now Board to Board the rival Vessels row;
The Billows lave the Skies, and Ocean groans below.

They reach'd the Mark; proud *Gyas* and his Train,
In Triumph rode the Victors of the Main: 21
But steering round, he charg'd his Pilot stand
More close to Shore, and skim along the Sand.

Let others bear to Sea. *Menætes* heard,
But secret shelves too cautiously he fear'd:
And fearing, sought the Deep; and still aloof he steer'd.   21

With louder Cries the Captain call'd again;
Bear to the rocky Shore, and shun the Main.

He spoke, and speaking at his stern he saw
The bold *Cloanthus* near the Shelvings draw;
Betwixt the mark and him the *Scylla* stood,   22
And in a closer Compass plow'd the Flood.

221 Flood.] Flood, *97 98*

He pass'd the Mark; and wheeling got before;
Gyas blasphem'd the Gods, devoutly swore,
Cry'd out for Anger, and his Hair he tore.
Mindless of others Lives, (so high was grown   225
His rising Rage,) and careless of his own:
The trembling Dotard to the Deck he drew,
Then hoisted up, and over-board he threw.
This done he seiz'd the Helm; his Fellows cheer'd;
Turn'd short upon the Shelfs, and madly steer'd.   230
   Hardly his Head, the plunging Pilot rears,
Clog'd with his Cloaths, and cumber'd with his Years:
Now dropping wet, he climbs the Cliff with Pain;
The Crowd that saw him fall, and float again,
Shout from the distant Shore; and loudly laught,   235
To see his heaving Breast disgorge the briny Draught.
The following *Centaur*, and the *Dolphin*'s Crew,
Their vanish'd hopes of Victory renew:
While *Gyas* lags, they kindle in the Race,
To reach the Mark; *Sergesthus* takes the place: 240
Mnestheus pursues; and while around they wind,
Comes up, not half his Gally's length behind.
Then, on the Deck amidst his Mates appear'd,
And thus their drooping Courages he cheer'd.
My Friends, and *Hector*'s Followers heretofore;   245
Exert your Vigour, tug the lab'ring Oar;
Stretch to your Stroaks, my still unconquer'd Crew,
Whom from the flaming Walls of *Troy* I drew.
In this, our common Int'rest, let me find
That strength of Hand, that courage of the Mind,   250
As when you stem'd the strong *Malæan* Flood,
And o're the *Syrtes* broken Billows row'd.
I seek not now the foremost Palm to gain;
Tho yet—But ah, that haughty Wish is vain!
Let those enjoy it whom the Gods ordain.   255
But to be last, the Lags of all the Race,
Redeem your selves and me from that Disgrace.
Now one and all, they tug amain; they row
At the full stretch, and shake the Brazen Prow.
The Sea beneath 'em sinks; their lab'ring sides   260

228 threw.] threw, *97 98*   237 *Centaur*] Centaur *97 98*

Are swell'd, and Sweat runs gutt'ring down in Tides.
Chance aids their daring with unhop'd Success;
Sergesthus, eager with his Beak, to press
Betwixt the Rival Gally and the Rock;
Shuts up th' unwieldy *Centaur* in the Lock.   2

The Vessel struck, and with the dreadful shock
Her Oars she shiver'd, and her Head she broke.
The trembling Rowers from their Banks arise,
And anxious for themselves renounce the Prize.
With Iron Poles they heave her off the Shores;   2
And gather, from the Sea, their floating Oars.
The Crew of *Mnestheus*, with elated Minds,
Urge their Success, and call the willing Winds:
Then ply their Oars, and cut their liquid way;
In larger Compass on the roomy Sea.   2

As when the Dove her Rocky Hold forsakes,
Rowz'd in a Fright, her sounding Wings she shakes;
The Cavern rings with clatt'ring; out she flies,
And leaves her Callow Care, and cleaves the Skies;
At first she flutters; but at length she springs,   2

To smoother flight, and shoots upon her Wings:
So *Mnestheus* in the *Dolphin* cuts the Sea,
And flying with a force, that force assists his Way.
Sergesthus in the *Centaur* soon he pass'd,
Wedg'd in the Rocky Sholes, and sticking fast.   2

In vain the Victor he with Cries implores,
And practices to row with shatter'd Oars.
Then *Mnestheus* bears with *Gyas*, and out-flies:
The Ship without a Pilot yields the Prize.
Unvanquish'd *Scylla* now alone remains;   2
Her he pursues; and all his vigour strains.

Shouts from the fav'ring Multitude arise,
Applauding *Echo* to the Shouts replies;
Shouts, Wishes, and Applause run ratling through the Skies.

These Clamours with disdain the *Scylla* heard;   2
Much grudg'd the Praise, but more the rob'd Reward:
Resolv'd to hold their own, they mend their pace;
All obstinate to dye, or gain the Race.
Rais'd with Success, the *Dolphin* swiftly ran,

(For they can Conquer who believe they can:) 300
Both urge their Oars, and Fortune both supplies;
And both, perhaps had shar'd an equal Prize;
When to the Seas *Cloanthus* holds his Hands,
And Succour from the Watry Pow'rs Demands:
Gods of the liquid Realms, on which I row, 305
If giv'n by you, the Lawrel bind my Brow,
Assist to make me guilty of my Vow.
A Snow-white Bull shall on your Shore be slain,
His offer'd Entrails cast into the Main;
And ruddy Wine from Golden Goblets thrown, 310
Your grateful Gift and my Return shall own.
The Quire of Nymphs, and *Phorcus* from below,
With Virgin *Panopea*, heard his Vow;
And old *Portunus*, with his breadth of Hand,
Push'd on, and sped the Gally to the Land. 315
Swift as a Shaft, or winged Wind, she flies;
And darting to the Port, obtains the Prize.
    The Herald summons all, and then proclaims
Cloanthus Conqu'ror of the Naval Games.
The Prince with Lawrel crowns the Victor's Head, 320
And three fat Steers are to his Vessel led;
The Ships Reward: with gen'rous Wine beside;
And Sums of Silver, which the Crew divide.
The Leaders are distinguish'd from the rest;
The Victor honour'd with a nobler Vest: 325
Where Gold and Purple strive in equal Rows;
And Needle-work its happy Cost bestows.
There, *Ganymede* is wrought with living Art,
Chasing thro' *Ida*'s Groves the trembling Hart:
Breathless he seems, yet eager to pursue; 330
When from aloft, descends in open view,
The Bird of *Jove*; and sowsing on his Prey,
With crooked Tallons bears the Boy away.
In vain, with lifted Hands, and gazing Eyes,
His Guards behold him soaring thro' the Skies; 335
And Dogs pursue his Flight, with imitated Cries.
    Mnestheus the second Victor was declar'd;
And summon'd there, the second Prize he shar'd:

338 shar'd:] shar'd. *97 98*

A Coat of Mail, which brave *Demoleus* bore;
More brave *Æneas* from his Shoulders tore;   } 34
In single Combat on the *Trojan* Shore.
This was ordain'd for *Mnestheus* to possess;
In War for his Defence; for Ornament in Peace.
Rich was the Gift, and glorious to behold;
But yet so pond'rous with its Plates of Gold,   34
That scarce two Servants cou'd the Weight sustain;   }
Yet, loaded thus, *Demoleus* o're the Plain   }
Pursu'd, and lightly seiz'd the *Trojan* Train.   }
The Third succeeding to the last Reward,
Two goodly Bowls of Massy Silver shar'd;   3
With Figures prominent, and richly wrought:
And two Brass Caldrons from *Dodona* brought.

   Thus, all rewarded by the Heroe's hands,
Their conqu'ring Temples bound with Purple Bands.
And now *Sergesthus*, clearing from the Rock,   3
Brought back his Gally shatter'd with the shock.
Forlorn she look'd, without an aiding Oar;
And howted, by the Vulgar, made to Shoar.
As when a Snake, surpris'd upon the Road,
Is crush'd athwart her Body by the load   3
Of heavy Wheels; or with a Mortal Wound
Her Belly bruis'd, and trodden to the Ground:
In vain, with loosen'd curls, she crawls along,
Yet fierce above, she brandishes her Tongue:
Glares with her Eyes, and bristles with her Scales,   3
But groveling in the Dust, her parts unsound she trails.
So slowly to the Port the *Centaur* tends,
But what she wants in Oars, with Sails amends:
Yet, for his Gally sav'd, the grateful Prince,
Is pleas'd th' unhappy Chief to recompence.   3
Pholoe, the *Cretan* Slave, rewards his Care,
Beauteous her self, with lovely Twins, as fair.

   From thence his way the *Trojan* Heroe bent,
Into the neighb'ring Plain, with Mountains pent;
Whose sides were shaded with surrounding Wood: 3
Full in the midst of this fair Vally stood

A Native Theatre, which rising slow,
By just degrees, o're-look'd the Ground below.
High on a Sylvan Throne the Leader sate;
A num'rous Train attend in Solemn State;   380
Here those, that in the rapid Course delight,
Desire of Honour, and the Prize invite.
The Rival Runners, without Order stand,
The *Trojans*, mix'd with the *Sicilian* Band.
First *Nisus*, with *Euryalus*, appears,   385
Euryalus a Boy of blooming Years;
With sprightly Grace, and equal Beauty crown'd:
Nisus, for Friendship to the Youth, renown'd.
Diores, next, of *Priam*'s Royal Race,
Then *Salius*, join'd with *Patron* took their Place: 390
But *Patron* in *Arcadia* had his Birth,
And *Salius* his, from *Acarnanian* Earth.
Then two *Sicilian* Youths, the Names of these
Swift *Helymus*, and lovely *Panopes*:
Both jolly Huntsmen, both in Forests bred,   395
And owning old *Acestes* for their Head.
With sev'ral others of Ignobler Name;
Whom Time has not deliver'd o're to Fame.
 To these the Heroe thus his Thoughts explain'd,
In Words, which gen'ral Approbation gain'd.   400

379–80 *transposed from S* 379 a Sylvan Throne the] the new rais'd Turfe their
S   381 that] who S Course] Race S 383–7 The Rival . . . crown'd:]
S *has*

> The *Trojans* and *Sicilians* mingled stand,
> With *Nisus* and *Euryalus*, the formost of the Band.
> *Euryalus* with youth and beauty crown'd,

388 Youth,] Boy S   389 Royal] Regal S   390 their] his S   391–2
But . . . Earth.] S *has*

> But from *Epirus* one deriv'd his birth,
> The other ow'd it to *Arcadian* Earth.

393 Names of these] name of this S   394 Swift *Helymus*, and lovely *Panopes*]
Was *Helimus*, of that was *Panopes* S 395 Both] Two S both in Forests] in
the Forest S 397 sev'ral] many S Ignobler] obscurer S 399–406 To
these . . . Steed] S *has*

> To these *Æneas* in the midst arose,
> And pleasingly did thus his mind expose.
> Not one of you shall unrewarded go;
> On each I will two *Cretan* Spears bestow,
> Pointed with polish'd Steel; a Battle-ax too,
> With Silver studded; these in common share,
> The formost three shall Olive Garlands wear:
> The Victor, who shall first the Race obtain,
> Shall for his Prize a well breath'd Courser gain,

One common Largess is for all design'd:
The Vanquish'd and the Victor shall be join'd.
Two Darts of polish'd Steel, and *Gnosian* Wood,
A Silver'd, studded Ax alike bestow'd.
The foremost three have Olive Wreaths decreed;   4
The first of these obtains a stately Steed
Adorn'd with Trappings; and the next in Fame,
The Quiver of an *Amazonian* Dame;
With feather'd *Thracian* Arrows well supply'd,   ⎫
A Golden Belt shall gird his Manly side;   ⎬ 4
Which with a sparkling Diamond shall be ty'd: ⎭
The third this *Grecian* Helmet shall content.
He said; to their appointed Base they went:
With beating Hearts th' expected Sign receive,
And, starting all at once, the Barrier leave.   4
Spread out, as on the winged Winds, they flew,
And seiz'd the distant Goal with greedy view.
Shot from the Crowd, swift *Nisus* all o're-pass'd;
Nor Storms, nor Thunder, equal half his haste.
The next, but tho' the next, yet far dis-join'd,   4
Came *Salius*, and *Euryalus* behind;
Then *Helymus*, whom young *Diores* ply'd,
Step after step, and almost side by side:
His Shoulders pressing, and in longer Space,
Had won, or left at least a dubious Race.   4

Now spent, the Goal they almost reach at last;
When eager *Nisus*, hapless in his haste,
Slip'd first, and slipping, fell upon the Plain,
Soak'd with the Blood of Oxen, newly slain:
The careless Victor had not mark'd his way;   4
But treading where the treach'rous Puddle lay,
His Heels flew up; and on the grassy Floor,
He fell, besmear'd with Filth, and Holy Gore.

404 Silver'd, studded] Silver'd studded *97 98:* silver-studded *Scott, Noyes. See Commentary*   407 and] to *S*   410–11 A Golden . . . ty'd:] Hung on a golden Belt, and with a Jewel ty'd: *S*   412 shall] must *S*   415 Barrier] Station *S* 416 winged] Wing of *S*   417 greedy] eager *S*   419 Nor] Not *S*   421 Came *Salius*, and *Euryalus* behind;] *S has*

                    Came *Salius*, then, a distant space behind
                    Euryalus the third.

422 Then] Next *S*   425 dubious] doubtful *S*   429 Soak'd] Moist *S* newly] lately *S*

Not mindless then, *Euryalus*, of thee,
Nor of the Sacred Bonds of Amity;   435
He strove th' immediate Rival's hope to cross;
And caught the Foot of *Salius* as he rose:
So *Salius* lay extended on the Plain;
Euryalus springs out, the Prize to gain;
And leaves the Crowd; applauding Peals attend   440
The Victor to the Goal, who vanquish'd by his Friend.
Next *Helymus*, and then *Diores* came;
By two Misfortunes made the third in Fame.
   But *Salius* enters; and, exclaiming loud
For Justice, deafens, and disturbs the Crowd: 445
Urges his Cause may in the Court be heard;
And pleads the Prize is wrongfully conferr'd.
But Favour for *Euryalus* appears;
His blooming Beauty, with his tender Tears,
Had brib'd the Judges for the promis'd Prize;   450
Besides *Diores* fills the Court with Cry's,
Who vainly reaches at the last Reward,
If the first Palm on *Salius* be conferr'd.
Then thus the Prince; let no Disputes arise:
Where Fortune plac'd it, I award the Prize.   455
But Fortune's Errors give me leave to mend,
At least to pity my deserving Friend.
He said, and from among the Spoils, he draws,
(Pond'rous with shaggy Main, and Golden Paws)
A Lyon's Hide; to *Salius* this he gives: 460
Nisus, with Envy sees the Gift, and grieves.
If such Rewards to vanquish'd Men are due,
He said, and Falling is to rise by you,
What Prize may *Nisus* from your Bounty claim,
Who merited the first Rewards and Fame?   465

436 Rival's hope to cross;] Rival to oppose, *S*   440 leaves] cuts *S*   441
Victor] Conqur'or *S*   vanquish'd by] conquer'd thro *S*   443 made] now *S*
449 with his tender] and his graceful *S*   450 for the promis'd Prize *98*: to
protect his Claim *S 97*   451 fills the Court with Cry's *98*: does as loud
exclaim *S 97*   456 But . . . mend] But give me leave, her Errours to amend
S   457 my] a *S*   458-61 He said . . . grieves.] *S has*

Thus having said,
A Lions Hide, amazing to behold,
Pond'rous with bristles, and with paws of gold,
He gave the Youth, which *Nisus* greiv'd to veiw:

463 He said] Said he *S*

In falling, both an equal Fortune try'd;
Wou'd Fortune for my Fall so well provide!
With this he pointed to his Face, and show'd
His Hands, and all his Habit smear'd with Blood.
Th' indulgent Father of the People smil'd;   4
And caus'd to be produc'd an ample Shield;
Of wond'rous Art by *Didymaon* wrought,
Long since from *Neptune*'s Bars in Triumph brought.
This giv'n to *Nisus*; he divides the rest;
And equal Justice, in his Gifts, express'd.   4
The Race thus ended, and Rewards bestow'd;
Once more the Prince bespeaks th' attentive Crowd.
If there be here, whose dauntless Courage dare
In Gauntlet fight, with Limbs and Body bare,
His Opposite sustain in open view,   4
Stand forth the Champion; and the Games renew.
Two Prizes I propose, and thus divide,
A Bull with gilded Horns, and Fillets ty'd,
Shall be the Portion of the conqu'ring Chief:
A Sword and Helm shall chear the Loser's Grief.   4
    Then haughty *Dares* in the Lists appears;
Stalking he strides, his Head erected bears:
His nervous Arms the weighty Gauntlet weild;
And loud Applauses echo thro' the Field.
Dares alone, in Combat us'd to stand   4
The match of mighty *Paris* hand to hand:
The same, at *Hector*'s Fun'rals undertook
Gygantick *Butes*, of th' *Amician* Stock;
And by the Stroak of his resistless Hand,
Stretch'd the vast Bulk upon the yellow Sand.   4
Such *Dares* was; and such he strod along,
And drew the Wonder of the gazing Throng.
His brawny Back, and ample Breast he shows;
His lifted Arms around his Head he throws;   ⎫
And deals, in whistling Air, his empty Blows.   ⎬   5
His Match is sought; but thro' the trembling Band, ⎭

466 an] did *S*   try'd;] try, *S*   467 for my Fall so well provide!] make me
fall as happily. *S*   469 all his Habit smear'd] body all besmear'd *S*   471 an
ample] a massie *S*   474–5 This . . . express'd.] *S has*
                    With this, the graceful Youth he gratifi'd;
                    Then the remaining presents did divide.

Not one dares answer to the proud Demand.
Presuming of his Force, with sparkling Eyes,
Already he devours the promis'd Prize.
He claims the Bull with awless Insolence;   505
And having seiz'd his Horns, accosts the Prince.
If none my matchless Valour dares oppose,
How long shall *Dares* wait his dastard Foes?
Permit me, Chief, permit without Delay,
To lead this uncontended Gift away.   510
The Crowd assents; and, with redoubled Cries,
For the proud Challenger demands the Prize.
   Acestes, fir'd with just Disdain, to see
The Palm usurp'd without a Victory;
Reproch'd *Entellus* thus, who sate beside,   515
And heard, and saw unmov'd, the *Trojan*'s Pride:
Once, but in vain, a Champion of Renown,
So tamely can you bear the ravish'd Crown?
A Prize in triumph born before your sight,
And shun for fear the danger of the Fight?   520
Where is our *Eryx* now, the boasted Name,
The God who taught your thund'ring Arm the Game;
Where now your baffled Honour, where the Spoil
That fill'd your House, and Fame that fill'd our Isle?
Entellus, thus: My Soul is still the same,   525
Unmov'd with Fear, and mov'd with Martial Fame:
But my chill Blood is curdled in my Veins;
And scarce the Shadow of a Man remains.
Oh, cou'd I turn to that fair Prime again,
That Prime, of which this Boaster is so vain,   530
The Brave who this decrepid Age defies,
Shou'd feel my force, without the promis'd Prize.
He said, and rising at the word, he threw
Two pond'rous Gauntlets down, in open view:
Gauntlets, which *Eryx* wont in Fight to wield,   535
And sheath his hands with in the listed field.
With Fear and Wonder seiz'd, the Crowd beholds
The Gloves of Death, with sev'n distinguish'd folds,
Of tough Bull Hides; the space within is spread
With Iron, or with loads of heavy Lead.   540
Dares himself was daunted at the sight,

Renounc'd his Challenge, and refus'd to fight.
Astonish'd at their weight the Heroe stands,
And poiz'd the pond'rous Engins in his hands.
What had your wonder, said *Entellus*, been,   54
Had you the Gauntlets of *Alcides* seen,
Or view'd the stern debate on this unhappy Green!
These which I bear, your Brother *Eryx* bore,
Still mark'd with batter'd Brains, and mingled Gore.
With these he long sustain'd th' *Herculean* Arm;   55
And these I weilded while my Blood was warm:
This languish'd Frame, while better Spirits fed,
E're Age unstrung my Nerves, or Time o'resnow'd my Head.
But if the Challenger these Arms refuse,
And cannot wield their weight, or dare not use;   55
If great *Æneas*, and *Acestes* joyn
In his Request, these Gauntlets I resign:
Let us with equal Arms perform the Fight,
And let him leave to Fear, since I resign my Right.
   This said, *Entellus* for the Strife prepares;   560
Strip'd of his quilted Coat, his Body bares:
Compos'd of mighty Bones and Brawn, he stands,
A goodly tow'ring Object on the Sands.
Then just *Æneas* equal Arms supply'd,
Which round their Shoulders to their Wrists they ty'd.   565
Both on the tiptoe stand, at full extent,
Their Arms aloft, their Bodies inly bent;
Their Heads from aiming Blows they bear a far;
With clashing Gauntlets then provoke the War.
One on his Youth and pliant Limbs relies;   570
One on his Sinews, and his Gyant size.
The last is stiff with Age, his Motion slow,
He heaves for Breath, he staggers to and fro;
And Clouds of issuing Smoak his Nostrils loudly blow.
Yet equal in Success, they ward, they strike;   575
Their ways are diff'rent, but their Art alike.
Before, behind, the blows are dealt; around
Their hollow sides the ratling Thumps resound.
A Storm of Strokes, well meant, with fury flies,
And errs about their Temples, Ears, and Eyes.   580

                560 Editor's paragraph

Nor always errs; for oft the Gauntlet draws
A sweeping stroke, along the crackling Jaws.
Heavy with Age, *Entellus* stands his Ground,
But with his warping Body wards the Wound.
His Hand, and watchful Eye keep even pace;   585
While *Dares* traverses, and shifts his place,
And like a Captain, who beleaguers round
Some strong built Castle, on a rising Ground,
Views all th' approaches with observing Eyes,
This, and that other part, in vain he tries;   590
And more on Industry, than Force relies.
With Hands on high, *Entellus* threats the Foe;
But *Dares* watch'd the Motion from below,
And slip'd aside, and shun'd the long descending Blow.
Entellus wasts his Forces on the Wind;   595
And thus deluded of the Stroke design'd,
Headlong, and heavy fell: his ample Breast,
And weighty Limbs, his ancient Mother press'd.
So falls a hollow Pine, that long had stood
On *Ida*'s height, or *Erymanthus* Wood,   600
Torn from the Roots: the diff'ring Nations rise,
And Shouts, and mingl'd Murmurs, rend the Skies.
Acestes runs, with eager haste, to raise
The fall'n Companion of his youthful Days:
Dauntless he rose, and to the Fight return'd: 605
With shame his glowing Cheeks, his Eyes with fury burn'd.
Disdain, and conscious Virtue fir'd his Breast;
And with redoubled Force his Foe he press'd.
He lays on load with either Hand, amain,
And headlong drives the *Trojan* o're the Plain.   610
Nor stops, nor stays; nor rest, nor Breath allows,
But Storms of Strokes descend about his Brows;
A ratling Tempest, and a Hail of Blows.
But now the Prince, who saw the wild Increase
Of Wounds, commands the Combatants to cease: 615
And bounds *Entellus* Wrath, and bids the Peace.
First to the *Trojan* spent with Toil he came,
And sooth'd his Sorrow for the suffer'd Shame.
What Fury seiz'd my Friend; the Gods, said he,

586 place,] place. *97 98*   587 round] round, *97 98*   619 Friend;] Friend, *97 98*

To him propitious, and averse to thee,   6.
Have giv'n his Arm superior Force to thine;
'Tis Madness to contend with Strength Divine.
The Gauntlet Fight thus ended, from the Shore,
His faithful Friends unhappy *Dares* bore:
His Mouth and Nostrils, pour'd a Purple Flood;   62
And pounded Teeth, came rushing with his Blood.
Faintly he stagger'd thro the hissing Throng;
And hung his Head, and trail'd his Legs along.
The Sword and Casque, are carry'd by his Train;
But with his Foe the Palm and Ox remain.   63

The Champion, then, before *Æneas* came,
Proud of his Prize; but prouder of his Fame;
O Goddess-born, and you *Dardanian* Host,
Mark with Attention, and forgive my Boast:
Learn what I was, by what remains; and know   63
From what impending Fate, you sav'd my Foe.
Sternly he spoke; and then confronts the Bull;
And, on his ample Forehead, aiming full,
The deadly Stroke descending, pierc'd the Skull.
Down drops the Beast; nor needs a second Wound: 64
But sprawls in pangs of Death; and spurns the Ground.
Then, thus: In *Dares* stead I offer this;
Eryx, accept a nobler Sacrifice:
Take the last Gift my wither'd Arms can yield,
Thy Gauntlets I resign; and here renounce the Field.   64

This done, *Æneas* orders, for the close,
The strife of Archers, with contending Bows.
The Mast, *Sergesthus* shatter'd Gally bore,
With his own Hands, he raises on the Shore.
A flutt'ring Dove upon the Top they tye,   65
The living Mark, at which their Arrows fly.
The rival Archers in a Line advance;
Their turn of Shooting to receive from Chance.
A Helmet holds their Names: The Lots are drawn,
On the first Scroll was read *Hippocoon*:   65
The People shout; upon the next was found
Young *Mnestheus*, late with Naval Honours crownd.
The third contain'd *Eurytion*'s Noble Name,
Thy Brother, *Pandarus*, and next in Fame:

Whom *Pallas* urg'd the Treaty to confound,   660
And send among the *Greeks* a feather'd Wound.
Acestes in the bottom, last remain'd;
Whom not his Age from Youthful Sports restrain'd.
Soon, all with Vigour bend their trusty Bows,
And from the Quiver each his Arrow chose,   665
Hippocoon's was the first: with forceful sway
It flew, and, whizzing, cut the liquid way:
Fix'd in the Mast the feather'd Weapon stands,
The fearful Pidgeon flutters in her Bands;
And the Tree trembled: and the shouting Cries   670
Of the pleas'd People, rend the vaulted Skies.
Then *Mnestheus* to the head his Arrow drove,
With lifted Eyes; and took his Aim above;
But made a glancing Shot, and miss'd the Dove.
Yet miss'd so narrow, that he cut the Cord   675
Which fasten'd, by the Foot, the flitting Bird.
The Captive thus releas'd, away she flies,
And beats with clapping Wings, the yielding Skies.
His Bow already bent, *Eurytion* stood,
And having first invok'd his Brother God,   680
His winged Shaft with eager haste he sped;
The fatal Message reach'd her as she fled:
She leaves her Life aloft, she strikes the Ground;
And renders back the Weapon in the Wound.
Acestes grudging at his Lot, remains,   685
Without a Prize to gratifie his Pains.
Yet shooting upward, sends his Shaft, to show
An Archer's Art, and boast his twanging Bow.
The featherd Arrow gave a dire Portent;
And latter Augures judge from this Event.   690
Chaf'd by the speed, it fir'd; and as it flew,
A Trail of following Flames, ascending drew:
Kindling they mount; and mark the shiny Way:
Across the Skies as falling Meteors play,
And vanish into Wind; or in a Blaze decay.   695
The *Trojans* and *Sicilians* wildly stare:
And trembling, turn their Wonder into Pray'r.
The *Dardan* Prince put on a smiling Face,

689 featherd *98*: pointed *97*

And strain'd *Acestes* with a close Embrace:
Then hon'ring him with Gifts above the rest,   700
Turn'd the bad Omen, nor his Fears confess'd.
The Gods, said he, this Miracle have wrought;
And order'd you the Prize without the Lot.
Accept this Goblet rough with figur'd Gold,
Which *Thracian Cisseus* gave my Sire of old: 705
This Pledge of ancient Amity receive,
Which to my second Sire I justly give.
He said, and with the Trumpets chearful sound,
Proclaim'd him Victor, and with Lawrel crown'd.
Nor good *Eurytion* envy'd him the Prize;   710
Tho' he transfix'd the Pidgeon in the Skies.
Who cut the Line, with second Gifts was grac'd;
The third was his, whose Arrow pierc'd the Mast.

   The Chief, before the Games were wholly done,
Call'd *Periphantes*, Tutor to his Son;   715
And whisper'd thus; with speed *Ascanius* find,
And if his Childish Troop be ready join'd;
On Horse-back let him grace his Grandsire's Day,
And lead his Equals arm'd, in just Array.
He said, and calling out, the Cirque he clears;   720
The Crowd withdrawn, an open Plain appears.
And now the Noble Youths, of Form Divine,
Advance before their Fathers, in a Line:
The Riders grace the Steeds; the Steeds with Glory shine.

   Thus marching on, in Military Pride,   725
Shouts of Applause resound from side to side.
Their Casques, adorn'd with Lawrel Wreaths, they wear,
Each brandishing aloft a Cornel Spear.
Some at their Backs their guilded Quivers bore;
Their Chains of burnish'd Gold hung down before.   730
Three graceful Troops they form'd upon the Green;
Three graceful Leaders at their Head were seen;
Twelve follow'd ev'ry Chief, and left a Space between.
The first young *Priam* led; a lovely Boy,
Whose Grandsire was th' unhappy King of *Troy*:   735

His Race in after times was known to Fame, }
New Honours adding to the *Latian* Name;
And well the Royal Boy his *Thracian* Steed became.
White were the Fetlocks of his Feet before;
And on his Front a snowy Star he bore: 740
Then beauteous *Atys*, with *Iulus* bred,
Of equal Age, the second Squadron led.
The last in Order, but the first in place,
First in the lovely Features of his Face;
Rode fair *Ascanius* on a fiery Steed, 745
Queen *Dido*'s Gift, and of the *Tyrian* breed.
Sure Coursers for the rest the King ordains;
With Golden Bitts adorn'd, and Purple Reins.
 The pleas'd Spectators peals of Shouts renew;
And all the Parents in the Children view: 750
Their Make, their Motions, and their sprightly Grace;
And Hopes and Fears alternate in their Face.
 Th' unfledg'd Commanders, and their Martial Train,
First make the Circuit of the sandy Plain,
Around their Sires: And at th' appointed Sign, 755
Drawn up in beauteous Order form a Line:
The second Signal sounds; the Troop divides,
In three distinguish'd parts, with three distinguish'd Guides.
Again they close, and once again dis-join,
In Troop to Troop oppos'd, and Line to Line. 760
They meet, they wheel, they throw their Darts afar
With harmless Rage, and well dissembled War.
Then in a round the mingl'd Bodies run;
Flying they follow, and pursuing shun.
Broken they break, and rallying, they renew 765
In other Forms the Military shew.
At last, in order, undiscern'd they join;
And march together, in a friendly Line.
And, as the *Cretan* Labyrinth of old,
With wand'ring Ways, and many a winding fold, 770
Involv'd the weary Feet, without redress,
In a round Error, which deny'd recess;
So fought the *Trojan* Boys in warlike Play,
Turn'd, and return'd, and still a diff'rent way.

770 Ways] Wave *98*

Thus Dolphins, in the Deep, each other chase,
In Circles, when they swim around the wat'ry Race.
This Game, these Carousels *Ascanius* taught;
And, building *Alba*, to the *Latins* brought.
Shew'd what he learn'd: The *Latin* Sires impart,
To their succeeding Sons, the graceful Art:
From these Imperial *Rome* receiv'd the Game;
Which *Troy*, the Youths the *Trojan* Troop, they name.
    Thus far the sacred Sports they celebrate:
But Fortune soon resum'd her ancient hate.
For while they pay the dead his Annual dues,
Those envy'd Rites *Saturnian Juno* views.
And sends the Goddess of the various bow,
To try new Methods of Revenge below:
Supplies the Winds to wing her Airy way;
Where in the Port secure the Navy lay.
Swiftly fair *Iris* down her Arch descends;
And undiscern'd her fatal Voyage ends.
She saw the gath'ring Crowd; and gliding thence,
The desart Shore, and Fleet without defence.
The *Trojan* Matrons on the Sands alone,
With Sighs and Tears, *Anchises* death bemoan.
Then, turning to the Sea their weeping Eyes,
Their pity to themselves, renews their Cries.
Alas! said one, what Oceans yet remain
For us to sail; what Labours to sustain!
All take the Word; and with a gen'ral groan,
Implore the Gods for Peace; and Places of their own.
The Goddess, great in Mischief, views their pains;
And in a Woman's Form her heav'nly Limbs restrains.
In Face and Shape, old *Beroe* she became,
Doriclus Wife, a venerable Dame;
Once bless'd with Riches, and a Mother's Name.
Thus chang'd, amidst the crying Crow'd she ran,
Mix'd with the Matrons, and these words began.
O wretched we, whom not the *Grecian* Pow'r,
Nor Flames destroy'd, in *Troy*'s unhappy hour!
O wretched we, reserv'd by Cruel Fate,
Beyond the Ruins of the sinking State!

772

78

78

79

79

80

80

81

783 Editor's paragraph

Now sev'n revolving Years are wholly run,
Since this improsp'rous Voyage we begun: 815
Since toss'd from Shores to Shores, from Lands to Lands,
Inhospitable Rocks and barren Sands;
Wand'ring in Exile, through the stormy Sea,
We search in vain for flying *Italy*.
Now Cast by Fortune on this kindred Land, 820
What shou'd our Rest, and rising Walls withstand,
Or hinder here to fix our banish'd Band?
O, Country lost, and Gods redeem'd in vain,
If still in endless Exile we remain!
Shall we no more the *Trojan* Walls renew, 825
Or Streams of some dissembl'd *Simois* view!
Haste, joyn with me, th' unhappy Fleet consume:
Cassandra bids, and I declare her doom.
In sleep I saw her; she supply'd my hands,
(For this I more than dreamt) with flaming Brands: 830
With these, said she, these wand'ring Ships destroy;
These are your fatal Seats, and this your *Troy*.
Time calls you now, the precious Hour employ.
Slack not the good Presage, while Heav'n inspires
Our Minds to dare, and gives the ready Fires. 835
See *Neptune*'s Altars minister their Brands;
The God is pleas'd; the God supplies our hands.
Then, from the Pile, a flaming Firr she drew,
And, toss'd in Air, amidst the Gallies threw.
Wrap'd in a maze, the Matrons wildly stare: 840
Then *Pyrgo*, reverenc'd for her hoary Hair,
Pyrgo, the Nurse of *Priam*'s num'rous Race,
No *Beroe* this, tho she belies her Face:
What Terrours from her frowning Front arise;
Behold a Goddess in her ardent Eyes! 845
What Rays around her heav'nly Face are seen,
Mark her Majestick Voice, and more than mortal Meen!
Beroe but now I left; whom pin'd with pain,
Her Age and Anguish from these Rites detain.
She said; the Matrons, seiz'd with new Amaze, 850
Rowl their malignant Eyes, and on the Navy gaze.
They fear, and hope, and neither part obey:

838 Firr] Fire *98. Cf. Æneis, ix. 85*

They hope the fated Land, but fear the fatal Way.
The Goddess, having done her Task below,
Mounts up on equal Wings, and bends her painted Bow.   8
Struck with the sight, and seiz'd with Rage Divine;
The Matrons prosecute their mad Design:
They shriek aloud, they snatch, with Impious Hands,
The food of Altars, Fires, and flaming Brands.
Green Boughs, and Saplings, mingled in their haste;   8
And smoaking Torches on the Ships they cast.
The Flame, unstop'd at first, more Fury gains;
And *Vulcan* rides at large with loosen'd Reins:
Triumphant to the painted Sterns he soars,
And seizes in his way, the Banks, and crackling Oars.   8
    Eumelus was the first, the News to bear,
While yet they crowd the Rural Theatre.
Then what they hear, is witness'd by their Eyes;
A storm of Sparkles, and of Flames arise.
Ascanius took th' Alarm, while yet he led   8
His early Warriors on his prancing Steed.
And spurring on, his Equals soon o'repass'd,
Nor cou'd his frighted Friends reclaim his haste.
Soon as the Royal Youth appear'd in view,
He sent his Voice before him as he flew;   8
What Madness moves you, Matrons, to destroy
The last Remainders of unhappy *Troy*!
Not hostile Fleets, but your own hopes you burn,
And on your Friends, your fatal Fury turn.
Behold your own *Ascanius*: while he said,   ⎫ 8
He drew his glitt'ring Helmet from his Head;   ⎬
In which the Youths to sportful Arms he led.   ⎭
By this, *Æneas* and his Train appear;
And now the Women, seiz'd with Shame and Fear,
Dispers'd, to Woods and Caverns take their Flight;   8
Abhor their Actions, and avoid the Light:
Their Friends acknowledge, and their Error find;
And shake the Goddess from their alter'd Mind.
    Not so the raging Fires their Fury cease;
But lurking in the Seams, with seeming Peace,   8
Work on their way, amid the smouldring Tow,

859 Fires *98*: Firs *97*   860 Boughs *98*: Leaves *97*   866 *Editor's paragraph*

Sure in Destruction, but in Motion slow.
The silent Plague, thro' the green Timber eats,
And vomits out a tardy Flame, by fits.
Down to the Keels, and upward to the Sails,   895
The Fire descends, or mounts; but still prevails:
Nor Buckets pour'd, nor strength of Human Hand,
Can the victorious Element withstand.

   The Pious Heroe rends his Robe, and throws
To Heav'n his Hands, and with his Hands his Vows.   900
O *Jove*, he cry'd, if Pray'rs can yet have place;
If thou abhorr'st not all the *Dardan* Race;
If any spark of Pity still remain;
If Gods are Gods, and not invok'd in vain;
Yet spare the Relicks of the *Trojan* Train.   905
Yet from the Flames our burning Vessels free:
Or let thy Fury fall alone on me.
At this devoted Head thy Thunder throw,
And send the willing Sacrifice below.

   Scarce had he said, when Southern Storms arise,   910
From Pole to Pole, the forky Lightning flies;
Loud ratling shakes the Mountains, and the Plain:
Heav'n bellies downward, and descends in Rain.
Whole Sheets of Water from the Clouds are sent,
Which hissing thro' the Planks, the Flames prevent;   915
And stop the fiery Pest: Four Ships alone
Burn to the wast; and for the Fleet attone.

   But doubtful thoughts the Hero's Heart divide;
If he should still in *Sicily* reside,
Forgetful of his Fates; or tempt the Main,   920
In hope the promis'd *Italy* to gain.
Then *Nautes*, old, and wise, to whom alone
The Will of Heav'n, by *Pallas* was fore-shown;
Vers'd in Portents, experienc'd and inspir'd,
To tell Events, and what the Fates requir'd: 925
Thus while he stood, to neither part inclin'd,
With chearful Words reliev'd his lab'ring Mind.
O Goddess-born, resign'd in ev'ry state,
With Patience bear, with Prudence push your Fate.
By suff'ring well, our Fortune we subdue;   930

915 prevent;] prevent: 97 98

Fly when she frowns, and when she calls pursue.
Your Friend *Acestes* is of *Trojan* Kind,
To him disclose the Secrets of your Mind:
Trust in his Hands your old and useless Train,
Too num'rous for the Ships which yet remain: 93
The feeble, old, indulgent of their Ease,
The Dames who dread the Dangers of the Seas,
With all the dastard Crew, who dare not stand
The shock of Battel with your Foes by Land;
Here you may build a common Town for all;   94
And from *Acestes* name, *Acesta* call.
The Reasons, with his Friend's Experience join'd,
Encourag'd much, but more disturb'd his Mind.

    'Twas dead of Night; when to his slumb'ring Eyes,
His Father's Shade descended from the Skies;   94
And thus he spoke: O more than vital Breath,
Lov'd while I liv'd, and dear ev'n after Death;
O Son, in various Toils and Troubles tost,
The King of Heav'n employs my careful Ghost
On his Commands; the God who sav'd from Fire   95
Your flaming Fleet, and heard your just desire:
The Wholsom Counsel of your Friend receive;
And here, the Coward Train, and Women leave:
The chosen Youth, and those who nobly dare,
Transport; to tempt the Dangers of the War.   95
The stern *Italians* will their Courage try;
Rough are their Manners, and their Minds are high.
But first to *Pluto*'s Palace you shall go,
And seek my Shade among the blest below.
For not with impious Ghosts my Soul remains,   96
Nor suffers, with the Damn'd, perpetual Pains;
But breaths the living Air of soft *Elysian* Plains.
The chast *Sybilla* shall your steps convey;
And Blood of offer'd Victims free the way.
There shall you know what Realms the Gods assign;   96
And learn the Fates and Fortunes of your Line.
But now, farewel; I vanish with the Night;
And feel the blast of Heav'ns approaching Light:
He said, and mix'd with Shades, and took his airy flight.

    944 *Editor's paragraph*   946 Breath,] Breath *97 98*

Whether so fast, the filial Duty cry'd, 970
And why, ah why, the wish'd Embrace deny'd!
He said, and rose: as holy Zeal inspires
He rakes hot Embers, and renews the Fires.
His Country Gods and *Vesta*, then adores
With Cakes and Incense; and their Aid implores. 975
Next, for his Friends, and Royal Host he sent,
Reveal'd his Vision and the Gods intent,
With his own Purpose: All, without delay,
The Will of *Jove*, and his Desires obey.
They list with Women each degenerate Name, 980
Who dares not hazard Life, for future Fame.
These they cashier; the brave remaining few,
Oars, Banks, and Cables half consum'd renew.
The Prince designs a City with the Plough;
The Lots their sev'ral Tenements allow. 985
This part is nam'd from *Ilium*, that from *Troy*;
And the new King ascends the Throne with Joy.
A chosen Senate from the People draws;
Appoints the Judges, and ordains the Laws.
Then on the top of *Eryx*, they begin 990
A rising Temple to the *Paphian* Queen:
Anchises, last, is honour'd as a God,
A Priest is added, annual Gifts bestow'd;
And Groves are planted round his blest Abode.
Nine days they pass in Feasts, their Temples crown'd; 995
And fumes of Incense in the Fanes abound.
Then, from the South arose a gentle Breeze,
That curl'd the smoothness of the glassy Seas:
The rising Winds, a ruffling Gale afford,
And call the merry Marriners aboard. 1000
   Now loud Laments along the Shores resound,
Of parting Friends in close Embraces bound.
The trembling Women, the degenerate Train,
Who shun'd the frightful dangers of the Main;
Ev'n those desire to sail, and take their share 1005
Of the rough Passage, and the promis'd War.
Whom Good *Æneas* chears; and recommends
To their new Master's Care, his fearful Friends.

991 A rising *98*: To raise a *97*   994 Abode. *98*: Abode, *97*

On *Eryx* Altars three fat Calves he lays;
A Lamb new fall'n to the stormy Seas;⠀⠀⠀⠀⠀} 10
Then slips his Haulsers, and his Anchors weighs.
High on the Deck, the Godlike Heroe stands;
With Olive crown'd; a Charger in his Hands;
Then cast the reeking Entrails in the brine,
And pour'd the Sacrifice of Purple Wine.⠀⠀⠀⠀⠀10
Fresh Gales arise, with equal Strokes they vye,
And brush the buxom Seas, and o're the Billows fly.
⠀⠀⠀Mean time the Mother-Goddess, full of Fears,
To *Neptune* thus address'd, with tender Tears.
The Pride of *Jove*'s Imperious Queen, the Rage,⠀⠀10
The malice which no Suff'rings can asswage,
Compel me to these Pray'rs: Since neither Fate,
Nor Time, nor Pity, can remove her hate.
Ev'n *Jove* is thwarted by his haughty Wife;
Still vanquish'd, yet she still renews the Strife.⠀⠀10
As if 'twere little to consume the Town
Which aw'd the World; and wore th' Imperial Crown:
She prosecutes the Ghost of *Troy* with Pains;
And gnaws, ev'n to the Bones, the last Remains.
Let her the Causes of her Hatred tell;⠀⠀⠀⠀⠀10
But you can witness its Effects too well.
You saw the Storm she rais'd on *Lybian* Floods,
That mix'd the mounting Billows with the Clouds.
When, bribing *Eolus*, she shook the Main;
And mov'd Rebellion in your wat'ry Reign.⠀⠀⠀⠀10
With Fury she possess'd the *Dardan* Dames;
To burn their Fleet with execrable Flames.
And forc'd *Æneas*, when his Ships were lost,
To leave his Foll'wers on a Foreign Coast.
For what remains, your Godhead I implore;⠀⠀⠀10
And trust my Son to your protecting Pow'r.
If neither *Jove*'s, nor Fate's decree withstand,
Secure his Passage to the *Latian* Land.
⠀⠀⠀Then thus the mighty Ruler of the Main,
What may not *Venus* hope, from *Neptune*'s Reign?⠀10
My Kingdom claims your Birth: my late Defence
Of your indanger'd Fleet, may claim your Confidence.
Nor less by Land than Sea, my Deeds declare,

How much your lov'd *Æneas* is my Care.
Thee *Xanthus*, and thee *Simois* I attest: 1050
Your *Trojan* Troops, when proud *Achilles* press'd,
And drove before him headlong on the Plain,
And dash'd against the Walls the trembling Train,
When Floods were fill'd with bodies of the slain:
When Crimson *Xanthus*, doubtful of his way,   1055
Stood up on ridges to behold the Sea;
New heaps came tumbling in, and choak'd his way:
When your *Æneas* fought, but fought with odds
Of Force unequal, and unequal Gods;
I spread a Cloud before the Victor's sight,   1060
Sustain'd the vanquish'd, and secur'd his flight.
Ev'n then secur'd him, when I sought with joy
The vow'd destruction of ungrateful *Troy*.
My Will's the same: Fair Goddess fear no more,
Your Fleet shall safely gain the *Latian* Shore: 1065
Their lives are giv'n; one destin'd Head alone
Shall perish, and for Multitudes attone.
Thus having arm'd with Hopes her anxious Mind,
His finny Team *Saturnian Neptune* join'd.
Then, adds the foamy Bridle to their Jaws;   1070
And to the loosen'd Reins permits the Laws.
High on the Waves his Azure Car he guides,
Its Axles thunder, and the Sea subsides;
And the smooth Ocean rowls her silent Tides.
The Tempests fly before their Father's face,   1075
Trains of inferiour Gods his Triumph grace;
And Monster Whales before their Master play,
And Quires of Tritons crowd the wat'ry way.
The Martial'd Pow'rs, in equal Troops divide,
To right and left: the Gods his better side   1080
Inclose, and on the worse the Nymphs and Nereids ride.
   Now smiling Hope, with sweet Vicissitude,
Within the Hero's Mind, his Joys renew'd.
He calls to raise the Masts, the Sheats display;
The Chearful Crew with diligence obey;   1085
They scud before the Wind, and sail in open Sea.
A Head of all the Master Pilot steers,
And as he leads, the following Navy veers.

The Steeds of Night had travell'd half the Sky,
The drowzy Rowers on their Benches lye;
When the soft God of Sleep, with easie flight,
Descends, and draws behind a trail of Light.
Thou *Palinurus* art his destin'd Prey;
To thee alone he takes his fatal way.
Dire Dreams to thee, and Iron Sleep he bears;
And lighting on thy Prow, the Form of *Phorbas* wears.
Then thus the Traytor God began his Tale:
The Winds, my Friend, inspire a pleasing gale;
The Ships, without thy Care, securely sail.
Now steal an hour of sweet Repose; and I
Will take the Rudder, and thy room supply.
To whom the yauning Pilot, half asleep;
Me dost thou bid to trust the treach'rous Deep!
The Harlot-smiles of her dissembling Face,
And to her Faith commit the *Trojan* Race?
Shall I believe the *Syren* South again,
And, oft betray'd, not know the Monster Main?
He said, his fasten'd Hands the Rudder keep,
And fix'd on Heav'n, his Eyes repel invading Sleep.
The God was wroth, and at his Temples threw
A Branch in *Lethe* dip'd, and drunk with *Stygian* Dew:
The Pilot, vanquish'd by the Pow'r Divine,
Soon clos'd his swimming Eyes, and lay supine.
Scarce were his Limbs extended at their length,
The God, insulting with superiour Strength,
Fell heavy on him, plung'd him in the Sea,
And, with the Stern, the Rudder tore away.
Headlong he fell, and strugling in the Main,
Cry'd out for helping hands, but cry'd in vain:
The Victor Dæmon mounts obscure in Air;
While the Ship sails without the Pilot's care.
On *Neptune*'s Faith the floating Fleet relies;
But what the Man forsook, the God supplies;
And o're the dang'rous Deep secure the Navy flies.
Glides by the *Syren*'s Cliffs, a shelfy Coast,
Long infamous for Ships, and Sailors lost;
And white with Bones: Th' impetuous Ocean roars;
And Rocks rebellow from the sounding Shores.

The watchful Heroe felt the knocks; and found
The tossing Vessel sail'd on shoaly Ground.   1130
Sure of his Pilot's loss, he takes himself
The Helm, and steers aloof, and shuns the Shelf.
Inly he griev'd; and groaning from the Breast,
Deplor'd his Death; and thus his Pain express'd:
For Faith repos'd on Seas, and on the flatt'ring Sky,   1135
Thy naked Corps is doom'd, on Shores unknown to lye.

THE SIXTH BOOK OF THE ÆNEIS

THE ARGUMENT

The Sibyl foretels Æneas *the Adventures he should meet with in* Italy. *She attends him to Hell; describing to him the various Scenes of that Place, and conducting him to his Father* Anchises. *Who instructs him in those sublime Mysteries of the Soul of the World, and the Transmigration: And shews him that glorious Race of Heroes, which was to descend from him, and his* 5 *Posterity.*

H E said, and wept: Then spread his Sails before
The Winds, and reach'd at length the *Cuman* Shore: ⎫
Their Anchors drop'd, his Crew the Vessels moor.   ⎭
They turn their Heads to Sea; their Sterns to Land;
And greet with greedy Joy th' *Italian* Strand.   5
Some strike from clashing Flints their fiery Seed;
Some gather Sticks, the kindled Flames to feed:
Or search for hollow Trees, and fell the Woods,
Or trace thro Valleys the discover'd Floods.
Thus, while their sev'ral Charges they fulfil,   10
The Pious Prince ascends the sacred Hill
Where *Phœbus* is ador'd; and seeks the Shade,
Which hides from sight, his venerable Maid.
Deep in a Cave the Sibyl makes abode;
Thence full of Fate returns, and of the God.   15
Thro *Trivia*'s Grove they walk; and now behold,
And enter now, the Temple roof'd with Gold.
When *Dedalus*, to fly the *Cretan* Shore,

1133 the *98*: his *97*
The Sixth Book. 18 fly *98*: shun *97*

His heavy Limbs on jointed Pinions bore,
(The first who sail'd in Air,) 'tis sung by Fame,
To the *Cumæan* Coast at length he came;
And, here alighting, built this costly Frame.
Inscrib'd to *Phœbus*, here he hung on high
The steerage of his Wings, that cut the Sky:
Then o're the lofty Gate his Art emboss'd
Androgeos Death, and Off'rings to his Ghost.
Sev'n Youths from *Athens* yearly sent, to meet
The Fate appointed by revengeful *Creet*.
And next to those the dreadful Urn was plac'd,
In which the destin'd Names, by Lots were cast:
The mournful Parents stand around in Tears;
And rising *Creet* against their Shore appears.
There too, in living Sculpture, might be seen
The mad Affection of the *Cretan* Queen:
Then how she cheats her bellowing Lover's Eye:
The rushing leap, the doubtful Progeny,
The lower part a Beast, a Man above,
The Monument of their polluted Love.
Nor far from thence he grav'd the wond'rous Maze;
A thousand Doors, a thousand winding Ways;
Here dwells the Monster, hid from Human View,
Not to be found, but by the faithful Clue:
'Till the kind Artist, mov'd with Pious Grief,
Lent to the loving Maid this last Relief.
And all those erring Paths describ'd so well,
That *Theseus* conquer'd, and the Monster fell.
Here hapless *Icarus* had found his part;
Had not the Father's Grief restrain'd his Art.
He twice essay'd to cast his Son in Gold;
Twice from his Hands he drop'd the forming Mould.
    All this with wond'ring Eyes *Æneas* view'd:
Each varying Object his Delight renew'd.
Eager to read the rest, *Achates* came,
And by his side the mad divining Dame;
The Priestess of the God, *Deiphobe* her Name.
Time suffers not, she said, to feed your Eyes
With empty Pleasures: haste the Sacrifice.

20

25

30

35

40

45

50

55

29 those *98*: these *97*   30 Names, *98*: Name *97*   53 Eager *98*: Prepar'd *97*

Sev'n Bullocks yet unyok'd, for *Phœbus* chuse,
And for *Diana* sev'n unspotted Ewes.
This said, the Servants urge the Sacred Rites;　　60
While to the Temple she the Prince invites.
A spacious Cave, within its farmost part,
Was hew'd and fashion'd by laborious Art,
Thro' the Hills hollow sides: Before the place,
A hundred Doors a hundred Entries grace:　　65
As many Voices issue; and the sound
Of Sibyl's Words as many times rebound.
Now to the Mouth they come: Aloud she cries,
This is the time, enquire your Destinies.
He comes, behold the God! Thus while she said,　　70
(And shiv'ring at the sacred Entry staid)
Her Colour chang'd, her Face was not the same,
And hollow Groans from her deep Spirit came.
Her Hair stood up; convulsive Rage possess'd
Her trembling Limbs, and heav'd her lab'ring Breast.　　75
Greater than Human Kind she seem'd to look:
And with an Accent, more than Mortal, spoke.
Her staring Eyes with sparkling Fury rowl;
When all the God came rushing on her Soul.
Swiftly she turn'd, and foaming as she spoke,　　80
Why this Delay, she cry'd; the Pow'rs invoke.
Thy Pray'rs alone can open this abode,
Else vain are my Demands, and dumb the God.
She said no more: The trembling *Trojans* hear;
O're-spread with a damp Sweat, and holy Fear.　　85
The Prince himself, with awful Dread possess'd,
His Vows to great *Apollo* thus address'd.
　　Indulgent God, propitious Pow'r to *Troy*,
Swift to relieve, unwilling to destroy;
Directed by whose Hand, the *Dardan* Dart　　90
Pierc'd the proud *Grecian*'s only Mortal part:
Thus far, by Fates Decrees, and thy Commands,
Through ambient Seas, and thro' devouring Sands,
Our exil'd Crew has sought th' *Ausonian* Ground:
And now, at length, the flying Coast is found.　　95
Thus far the Fate of *Troy*, from place to place,

63 Art,] Art. *97 98*　　88 *Editor's paragraph*

With Fury has pursu'd her wand'ring Race:
Here cease ye Pow'rs, and let your Vengeance end,
Troy is no more, and can no more offend.
And thou, O sacred Maid, inspir'd to see   1●
Th' Event of things in dark Futurity;
Give me, what Heav'n has promis'd to my Fate,
To conquer and command the *Latian* State:
To fix my wand'ring Gods; and find a place
For the long Exiles of the *Trojan* Race.   1●
Then shall my grateful Hands a Temple rear
To the twin Gods, with Vows and solemn Pray'r;
And Annual Rites, and Festivals, and Games,
Shall be perform'd to their auspicious Names.
Nor shalt thou want thy Honours in my Land,   1?
For there thy faithful Oracles shall stand,
Preserv'd in Shrines: and ev'ry Sacred Lay,
Which, by thy Mouth, *Apollo* shall convey.
All shall be treasur'd, by a chosen Train
Of holy Priests, and ever shall remain.   1.
But, oh! commit not thy prophetick Mind
To flitting Leaves, the sport of ev'ry Wind:
Lest they disperse in Air our empty Fate:
Write not, but, what the Pow'rs ordain, relate.
    Strugling in vain, impatient of her Load,   1.
And lab'ring underneath the pond'rous God,
The more she strove to shake him from her Breast,
With more, and far superior Force he press'd:
Commands his Entrance, and without Controul,
Usurps her Organs, and inspires her Soul.   1?
Now, with a furious Blast, the hundred Doors
Ope of themselves; a rushing Whirlwind roars
Within the Cave; and Sibyl's Voice restores.
    Escap'd the Dangers of the wat'ry Reign,
Yet more, and greater Ills, by Land remain.   1?
The Coast so long desir'd, (nor doubt th' Event)
Thy Troops shall reach, but having reach'd, repent.
Wars, horrid Wars I view; a field of Blood;
And *Tyber* rolling with a Purple Flood.
Simois nor *Xanthus* shall be wanting there;   1?
A new *Achilles* shall in Arms appear:

And he, too, Goddess-born: fierce *Juno*'s Hate,
Added to hostile Force, shall urge thy Fate.
To what strange Nations shalt not thou resort,
Driv'n to sollicite Aid at ev'ry Court!   140
The Cause the same which *Ilium* once oppress'd,
A foreign Mistress, and a foreign Guest.
But thou, secure of Soul, unbent with Woes,
The more thy Fortune frowns, the more oppose.
The dawnings of thy Safety, shall be shown,   145
From whence thou least shalt hope, a *Grecian* Town.

   Thus, from the dark Recess, the Sibyl spoke,
And the resisting Air the Thunder broke;
The Cave rebellow'd; and the Temple shook.
Th' ambiguous God, who rul'd her lab'ring Breast,   150
In these mysterious Words his Mind exprest:
Some Truths reveal'd, in Terms involv'd the rest.
At length her Fury fell; her foaming ceas'd,
And, ebbing in her Soul, the God decreas'd.
Then thus the Chief: no Terror to my view,   155
No frightful Face of Danger can be new.
Inur'd to suffer, and resolv'd to dare,
The Fates, without my Pow'r, shall be without my Care.
This let me crave, since near your Grove the Road
To Hell lies open, and the dark Abode,   160
Which *Acheron* surrounds, th' innavigable Flood:
Conduct me thro' the Regions void of Light,
And lead me longing to my Father's sight.
For him, a thousand Dangers I have sought;
And, rushing where the thickest *Grecians* fought,   165
Safe on my Back the sacred Burthen brought.
He, for my sake, the raging Ocean try'd,
And Wrath of Heav'n; my still auspicious Guide;
And bore beyond the strength decrepid Age supply'd.
Oft since he breath'd his last, in dead of Night,   170
His reverend Image stood before my sight;
Enjoin'd to seek below, his holy Shade;
Conducted there, by your unerring aid.
But you, if pious Minds by Pray'rs are won,
Oblige the Father, and protect the Son.   175

Yours is the Pow'r; nor *Proserpine* in vain
Has made you Priestess of her nightly Reign.
If *Orpheus*, arm'd with his enchanting Lyre,
The ruthless King with Pity could inspire;
And from the Shades below redeem his Wife: 18
If *Pollux*, off'ring his alternate Life,
Cou'd free his Brother; and can daily go
By turns aloft, by turns descend below:
Why name I *Theseus*, or his greater Friend,
Who trod the downward Path, and upward cou'd ascend! 18
Not less than theirs, from *Jove* my Lineage came:
My Mother greater, my Descent the same.
So pray'd the *Trojan* Prince; and while he pray'd
His Hand upon the holy Altar laid.

    Then thus reply'd the Prophetess Divine: 19
O Goddess-born! of Great *Anchises* Line;
The Gates of Hell are open Night and Day;
Smooth the Descent, and easie is the Way:
But, to return, and view the chearful Skies;
In this the Task, and mighty Labour lies.   19
To few great *Jupiter* imparts this Grace:
And those of shining Worth, and Heav'nly Race.
Betwixt those Regions, and our upper Light,
Deep Forrests, and impenetrable Night
Possess the middle space: Th' Infernal Bounds   20
Cocytus, with his sable Waves, surrounds.
But if so dire a Love your Soul invades,
As twice below to view the trembling Shades;
If you so hard a Toil will undertake,
As twice to pass th' innavigable Lake;   20
Receive my Counsel. In the Neighb'ring Grove
There stands a Tree; the Queen of *Stygian Jove*
Claims it her own; thick Woods, and gloomy Night,
Conceal the happy Plant from Humane sight.
One Bough it bears; but, wond'rous to behold;   210
The ductile Rind, and Leaves, of Radiant Gold:
This, from the vulgar Branches must be torn,
And to fair *Proserpine*, the Present born:

   190 *Editor's paragraph*   202 invades,] invades; *97 98*

E're leave be giv'n to tempt the neather Skies:
The first thus rent, a second will arise;   215
And the same Metal the same room supplies.
Look round the Wood, with lifted Eyes, to see
The lurking Gold upon the fatal Tree:
Then rend it off, as holy Rites command:
The willing Metal will obey thy hand,   220
Following with ease, if, favour'd by thy Fate,
Thou art foredoom'd to view the *Stygian* State:
If not, no labour can the Tree constrain:
And strength of stubborn Arms, and Steel are vain.
Besides, you know not, while you here attend   225
Th' unworthy Fate of your unhappy Friend:
Breathless he lies: And his unbury'd Ghost,
Depriv'd of Fun'ral Rites, pollutes your Host.
Pay first his Pious Dues: And for the dead,
Two sable Sheep around his Herse be led.   230
Then, living Turfs upon his Body lay;
This done, securely take the destin'd Way,
To find the Regions destitute of Day.
    She said: and held her Peace. *Æneas* went
Sad from the Cave, and full of Discontent;   235
Unknowing whom the sacred Sibyl meant.
Achates, the Companion of his Breast,
Goes grieving by his side; with equal Cares oppress'd.
Walking, they talk'd, and fruitlesly divin'd
What Friend, the Priestess by those Words design'd.   240
But soon they found an Object to deplore;
Misenus lay extended on the Shore.
Son to the God of Winds; none so renown'd,
The Warrior Trumpet in the Field to sound:
With breathing Brass to kindle fierce Alarms;   245
And rouze to dare their Fate, in honourable Arms.
He serv'd great *Hector*; and was ever near;
Not with his Trumpet only, but his Spear.
But, by *Pelides* Arms, when *Hector* fell,
He chose *Æneas*, and he chose as well.   250
Swoln with Applause, and aiming still at more,
He now provokes the Sea Gods from the Shore;

    234 *Editor's paragraph*   243 to] of *98*

With Envy *Triton* heard the Martial sound,
And the bold Champion, for his Challenge, drown'd.
Then cast his mangled Carcass on the Strand:　　　　　25
The gazing Crowd around the Body stand.
All weep, but most *Æneas* mourns his Fate;
And hastens to perform the Funeral state.
In Altar-wise, a stately Pile they rear;
The Basis broad below, and top advanc'd in Air.　　　26
An ancient Wood, fit for the Work design'd,
(The shady Covert of the Salvage Kind)
The *Trojans* found: The sounding Axe is ply'd:
Firs, Pines, and Pitch-Trees, and the tow'ring Pride
Of Forest Ashes, feel the fatal Stroke:　　　　　26
And piercing Wedges cleave the stubborn Oak.
Huge Trunks of Trees, fell'd from the steepy Crown
Of the bare Mountains, rowl with Ruin down.
Arm'd like the rest the *Trojan* Prince appears:
And, by his pious Labour, urges theirs.　　　　　27

　　Thus while he wrought, revolving in his Mind,
The ways to compass what his Wish design'd,
He cast his Eyes upon the gloomy Grove;
And then with Vows implor'd the Queen of Love.
O may thy Pow'r, propitious still to me,　　　　　27
Conduct my steps to find the fatal Tree,
In this deep Forest; since the Sibyl's Breath
Foretold, alas! too true, *Misenus* Death.
Scarce had he said, when full before his sight
Two Doves, descending from their Airy Flight,　　　　28
Secure upon the grassy Plain alight.
He knew his Mother's Birds: and thus he pray'd:
Be you my Guides, with your auspicious Aid:
And lead my Footsteps, 'till the Branch be found,
Whose glittering Shadow guilds the sacred Ground:　　　28
And thou, great Parent! with Cœlestial Care,
In this Distress, be present to my Pray'r.
Thus having said, he stop'd: With watchful sight,
Observing still the motions of their Flight,

271 *Editor's paragraph*　　　289 Flight,] Flight. *97 98*

What course they took, what happy Signs they shew.　〕290
They fed, and flutt'ring by degrees, withdrew
Still farther from the Place; but still in view.　〕
Hopping, and flying, thus they led him on
To the slow Lake; whose baleful Stench to shun,
They wing'd their Flight aloft; then, stooping low,　　295
Perch'd on the double Tree, that bears the golden Bough.
Thro' the green Leafs the glitt'ring Shadows glow;
As on the sacred Oak, the wintry Misleto:
Where the proud Mother views her precious Brood;
And happier Branches, which she never sow'd.　　300
Such was the glitt'ring; such the ruddy Rind,
And dancing Leaves, that wanton'd in the Wind.
He seiz'd the shining Bough with griping hold;
And rent away, with ease, the ling'ring Gold.
Then, to the Sibyl's Palace bore the Prize.　〕305
Mean time, the Trojan Troops, with weeping Eyes,　〕
To dead *Misenus* pay his Obsequies.　〕

　First, from the Ground, a lofty Pile they rear,
Of Pitch-trees, Oaks, and Pines, and unctuous Firr:
The Fabrick's Front with Cypress Twigs they strew;　　310
And stick the sides with Boughs of baleful Yeugh.
The topmost part, his glitt'ring Arms adorn;
Warm Waters, then, in brazen Caldrons born,
Are pour'd to wash his Body, Joint by Joint:
And fragrant Oils the stiffen'd Limbs anoint.　　315
With Groans and Cries *Misenus* they deplore:
Then on a Bier, with Purple cover'd o're,
The breathless Body, thus bewail'd, they lay:　〕
And fire the Pile, their Faces turn'd away:　〕
(Such reverend Rites their Fathers us'd to pay.)　〕320
Pure Oyl, and Incense, on the Fire they throw:
And Fat of Victims, which his Friends bestow.
These Gifts, the greedy Flames to Dust devour;
Then, on the living Coals, red Wine they pour:
And last, the Relicks by themselves dispose;　　325
Which in a brazen Urn the Priests inclose.
Old *Chorineus* compass'd thrice the Crew;
And dip'd an Olive Branch in holy Dew;

　　　308 *Editor's paragraph*

Which thrice he sprinkl'd round; and thrice aloud
Invok'd the dead, and then dismiss'd the Crowd.
    But good *Æneas* order'd on the Shore
A stately Tomb; whose top a Trumpet bore:
A Souldier's Fauchion, and a Sea-man's Oar.
Thus was his Friend interr'd: And deathless Fame
Still to the lofty Cape consigns his Name.
    These Rites perform'd, the Prince, without delay,
Hastes to the neather World, his destin'd Way.
Deep was the Cave; and downward as it went
From the wide Mouth, a rocky rough Descent;
And here th' access a gloomy Grove defends;
And there th' unnavigable Lake extends.
O're whose unhappy Waters, void of Light,
No Bird presumes to steer his Airy Flight;
Such deadly Stenches from the depth arise,
And steaming Sulphur, that infects the Skies.
From hence the *Grecian* Bards their Legends make,
And give the name *Avernus* to the Lake.
Four sable Bullocks, in the Yoke untaught,
For Sacrifice the pious Heroe brought.
The Priestess pours the Wine betwixt their Horns:
Then cuts the curling Hair; that first Oblation burns.
Invoking *Hecate* hither to repair;
(A pow'rful Name in Hell, and upper Air.)
The sacred Priests with ready Knives bereave
The Beasts of Life; and in full Bowls receive
The streaming Blood: A Lamb to Hell and Night,
(The sable Wool without a streak of white)
Æneas offers: And, by Fates decree,
A barren Heifar, *Proserpine* to thee.
With Holocausts he *Pluto*'s Altar fills:
Sev'n brawny Bulls with his own Hand he kills:
Then on the broiling Entrails Oyl he pours;
Which, ointed thus, the raging Flame devours.
Late, the Nocturnal Sacrifice begun;
Nor ended, 'till the next returning Sun.
Then Earth began to bellow, Trees to dance;
And howling Dogs in glimm'ring Light advance;
E're *Hecate* came: Far hence be Souls prophane,

The Sibyl cry'd, and from the Grove abstain.
Now, *Trojan*, take the way thy Fates afford: 370
Assume thy Courage, and unsheath thy Sword.
She said, and pass'd along the gloomy Space:
The Prince pursu'd her Steps with equal pace.

    Ye Realms, yet unreveal'd to human sight,
Ye Gods, who rule the Regions of the Night, -   375
Ye gliding Ghosts, permit me to relate
The mystick Wonders of your silent State.

    Obscure they went thro dreery Shades, that led
Along the waste Dominions of the dead:
Thus wander Travellers in Woods by Night,   380
By the Moon's doubtful, and malignant Light:
When *Jove* in dusky Clouds involves the Skies;
And the faint Crescent shoots by fits before their Eyes.

    Just in the Gate, and in the Jaws of Hell,
Revengeful Cares, and sullen Sorrows dwell;   385
And pale Diseases, and repining Age;
Want, Fear, and Famine's unresisted rage.
Here Toils, and Death, and Death's half-brother, Sleep,
Forms terrible to view, their Centry keep:
With anxious Pleasures of a guilty Mind,   390
Deep Frauds before, and open Force behind:
The Furies Iron Beds, and Strife that shakes
Her hissing Tresses, and unfolds her Snakes.
Full in the midst of this infernal Road,
An Elm displays her dusky Arms abroad;   395
The God of Sleep there hides his heavy Head:
And empty Dreams on ev'ry Leaf are spread.
Of various Forms unnumber'd Specters more;
Centaurs, and double Shapes, besiege the Door:
Before the Passage horrid *Hydra* stands,   400
And *Briareus* with all his hundred Hands:
Gorgons, *Geryon* with his triple Frame;
And vain *Chimæra* vomits empty Flame.
The Chief unsheath'd his shining Steel, prepar'd,
Tho seiz'd with sudden Fear, to force the Guard.   405
Off'ring his brandish'd Weapon at their Face;
Had not the Sibyl stop'd his eager Pace,
And told him what those empty Fantomes were;

Forms without Bodies, and impassive Air.
Hence to deep *Acheron* they take their way;   41
Whose troubled Eddies, thick with Ooze and Clay,
Are whirl'd aloft, and in *Cocytus* lost:
There *Charon* stands, who rules the dreary Coast:
A sordid God; down from his hoary Chin
A length of Beard descends; uncomb'd, unclean: 41
His Eyes, like hollow Furnaces on Fire:
A Girdle, foul with grease, binds his obscene Attire.
He spreads his Canvas, with his Pole he steers;
The Freights of flitting Ghosts in his thin Bottom bears.
He look'd in Years; yet in his Years were seen   42(
A youthful Vigour, and Autumnal green.
An Airy Crowd came rushing where he stood;
Which fill'd the Margin of the fatal Flood.
Husbands and Wives, Boys and unmarry'd Maids;
And mighty Heroes more Majestick Shades.   42:
And Youths, intomb'd before their Fathers Eyes,
With hollow Groans, and Shrieks, and feeble Cries:
Thick as the Leaves in Autumn strow the Woods:
Or Fowls, by Winter forc'd, forsake the Floods,
And wing their hasty flight to happier Lands: ⎫ 43(
Such, and so thick, the shiv'ring Army stands: ⎬
And press for passage with extended hands.   ⎭

   Now these, now those, the surly Boatman bore:
The rest he drove to distance from the Shore.
The Heroe, who beheld with wond'ring Eyes,   43\$
The Tumult mix'd with Shrieks, Laments, and Cries;
Ask'd of his Guide, what the rude Concourse meant?
Why to the Shore the thronging People bent?
What Forms of Law, among the Ghosts were us'd?
Why some were ferry'd o're, and some refus'd?   440

   Son of *Anchises*, Offspring of the Gods,
The Sibyl said; you see the *Stygian* Floods,
The Sacred Stream, which Heav'n's Imperial State
Attests in Oaths, and fears to violate.
The Ghosts rejected, are th' unhappy Crew   445
Depriv'd of Sepulchers, and Fun'ral due.
The Boatman *Charon*; those, the bury'd host,

He Ferries over to the Farther Coast.
Nor dares his Transport Vessel cross the Waves,
With such whose Bones are not compos'd in Graves.   450
A hundred years they wander on the Shore,
At length, their Pennance done, are wafted o're.
　　The *Trojan* Chief his forward pace repress'd;
Revolving anxious Thoughts within his Breast.
He saw his Friends, who whelm'd beneath the Waves,   455
Their Fun'ral Honours claim'd, and ask'd their quiet Graves.
The lost *Leucaspis* in the Crowd he knew;
And the brave Leader of the *Lycian* Crew:
Whom, on the *Tyrrhene* Seas, the Tempests met;
The Sailors master'd, and the Ship o'reset.   460
Amidst the Spirits *Palinurus* press'd;
Yet fresh from life; a new admitted Guest.
Who, while he steering view'd the Stars, and bore
His Course from *Affrick*, to the *Latian* Shore,
Fell headlong down. The *Trojan* fix'd his view;   465
And scarcely through the gloom the sullen Shadow knew.
Then thus the Prince. What envious Pow'r, O Friend,
Brought your lov'd life to this disastrous end?
For *Phœbus*, ever true in all he said,
Has, in your fate alone, my Faith betray'd.   470
The God foretold you shou'd not die, before
You reach'd, secure from Seas, th' *Italian* Shore.
Is this th' unerring Pow'r? The Ghost reply'd,
Nor *Phœbus* flatter'd, nor his Answers ly'd;
Nor envious Gods have sent me to the Deep: 475
But while the Stars, and course of Heav'n I keep,
My weary'd Eyes were seiz'd with fatal sleep.
I fell; and with my weight, the Helm constrain'd,
Was drawn along, which yet my gripe retain'd.
Now by the Winds, and raging Waves, I swear,   480
Your Safety, more than mine, was then my Care:
Lest, of the Guide bereft, the Rudder lost,
Your Ship shou'd run against the rocky Coast.
Three blust'ring Nights, born by the Southern blast,
I floated; and discover'd Land at last: 485

453 *Editor's paragraph*   470 betray'd.] betray'd? *97 98*   472 Shore.] Shore?
97 98

High on a Mounting Wave, my head I bore:
Forcing my Strength, and gath'ring to the Shore:
Panting, but past the danger, now I seiz'd
The Craggy Cliffs, and my tyr'd Members eas'd:
While, cumber'd with my dropping Cloaths, I lay,
The cruel Nation, covetous of Prey,
Stain'd with my Blood th' unhospitable Coast:
And now, by Winds and Waves, my lifeless Limbs are tost.
Which O avert, by yon Etherial Light
Which I have lost, for this eternal Night:
Or if by dearer tyes you may be won,
By your dead Sire, and by your living Son,
Redeem from this Reproach, my wand'ring Ghost;
Or with your Navy seek the *Velin* Coast:
And in a peaceful Grave my Corps compose:
Or, if a nearer way your Mother shows,
Without whose Aid, you durst not undertake
This frightful Passage o're the *Stygian* Lake;
Lend to this Wretch your Hand, and waft him o're
To the sweet Banks of yon forbidden Shore.
Scarce had he said, the Prophetess began;
What Hopes delude thee, miserable Man?
Think'st thou thus unintomb'd to cross the Floods,
To view the Furies, and Infernal Gods;
And visit, without leave, the dark abodes?
Attend the term of long revolving Years:
Fate, and the dooming Gods, are deaf to Tears.
This Comfort of thy dire Misfortune take;
The Wrath of Heav'n, inflicted for thy sake,
With Vengeance shall pursue th' inhumane Coast.
Till they propitiate thy offended Ghost,
And raise a Tomb, with Vows, and solemn Pray'r;
And *Palinurus* name the Place shall bear.
This calm'd his Cares: sooth'd with his future Fame;
And pleas'd to hear his propagated Name.
Now nearer to the *Stygian* Lake they draw:
Whom from the Shore, the surly Boatman saw:
Observ'd their Passage thro' the shady Wood;
And mark'd their near Approaches to the Flood:

519 calm'd] claim'd *98*

Then thus he call'd aloud, inflam'd with Wrath; 525
Mortal, what e're, who this forbidden Path
In Arms presum'st to tread, I charge thee stand,
And tell thy Name, and Buis'ness in the Land.
Know this, the Realm of Night; the *Stygian* Shore:
My Boat conveys no living Bodies o're: 530
Nor was I pleas'd great *Theseus* once to bear;
Who forc'd a Passage with his pointed Spear;
Nor strong *Alcides*: Men of mighty Fame;
And from th' immortal Gods their Lineage came.
In Fetters one the barking Porter ty'd, 535
And took him trembling from his Sov'raign's side:
Two sought by Force to seize his beauteous Bride.
To whom the Sibyl thus, compose thy Mind:
Nor Frauds are here contriv'd, nor Force design'd.
Still may the Dog the wand'ring Troops constrain 540
Of Airy Ghosts; and vex the guilty Train;
And with her grisly Lord his lovely Queen remain.
The *Trojan* Chief, whose Lineage is from *Jove*,
Much fam'd for Arms, and more for filial Love,
Is sent to seek his Sire, in your *Elisian* Grove. 545
If neither Piety, nor Heav'n's Command,
Can gain his Passage to the *Stygian* Strand,
This fatal Present shall prevail, at least;
Then shew'd the shining Bough, conceal'd within her Vest.
No more was needful: for the gloomy God 550
Stood mute with Awe, to see the Golden Rod:
Admir'd the destin'd Off'ring to his Queen;
(A venerable Gift so rarely seen.)
His Fury thus appeas'd, he puts to Land:
The Ghosts forsake their Seats, at his Command: 555
He clears the Deck, receives the mighty Freight,
The leaky Vessel groans beneath the weight.
Slowly she sails; and scarcely stems the Tides:
The pressing Water pours within her sides.
His Passengers at length are wafted o're; 560
Expos'd in muddy Weeds, upon the miry Shore.
    No sooner landed, in his Den they found

533 *Alcides*:] *Alcides*, 97 98   558 she *Scott-Saintsbury, Noyes*: he 97 98
562 *Editor's paragraph*

The triple Porter of the *Stygian* Sound:
Grim *Cerberus*; who soon began to rear
His crested Snakes, and arm'd his bristling Hair.   5
The prudent Sibyl had before prepar'd
A Sop, in Honey steep'd, to charm the Guard.
Which, mix'd with pow'rful Drugs, she cast before
His greedy grinning Jaws, just op'd to roar:
With three enormous Mouths he gapes; and streight,   5
With Hunger prest, devours the pleasing Bait.
Long draughts of Sleep his monstrous Limbs enslave;
He reels, and falling, fills the spacious Cave.
The Keeper charm'd, the Chief without Delay
Pass'd on, and took th' irremeable way.   5
Before the Gates, the Cries of Babes new born,
Whom Fate had from their tender Mothers torn,
Assault his Ears: Then those, whom Form of Laws
Condemn'd to die, when Traitors judg'd their Cause.
Nor want they Lots, nor Judges to review   5
The wrongful Sentence, and award a new.
Minos, the strict Inquisitor, appears;
And Lives and Crimes, with his Assessors, hears.
Round, in his Urn, the blended Balls he rowls;
Absolves the Just, and dooms the Guilty Souls.   5
The next in Place, and Punishment, are they
Who prodigally throw their Souls away.
Fools, who repining at their wretched State,
And loathing anxious life, suborn'd their Fate.
With late Repentance, now they wou'd retrieve   5
The Bodies they forsook, and wish to live.
Their Pains and Poverty desire to bear,
To view the Light of Heav'n, and breath the vital Air:
But Fate forbids; the *Stygian* Floods oppose;
And, with nine circling Streams, the captive Souls inclose. 5
    Not far from thence, the mournful Fields appear;
So call'd, from Lovers that inhabit there.
The Souls, whom that unhappy Flame invades,
In secret Solitude, and Myrtle Shades,
Make endless Moans, and pining with Desire,   6
Lament too late, their unextinguish'd Fire.
Here *Procris*, *Eryphile* here, he found

Baring her Breast, yet bleeding with the Wound
Made by her Son. He saw *Pasiphae* there,
With *Phædra*'s Ghost, a foul incestuous pair;   605
There *Laodamia*, with *Evadne*, moves:
Unhappy both; but loyal in their Loves.
Cæneus, a Woman once, and once a Man;
But ending in the Sex she first began.
Not far from these *Phœnician Dido* stood;   610
Fresh from her Wound, her Bosom bath'd in Blood.
Whom, when the *Trojan* Heroe hardly knew,
Obscure in Shades, and with a doubtful view,
(Doubtful as he who sees thro' dusky Night,
Or thinks he sees the Moon's uncertain Light:)   615
With Tears he first approach'd the sullen Shade;
And, as his Love inspir'd him, thus he said.
Unhappy Queen! then is the common breath
Of Rumour true, in your reported Death,
And I, alas, the Cause! By Heav'n, I vow,   620
And all the Pow'rs that rule the Realms below,
Unwilling I forsook your friendly State:
Commanded by the Gods, and forc'd by Fate.
Those Gods, that Fate, whose unresisted Might ⎫
Have sent me to these Regions, void of Light, ⎬ 625
Thro' the vast Empire of eternal Night.   ⎭
Nor dar'd I to presume, that, press'd with Grief,
My Flight should urge you to this dire Relief.
Stay, stay your Steps, and listen to my Vows:
'Tis the last Interview that Fate allows!   630
In vain he thus attempts her Mind to move,
With Tears, and Pray'rs, and late repenting Love.
Disdainfully she look'd; then turning round,
But fix'd her Eyes unmov'd upon the Ground.
And, what he says, and swears, regards no more   635
Than the deaf Rocks, when the loud Billows roar.
But whirl'd away, to shun his hateful sight,
Hid in the Forest, and the Shades of Night.
Then sought *Sicheus*, thro' the shady Grove,
Who answer'd all her Cares, and equal'd all her Love.   640
    Some pious Tears the pitying Heroe paid;

606 There *98*: Chast *97*   614 sees] runs *98*   641 *Editor's paragraph*

And follow'd with his Eyes the flitting Shade.
Then took the forward Way, by Fate ordain'd,
And, with his Guide, the farther Fields attain'd;
Where, sever'd from the rest, the Warrior Souls remain'd.   645
Tideus he met, with *Meleager*'s Race;
The Pride of Armies, and the Souldier's Grace;
And pale *Adrastus* with his ghastly Face.
Of *Trojan* Chiefs he view'd a num'rous Train:
All much lamented, all in Battel slain.   650
Glaucus and *Medon*, high above the rest,
Antenor's Sons, and *Ceres* sacred Priest:
And proud *Ideus*, *Priam*'s Charioteer;
Who shakes his empty Reins, and aims his Airy Spear.
The gladsome Ghosts, in circling Troops, attend,   655
And with unweary'd Eyes behold their Friend.
Delight to hover near; and long to know
What buis'ness brought him to the Realms below.
    But *Argive* Chiefs, and *Agamemnon*'s Train,
When his refulgent Arms flash'd thro' the shady Plain,   660
Fled from his well known Face, with wonted Fear,
As when his thund'ring Sword, and pointed Spear,
Drove headlong to their Ships, and glean'd the routed Reer.
They rais'd a feeble Cry, with trembling Notes:
But the weak Voice deceiv'd their gasping Throats.   665
Here *Priam*'s Son, *Deiphobus*, he found:
Whose Face and Limbs were one continu'd Wound.
Dishonest, with lop'd Arms, the Youth appears:
Spoil'd of his Nose, and shorten'd of his Ears.
He scarcely knew him, striving to disown   670
His blotted Form, and blushing to be known.
And therefore first began. O *Teucer*'s Race,
Who durst thy faultless Figure thus deface?
What heart cou'd wish, what hand inflict this dire Disgrace?
Twas fam'd, that in our last and fatal Night,   675
Your single Prowess long sustain'd the Fight:
Till tir'd, not forc'd, a glorious Fate you chose:
And fell upon a Heap of slaughter'd Foes.
But in remembrance of so brave a Deed,
A Tomb, and Fun'ral Honours I decreed: 680
Thrice call'd your *Manes*, on the *Trojan* Plains:

The place your Armour, and your Name retains.
Your Body too I sought; and had I found,
Design'd for Burial in your Native Ground.
    The Ghost reply'd, your Piety has paid   685
All needful Rites, to rest my wand'ring Shade:
But cruel Fate, and my more cruel Wife,
To *Grecian* Swords betray'd my sleeping Life.
These are the Monuments of *Helen*'s Love:
The Shame I bear below, the Marks I bore above.   690
You know in what deluding Joys we past
The Night, that was by Heav'n decreed our last.
For when the fatal Horse, descending down,
Pregnant with Arms, o'rewhelm'd th' unhappy Town;
She feign'd Nocturnal Orgyes: left my Bed,   695
And, mix'd with *Trojan* Dames, the Dances led.
Then, waving high her Torch, the Signal made,
Which rouz'd the *Grecians* from their Ambuscade.
With Watching overworn, with Cares opprest,
Unhappy I had laid me down to rest;   700
And heavy Sleep my weary Limbs possess'd.
Mean time my worthy Wife, our Arms mislay'd;
And from beneath my head my Sword convey'd:
The Door unlatch'd; and with repeated calls,
Invites her former Lord within my walls.   705
Thus in her Crime her confidence she plac'd:
And with new Treasons wou'd redeem the past.
What need I more, into the Room they ran;
And meanly murther'd a defenceless Man.
Ulysses, basely born, first led the way: 710
Avenging Pow'rs! with Justice if I pray,
That Fortune be their own another day.
    But answer you; and in your turn relate,
What brought you, living, to the *Stygian* State?
Driv'n by the Winds and Errors of the Sea,   715
Or did you Heav'ns Superior Doom obey?
Or tell what other Chance conducts your way?
To view, with Mortal Eyes, our dark Retreats,
Tumults and Torments of th' Infernal Seats?
    While thus, in talk, the flying Hours they pass,   720

720 *Editor's paragraph*

The Sun had finish'd more than half his Race:
And they, perhaps, in Words and Tears had spent
The little time of stay, which Heav'n had lent.
But thus the Sibyl chides their long delay;
Night rushes down, and headlong drives the Day: 725
Tis here, in different Paths, the way divides:
The right, to *Pluto*'s Golden Palace guides:
The left to that unhappy Region tends,
Which to the depth of *Tartarus* descends;
The Seat of Night profound, and punish'd Fiends.   730
Then thus *Deiphobus*: O Sacred Maid!
Forbear to chide; and be your Will Obey'd:
Lo to the secret Shadows I retire,
To pay my Penance 'till my Years expire.
Proceed Auspicious Prince, with Glory Crownd,   735
And born to better Fates than I have found.
He said; and while he said, his Steps he turn'd
To Secret Shadows; and in silence Mourn'd.

    The Heroe, looking on the left, espy'd
A lofty Tow'r, and strong on ev'ry side   740
With treble Walls, which *Phlegethon* surrounds,
Whose fiery Flood the burning Empire bounds:
And press'd betwixt the Rocks, the bellowing noise resounds.
Wide is the fronting Gate, and rais'd on high
With Adamantine Columns, threats the Sky.   745
Vain is the force of Man, and Heav'ns as vain,
To crush the Pillars which the Pile sustain.
Sublime on these a Tow'r of Steel is rear'd;
And dire *Tisiphone* there keeps the Ward:
Girt in her sanguine Gown, by Night and Day,   750
Observant of the Souls that pass the downward way:
From hence are heard the Groans of Ghosts, the pains
Of sounding Lashes, and of dragging Chains.
The *Trojan* stood astonish'd at their Cries;
And ask'd his Guide, from whence those Yells arise?   755
And what the Crimes and what the Tortures were,
And loud Laments that rent the liquid Air?
    She thus reply'd: The chast and holy Race,
Are all forbidden this polluted Place.

739 *Editor's paragraph*   749 Ward:] Ward. *97 98*   **758** *Editor's paragraph*

But *Hecate*, when she gave to rule the Woods,   760
Then led me trembling thro' these dire Abodes:
And taught the Tortures of th' avenging Gods.
These are the Realms of unrelenting Fate:
And awful *Rhadamanthus* rules the State.
He hears and judges each committed Crime;   765
Enquires into the Manner, Place, and Time.
The conscious Wretch must all his Acts reveal:
Loath to confess, unable to conceal:
From the first Moment of his vital Breath,
To his last Hour of unrepenting Death.   770
Straight, o're the guilty Ghost, the Fury shakes
The sounding Whip, and brandishes her Snakes:
And the pale Sinner, with her Sisters, takes.
Then, of it self, unfolds th' Eternal Door:
With dreadful Sounds the brazen Hinges roar.   775
You see, before the Gate, what stalking Ghost
Commands the Guard, what Centries keep the Post:
More formidable *Hydra* stands within;
Whose Jaws with Iron Teeth severely grin.
The gaping Gulph, low to the Centre lies;   780
And twice as deep as Earth is distant from the Skies.
The Rivals of the Gods, the *Titan* Race,
Here sing'd with Lightning, rowl within th' unfathom'd space.
Here lye th' *Alœan* Twins, (I saw them both)
Enormous Bodies, of Gigantick Growth;   785
Who dar'd in Fight the Thund'rer to defy;
Affect his Heav'n, and force him from the Sky.
Salmoneus, suff'ring cruel Pains, I found,
For emulating *Jove*; the ratling Sound
Of Mimick Thunder, and the glitt'ring Blaze   790
Of pointed Lightnings, and their forky Rays.
Through *Elis*, and the *Grecian* Towns he flew:
Th' audacious Wretch four fiery Coursers drew:
He wav'd a Torch aloft, and, madly vain,
Sought Godlike Worship from a Servile Train.   795
Ambitious Fool, with horny Hoofs to pass
O're hollow Arches, of resounding Brass;
To rival Thunder, in its rapid Course:
And imitate inimitable Force.

But he, the King of Heav'n, obscure on high,　　　　　800
Bar'd his red Arm, and launching from the Sky
His writhen Bolt, not shaking empty Smoak,
Down to the deep Abyss the flaming Felon strook.
There *Tityus* was to see; who took his Birth
From Heav'n, his Nursing from the foodful Earth.　　805
Here his Gygantic Limbs, with large Embrace,
Infold nine Acres of Infernal Space.
A rav'nous Vulture in his open'd side,
Her crooked Beak and cruel Tallons try'd:
Still for the growing Liver dig'd his Breast;　　　　810
The growing Liver still supply'd the Feast.
Still are his Entrails fruitful to their Pains:
Th' immortal Hunger lasts, th' immortal Food remains.
Ixion and *Perithous* I cou'd name;
And more *Thessalian* Chiefs of mighty Fame.　　　　815
High o're their Heads a mould'ring Rock is plac'd,
That promises a fall; and shakes at ev'ry Blast.
They lye below, on Golden Beds display'd,
And genial Feasts, with Regal Pomp, are made.
The Queen of Furies by their sides is set;　　　　　820
And snatches from their Mouths th' untasted Meat.
Which, if they touch, her hissing Snakes she rears:
Tossing her Torch, and thund'ring in their Ears.
Then they, who Brothers better Claim disown,
Expel their Parents, and usurp the Throne;　　　　825
Defraud their Clients, and to Lucre sold,
Sit brooding on unprofitable Gold:
Who dare not give, and ev'n refuse to lend
To their poor Kindred, or a wanting Friend:
Vast is the Throng of these; nor less the Train　　830
Of lustful Youths, for foul Adultry slain.
Hosts of Deserters, who their Honour sold,
And basely broke their Faith for Bribes of Gold:
All these within the Dungeon's depth remain:
Despairing Pardon, and expecting Pain.　　　　　835
Ask not what Pains; nor farther seek to know
Their Process, or the Forms of Law below.
Some rowl a weighty Stone; some laid along,
And bound with burning Wires, on Spokes of Wheels are hung.

Unhappy *Theseus*, doom'd for ever there, 840
Is fix'd by Fate on his Eternal Chair:
And wretched *Phlegias* warns the World with Cries;
(Cou'd Warning make the World more just or wise,)
Learn Righteousness, and dread th' avenging Deities.
To Tyrants others have their Country sold, 845
Imposing Foreign Lords, for Foreign Gold:
Some have old Laws repeal'd, new Statutes made;
Not as the People pleas'd, but as they paid.
With Incest some their Daughters Bed prophan'd,
All dar'd the worst of Ills, and what they dar'd, attain'd. 850
Had I a hundred Mouths, a hundred Tongues,
And Throats of Brass, inspir'd with Iron Lungs,
I could not half those horrid Crimes repeat:
Nor half the Punishments those Crimes have met.
But let us haste our Voyage to pursue; 855
The Walls of *Pluto*'s Palace are in view.
The Gate, and Iron Arch above it, stands:
On Anvils labour'd by the *Cyclops* Hands.
Before our farther way the Fates allow,
Here must we fix on high the Golden Bough. 860
   She said, and thro' the gloomy Shades they past,
And chose the middle Path: Arriv'd at last,
The Prince, with living Water, sprinkl'd o're
His Limbs, and Body; then approach'd the Door.
Possess'd the Porch, and on the Front above 865
He fix'd the fatal Bough, requir'd by *Pluto*'s Love.
These Holy Rites perform'd, they took their Way,
Where long extended Plains of Pleasure lay.
The verdant Fields with those of Heav'n may vye;
With *Æther* vested, and a Purple Sky: 870
The blissful Seats of Happy Souls below:
Stars of their own, and their own Suns they know.
Their Airy Limbs in Sports they exercise,
And, on the Green, contend the Wrestler's Prize.
Some, in Heroick Verse, divinely sing; 875
Others in artful Measures lead the ring.
The *Thracian* Bard, surrounded by the rest,
There stands conspicuous in his flowing Vest.

857 stands:] stands *98*   861 *Editor's paragraph*

His flying Fingers, and harmonious Quill,
Strike sev'n distinguish'd Notes, and sev'n at once they fill.   880
Here found they *Teucer*'s old Heroick Race;
Born better times and happier Years to grace.
Assaracus and *Ilus* here enjoy
Perpetual Fame, with him who founded *Troy*.
The Chief beheld their Chariots from afar;   885
Their shining Arms, and Coursers train'd to War:
Their Lances fix'd in Earth, their Steeds around,
Free from their Harness, graze the flow'ry Ground.
The love of Horses which they had, alive,
And care of Chariots, after Death survive.   890
Some chearful Souls, were feasting on the Plain;
Some did the Song, and some their Choir maintain:
Beneath a Laurel Shade, where mighty *Po*
Mounts up to Woods above, and hides his Head below.
Here Patriots live, who, for their Countries good,   895
In fighting Fields, were prodigal of Blood:
Priests of unblemish'd Lives here make Abode;
And Poets worthy their inspiring God:
And searching Wits, of more Mechanick parts,
Who grac'd their Age with new invented Arts.   900
Those who, to worth, their Bounty did extend;
And those who knew that Bounty to commend.
The Heads of these with holy Fillets bound;
And all their Temples were with Garlands crown'd.

To these the Sibyl thus her Speech address'd: 905
And first, to him surrounded by the rest;
Tow'ring his Height, and ample was his Breast:
Say happy Souls, Divine *Musæus* say,
Where lives *Anchises*, and where lies our Way
To find the Heroe, for whose only sake   910
We sought the dark Abodes, and cross'd the bitter Lake?
To this the Sacred Poet thus reply'd;
In no fix'd place the Happy Souls reside.
In Groves we live; and lye on mossy Beds
By Crystal Streams, that murmur through the Meads: 915
But pass yon easie Hill, and thence descend,
The Path conducts you to your Journeys end.

This said, he led them up the Mountains brow,
And shews them all the shining Fields below;
They wind the Hill, and thro' the blissful Meadows go.　920
But old *Anchises*, in a flow'ry Vale,
Review'd his muster'd Race; and took the Tale:
Those Happy Spirits, which ordain'd by Fate,
For future Beings, and new Bodies wait.
With studious Thought observ'd th' illustrious Throng;　925
In Nature's Order as they pass'd along.
Their Names, their Fates, their Conduct, and their Care,
In peaceful Senates, and successful War.
He, when *Æneas* on the Plain appears,
Meets him with open Arms, and falling Tears.　930
Welcome, he said, the Gods undoubted Race,
O long expected, to my dear Embrace;
Once more 'tis giv'n me to behold your Face!
The Love, and Pious Duty which you pay,
Have pass'd the Perils of so hard a way.　935
'Tis true, computing times, I now believ'd
The happy Day approach'd; nor are my Hopes deceiv'd.
What length of Lands, what Oceans have you pass'd,
What Storms sustain'd, and on what Shores been cast?
How have I fear'd your Fate! But fear'd it most,　940
When Love assail'd you, on the *Lybian* Coast.
To this, the Filial Duty thus replies;
Your sacred Ghost, before my sleeping Eyes,
Appear'd; and often urg'd this painful Enterprise.
After long tossing on the *Tyrrhene* Sea,　945
My Navy rides at Anchor in the Bay.
But reach your Hand, oh Parent Shade, nor shun
The dear Embraces of your longing Son!
He said; and falling Tears his Face bedew:
Then thrice, around his Neck, his Arms he threw;　950
And thrice the flitting Shadow slip'd away;
Like Winds, or empty Dreams that fly the Day.
　Now in a secret Vale, the *Trojan* sees
A sep'rate Grove, thro' which a gentle Breeze
Plays with a passing Breath, and whispers thro' the Trees.　955

922 Tale:] Tale. *97 98*　　931 Gods] God's *98*　　932 expected,] expected
97 98　　953–1247 *Editor's paragraphs*

And just before the Confines of the Wood,
The gliding *Lethe* leads her silent Flood.
About the Boughs an Airy Nation flew,
Thick as the humming Bees, that hunt the Golden Dew;
In Summer's heat, on tops of Lillies feed,
And creep within their Bells, to suck the balmy Seed.
The winged Army roams the Fields around;
The Rivers and the Rocks remurmur to the sound.
Æneas wond'ring stood: Then ask'd the Cause,
Which to the Stream the Crowding People draws.
Then thus the Sire. The Souls that throng the Flood
Are those, to whom, by Fate, are other Bodies ow'd:
In *Lethe*'s Lake they long Oblivion tast;
Of future Life secure, forgetful of the Past.
Long has my Soul desir'd this time, and place,
To set before your sight your glorious Race.
That this presaging Joy may fire your Mind,
To seek the Shores by Destiny design'd.
O Father, can it be, that Souls sublime,
Return to visit our Terrestrial Clime?
And that the Gen'rous Mind, releas'd by Death,
Can Covet lazy Limbs, and Mortal Breath?
    Anchises then, in order, thus begun
To clear those Wonders to his Godlike Son.
Know first, that Heav'n, and Earth's compacted Frame,
And flowing Waters, and the starry Flame,
And both the Radiant Lights, one Common Soul
Inspires, and feeds, and animates the whole.
This Active Mind infus'd through all the Space,
Unites and mingles with the mighty Mass.
Hence Men and Beasts the Breath of Life obtain;
And Birds of Air, and Monsters of the Main.
Th' Etherial Vigour is in all the same,
And every Soul is fill'd with equal Flame:
As much as Earthy Limbs, and gross allay
Of Mortal Members, subject to decay,
Blunt not the Beams of Heav'n and edge of Day.
From this course Mixture of Terrestrial parts,
Desire, and Fear, by turns possess their Hearts:

962 Fields] Field *98*

And Grief, and Joy: Nor can the groveling Mind, ⎫ 995
In the dark Dungeon of the Limbs confin'd, ⎬
Assert the Native Skies; or own its heav'nly Kind. ⎭
Nor Death it self can wholly wash their Stains;
But long contracted Filth, ev'n in the Soul remains.
The Reliques of inveterate Vice they wear; 1000
And Spots of Sin obscene, in ev'ry Face appear.
For this are various Penances enjoyn'd;
And some are hung to bleach, upon the Wind;
Some plung'd in Waters, others purg'd in Fires,
Till all the Dregs are drain'd; and all the Rust expires: 1005
All have their *Manes*, and those *Manes* bear: ⎫
The few, so cleans'd to these Abodes repair: ⎬
And breath, in ample Fields, the soft *Elysian* Air. ⎭
Then are they happy, when by length of time
The Scurf is worn away, of each committed Crime. 1010
No Speck is left, of their habitual Stains;
But the pure Æther of the Soul remains.
But, when a Thousand rowling Years are past,
(So long their Punishments and Penance last;)
Whole Droves of Minds are, by the driving God, 1015
Compell'd to drink the deep *Lethæan* Flood:
In large forgetful draughts to steep the Cares
Of their past Labours, and their Irksom Years.
That, unrememb'ring of its former Pain,
The Soul may suffer mortal Flesh again. 1020
    Thus having said; the Father Spirit, leads
The Priestess and his Son through Swarms of Shades,
And takes a rising Ground, from thence to see
The long Procession of his Progeny.
Survey (pursu'd the Sire) this airy Throng; 1025
As, offer'd to thy view, they pass along.
These are th' *Italian* Names, which Fate will join
With ours, and graff upon the *Trojan* Line.
Observe the Youth who first appears in sight;
And holds the nearest Station to the Light: 1030
Already seems to snuff the vital Air;
And leans just forward, on a shining Spear;

Silvius is he: thy last begotten Race;
But first in order sent, to fill thy place,
An *Alban* Name; but mix'd with *Dardan* Blood;   10
Born in the Covert of a shady Wood:
Him fair *Lavinia*, thy surviving Wife,
Shall breed in Groves, to lead a solitary Life.
In *Alba* he shall fix his Royal Seat:
And, born a King, a Race of Kings beget.   10.
Then *Procas*, Honour of the *Trojan* Name,
Capys, and *Numitor*, of endless Fame.
A second *Silvius* after these appears;
Silvius Æneas, for thy Name he bears.
For Arms and Justice equally renown'd;   10.
Who, late restor'd, in *Alba* shall be crown'd.
How great they look, how vig'rously they wield
Their weighty Lances, and sustain the Shield!
But they, who crown'd with Oaken Wreaths appear,
Shall *Gabian* Walls, and strong *Fidena* rear: 10.
Nomentum, *Bola*, with *Pometia*, found;
And raise *Colatian* Tow'rs on Rocky Ground.
All these shall then be Towns of mighty Fame;
Tho' now they lye obscure; and Lands without a Name.
See *Romulus* the great, born to restore   10.
The Crown that once his injur'd Grandsire wore.
This Prince, a Priestess of our Blood shall bear;
And like his Sire in Arms he shall appear.
Two rising Crests his Royal Head adorn;
Born from a God, himself to Godhead born.   100
His Sire already signs him for the Skies,
And marks his Seat amidst the Deities.
Auspicious Chief! thy Race in times to come
Shall spread the Conquests of Imperial *Rome*.
Rome whose ascending Tow'rs shall Heav'n invade;   100
Involving Earth and Ocean in her Shade.
High as the Mother of the Gods in place;
And proud, like her, of an Immortal Race.
Then when in Pomp she makes the *Phrygian* round;
With Golden Turrets on her Temples crown'd: 107
A hundred Gods her sweeping Train supply;

1057 our] your *98*   1062 his] the *98*

Her Offspring all, and all command the Sky.

   Now fix your Sight, and stand intent, to see
Your *Roman* Race, and *Julian* Progeny.
The mighty *Cæsar* waits his vital Hour;   1075
Impatient for the World, and grasps his promis'd Pow'r.
But next behold the Youth of Form Divine,
Cæsar himself, exalted in his Line;
Augustus, promis'd oft, and long foretold,
Sent to the Realm that *Saturn* rul'd of old;   1080
Born to restore a better Age of Gold.
Affrick, and *India*, shall his Pow'r obey,
He shall extend his propagated Sway,
Beyond the Solar Year; without the starry Way.
Where *Atlas* turns the rowling Heav'ns around;   1085
And his broad Shoulders with their Lights are crown'd.
At his fore-seen Approach, already quake
The *Caspian* Kingdoms, and *Mæotian* Lake.
Their Seers behold the Tempest from afar;
And threatning Oracles denounce the War.   1090
Nile hears him knocking at his sev'nfold Gates;
And seeks his hidden Spring, and fears his Nephews Fates.
Nor *Hercules* more Lands or Labours knew,
Not tho' the brazen-footed Hind he slew;
Freed *Erymanthus* from the foaming Boar,   1095
And dip'd his Arrows in *Lernæan* Gore.
Nor *Bacchus*, turning from his *Indian* War,
By Tygers drawn triumphant in his Car,
From *Nisas* top descending on the Plains;
With curling Vines around his purple Reins.   1100
And doubt we yet thro' Dangers to pursue
The Paths of Honour, and a Crown in view?

   But what's the Man, who from afar appears,
His Head with Olive crown'd, his Hand a Censer bears?
His hoary Beard, and holy Vestments bring   1105
His lost Idea back: I know the *Roman* King.
He shall to peaceful *Rome* new Laws ordain:
Call'd from his mean abode, a Scepter to sustain.
Him, *Tullus* next in Dignity succeeds;
An active Prince, and prone to Martial Deeds.   1110

1092 Nephews] Nephew's *97 98*   1099 *Nisas*] *Nisus 97 98*

He shall his Troops for fighting Fields prepare,
Disus'd to Toils, and Triumphs of the War.
By dint of Sword his Crown he shall increase;
And scour his Armour from the Rust of Peace.
Whom *Ancus* follows, with a fawning Air;   11
But vain within, and proudly popular.
Next view the *Tarquin* Kings: Th' avenging Sword
Of *Brutus*, justly drawn, and *Rome* restor'd.
He first renews the Rods, and Axe severe;
And gives the Consuls Royal Robes to wear.   11.
His Sons, who seek the Tyrant to sustain,
And long for Arbitrary Lords again,
With Ignominy scourg'd, in open sight,
He dooms to Death deserv'd; asserting Publick Right.
Unhappy Man, to break the Pious Laws   11.
Of Nature, pleading in his Children's Cause!
Howe're the doubtful Fact is understood,   ⎤
'Tis Love of Honour, and his Country's good: ⎬
The Consul, not the Father, sheds the Blood.   ⎦
Behold *Torquatus* the same Track pursue;   11
And next, the two devoted *Decij* view.
The *Drusian* Line, *Camillus* loaded home
With Standards well redeem'd, and foreign Foes o'recome.
The Pair you see in equal Armour shine;
Now, Friends below, in close Embraces join: 11
But when they leave the shady Realms of Night,
And, cloath'd in Bodies, breath your upper Light,
With mortal Hate each other shall pursue:
What Wars, what Wounds, what Slaughter shall ensue!
From *Alpine* Heights the Father first descends;   ⎤ 11
His Daughter's Husband in the Plain attends: ⎬
His Daughter's Husband arms his Eastern Friends.   ⎦
Embrace again, my Sons, be Foes no more:
Nor stain your Country with her Childrens Gore.
And thou, the first, lay down thy lawless claim;   11.
Thou, of my Blood, who bear'st the *Julian* Name.
Another comes, who shall in Triumph ride;

1111 He . . . prepare 98: For fighting Fields his Troops he shall prepare 97
1131 two 97 (*errata*): three 97 (*text*)   1135-7 Now . . . Light,] (Now . . .
Light,) 97 98

And to the Capitol his Chariot guide;
From conquer'd *Corinth*, rich with *Grecian* Spoils.
And yet another, fam'd for Warlike Toils,   1150
On *Argos* shall impose the *Roman* Laws:
And, on the *Greeks*, revenge the *Trojan* Cause:
Shall drag in Chains their *Achillæan* Race;   ⎫
Shall vindicate his Ancestors Disgrace: ⎬
And *Pallas*, for her violated Place.   ⎭ 1155
Great *Cato* there, for Gravity renown'd,
And conqu'ring *Cossus* goes with Lawrels crown'd.
Who can omit the *Gracchi*, who declare
The *Scipio's* Worth, those Thunderbolts of War,
The double Bane of *Carthage*? Who can see,   1160
Without esteem for virtuous Poverty,
Severe *Fabritius*, or can cease t' admire
The Ploughman Consul in his Course Attire!
Tir'd as I am, my Praise the *Fabij* claim;
And thou great Heroe, greatest of thy Name;   1165
Ordain'd in War to save the sinking State,
And, by Delays, to put a stop to Fate!
Let others better mold the running Mass   ⎫
Of Mettals, and inform the breathing Brass;   ⎬
And soften into Flesh a Marble Face: ⎭ 1170
Plead better at the Bar; describe the Skies,
And when the Stars descend, and when they rise.
But, *Rome*, 'tis thine alone, with awful sway,   ⎫
To rule Mankind; and make the World obey;   ⎬
Disposing Peace, and War, thy own Majestick Way.   ⎭ 1175
To tame the Proud, the fetter'd Slave to free;
These are Imperial Arts, and worthy thee.
    He paus'd: And while with wond'ring Eyes they view'd
The passing Spirits, thus his Speech renew'd.
See great *Marcellus*! how, untir'd in Toils,   1180
He moves with Manly grace, how rich with Regal Spoils!
He, when his Country, (threaten'd with Alarms,)
Requires his Courage, and his Conqu'ring Arms,
Shall more than once the *Punic* Bands affright:
Shall kill the *Gaulish* King in single Fight: 1185
Then, to the Capitol in Triumph move,
And the third Spoils shall grace *Feretrian Jove*.

Æneas, here, beheld of Form Divine
A Godlike Youth, in glitt'ring Armour shine:
With great *Marcellus* keeping equal pace;   11
But gloomy were his Eyes, dejected was his Face:
He saw, and, wond'ring, ask'd his airy Guide,
What, and of whence was he, who press'd the Hero's side?
His Son, or one of his Illustrious Name,
How like the former, and almost the same: 11
Observe the Crowds that compass him around;
All gaze, and all admire, and raise a shouting sound:
But hov'ring Mists around his Brows are spread,
And Night, with sable Shades, involves his Head.
Seek not to know (the Ghost reply'd with Tears)   12
The Sorrows of thy Sons, in future Years.
This Youth (the blissful Vision of a day)
Shall just be shown on Earth, and snatch'd away.
The Gods too high had rais'd the *Roman* State;
Were but their Gifts as permanent as great.   12
What groans of Men shall fill the *Martian* Field!
How fierce a Blaze his flaming Pile shall yield!
What Fun'ral Pomp shall floating *Tiber* see,
When, rising from his Bed, he views the sad Solemnity!
No Youth shall equal hopes of Glory give: 12
No Youth afford so great a Cause to grieve.
The *Trojan* Honour, and the *Roman* Boast;
Admir'd when living, and Ador'd when lost!
Mirror of ancient Faith in early Youth!
Undaunted Worth, Inviolable Truth!   12
No Foe unpunish'd in the fighting Field,
Shall dare thee Foot to Foot, with Sword and Shield.
Much less, in Arms oppose thy matchless Force,
When thy sharp Spurs shall urge thy foaming Horse.
Ah, cou'dst thou break through Fates severe Decree,   12
A new *Marcellus* shall arise in thee!
Full Canisters of fragrant Lillies bring,
Mix'd with the Purple Roses of the Spring:
Let me with Fun'ral Flow'rs his Body strow;
This Gift which Parents to their Children owe,   122
This unavailing Gift, at least I may bestow!

  Thus having said, He led the Heroe round

The confines of the blest *Elysian* Ground.
Which, when *Anchises* to his Son had shown,
And fir'd his Mind to mount the promis'd Throne,   1230
He tells the future Wars, ordain'd by Fate;
The Strength and Customs of the *Latian* State:
The Prince, and People: And fore-arms his Care
With Rules, to push his Fortune, or to bear.
Two Gates the silent House of Sleep adorn;   1235
Of polish'd Iv'ry this, that of transparent Horn:
True Visions through transparent Horn arise;
Through polish'd Iv'ry pass deluding Lyes.
Of various things discoursing as he pass'd,
Anchises hither bends his Steps at last.   1240
Then, through the Gate of Iv'ry, he dismiss'd
His valiant Offspring, and Divining Guest.
Streight to the Ships *Æneas* took his way;
Embarqu'd his Men, and skim'd along the Sea:
Still Coasting, till he gain'd *Cajeta*'s Bay.   1245
At length on Oozy ground his Gallies moor:
Their Heads are turn'd to Sea, their Sterns to Shoar.

THE SEVENTH BOOK OF THE ÆNEIS

THE ARGUMENT

King Latinus *entertains* Æneas, *and promises him his only Daughter,* Lavinia, *the Heiress of his Crown.* Turnus *being in Love with her, favour'd by her Mother, and stir'd up by* Juno, *and* Alecto, *breaks the Treaty which was made, and engages in his Quarrel,* Mezentius, Camilla, Messapus, *and many others of the Neighbouring Princes; whose Forces and the Names of their* 5 *Commanders are here particularly related.*

AND thou, O Matron of Immortal Fame!
Here Dying, to the Shore hast left thy Name:
Cajeta still the place is call'd from thee,
The Nurse of great *Æneas* Infancy.
Here rest thy Bones in rich *Hesperia*'s Plains,   5
Thy Name ('tis all a Ghost can have) remains.

1237–8 True . . . Lyes.] *Wanting in* 97 'by the carelessness of the *Amanuensis*' *and supplied in Dryden's notes to* 97 'out of the Original Copy'
 The Seventh Book. The Argument. 5 others] other 98

Now, when the Prince her Fun'ral Rites had paid,
He plough'd the *Tyrrhene* Seas with Sails display'd.
From Land a gentle Breeze arose by Night,
Serenely shone the Stars, the Moon was bright,   10
And the Sea trembled with her Silver Light.
Now near the Shelves of *Circe*'s Shores they run,
(*Circe* the rich, the Daughter of the Sun)
A dang'rous Coast: The Goddess wasts her Days
In joyous Songs, the Rocks resound her Lays: 15
In spinning, or the Loom, she spends the Night,
And Cedar Brands supply her Father's Light.
From hence were heard, (rebellowing to the Main,)
The Roars of Lyons that refuse the Chain,
The Grunts of Bristled Boars, and Groans of Bears,   20
And Herds of Howling Wolves that stun the Sailors Ears.
These from their Caverns, at the close of Night,
Fill the sad Isle with Horror and Affright.
Darkling they mourn their Fate, whom *Circe*'s Pow'r
(That watch'd the Moon, and Planetary Hour)   25
With Words and wicked Herbs, from Human Kind
Had alter'd, and in Brutal Shapes confin'd.
Which Monsters, lest the *Trojans* pious Host
Shou'd bear, or touch upon th' inchanted Coast;
Propitious *Neptune* steer'd their Course by Night,   30
With rising Gales, that sped their happy Flight.
Supply'd with these, they skim the sounding Shore,
And hear the swelling Surges vainly roar.
Now when the rosie Morn began to rise,
And wav'd her Saffron Streamer thro' the Skies;   35
When *Thetis* blush'd in Purple, not her own,
And from her Face the breathing Winds were blown:
A sudden Silence sate upon the Sea,
And sweeping Oars, with Strugling, urge their Way.
The *Trojan*, from the Main beheld a Wood,   40
Which thick with Shades, and a brown Horror, stood:
Betwixt the Trees the *Tyber* took his Course,
With Whirlpools dimpled; and with downward Force
That drove the Sand along, he took his Way,
And rowl'd his yellow Billows to the Sea.   45
About him, and above, and round the Wood,

The Birds that haunt the Borders of his Flood;
That bath'd within, or bask'd upon his side,
To tuneful Songs their narrow Throats apply'd.
The Captain gives Command, the joyful Train   50
Glide thro' the gloomy Shade, and leave the Main.
    Now, *Erato*, thy Poet's Mind inspire,
And fill his Soul with thy Cœlestial Fire.
Relate what *Latium* was, her ancient Kings:
Declare the past, and present State of things,   55
When first the *Trojan* Fleet *Ausonia* sought;
And how the Rivals lov'd, and how they fought.
These are my Theme, and how the War began,
And how concluded by the Godlike Man.
For I shall sing of Battels, Blood, and Rage,   60
Which Princes, and their People did engage:
And haughty Souls, that mov'd with mutual Hate,
In fighting Fields pursu'd and found their Fate:
That rouz'd the *Tyrrhene* Realm with loud Alarms,
And peaceful *Italy* involv'd in Arms.   65
A larger Scene of Action is display'd,
And, rising hence, a greater Work is weigh'd.
    Latinus old and mild, had long possess'd
The *Latian* Scepter, and his People bless'd:
His Father *Faunus*: a *Laurentian* Dame   70
His Mother, fair *Marica* was her Name.
But *Faunus* came from *Picus*, *Picus* drew
His Birth from *Saturn*, if Records be true.
Thus King *Latinus*, in the third Degree,
Had *Saturn* Author of his Family.   75
But this old peaceful Prince, as Heav'n decreed,
Was bless'd with no Male Issue to succeed:
His Sons in blooming Youth were snatch'd by Fate;
One only Daughter heir'd the Royal State.
Fir'd with her Love, and with Ambition led,   80
The neighb'ring Princes court her nuptial Bed.
Among the Crowd, but far above the rest,
Young *Turnus* to the Beauteous Maid address'd.
Turnus, for high Descent, and graceful Meen,
Was first, and favour'd by the *Latian* Queen: 85

84 high *98*: great *97*

With him she strove to join *Lavinia*'s Hand:
But dire Portents the purpos'd Match withstand.
   Deep in the Palace, of long Growth there stood
A Lawrels Trunk, a venerable Wood;
Where Rites Divine were paid; whose holy Hair   90
Was kept, and cut with superstitious Care.
This Plant *Latinus*, when his Town he wall'd,
Then found, and from the Tree *Laurentum* call'd:
And last in Honour of his new Abode,
He vow'd the Lawrel, to the Lawrel's God.   95
It happen'd once, (a bodeing Prodigy,)
A swarm of Bees, that cut the liquid Sky,
Unknown from whence they took their airy flight,
Upon the topmost Branch in Clouds alight:
There, with their clasping Feet together clung,   100
And a long Cluster from the Lawrel hung.
An ancient Augur prophesy'd from hence:
Behold on *Latian* Shores a foreign Prince!
From the same parts of Heav'n his Navy stands,
To the same parts on Earth: his Army lands;   10
The Town he conquers, and the Tow'r commands.
Yet more, when fair *Lavinia* fed the Fire
Before the Gods, and stood beside her Sire;
Strange to relate, the Flames, involv'd in Smoke
Of Incense, from the sacred Altar broke;   110
Caught her dishevell'd Hair, and rich Attire;
Her Crown and Jewels crackled in the Fire:
From thence the fuming Trail began to spread,
And lambent Glories danc'd about her Head.
This new Portent the Seer with Wonder views;   11
Then pausing, thus his Prophecy renews.
The Nymph who scatters flaming Fires around,
Shall shine with Honour, shall herself be crown'd:
But, caus'd by her irrevocable Fate,
War shall the Country waste, and change the State.   120
   Latinus, frighted with this dire Ostent,
For Counsel to his Father *Faunus* went:
And sought the Shades renown'd for Prophecy,
Which near *Albunea*'s sulph'rous Fountain lye.

To these the *Latian,* and the *Sabine* Land   125
Fly, when distress'd, and thence Relief demand.
The Priest on Skins of Off'rings takes his Ease;
And nightly Visions in his Slumber sees:
A swarm of thin aerial Shapes appears,
And, flutt'ring round his Temples, deafs his Ears: 130
These he consults, the future Fates to know,
From Pow'rs above, and from the Fiends below.
Here, for the Gods advice, *Latinus* flies,
Off'ring a hundred Sheep for Sacrifice:
Their wooly Fleeces, as the Rites requir'd,   135
He laid beneath him, and to Rest retir'd.
No sooner were his Eyes in Slumber bound,
When, from above, a more than Mortal Sound
Invades his Ears; and thus the Vision spoke:
Seek not, my Seed, in *Latian* Bands to Yoke   } 140
Our fair *Lavinia,* nor the Gods provoke.
A foreign Son upon thy Shore descends,
Whose Martial Fame from Pole to Pole extends.
His Race in Arms, and Arts of Peace renown'd,
Not *Latium* shall contain, nor *Europe* bound: } 145
'Tis theirs what e're the Sun surveys around.
These Answers in the silent Night receiv'd,
The King himself divulg'd, the Land believ'd:
The Fame through all the Neighb'ring Nations flew,
When now the *Trojan* Navy was in view.   150
    Beneath a shady Tree the Heroe spread
His Table on the Turf, with Cakes of Bread;   }
And, with his Chiefs, on Forest Fruits he fed.
They sate, and (not without the God's Command)
Their homely Fare dispatch'd; the hungry Band   155
Invade their Trenchers next, and soon devour,
To mend the scanty Meal, their Cakes of Flow'r.
Ascanius this observ'd, and, smiling, said,
See, we devour the Plates on which we fed.
The Speech had Omen, that the *Trojan* Race   160
Shou'd find Repose, and this the Time and Place.
Æneas took the Word, and thus replies;
(Confessing Fate with Wonder in his Eyes)

142 thy] the *98*

All hail, O Earth! all hail my household Gods,
Behold the destin'd place of your Abodes!   16
For thus *Anchises* prophesy'd of old,
And this our fatal place of Rest foretold.
"When on a Foreign Shore, instead of Meat,
"By Famine forc'd, your Trenchers you shall eat;
"Then Ease your weary *Trojans* will attend: 17
"And the long Labours of your Voyage end.
"Remember on that happy Coast to build:
"And with a Trench inclose the fruitful Field.
This was that Famine, this the fatal place,
Which ends the Wand'ring of our exil'd Race.   17
Then, on to Morrow's Dawn, your Care employ,
To search the Land, and where the Cities lye,
And what the Men; but give this Day to Joy.

Now pour to *Jove*, and after *Jove* is blest,
Call great *Anchises* to the Genial Feast: 18
Crown high the Goblets with a chearful Draught;
Enjoy the present Hour, adjourn the future Thought.

Thus having said, the Heroe bound his Brows,
With leafy Branches, then perform'd his Vows:
Adoring first the Genius of the Place;   18
Then Earth, the Mother of the Heav'nly Race;
The Nymphs, and native Godheads yet unknown,
And Night, and all the Stars that guild her sable Throne.
And ancient *Cybel*, and *Idæan Jove*;
And last his Sire below, and Mother Queen above.   19

Then Heav'ns high Monarch thundred thrice aloud,
And thrice he shook aloft, a Golden Cloud.
Soon thro' the joyful Camp a Rumor flew,
The time was come their City to renew:
Then ev'ry Brow with chearful Green is crown'd,   19
The Feasts are doubl'd, and the Bowls go round.

When next the rosie Morn disclos'd the Day,
The Scouts to sev'ral parts divide their Way,
To learn the Natives Names, their Towns, explore
The Coasts, and Trendings of the crooked Shore: 200
Here *Tyber* flows, and here *Numicus* stands,
Here warlike *Latins* hold the happy Lands.

183 Brows,] Brows. *97 98*

The Pious Chief, who sought by peaceful Ways,
To found his Empire, and his Town to raise;
A hundred Youths from all his Train selects;   205
And to the *Latian* Court their Course directs:
(The spacious Palace where their Prince resides;)
And all their heads with Wreaths of Olive hides.
They go commission'd to require a Peace;
And carry Presents to procure Access.   210
Thus while they speed their Pace, the Prince designs
His new elected Seat, and draws the Lines:
The *Trojans* round the place a Rampire cast,
And Palisades about the Trenches plac'd.

Mean time the Train, proceeding on their way,   215
From far the Town, and lofty Tow'rs survey:
At length approach the Walls: without the Gate
They see the Boys, and *Latian* Youth debate
The Martial Prizes on the dusty Plain;
Some drive the Cars, and some the Coursers rein: 220
Some bend the stubborn Bow for Victory;
And some with Darts their active Sinews try.
A posting Messenger dispatch'd from hence,
Of this fair Troop advis'd their aged Prince;
That foreign Men, of mighty Stature, came;   225
Uncouth their Habit, and unknown their Name.
The King ordains their entrance, and ascends
His Regal Seat, surrounded by his Friends.
The Palace built by *Picus*, vast and Proud,
Supported by a hundred Pillars stood;   } 230
And round incompass'd with a rising Wood.
The Pile o'relook'd the Town, and drew the sight;
Surpriz'd at once with Reverence and Delight.
There Kings receiv'd the Marks of Sov'raign Pow'r:
In State the Monarchs march'd, the Lictors bore   } 235
Their Awful Axes, and the Rods before.
Here the Tribunal stood, the House of Pray'r;
And here the sacred Senators repair:
All at large Tables, in long order set,
A Ram their Off'ring, and a Ram their Meat.   240
Above the Portal, Carv'd in Cedar Wood,

205 selects *98*: elects *97*   230 stood;] stood *97*: stood: *98*

Plac'd in their Ranks, their Godlike Grandsires stood.
Old *Saturn*, with his crooked Scythe, on high;
And *Italus*, that led the Colony:
And ancient *Janus*, with his double Face,   24
And Bunch of Keys, the Porter of the place.
There good *Sabinus*, planter of the Vines,
On a short Pruning-hook his Head reclines:
And studiously surveys his gen'rous Wines.
Then Warlike Kings, who for their Country fought,   25
And honourable Wounds from Battel brought.
Around the Posts hung Helmets, Darts, and Spears;
And Captive Chariots, Axes, Shields, and Bars,
And broken Beaks of Ships, the Trophies of their Wars.
Above the rest, as Chief of all the Band,   25
Was *Picus* plac'd, a Buckler in his hand;
His other wav'd a long divining Wand.
Girt in his Gabin Gown the Heroe sate:
Yet could not with his Art avoid his Fate.
For *Circe* long had lov'd the Youth in vain,   26
Till Love, refus'd, converted to Disdain:
Then mixing pow'rful Herbs, with Magic Art,
She chang'd his Form, who cou'd not change his heart.
Constrain'd him in a Bird, and made him fly,
With party-colour'd Plumes, a Chattring Pye.   26

  In this high Temple, on a Chair of State,
The Seat of Audience, old *Latinus* sate;
Then gave admission to the *Trojan* Train,
And thus, with pleasing accents, he began.
Tell me, ye *Trojans*, for that Name you own,   27
Nor is your Course upon our Coasts unknown;
Say what you seek, and whither were you bound?
Were you by stress of Weather cast a-ground?
Such dangers as on Seas are often seen,
And oft befall to miserable Men?   27
Or come, your Shipping in our Ports to lay,
Spent and disabl'd in so long a way?
Say what you want, the *Latians* you shall find
Not forc'd to Goodness, but by Will inclin'd:
For since the time of *Saturn*'s holy Reign,   28

His Hospitable Customs we retain.
I call to mind, (but Time the Tale has worn,)
Th' *Arunci* told; that *Dardanus*, tho' born
On *Latian* Plains, yet sought the *Phrygian* Shore,
And *Samothracia*, *Samos* call'd before: 285
From *Tuscan Coritum* he claim'd his Birth,
But after, when exempt from Mortal Earth,
From thence ascended to his kindred Skies,
A God, and as a God augments their Sacrifice.

  He said. *Ilioneus* made this Reply,   290
O King, of *Faunus* Royal Family!
Nor Wint'ry Winds to *Latium* forc'd our way,
Nor did the Stars our wand'ring Course betray.
Willing we sought your Shores, and hither bound,
The Port so long desir'd, at length we found.   295
From our sweet Homes and ancient Realms expell'd;
Great as the greatest that the Sun beheld.
The God began our Line, who rules above,
And as our Race, our King descends from *Jove*:
And hither are we come, by his Command,   300
To crave Admission in your happy Land.
How dire a Tempest, from *Mycenæ* pour'd,
Our Plains, our Temples, and our Town devour'd;
What was the Waste of War, what fierce Alarms
Shook *Asia*'s Crown with *Europæan* Arms;   305
Ev'n such have heard, if any such there be,
Whose Earth is bounded by the frozen Sea:
And such as born beneath the burning Sky,
And sultry Sun, betwixt the Tropicks lye.
From that dire Deluge, through the wat'ry Waste,   310
Such length of Years, such various Perils past:
At last escap'd, to *Latium* we repair,
To beg what you without your Want may spare; }
The common Water, and the common Air.
Sheds which our selves will build, and mean abodes,   315
Fit to receive and serve our banish'd Gods.
Nor our Admission shall your Realm disgrace,
Nor length of time our Gratitude efface.
Besides, what endless Honour you shall gain

    290 *Editor's paragraph*   309 Sun,] Sun *97 98*

To save and shelter *Troy*'s unhappy Train.   32
Now, by my Sov'raign, and his Fate I swear,
Renown'd for Faith in Peace, for Force in War;
Oft our Alliance other Lands desir'd,
And what we seek of you, of us requir'd.
Despise not then, that in our Hands we bear   32
These Holy Boughs, and sue with Words of Pray'r.
Fate and the Gods, by their supreme Command,
Have doom'd our Ships to seek the *Latian* Land.
To these abodes our Fleet *Apollo* sends;
Here *Dardanus* was born, and hither tends: 33
Where *Thuscan Tyber* rowls with rapid Force,
And where *Numicus* opes his Holy Source.
Besides our Prince presents, with his Request,
Some small Remains of what his Sire possess'd.
This Golden Charger, snatch'd from burning *Troy*,   33
Anchises did in Sacrifice employ:
This Royal Robe, and this *Tiara* wore
Old *Priam*, and this Golden Scepter bore
In full Assemblies, and in solemn Games;
These Purple Vests were weav'd by *Dardan* Dames.   34
   Thus while he spoke, *Latinus* rowld around
His Eyes, and fix'd a while upon the Ground.
Intent he seem'd, and anxious in his Breast;
Not by the Scepter mov'd, or Kingly Vest:
But pond'ring future Things of wond'rous Weight;   3.
Succession, Empire, and his Daughter's Fate:
On these he mus'd within his thoughtful Mind;
And then revolv'd what *Faunus* had divin'd.
This was the Foreign Prince, by Fate decreed
To share his Scepter, and *Lavinia*'s Bed: 3.
This was the Race, that sure Portents foreshew
To sway the World, and Land and Sea subdue.
At length he rais'd his chearful Head, and spoke:
The Pow'rs, said he, the Pow'rs we both invoke,
To you, and yours, and mine, propitious be,   3.
And firm our Purpose with their Augury.
Have what you ask; your Presents I receive,
Land where, and when you please, with ample Leave:
Partake and use my Kingdom as your own;

All shall be yours, while I command the Crown. 360
And if my wish'd Alliance please your King,
Tell him he shou'd not send the Peace, but bring:
Then let him not a Friend's Embraces fear;
The Peace is made when I behold him here.
Besides this Answer, tell my Royal Guest, 365
I add to his Commands, my own Request:
One only Daughter heirs my Crown and State,
Whom, not our Oracles, nor Heav'n, nor Fate,
Nor frequent Prodigies permit to join
With any Native of th' *Ausonian* Line. 370
A foreign Son-in-Law shall come from far,
(Such is our Doom) a Chief renown'd in War:
Whose Race shall bear aloft the *Latian* Name,
And through the conquer'd World diffuse our Fame.
Himself to be the Man the Fates require, 375
I firmly judge, and what I judge, desire.

He said, and then on each bestow'd a Steed;
Three hundred Horses, in high Stables fed,
Stood ready, shining all, and smoothly dress'd;
Of these he chose the fairest and the best, 380
To mount the *Trojan* Troop; at his Command,
The Steeds caparison'd with Purple stand;
With Golden Trappings, glorious to behold,
And champ betwixt their Teeth the foaming Gold.
Then to his absent Guest the King decreed 385
A pair of Coursers born of Heav'nly Breed:
Who from their Nostrils breath'd Etherial Fire;
Whom *Circe* stole from her Cœlestial Sire:
By substituting Mares, produc'd on Earth,
Whose Wombs conceiv'd a more than Mortal Birth. 390
These draw the Chariot which *Latinus* sends;
And the rich Present to the Prince commends.
Sublime on stately Steeds the *Trojans* born,
To their expecting Lord with Peace return.

But jealous *Juno*, from *Pachynus* height, 395
As she from *Argos* took her airy Flight,
Beheld, with envious Eyes, this hateful Sight.
She saw the *Trojan*, and his joyful Train

377 *Editor's paragraph*

Descend upon the Shore, desert the Main;
Design a Town, and with unhop'd Success   4C
Th' Embassadors return with promis'd Peace.
Then pierc'd with Pain, she shook her haughty Head,
Sigh'd from her inward Soul; and thus she said.
O hated Off-spring of my *Phrygian* Foes!
O Fates of *Troy*, which *Juno*'s Fates oppose!   4C
Cou'd they not fall unpity'd, on the Plain,
But slain revive, and taken, scape again?
When execrable *Troy* in Ashes lay,
Thro' Fires, and Swords, and Seas, they forc'd their Way.
Then vanquish'd *Juno* must in vain contend,   4I
Her Rage disarm'd, her Empire at an end.
Breathless and tir'd, is all my Fury spent,
Or does my glutted Spleen at length relent?
As if 'twere little from their Town to chase,
I thro' the Seas pursu'd their exil'd Race: 4I
Ingag'd the Heav'ns, oppos'd the Stormy Main;
But Billows roar'd, and Tempests rag'd in vain.
What have my *Scylla's* and my *Sirtes* done,
When these they overpass, and those they shun?
On *Tyber*'s Shores they land, secure of Fate,   42
Triumphant o're the Storms and *Juno*'s Hate.
Mars cou'd in mutual Blood the *Centaurs* bath,
And *Jove* himself gave way to *Cynthia*'s Wrath;
Who sent the tusky Boar to *Calydon*:
What great Offence had either People done?   42
But I, the Consort of the Thunderer,
Have wag'd a long and unsuccessful War:
With various Arts and Arms in vain have toil'd,
And by a Mortal Man at length am foil'd.
If native Pow'r prevail not, shall I doubt   43
To seek for needful Succour from without:
If *Jove* and Heav'n my just Desires deny,
Hell shall the Pow'r of Heav'n and *Jove* supply.
Grant that the Fates have firm'd, by their Decree,
The *Trojan* Race to reign in *Italy*;   43
At least I can defer the Nuptial Day,
And with protracted Wars the Peace delay:
With Blood the dear Alliance shall be bought;

And both the People near Destruction brought.
So shall the Son-in-Law, and Father join, 440
With Ruin, War, and Waste of either Line.
O fatal Maid! thy Marriage is endow'd
With *Phrygian*, *Latian*, and *Rutulian* Blood!
Bellona leads thee to thy Lover's Hand,
Another Queen brings forth another Brand; 445
To burn with foreign Fires another Land!
A second *Paris*, diff'ring but in Name,
Shall fire his Country with a second Flame.
 Thus having said, she sinks beneath the Ground,
With furious haste, and shoots the *Stygian* Sound; 450
To rowze *Alecto* from th' Infernal Seat
Of her dire Sisters, and their dark Retreat.
This Fury, fit for her Intent, she chose;
One who delights in Wars, and Human Woes.
Ev'n *Pluto* hates his own mishapen Race: 455
Her Sister-Furies fly her hideous Face:
So frightful are the Forms the Monster takes,
So fierce the Hissings of her speckled Snakes.
Her *Juno* finds, and thus inflames her Spight:
O Virgin Daughter of Eternal Night, 460
Give me this once thy Labour, to sustain
My Right, and execute my just disdain.
Let not the *Trojans*, with a feign'd Pretence
Of proffer'd Peace, delude the *Latian* Prince:
Expel from *Italy* that odious Name, 465
And let not *Juno* suffer in her Fame.
'Tis thine to ruin Realms, o'return a State,
Betwixt the dearest Friends to raise Debate;
And kindle kindred Blood to mutual Hate.
Thy Hand o're Towns the fun'ral Torch displays, 470
And forms a thousand Ills ten thousand Ways.
Now shake from out thy fruitful Breast, the Seeds
Of Envy, Discord, and of Cruel Deeds:
Confound the Peace establish'd, and prepare
Their Souls to Hatred, and their Hands to War. 475
 Smear'd as she was with black *Gorgonean* Blood,

The Fury sprang above the *Stygian* Flood:
And on her wicker Wings, sublime through Night,
She to the *Latian* Palace took her Flight.
There sought the Queen's Apartment, stood before   480
The peaceful Threshold, and besieg'd the Door.
Restless *Amata* lay, her swelling Breast
Fir'd with Disdain for *Turnus* dispossest,
And the new Nuptials of the *Trojan* Guest.
From her black bloody Locks the Fury shakes   485
Her darling Plague, the Fav'rite of her Snakes:
With her full Force she threw the pois'nous Dart,
And fix'd it deep within *Amata*'s Heart.
That thus envenom'd she might kindle Rage,
And sacrifice to Strife her House and Husbands Age.   490
Unseen, unfelt, the fiery Serpent skims
Betwixt her Linnen, and her naked Limbs.
His baleful Breath inspiring, as he glides,
Now like a Chain around her Neck he rides;
Now like a Fillet to her Head repairs,   495
And with his Circling Volume folds her Hairs.
At first the silent Venom slid with ease,
And seiz'd her cooler Senses by degrees;
Then e're th' infected Mass was fir'd too far,
In Plaintive Accents she began the War: 500
And thus bespoke her Husband; Shall, she said,
A wandring Prince enjoy *Lavinia*'s Bed?
If Nature plead not in a Parent's Heart,
Pity my Tears, and pity her Desert:
I know, my dearest Lord, the time will come,   505
You wou'd, in vain, reverse your Cruel doom:
The faithless Pirate soon will set to Sea,
And bear the Royal Virgin far away!
A Guest like him, a *Trojan* Guest before,
In shew of friendship, sought the *Spartan* Shore;   510
And ravish'd *Helen* from her Husband bore.
Think on a King's inviolable Word;
And think on *Turnus*, her once plighted Lord:
To this false Foreigner you give your Throne,
And wrong a Friend, a Kinsman, and a Son.   515
Resume your ancient Care; and if the God

Your Sire, and you, resolve on Foreign Blood:
Know all are Foreign, in a larger Sense,
Not born your Subjects, or deriv'd from hence.
Then if the Line of *Turnus* you retrace;   520
He springs from *Inachus* of *Argive* Race.
  But when she saw her Reasons idly spent,
And cou'd not move him from his fix'd Intent;
She flew to rage; for now the Snake possess'd
Her vital parts, and poison'd all her Breast;   525
She raves, she runs with a distracted pace,
And fills, with horrid howls, the public Place.
And, as young Striplings whip the Top for sport,
On the smooth Pavement of an empty Court;
The wooden Engine flies and whirls about,   530
Admir'd, with Clamours, of the Beardless rout;
They lash aloud, each other they provoke,
And lend their little Souls at ev'ry stroke:
Thus fares the Queen, and thus her fury blows
Amidst the Crowd, and kindles as she goes.   535
Nor yet content, she strains her Malice more,
And adds new Ills to those contriv'd before:
She flies the Town, and, mixing with a throng
Of madding Matrons, bears the Bride along:
Wand'ring through Woods and Wilds, and devious ways, 540
And with these Arts the *Trojan* Match delays.
She feign'd the Rites of *Bacchus*; cry'd aloud,
And to the Buxom God the Virgin vow'd.
Evoe, O *Bacchus* thus began the Song,
And *Evoe*! answer'd all the Female Throng: 545
O Virgin! worthy thee alone, she cry'd;
O worthy thee alone, the Crew reply'd.
For thee she feeds her Hair, she leads thy Dance,
And with thy winding Ivy wreaths her Lance.
Like fury seiz'd the rest; the progress known,   550
All seek the Mountains, and forsake the Town:
All Clad in Skins of Beasts the Jav'lin bear,
Give to the wanton Winds their flowing Hair:
And shrieks and showtings rend the suff'ring Air.

522 *Editor's paragraph*   542 *Bacchus*;] *Bacchus*! 97 98   549 wreaths 97
(*errata*): crowns 97 (*text*)   554 suff'ring 98: passive 97

The Queen, her self, inspir'd with Rage Divine,   555
Shook high above her head a flaming Pine:
Then rowl'd her haggar'd Eyes around the throng,
And sung, in *Turnus* Name, the Nuptial Song:
Io ye *Latian* Dames, if any here
Hold your unhappy Queen, *Amata*, dear;   560
If there be here, she said, who dare maintain
My Right, nor think the Name of Mother vain:
Unbind your Fillets, loose your flowing Hair,
And *Orgies*, and Nocturnal Rites prepare.
Amata's Breast the Fury thus invades,   565
And fires with Rage, amid the Silvan Shades.
Then when she found her Venom spread so far,
The Royal House embroil'd in Civil War:
Rais'd on her dusky Wings she cleaves the Skies,
And seeks the Palace where young *Turnus* lies.   570
His Town, as Fame reports, was built of old
By *Danae*, pregnant with Almighty Gold:
Who fled her Father's Rage, and with a Train
Of following *Argives*, thro' the stormy Main,
Driv'n by the *Southern* Blasts, was fated here to reign.   575
'Twas *Ardua* once, now *Ardea*'s Name it bears:
Once a fair City, now consum'd with Years.
Here in his lofty Palace *Turnus* lay,
Betwixt the Confines of the Night and Day,
Secure in Sleep: The Fury laid aside   580
Her Looks and Limbs, and with new methods try'd,
The foulness of th' infernal Form to hide.
Prop'd on a Staff, she takes a trembling Meen,
Her Face is furrow'd, and her Front obscene:
Deep dinted Wrinckles on her Cheek she draws,   585
Sunk are her Eyes, and toothless are her Jaws:
Her hoary Hair with holy Fillets bound,
Her Temples with an Olive Wreath are crown'd.
Old *Calibe*, who kept the sacred Fane
Of *Juno*, now she seem'd, and thus began,   590
Appearing in a Dream, to rouze the careless Man.
Shall *Turnus* then such endless Toil sustain,
In fighting Fields, and conquer Towns in vain:

560 Hold] Hold, *97 98*   589 *Calibe 98: Chalibe 97*

Win, for a *Trojan* Head to wear the Prize,
Usurp thy Crown, enjoy thy Victories? 595
The Bride and Scepter which thy Blood has bought,
The King transfers, and Foreign Heirs are sought:
Go now, deluded Man, and seek again
New Toils, new Dangers on the dusty Plain.
Repel the *Tuscan* Foes, their City seize, 600
Protect the *Latians* in luxurious Ease.
This Dream all-pow'rful *Juno* sends, I bear
Her mighty Mandates, and her Words you hear.
Haste, arm your *Ardeans*, issue to the Plain,
With Fate to friend, assault the *Trojan* Train: 605
Their thoughtless Chiefs, their painted Ships that lye
In *Tyber*'s Mouth, with Fire and Sword destroy.
The *Latian* King, unless he shall submit,
Own his old Promise, and his new forget;
Let him, in Arms, the Pow'r of *Turnus* prove, 610
And learn to fear whom he disdains to love:
For such is Heav'ns Command. The youthful Prince
With Scorn reply'd, and made this bold Defence.
You tell me, Mother, what I knew before,
The *Phrygian* Fleet is landed on the Shore: 615
I neither fear, nor will provoke the War;
My Fate is *Juno*'s most peculiar Care.
But Time has made you dote, and vainly tell
Of Arms imagin'd, in your lonely Cell:
Go, be the Temple and the Gods your Care, 620
Permit to Men the Thought of Peace and War.
   These haughty Words *Alecto*'s Rage provoke,
And frighted *Turnus* trembled as she spoke.
Her Eyes grow stiffen'd, and with Sulphur burn,
Her hideous Looks, and hellish Form return: 625
Her curling Snakes, with Hissings fill the Place,
And open all the Furies of her Face:
Then, darting Fire from her malignant Eyes,
She cast him backward as he strove to rise,
And, ling'ring, sought to frame some new Replies. 630

611 love:] Love. *97 98*

High on her Head she rears two twisted Snakes,
Her Chains she rattles, and her Whip she shakes;
And churning bloody Foam, thus loudly speaks.
Behold whom Time has made to dote, and tell
Of Arms, imagin'd in her lonely Cell: 6.
Behold the Fates Infernal Minister;
War, Death, Destruction, in my Hand I bear.
    Thus having said, her smould'ring Torch impress'd,
With her full Force, she plung'd into his Breast.
Aghast he wak'd, and, starting from his Bed,   6
Cold Sweat, in clammy Drops, his Limbs o'respread.
Arms, Arms, he cries, my Sword and Shield prepare;
He breaths Defiance, Blood, and Mortal War.
So when with crackling Flames a Cauldron fries,
The bubling Waters from the Bottom rise: 6
Above the Brims they force their fiery way;
Black Vapours climb aloft, and cloud the Day.
    The Peace polluted thus, a chosen Band
He first commissions to the *Latian* Land;
In threatning Embassy: Then rais'd the rest,   6
To meet in Arms th' intruding *Trojan* Guest:
To force the Foes from the *Lavinian* Shore,
And *Italy*'s indanger'd Peace restore.
Himself alone, an equal Match he boasts,
To fight the *Phrygian* and *Ausonian* Hoasts.   6
The Gods invok'd, the *Rutuli* prepare
Their Arms, and warm each other to the War.
His Beauty these, and those his blooming Age,
The rest his House, and his own Fame ingage.
    While *Turnus* urges thus his Enterprise;   6
The *Stygian* Fury to the *Trojans* flies:
New Frauds invents, and takes a steepy Stand,
Which overlooks the Vale with wide Command;
Where fair *Ascanius*, and his youthful Train,
With Horns and Hounds a hunting Match ordain,   6
And pitch their Toils around the shady Plain.
The Fury fires the Pack; they snuff, they vent,
And feed their hungry Nostrils with the Scent.
'Twas of a well grown Stag, whose Antlers rise

668 feed *97* (*errata*): fill *97* (*text*)

High o're his Front, his Beams invade the Skies: 670
From this light Cause, th' Infernal Maid prepares
The Country Churls to Mischief, Hate, and Wars.
　　The stately Beast, the Two *Tyrrheidæ* bred,
Snatch'd from his Dam, and the tame Youngling fed.
Their Father *Tyrrheus* did his Fodder bring,   675
Tyrrheus, chief Ranger to the *Latian* King:
Their Sister *Silvia* cherish'd with her Care
The little Wanton, and did Wreaths prepare
To hang his budding Horns: with Ribbons ty'd
His tender Neck, and comb'd his silken Hide;   680
And bath'd his Body. Patient of Command,
In time he grew, and growing us'd to Hand.
He waited at his Master's Board for Food;
Then sought his salvage Kindred in the Wood:
Where grazing all the Day, at Night he came   685
To his known Lodgings, and his Country Dame.
　　This household Beast, that us'd the Woodland Grounds,
Was view'd at first by the young Hero's Hounds;
As down the Stream he swam, to seek Retreat
In the cool Waters, and to quench his Heat.   690
Ascanius young, and eager of his Game,
Soon bent his Bow, uncertain in his Aim:
But the dire Fiend the fatal Arrow guides,
Which pierc'd his Bowels thro' his panting sides.
The bleeding Creature issues from the Floods,   695
Possess'd with Fear, and seeks his known abodes;
His old familiar Hearth, and household Gods.
He falls, he fills the House with heavy Groans,
Implores their Pity, and his Pain bemoans.
Young *Silvia* beats her Breast, and cries aloud   700
For Succour, from the clownish Neighbourhood:
The Churls assemble; for the Fiend, who lay
In the close Woody Covert, urg'd their way.
One with a Brand, yet burning from the Flame;
Arm'd with a knotty Club, another came: 705
What e're they catch or find, without their Care,
Their Fury makes an Instrument of War.
Tyrrheus, the Foster-Father of the Beast,
Then clench'd a Hatchet in his horny Fist:

But held his Hand from the descending Stroke,
And left his Wedge within the cloven Oak,
To whet their Courage, and their Rage provoke.
And now the Goddess, exercis'd in Ill,
Who watch'd an Hour to work her impious Will,
Ascends the Roof, and to her crooked Horn,
Such as was then by *Latian* Shepherds born,
Adds all her Breath; the Rocks and Woods around,
And Mountains, tremble at th' infernal Sound.
The Sacred Lake of *Trivia* from afar,
The *Veline* Fountains, and sulphureous *Nar*,
Shake at the baleful Blast, the Signal of the War.
Young Mothers wildly stare, with Fear possess'd,
And strain their helpless Infants to their Breast.

   The Clowns, a boist'rous, rude, ungovern'd Crew,
With furious haste to the loud Summons flew.
The Pow'rs of *Troy* then issuing on the Plain,
With fresh Recruits their youthful Chief sustain:
Not theirs a raw and unexperienc'd Train,
But a firm Body of embattel'd Men.
At first, while Fortune favour'd neither side,
The Fight with Clubs and burning Brands was try'd:
But now, both Parties reinforc'd, the Fields
Are bright with flaming Swords and brazen Shields.
A shining Harvest either Host displays,
And shoots against the Sun with equal Rays.

   Thus when a black-brow'd Gust begins to rise,
White Foam at first on the curl'd Ocean fries;
Then roars the Main, the Billows mount the Skies:
'Till by the Fury of the Storm full blown,
The muddy Bottom o're the Clouds is thrown.
   First *Almon* falls, old *Tyrrheus* eldest Care,
Pierc'd with an Arrow from the distant War:
Fix'd in his Throat the flying Weapon stood,
And stop'd his Breath, and drank his vital Blood.
Huge Heaps of slain around the Body rise;
Among the rest, the rich *Galesus* lyes:
A good old Man, while Peace he preach'd in vain,

71
71
72
72
73
735
740
745

Amidst the Madness of th' unruly Train:
Five Heards, five bleating Flocks his Pastures fill'd,
His Lands a hundred Yoke of Oxen till'd.   750
Thus, while in equal Scales their Fortune stood,
The Fury bath'd them in each others Blood.
Then having fix'd the Fight, exulting flies,
And bears fulfill'd her Promise to the Skies.
To *Juno* thus she speaks; Behold, 'tis done,   755
The Blood already drawn, the War begun;
The Discord is compleat, nor can they cease
The dire Debate, nor you command the Peace.
Now since the *Latian* and the *Trojan* Brood
Have tasted Vengeance, and the Sweets of Blood;   760
Speak, and my Pow'r shall add this Office more:
The Neighb'ring Nations of th' *Ausonian* Shore
Shall hear the dreadful Rumour, from afar,
Of arm'd Invasion, and embrace the War.
Then *Juno* thus; The grateful Work is done,   765
The Seeds of Discord sow'd, the War begun:
Frauds, Fears, and Fury have possess'd the State,
And fix'd the Causes of a lasting Hate:
A bloody *Hymen* shall th' Alliance join
Betwixt the *Trojan* and *Ausonian* Line: 770
But thou with Speed to Night and Hell repair,
For not the Gods, nor angry *Jove* will bear
Thy lawless wand'ring walks, in upper Air.
Leave what remains to me. *Saturnia* said:
The sullen Fiend her sounding Wings display'd;   775
Unwilling left the Light, and sought the neather Shade.
In midst of *Italy*, well known to Fame,
There lies a Lake, *Amsanctus* is the Name,
Below the lofty Mounts: On either side
Thick Forrests, the forbidden Entrance hide: 780
Full in the Centre of the sacred Wood
An Arm arises of the *Stygian* Flood;
Which, breaking from beneath with bellowing sound,
Whirls the black Waves and rattling Stones around.
Here *Pluto* pants for Breath from out his Cell,   785
And opens wide the grinning Jaws of Hell.

748 Train: *98*: Train. *97*

To this Infernal Lake the Fury flies;
Here hides her hated Head, and frees the lab'ring Skies.
    Saturnian Juno now, with double Care,
Attends the fatal Process of the War.   7⁹
The Clowns return'd, from Battel bear the slain,
Implore the Gods, and to their King complain.
The Corps of *Almon* and the rest are shown,
Shrieks, Clamours, Murmurs fill the frighted Town.
Ambitious *Turnus* in the Press appears,   7⁹
And, aggravating Crimes, augments their Fears:
Proclaims his Private Injuries aloud,   ⎫
A Solemn Promise made, and disavow'd;   ⎬
A foreign Son is sought, and a mix'd Mungril Brood.   ⎭
Then they, whose Mothers, frantick with their Fear,   ⎫ 8⁰
In Woods and Wilds the Flags of *Bacchus* bear,   ⎬
And lead his Dances with dishevell'd hair,   ⎭
Increase the Clamour, and the War demand,
(Such was *Amata*'s Interest in the Land)
Against the Public Sanctions of the Peace,   8⁰
Against all Omens of their ill Success;
With Fates averse, the Rout in Arms resort,
To Force their Monarch, and insult the Court.
But like a Rock unmov'd, a Rock that braves
The rageing Tempest and the rising Waves,   81
Prop'd on himself he stands: His solid sides
Wash off the Sea-weeds, and the sounding Tides:
So stood the Pious Prince unmov'd: and long
Sustain'd the madness of the noisie Throng.
But when he found that *Juno*'s Pow'r prevail'd,   81
And all the Methods of cool Counsel fail'd,
He calls the Gods to witness their offence,
Disclaims the War, asserts his Innocence.
Hurry'd by Fate, he cries, and born before
A furious Wind, we leave the faithful Shore: 82
O more than Madmen! you your selves shall bear
The guilt of Blood and Sacrilegious War:
Thou, *Turnus*, shalt attone it by thy Fate,
And pray to Heav'n for Peace, but pray too late.
For me, my stormy Voyage at an end,   82

        789 *Editor's paragraph*   822 Blood] Blood, *98*

I to the Port of Death securely tend.
The Fun'ral Pomp which to your Kings you pay,
Is all I want, and all you take away.
He said no more, but in his Walls confin'd,
Shut out the Woes which he too well divin'd: 830
Nor with the rising Storm wou'd vainly strive,
But left the Helm, and let the Vessel drive.

   A solemn Custom was observ'd of old,
Which *Latium* held, and now the *Romans* hold;
Their Standard, when in fighting Fields they rear   } 835
Against the fierce *Hircanians*, or declare
The *Scythian*, *Indian*, or *Arabian* War:
Or from the boasting *Parthians* wou'd regain
Their Eagles lost in *Carrhæ*'s bloody Plain:
Two Gates of Steel (the Name of *Mars* they bear,   840
And still are worship'd with religious Fear;)
Before his Temple stand: The dire abode,
And the fear'd Issues of the furious God,
Are fenc'd with Brazen Bolts; without the Gates,
The wary Guardian *Janus* doubly waits.   845
Then, when the sacred Senate votes the Wars,
The *Roman* Consul their Decree declares,
And in his Robes the sounding Gates unbars.
The Youth in Military Shouts arise,
And the loud Trumpets break the yielding Skies.   850
These Rites of old by Sov'raign Princes us'd,
Were the King's Office, but the King refus'd.
Deaf to their Cries, nor wou'd the Gates unbar
Of sacred Peace, or loose th' imprison'd War:
But hid his Head, and, safe from loud Alarms,   855
Abhor'd the wicked Ministry of Arms.
Then Heav'ns Imperious Queen shot down from high;
At her Approach the Brazen Hinges fly,
The Gates are forc'd, and ev'ry falling Bar,
And like a Tempest issues out the War.   860
The peaceful Cities of th' *Ausonian* Shore,
Lull'd in their Ease, and undisturb'd before;
Are all on Fire, and some with studious Care,

833 *Editor's paragraph*   840–1 bear, . . . Fear;)] bear) . . . Fear; *97 98*
857 shot *98*: came *97*

Their restiff Steeds in sandy Plains prepare:
Some their soft Limbs in painful Marches try,   8
And War is all their Wish, and Arms the gen'ral Cry.
Part scour the rusty Shields with Seam, and part
New grind the blunted Ax, and point the Dart:
With Joy they view the waving Ensigns fly,
And hear the Trumpet's Clangor pierce the Sky.   8
Five Cities forge their Arms: th' *Atinian* Pow'rs,
Antemnæ, *Tybur* with her lofty Tow'rs,
Ardea the proud, the *Crustumerian* Town:
All these of old were places of Renown.
Some hammer Helmets for the fighting Field,   8
Some twine young Sallows to support the Shield;
The Croslet some, and some the Cuishes mould,
With Silver plated, and with ductile Gold.
The rustick Honours of the Scythe and Share,
Give place to Swords and Plumes, the Pride of War.   88
Old Fauchions are new temper'd in the Fires:
The sounding Trumpet ev'ry Soul inspires.
The Word is giv'n, with eager Speed they lace
The shining Head-piece, and the Shield embrace.
The neighing Steeds are to the Chariot ty'd,   88
The trusty Weapon sits on ev'ry side.
    And now the mighty Labour is begun,
Ye Muses open all your *Helicon*.
Sing you the Chiefs that sway'd th' *Ausonian* Land,
Their Arms, and Armies under their Command: 89
What Warriours in our ancient Clime were bred,
What Souldiers follow'd, and what Heroes led.
For well you know, and can record alone,
What Fame to future times conveys but darkly down.
    Mezentius first appear'd upon the Plain,   89
Scorn sate upon his Brows, and sour Disdain;
Defying Earth and Heav'n: *Etruria* lost,
He brings to *Turnus* Aid his baffled Host.
The charming *Lausus*, full of youthful Fire,
Rode in the Rank, and next his sullen Sire: 90
To *Turnus* only second in the Grace
Of Manly Meen, and features of the Face.

898 *Turnus*] *Turnus's* 97 98

A skilful Horseman, and a Huntsman bred,
With Fates averse a thousand Men he led:
His Sire unworthy of so brave a Son;   905
Himself well worthy of a happier Throne.
  Next *Aventinus* drives his Chariot round
The *Latian* Plains, with Palms and Lawrels crown'd.
Proud of his Steeds he smoaks along the Field,
His Father's *Hydra* fills his ample Shield.   910
A hundred Serpents hiss about the Brims;
The Son of *Hercules* he justly seems,
By his broad Shoulders and Gigantick Limbs.
Of Heav'nly part, and part of Earthly Blood,
A mortal Woman mixing with a God.   915
For strong *Alcides*, after he had slain
The triple *Geryon*, drove from conquer'd *Spain*
His captive Herds, and thence in Triumph led;
On *Tuscan Tyber*'s flow'ry Banks they fed.
Then on Mount *Aventine*, the Son of *Jove*   920
The Priestess *Rhea* found, and forc'd to Love.
  For Arms his Men long Piles and Jav'lins bore,
And Poles with pointed Steel their Foes in Battel gore.
Like *Hercules* himself, his Son appears,
In Salvage Pomp: a Lyon's Hide he wears;   925
About his Shoulders hangs the shaggy Skin,
The Teeth, and gaping Jaws severely grin.
Thus like the God his Father, homely drest,
He strides into the Hall, a horrid Guest.
  Then two Twin-Brothers from fair *Tybur* came,   930
(Which from their Brother *Tyburs* took the Name,)
Fierce *Coras*, and *Catillus*, void of Fear,
Arm'd *Argive* Horse they led, and in the Front appear.
Like Cloud-born *Centaurs*, from the Mountain's height,
With rapid Course descending to the Fight;   935
They rush along, the ratling Woods give way,
The Branches bend before their sweepy Sway.
  Nor was *Præneste*'s Founder wanting there,
Whom Fame reports the Son of *Mulciber*:

910 his] the *98*   925 Pomp: *98*: Pomp *97*

Found in the Fire, and foster'd in the Plains;   } 940
A Shepherd and a King at once he reigns,
And leads to *Turnus* Aid his Country Swains.
His own *Præneste* sends a chosen Band,
With those who plough *Saturnia's Gabine* Land:
Besides the Succour which cold *Anien* yields,   945
The Rocks of *Hernicus*, and dewy Fields;
Anagnia fat, and Father *Amasene*,
A num'rous Rout, but all of naked Men:
Nor Arms they wear, nor Swords and Bucklers wield,
Nor drive the Chariot thro' the dusty Field: 950
But whirle from Leathern Slings huge Balls of Lead;
And Spoils of yellow Wolves adorn their Head:
The Left Foot naked, when they march to fight,
But in a Bull's raw Hide they sheath the Right.
   Messapus next, (great *Neptune* was his Sire)   955
Secure of Steel, and fated from the Fire;
In Pomp appears: And with his Ardour warms
A heartless Train, unexercis'd in Arms:
The just *Faliscans* he to Battel brings,
And those who live where Lake *Ciminia* springs;   960
And where *Feronia's* Grove and Temple stands,
Who till *Fescennian* or *Flavinian* Lands:
All these in order march, and marching sing
The warlike Actions of their Sea-born King.
Like a long Team of Snowy Swans on high,   965
Which clap their Wings, and cleave the liquid Sky,
When homeward from their wat'ry Pastures born,
They sing, and *Asia's* Lakes their Notes return.
Not one who heard their Musick from afar,
Wou'd think these Troops an Army train'd to War: 970
But Flocks of Fowl, that when the Tempests roar,
With their hoarse gabling seek the silent Shoar.
   Then *Clausus* came, who led a num'rous Band
Of Troops embody'd, from the *Sabine* Land:
And in himself alone, an Army brought,   975
'Twas he the noble *Claudian* Race begot:
The *Claudian* Race, ordain'd, in times to come,
To share the Greatness of Imperial *Rome*.

He led the *Cures* forth of old Renown,
Mutuscans from their Olive-bearing Town; 980
And all th' *Eretian* Pow'rs: Besides a Band
That follow'd from *Velinum*'s dewy Land:
And *Amiternian* Troops, of mighty Fame,
And Mountaineers, that from *Severus* came.
And from the craggy Cliffs of *Tetrica*, 985
And those where yellow *Tyber* takes his way,
And where *Himella*'s wanton Waters play.
Casperia sends her Arms, with those that lye
By *Fabaris*, and fruitful *Foruli*:
The warlike Aids of *Horta* next appear, 990
And the cold *Nursians* come to close the Reer:
Mix'd with the Natives born of *Latine* Blood,
Whom *Allia* washes with her fatal Flood.
Not thicker Billows beat the *Lybian* Main,
When pale *Orion* sets in wint'ry Rain; 995
Not thicker Harvests on rich *Hermus* rise,
Or *Lycian* Fields, when *Phœbus* burns the Skies;
Than stand these Troops: Their Bucklers ring around,
Their Trampling turns the Turf, and shakes the solid Ground.

   High in his Chariot then *Halesus* came, 1000
A Foe by Birth to *Troy*'s unhappy Name;
From *Agamemnon* born; to *Turnus* Aid,
A thousand Men the youthful Heroe led;
Who till the *Massick* Soil, for Wine renown'd,
And fierce *Auruncans* from their Hilly Ground: 1005
And those who live by *Sidicinian* Shores,
And where, with shoaly Foords *Vulturnus* roars;
Cales and *Osca*'s old Inhabitants,
And rough *Saticulans* inur'd to Wants:
Light demi-Launces from afar they throw, 1010
Fasten'd with Leathern Thongs to gaul the Foe.
Short crooked Swords in closer Fight they wear,
And on their warding Arm light Bucklers bear.

   Nor *Oebalus*, shalt thou be left unsung,
From Nymph *Sebethis* and old *Telon* sprung: 1015
Who then in *Teleboan Capri* reign'd,
But that short Isle th' ambitious Youth disdain'd;

1001 Name;] Name: *97 98*   1015 *Sebethis*] *Semethis 97 98*

And o're *Campania* stretch'd his ample Sway;
Where swelling *Sarnus* seeks the *Tyrrhene* Sea:
O're *Batulum*, and where *Abella* sees,   102
From her high Tow'rs, the Harvest of her Trees.
And these (as was the *Teuton* use of old)
Wield Brazen Swords, and Brazen Bucklers hold:
Sling weighty Stones when from afar they fight;
Their Casques are Cork, a Covering thick and light.   102
Next these in Rank, the warlike *Ufens* went,
And led the Mountain Troops that *Nursia* sent.
The rude *Equicolæ* his Rule obey'd,
Hunting their Sport, and Plund'ring was their Trade.
In Arms they plough'd, to Battel still prepar'd;   103
Their Soil was barren, and their Hearts were hard.

    Umbro the Priest the proud *Marrubians* led,
By King *Archippus* sent to *Turnus* aid;
And peaceful Olives crown'd his hoary head.
His Wand and holy Words, the Viper's rage,   103
And venom'd wounds of Serpents, cou'd asswage.
He, when he pleas'd with powerful Juice to steep
Their Temples, shut their Eyes in pleasing Sleep.
But vain were *Marsian* Herbs, and Magick Art,
To cure the Wound giv'n by the *Dardan* Dart.   104
Yet his untimely Fate, th' *Angitian* Woods
In sighs remurmur'd, to the *Fucine* Floods.

    The Son of fam'd *Hippolitus* was there;
Fam'd as his Sire, and as his Mother fair.
Whom in *Egerian* Groves *Aricia* bore,   104
And nurs'd his Youth along the Marshy Shore:
Where great *Diana*'s peaceful Altars flame,
In fruitful Fields, and *Virbius* was his Name.
Hippolitus, as old Records have said,
Was by his Stepdam sought to share her Bed: 10
But when no Female Arts his Mind cou'd move,
She turn'd to furious Hate her impious Love.
Torn by Wild Horses on the sandy Shore,
Another's Crimes th' unhappy Hunter bore;
Glutting his Father's Eyes with guiltless gore.   10

1018 *Campania* 98: *Campagnia* 97   1022 And 98: All 97   1036 wounds]
wound 98   1043 *Editor's paragraph*

But chast *Diana*, who his death deplor'd,
With *Æsculapian* Herbs his life restor'd.
Then *Jove*, who saw from high, with just disdain,
The dead inspir'd with Vital Breath again,
Struck to the Center with his flaming Dart   1060
Th' unhappy Founder of the Godlike Art.
But *Trivia* kept in secret Shades alone,
Her care, *Hippolitus*, to Fate unknown;
And call'd him *Virbius* in th' *Egerian* Grove:
Where then he liv'd obscure, but safe from *Jove*.   1065
For this, from *Trivia*'s Temple and her Wood,
Are Coursers driv'n, who shed their Master's Blood;
Affrighted by the Monsters of the Flood.
His Son, the Second *Virbius*, yet retain'd
His Fathers Art, and Warrior Steeds he rein'd.   1070
   Amid the Troops, and like the leading God,
High o're the rest in Arms the Graceful *Turnus* rode:
A triple Pile of Plumes his Crest adorn'd,
On which with belching Flames *Chimæra* burn'd:
The more the kindled Combat, rises high'r,   1075
The more with fury burns the blazing Fire.
Fair *Io* grac'd his Shield, but *Io* now
With Horns exalted stands, and seems to lowe:
(A noble charge) her Keeper by her side,
To watch her Walks his hundred Eyes apply'd.   1080
And on the Brims her Sire, the wat'ry God,
Rowl'd from a Silver Urn his Crystal Flood.
A Cloud of Foot succeeds, and fills the Fields
With Swords and pointed Spears, and clatt'ring Shields;
Of *Argives*, and of old *Sicanian* Bands,   1085
And those who Plow the rich *Rutulian* Lands;
Auruncan Youth and those *Sacrana* yields,
And the proud *Labicans* with painted Shields.
And those who near *Numician* Streams reside,
And those whom *Tyber*'s holy Forests hide;   1090
Or *Circes* Hills from the main Land divide.
Where *Ufens* glides along the lowly Lands,
Or the black Water of *Pomptina* stands.

1071 *Editor's paragraph*   1075 The more . . . high'r *98*: The more the Winds
his kindled Course inspire *97*   1076 burns *98*: burn'd *97*

Last from the *Volscians* fair *Camilla* came;
And led her warlike Troops, a Warriour Dame: 1
Unbred to Spinning, in the Loom unskill'd,
She chose the nobler *Pallas* of the Field.
Mix'd with the first, the fierce *Virago* fought,
Sustain'd the Toils of Arms, the Danger sought:
Outstrip'd the Winds in speed upon the Plain, 1
Flew o're the Fields, nor hurt the bearded Grain:
She swept the Seas, and as she skim'd along,
Her flying Feet unbath'd on Billows hung.
Men, Boys, and Women stupid with Surprise,
Where e're she passes, fix their wond'ring Eyes: 1
Longing they look, and gaping at the Sight,
Devour her o're and o're with vast Delight.
Her Purple Habit sits with such a Grace
On her smooth Shoulders, and so suits her Face:
Her Head with Ringlets of her Hair is crown'd, 1
And in a Golden Caul the Curls are bound.
She shakes her Myrtle Jav'lin: And, behind,
Her *Lycian* Quiver dances in the Wind.

THE EIGHTH BOOK OF THE ÆNEIS

THE ARGUMENT

The War *being now begun, both the Generals make all possible Preparations.*
Turnus sends to Diomedes. *Æneas goes in Person to beg Succours from*
Evander *and the* Tuscans. Evander *receives him kindly, furnishes him with*
Men, *and sends his Son* Pallas *with him.* Vulcan, *at the Request of* Venus,
makes Arms for her Son Æneas, *and draws on his Shield the most memorable*
Actions of his Posterity.

WHEN *Turnus* had assembled all his Pow'rs;
His Standard planted on *Laurentum*'s Tow'rs;
When now the sprightly Trumpet, from afar,
Had giv'n the Signal of approaching War;
Had rouz'd the neighing Steeds to scour the Fields,
While the fierce Riders clatter'd on their Shields:

1094 *Editor's paragraph*
The Eighth Book. 4 War;] War, *97 98*   6 Shields:] Shields, *97 98*

Trembling with Rage, the *Latian* Youth prepare
To join th' Allies, and headlong rush to War.
Fierce *Ufens*, and *Messapus*, led the Crowd;
With bold *Mezentius*, who blasphem'd aloud.   10
These, thro the Country took their wastful Course;
The Fields to forage, and to gather Force.
Then *Venulus* to *Diomede* they send,
To beg his Aid *Ausonia* to defend:
Declare the common Danger; and inform   15
The *Grecian* Leader of the growing Storm:
Æneas landed on the *Latian* Coast,
With banish'd Gods, and with a baffled Hoast;
Yet now aspir'd to Conquest of the State;
And claim'd a Title from the Gods and Fate: 20
What num'rous Nations in his Quarrel came,
And how they spread his formidable Name.
What he design'd, what Mischiefs might arise,
If Fortune favour'd his first Enterprise,
Was left for him to weigh: whose equal Fears,   25
And common Interest was involv'd in theirs.
While *Turnus* and th' Allies thus urge the War,
The *Trojan* floating in a Flood of Care,
Beholds the Tempest which his Foes prepare.
This way and that he turns his anxious Mind;   30
Thinks, and rejects the Counsels he design'd.
Explores himself in vain, in ev'ry part,
And gives no rest to his distracted Heart.
So when the Sun by Day, or Moon by Night,
Strike, on the polish'd Brass, their trembling Light,   35
The glitt'ring Species here and there divide;
And cast their dubious Beams from side to side:
Now on the Walls, now on the Pavement play,
And to the Cieling flash the glaring Day.
    'Twas Night: And weary Nature lul'd asleep   40
The Birds of Air, and Fishes of the Deep;
And Beasts, and Mortal Men: The *Trojan* Chief
Was laid on *Tyber*'s Banks, oppress'd with Grief,
And found in silent Slumber late Relief.

---

20 Fate:] Fate. *97 98*   22 Name.] Name: *97 98*   23 Mischiefs] Mischief *98*
34 *paragraph 97 98*   40 *Editor's paragraph*

Then, thro' the Shadows of the Poplar Wood,
Arose the Father of the *Roman* Flood;
An Azure Robe was o're his Body spread,
A Wreath of shady Reeds adorn'd his Head:
Thus, manifest to Sight, the God appear'd;
And with these pleasing Words his Sorrow chear'd.
Undoubted Off-spring of Etherial Race,
O long expected in this promis'd Place,
Who, thro the Foes, hast born thy banish'd Gods,
Restor'd them to their Hearths, and old Abodes;
This is thy happy Home! The Clime where Fate
Ordains thee to restore the *Trojan* State.
Fear not, the War shall end in lasting Peace;
And all the Rage of haughty *Juno* cease.
   And that this nightly Vision may not seem
Th' Effect of Fancy, or an idle Dream,
A Sow beneath an Oak shall lye along;
All white her self, and white her thirty Young.
When thirty rowling Years have run their Race,
Thy Son, *Ascanius*, on this empty Space,
Shall build a Royal Town, of lasting Fame;
Which from this Omen shall receive the Name.
Time shall approve the Truth: For what remains,
And how with sure Success to crown thy Pains,
With Patience next attend. A banish'd Band,
Driv'n with *Evander* from th' *Arcadian* Land,
Have planted here: and plac'd on high their Walls;
Their Town the Founder, *Palanteum* calls;
Deriv'd from *Pallas*, his great Grandsire's Name:
But the fierce *Latians* old Possession claim;
With War infesting the new Colony:
These make thy Friends, and on their Aid rely.
To thy free Passage I submit my Streams:
Wake Son of *Venus* from thy pleasing Dreams;
And, when the setting Stars are lost in Day,
To *Juno's* Pow'r thy just Devotion pay.
With Sacrifice the wrathful Queen appease;
Her Pride at length shall fall, her Fury cease.
When thou return'st victorious from the War,

Perform thy Vows to me with grateful Care.
The God am I, whose yellow Water flows 85
Around these Fields, and fattens as it goes:
Tyber my Name: among the rowling Floods,
Renown'd on Earth, esteem'd among the Gods.
This is my certain Seat: In Times to come,
My Waves shall wash the Walls of mighty *Rome*. 90
 He said; and plung'd below, while yet he spoke:
His Dream *Æneas* and his Sleep forsook.
He rose, and looking up, beheld the Skies
With Purple blushing, and the Day arise.
Then, Water in his hollow Palm he took, 95
From *Tyber*'s Flood; and thus the Pow'rs bespoke.
Laurentian Nymphs, by whom the Streams are fed,
And Father *Tyber*, in thy sacred Bed
Receive *Æneas*; and from Danger keep.
Whatever Fount, whatever holy deep, 100
Conceals thy wat'ry Stores; where e're they rise,
And, bubling from below, salute the Skies:
Thou King of horned Floods, whose plenteous Urn
Suffices Fatness to the fruitful Corn,
For this thy kind Compassion of our Woes, 105
Shalt share my Morning Song, and Ev'ning Vows.
But, oh! be present to thy Peoples Aid;
And firm the gracious Promise thou hast made.
Thus having said, two Gallies, from his Stores,
With Care he chuses; Mans, and fits with Oars. 110
Now on the Shore the fatal Swine is found:
Wond'rous to tell; she lay along the Ground:
Her well fed Offspring at her Udders hung;
She white her self, and white her thirty young.
Æneas takes the Mother, and her Brood, 115
And all on *Juno*'s Altar are bestow'd.
 The foll'wing Night, and the succeeding Day,
Propitious *Tyber* smooth'd his wat'ry Way:
He rowld his River back; and pois'd he stood;
A gentle Swelling, and a peaceful Flood. 120
The *Trojans* mount their Ships; they put from Shore,
Born on the Waves, and scarcely dip an Oar.

  91 *Editor's paragraph* 117 *Editor's paragraph*

Shouts from the Land give Omen to their Course;
And the pitch'd Vessels glide with easie Force.
The Woods and Waters, wonder at the Gleam 125
Of Shields, and painted Ships, that stem the Stream.
One Summer's Night, and one whole Day they pass,
Betwixt the green-wood Shades; and cut the liquid Glass.
The fiery Sun had finish'd half his Race;
Look'd back, and doubted in the middle Space: 130
When they from far beheld the rising Tow'rs,
The Tops of Sheds, and Shepherds lowly Bow'rs:
Thin as they stood, which, then of homely Clay,
Now rise in Marble, from the *Roman* Sway.
These Cots, (*Evander*'s Kingdom, mean and poor) 135
The *Trojan* saw; and turn'd his Ships to Shore.
'Twas on a solemn Day: Th' *Arcadian* States,
The King and Prince without the City Gates,
Then paid their Off'rings in a sacred Grove,
To *Hercules*, the Warrior Son of *Jove*. 140
Thick Clouds of rowling Smoke involve the Sky's:
And Fat of Entrails on his Altar fry's.
    But when they saw the Ships that stemm'd the Flood,
And glitter'd thro' the Covert of the Wood,
They rose with Fear; and left th' unfinish'd Feast: 145
'Till dauntless *Pallas* reassur'd the rest,
To pay the Rites. Himself without delay
A Jav'lin seiz'd, and singly took his Way.
Then gain'd a rising Ground; and call'd from far.
Resolve me, Strangers, whence, and what you are; ⎫
Your Buis'ness here; and bring you Peace or War? ⎬ 150
High on the Stern, *Æneas* took his Stand, ⎭
And held a Branch of Olive in his Hand;
While thus he spoke. The *Phrygians* Arms you see;
Expell'd from *Troy*, provok'd in *Italy* 155
By *Latian* Foes, with War unjustly made:
At first affianc'd, and at last betray'd.
This Message bear: The *Trojans* and their Chief
Bring holy Peace; and beg the King's Relief.
Struck with so great a Name, and all on fire, 160
The Youth Replies, Whatever you require,

141 Sky's *98*: Sky *97*   142 fry's *98*: fry *97*   148 singly] signally *98*

Your Fame exacts: Upon our Shores descend,
A welcome Guest, and what you wish, a Friend.
He said; and downward hasting to the Strand,
Embrac'd the Stranger Prince, and join'd his Hand.   165
   Conducted to the Grove, *Æneas* broke
The silence first, and thus the King bespoke.
Best of the *Greeks*, to whom, by Fates Command,
I bear these peaceful Branches in my hand;
Undaunted I approach you; though I know   170
Your Birth is *Grecian*, and your Land my Foe:
From *Atreus* tho' your ancient Lineage came;
And both the Brother Kings your Kindred claim:
Yet, my self-conscious Worth, your high Renown,
Your Vertue, through the Neighb'ring Nations blown,   175
Our Fathers mingl'd Blood, *Apollo*'s Voice,
Have led me hether, less by Need than Choice.
Our Founder *Dardanus*, as Fame has sung,
And *Greeks* acknowledge, from *Electra* sprung:
Electra from the Loins of *Atlas* came;   180
Atlas whose Head sustains the Starry Frame.
Your Sire is *Mercury*; whom long before
On cold *Cyllene*'s top fair *Maja* bore.
Maja the fair, on Fame if we rely,
Was *Atlas* Daughter, who sustains the Sky.   185
Thus from one common Source our Streams divide:
Ours is the *Trojan*, yours th' *Arcadian* side.
Rais'd by these Hopes, I sent no News before:
Nor ask'd your leave, nor did your Faith implore;
But come, without a Pledg, my own Ambassador.   190
The same *Rutulians*, who with Arms pursue
The *Trojan* Race, are equal Foes to you.
Our Host expell'd, what farther Force can stay
The Victor Troops from Universal Sway?
Then will they stretch their Pow'r athwart the Land;   195
And either Sea from side to side command.
Receive our offer'd Faith: and give us thine;
Ours is a gen'rous, and experienc'd Line:
We want not Hearts, nor Bodies for the War;
In Council cautious, and in Fields we dare.   200

166–416 *Editor's paragraphs*   189 your leave] you leave *98*

He said; and while he spoke, with piercing Eyes,
Evander view'd the Man with vast surprize.
Pleas'd with his Action, ravish'd with his Face,
Then answer'd briefly, with a Royal grace.
O Valiant Leader of the *Trojan* Line,   20
In whom the Features of thy Father shine;
How I recall *Anchises*, how I see
His Motions, Meen, and all my Friend in thee!
Long tho it be, 'tis fresh within my Mind,
When *Priam*, to his Sister's Court design'd   21◦
A welcome Visit, with a friendly stay;
And, through th' *Arcadian* Kingdom took his way.
Then, past a Boy, the callow Down began
To shade my Chin, and call me first a Man.
I saw the shining Train, with vast delight,   21
And *Priam*'s goodly Person pleas'd my sight:
But great *Anchises*, far above the rest,
With awful Wonder fir'd my Youthful Breast.
I long'd to join, in Friendship's holy Bands,
Our mutual Hearts, and plight our mutual Hands.   22
I first accosted him: I su'd, I sought,
And, with a loving force, to *Pheneus* brought.
He gave me, when at length constrain'd to go,
A *Lycian* Quiver, and a *Gnossian* Bow:
A Vest embroyder'd, glorious to behold,   22⟩
And two rich Bridles, with their Bits of Gold,
Which my Son's Coursers in obedience hold.
The League you ask I offer, as your Right:
And when to Morrow's Sun reveals the Light,
With swift Supplies you shall be sent away: 23⟩
Now celebrate, with us, this solemn Day;
Whose Holy Rites admit no long Delay.
Honour our Annual Feast; and take your Seat
With friendly Welcome, at a homely Treat.
Thus having said, the Bowls (remov'd for Fear)   23
The Youths replac'd; and soon restor'd the Chear.
On sods of Turf he set the Souldiers round;
A Maple Throne, rais'd higher from the Ground,
Receiv'd the *Trojan* Chief: And o're the Bed,
A Lyon's shaggy Hide for Ornament they spread.   24◦

The Loaves were serv'd in Canisters; the Wine
In Bowls, the Priest renew'd the Rites Divine:
Broil'd Entrails are their Food; and Beefs continu'd Chine.
But, when the Rage of Hunger was repress'd,
Thus spoke *Evander* to his Royal Guest.   245
    These Rites, these Altars, and this Feast, O King,
From no vain Fears, or Superstition spring:
Or blind Devotion, or from blinder Chance;
Or heady Zeal, or brutal Ignorance:
But, sav'd from Danger, with a grateful Sence,   250
The Labours of a God we recompence.
See, from afar, yon Rock that mates the Sky;
About whose Feet such Heaps of Rubbish lye:
Such indigested Ruin; bleak and bare,
How desart now it stands, expos'd in Air!   255
'Twas once a Robber's Den; inclos'd around
With living Stone, and deep beneath the Ground.
The Monster *Cacus*, more than half a Beast,
This Hold, impervious to the Sun, possess'd.
The Pavement ever foul with Human Gore;   260
Heads, and their mangled Members, hung the Door.
Vulcan this Plague begot: And, like his Sire,
Black Clouds he belch'd, and flakes of livid Fire.
Time, long expected, eas'd us of our Load:
And brought the needful Presence of a God.   265
Th' avenging Force of *Hercules*, from *Spain*,
Arriv'd in Triumph, from *Geryon* slain;
Thrice liv'd the Gyant, and thrice liv'd in vain.
His Prize, the lowing Herds, *Alcides* drove
Near *Tyber*'s Bank, to graze the shady Grove.   270
Allur'd with Hope of Plunder, and intent
By Force to rob, by Fraud to circumvent;
The brutal *Cacus*, as by Chance they stray'd,
Four Oxen thence, and four fair Kine convey'd.
And, lest the printed Footsteps might be seen,   275
He drag'd 'em backwards to his rocky Den.
The Tracks averse, a lying Notice gave;
And led the Searcher backward from the Cave.
Mean time the Herdsman Heroe shifts his place:
To find fresh Pasture, and untrodden Grass.   280

The Beasts, who miss'd their Mates, fill'd all around
With Bellowings, and the Rocks restor'd the Sound.
One Heifar who had heard her Love complain,
Roar'd from the Cave; and made the Project vain.
Alcides found the Fraud: With Rage he shook,   285
And toss'd about his Head his knotted Oak.
Swift as the Winds, or *Scythian* Arrows flight,
He clomb, with eager haste, th' Aerial height.
Then first we saw the Monster mend his Pace:
Fear in his Eyes, and Paleness in his Face,   290
Confess'd the Gods approach: Trembling he springs,
As Terror had increas'd his Feet with Wings:
Nor stay'd for Stairs; but down the Depth he threw
His Body; on his Back the Door he drew.
The Door, a Rib of living Rock; with Pains   295
His Father hew'd it out, and bound with Iron Chains.
He broke the heavy Lincks; the Mountain clos'd;
And Bars and Leavers to his Foe oppos'd.
The Wretch had hardly made his Dungeon fast;
The fierce Avenger came with bounding haste: 300
Survey'd the Mouth of the forbidden hold;
And here and there his raging Eyes he rowl'd.
He gnash'd his Teeth; and thrice he compass'd round
With winged speed the Circuit of the Ground.
Thrice at the Cavern's Mouth he pull'd in vain,   305
And, panting, thrice desisted from his Pain.
A pointed flinty Rock, all bare, and black,
Grew gibbous from behind the Mountains Back:
Owls, Ravens, all ill Omens of the Night,
Here built their Nests, and hether wing'd their Flight.   310
The leaning Head hung threat'ning o're the Flood:
And nodded to the left: The Heroe stood
Adverse, with planted Feet, and from the right,
Tugg'd at the solid Stone with all his might.
Thus heav'd, the fix'd Foundations of the Rock   315
Gave way: Heav'n echo'd at the ratling Shock.
Tumbling it choak'd the Flood: On either side
The Banks leap backward; and the Streams divide.
The Sky shrunk upward with unusual Dread:
And trembling *Tyber* div'd beneath his Bed.   320

The Court of *Cacus* stands reveal'd to sight;
The Cavern glares with new admitted Light.
So the pent Vapours with a rumbling Sound
Heave from below; and rend the hollow Ground:
A sounding Flaw succeeds: And from on high,   325
The Gods, with Hate behold the neather Sky:
The Ghosts repine at violated Night;
And curse th' invading Sun; and sicken at the sight.
The graceless Monster caught in open Day,
Inclos'd, and in Despair to fly away;   330
Howls horrible from underneath, and fills
His hollow Palace, with unmanly Yells.
The Heroe stands above; and from afar
Plies him with Darts, and Stones, and distant War.
He, from his Nostrils, and huge Mouth, expires   335
Black Clouds of Smoke, amidst his Father's Fires.
Gath'ring, with each repeated Blast, the Night:
To make uncertain Aim, and erring Sight.
The wrathful God, then plunges from above,
And where in thickest Waves the Sparkles drove,   340
There lights; and wades thro Fumes, and gropes his Way;
Half sing'd, half stifled, 'till he grasps his Prey.
The Monster, spewing fruitless Flames, he found;
He squeez'd his Throat, he writh'd his Neck around,
And in a Knot his cripled Members bound.   345
Then, from their Sockets, tore his burning Eyes;
Rowld on a heap the breathless Robber lyes.
The Doors, unbarr'd, receive the rushing Day;
And thorough Lights disclose the ravish'd Prey.
The Bulls redeem'd, breathe open Air agen;   350
Next, by the Feet, they drag him from his Den.
The wond'ring Neighbourhood, with glad surprize,
Behold his shagged Breast, his Gyant Size,
His Mouth that flames no more, and his extinguish'd Eyes.
From that auspicious Day, with Rites Divine,   355
We worship at the Hero's Holy Shrine.
Potitius first ordain'd these annual Vows;
As Priests, were added the *Pinarian* House:

326 behold *Scott:* beheld *97 98*   353 Behold] Beheld *98*   357 Vows;]
Vows, *97 98*

Who rais'd this Altar in the Sacred Shade;
Where Honours, ever due, for ever shall be paid.   360
For these Deserts, and this high Virtue shown,
Ye warlike Youths, your Heads with Garlands crown.
Fill high the Goblets with a sparkling Flood:
And with deep Draughts invoke our common God.
    This said, a double Wreath *Evander* twin'd: 365
And Poplars black and white his Temples bind.
Then Brims his ample Bowl: With like Design
The rest invoke the Gods, with sprinkled Wine.
Mean time the Sun descended from the Skies;
And the bright Evening-Star began to rise.   370
And now the Priests, *Potitius* at their Head,
In Skins of Beasts involv'd, the long Procession led:
Held high the flaming Tapers in their Hands;
As Custom had prescrib'd their holy Bands:
Then with a second Course the Tables load: 375
And with full Chargers offer to the God.
The *Salij* sing; and cense his Altars round
With *Saban* Smoke, their Heads with Poplar bound.
One Choire of old, another of the young;
To dance, and bear the Burthen of the Song.   380
The Lay records the Labours, and the Praise,
And all th' Immortal Acts of *Hercules*.
First, how the mighty Babe, when swath'd in Bands,
The Serpents strangled, with his Infant Hands:
Then, as in Years, and matchless Force he grew,   385
Th' *Oechalian* Walls, and *Trojan* overthrew.
Besides a thousand Hazards they relate,
Procur'd by *Juno*'s, and *Euristheus* Hate.
Thy Hands, unconquer'd Heroe, cou'd subdue
The Cloud-born *Centaurs*, and the Monster Crew.   390
Nor thy resistless Arm the Bull withstood:
Nor He the roaring Terror of the Wood.
The triple Porter of the *Stygian* Seat,
With lolling Tongue, lay fawning at thy Feet:
And, seiz'd with Fear, forgot his mangled Meat.   395
Th' Infernal Waters trembled at thy Sight;
Thee, God, no face of Danger cou'd Affright.

388 *Euristheus*] *Euristheus*'s 97 98

Not huge *Typhœus*, nor th' unnumber'd Snake,
Increas'd with hissing Heads, in *Lerna*'s Lake.
Hail *Jove*'s undoubted Son! An added Grace   400
To Heav'n, and the great Author of thy Race.
Receive the grateful Off'rings, which we pay,
And smile propitious on thy solemn Day.
In Numbers, thus, they sung: Above the rest,
The Den, and Death of *Cacus* crown the Feast.   405
The Woods to hollow Vales convey the Sound;
The Vales to Hills, and Hills the Notes rebound.
    The Rites perform'd, the chearful Train retire.
Betwixt young *Pallas*, and his aged Sire
The *Trojan* pass'd, the City to survey;   410
And pleasing Talk beguil'd the tedious Way.
The Stranger cast around his curious Eyes;
New Objects viewing still, with new Surprise.
With greedy Joy enquires of various Things;
And Acts and Monuments of Ancient Kings.   415
    Then thus the Founder of the *Roman* Tow'rs:
These Woods were first the Seat of *Silvan* Pow'rs,
Of Nymphs, and Fauns, and salvage Men, who took
Their Birth from Trunks of Trees, and stubborn Oak.
Nor Laws they knew, nor Manners, nor the Care   420
Of lab'ring Oxen, or the shining Share:
Nor Arts of Gain, nor what they gain'd to spare.
Their Exercise the Chase: the running Flood
Supply'd their Thirst; the Trees supply'd their Food.
Then *Saturn* came, who fled the Pow'r of *Jove*,   425
Robb'd of his Realms, and banish'd from above.
The Men, dispers'd on Hills, to Towns he brought;
And Laws ordain'd, and Civil Customs taught:
And *Latium* call'd the Land where safe he lay,
From his Unduteous Son, and his Usurping Sway.   430
With his mild Empire, Peace and Plenty came:
And hence the Golden Times deriv'd their name.
A more degenerate, and discolour'd Age,
Succeeded this, with Avarice and Rage.
Th' *Ausonians*, then, and bold *Sicanians* came;   435
And *Saturn*'s Empire often chang'd the name.

402 grateful *98*: gratful *97*

Then Kings, Gygantick *Tybris*, and the rest,
With Arbitrary Sway the Land oppress'd.
For *Tybers* flood was *Albula* before:
Till, from the Tyrants Fate, his name it bore.   440
I last arriv'd, driv'n from my native home,
By Fortune's Pow'r, and Fate's resistless Doom.
Long toss'd on Seas I sought this happy Land:
Warn'd by my Mother Nymph, and call'd by Heav'ns Command.
    Thus, walking on, he spoke: and shew'd the Gate,   44
Since call'd *Carmental* by the *Roman* State;
Where stood an Altar, Sacred to the Name
Of old *Carmenta*, the Prophetick Dame:
Who to her Son foretold th' *Ænean* Race,
Sublime in Fame, and *Rome*'s Imperial Place.   45
Then shews the Forest, which in after times,
Fierce *Romulus*, for perpetrated Crimes,
A Sacred Refuge made: with this, the Shrine
Where *Pan* below the Rock had Rites Divine.
Then tells of *Argus* death, his murder'd Guest,   45
Whose Grave, and Tomb, his Innocence attest.
Thence, to the steep *Tarpeian* Rock he leads;
Now Roof'd with Gold; then thatch'd with homely Reeds.
A Reverent fear (such Superstition reigns
Among the rude) ev'n then possess'd the Swains.   46
Some God they knew, what God they cou'd not tell,
Did there amidst the sacred horrour dwell.
Th' *Arcadians* thought him *Jove*; and said they saw
The mighty Thund'rer with Majestick awe;
Who shook his Shield, and dealt his Bolts around;   46
And scatter'd Tempests on the teeming Ground.
Then saw two heaps of Ruins; once they stood
Two stately Towns, on either side the Flood.
Saturnia's and *Janicula*'s Remains:
And, either place, the Founder's Name retains.   47
Discoursing thus together, they resort
Where poor *Evander* kept his Country Court.
They view'd the ground of *Rome*'s litigious Hall;
Once Oxen low'd, where now the Lawyers bawl.
Then, stooping, through the Narrow Gate they press'd,   47
When thus the King bespoke his *Trojan* Guest.

Mean as it is, this Palace, and this Door,
Receiv'd *Alcides*, then a Conquerour.
Dare to be poor: accept our homely Food
Which feasted him; and emulate a God.   480
Then, underneath a lowly Roof, he led
The weary Prince; and laid him on a Bed:
The stuffing Leaves, with Hides of Bears o'respread.

   Now Night had shed her silver Dews around,
And with her sable Wings embrac'd the Ground,   485
When Love's fair Goddess, anxious for her Son,
(New Tumults rising, and new Wars begun)
Couch'd with her Husband, in his Golden Bed,
With these alluring Words invokes his aid.
And, that her pleasing Speech his Mind may move,   490
Inspires each accent with the Charms of Love.
While Cruel Fate conspir'd with *Grecian* Pow'rs,
To level with the Ground the *Trojan* Tow'rs;
I ask'd not Aid th' unhappy to restore:
Nor did the Succour of thy Skill implore.   495
Nor urg'd the Labours of my Lord in vain;
A sinking Empire longer to sustain.
Tho' much I ow'd to *Priam*'s House; and more
The Dangers of *Æneas* did deplore.
But now by *Jove*'s Command, and Fates Decree,   500
His Race is doom'd to reign in *Italy*;
With humble Suit I beg thy needful Art,
O still propitious Pow'r, that rules my Heart!
A Mother kneels a suppliant for her Son.
By *Thetis* and *Aurora* thou wert won   505

---

483 with 98: which 97   484–9 Now . . . aid.] *The version in* Sylvæ *opens*
    Now Night with Sable wings the World o'respread;
    But *Venus*, not in vain, surpriz'd with dread
    Of *Latian* arms, before the tempest breaks,
    Her Husbands timely succour thus bespeaks,
    Couch'd in his golden Bed:—
490–1 And . . . Love.] (And . . . Love:) *S*   491 each accent with the] it with
diviner *S*   492 Cruel] adverse *S*   494 ask'd not] begg'd no *S*   495 the
Succour of thy Skill] thy succour, nor thy art *S*   496–7 Nor . . . sustain.]
S has
    Nor sought, their sinking Empire to sustain,
    To urge the labour of my Lord in vain.
502 beg] ask *S*   503 that rules] O Soveraign of *S*   504 kneels] stands *S*
her] a *S*   505 *Thetis* and *Aurora*] silver footed *Thetis S*

To forge impenetrable Shields; and grace,
With fated Arms, a less illustrious Race.
Behold, what haughty Nations are combin'd
Against the Relicks of the *Phrygian* Kind;
With Fire and Sword my People to destroy;   51
And conquer *Venus* twice, in conqu'ring *Troy*.
She said; and strait her Arms, of snowy hue,
About her unresolving Husband threw.
Her soft Embraces soon infuse Desire:
His Bones and Marrow sudden Warmth inspire;   } 51
And all the Godhead feels the wonted Fire.
Not half so swift the ratling Thunder flies,
Or forky Lightnings flash along the Skies.
The Goddess, proud of her successful Wiles,
And conscious of her Form, in secret Smiles.   52
Then thus, the Pow'r, obnoxious to her Charms,
Panting, and half dissolving in her Arms:
Why seek you Reasons for a Cause so just;
Or your own Beauties, or my Love distrust?
Long since, had you requir'd my helpful Hand,   52
Th' Artificer, and Art you might command,
To labour Arms for *Troy*: Nor *Jove*, nor Fate,
Confin'd their Empire to so short a Date.
And, if you now desire new Wars to wage,
My Skill I promise; and my Pains engage.   53
Whatever melting Metals can conspire,
Or breathing Bellows, or the forming Fire,
Is freely yours: Your anxious Fears remove:
And think no Task is difficult to Love.

506–9 To forge . . . Kind;] *S has*

> For fierce *Achilles*, and the rosie Morn
> Mov'd thee with Armes her *Memnon* to adorn;
> Are these my tears, less pow'rful on thy mind?
> Behold what warlike Nations are combin'd,

511 And . . . *Troy*.] And twice to triumph over *Me* and *Troy*. *S*   517 ratling]
rowling *S*   518 forky Lightnings] streaks of lightning *S*   519 proud of]
pleas'd with *S*   520 Form, in secret] conqu'ring Beauty, *S*   521 Pow'r,
obnoxious to] good old God, (sooth'd with *S*   522 Arms:] arms:) *S*   524
Beauties] beauty *S*   526 Th' Artificer, and Art you might] You might the
Artist, and his Art *S*   527 To labour Arms for *Troy*: Nor *Jove*, nor] To arm
your *Trojans*: nor did *Jove* or *S*   528 Confin'd] Confine *S*   530 My Skill
I promise; and my Pains] My care, my skill, my labour I *S*   533 Is freely
yours: Your anxious Fears] I freely promise; all your doubts *S*

Trembling he spoke; and eager of her Charms,　　　535
He snatch'd the willing Goddess to his Arms;
'Till in her Lap infus'd, he lay possess'd
Of full Desire, and sunk to pleasing Rest.
Now when the Night her middle race had rode;
And his first Slumber had refresh'd the God;　　　540
The time when early Housewifes leave the Bed;
When living Embers on the Hearth they spred;
Supply the Lamp, and call the Maids to rise,
With yawning Mouths, and with half open'd Eyes;
They ply the Distaff by the winking Light;　　　545
And to their daily Labour add the Night:
Thus frugally they earn their Childrens Bread;
And uncorrupted keep the Nuptial Bed:
Not less concern'd, nor at a later Hour,
Rose from his downy Couch the forging Pow'r.　　　550
　　Sacred to *Vulcan*'s Name an Isle there lay,
Betwixt *Sicilia*'s Coasts and *Lipare*;
Rais'd high on smoaking Rocks, and deep below,
In hollow Caves the Fires of *Ætna* glow.
The *Cyclops* here their heavy Hammers deal;　　　555
Loud Strokes, and hissings of tormented Steel
Are heard around: The boyling Waters roar;
And smoaky Flames thro' fuming Tunnels soar.
Hether, the Father of the Fire, by Night,
Through the brown Air precipitates his Flight.　　　560
On their Eternal Anvils here he found
The Brethren beating, and the Blows go round:
A load of pointless Thunder now there lies
Before their Hands, to ripen for the Skies:
These Darts, for angry *Jove*, they dayly cast:　　　565
Consum'd on Mortals with prodigious waste.
Three Rays of writhen Rain, of Fire three more,
Of winged *Southern* Winds, and cloudy Store
As many parts, the dreadful Mixture frame:
And Fears are added, and avenging Flame.　　　570
Inferior Ministers, for *Mars* repair

535 Trembling he spoke; and eager of] He said; and eager to enjoy *S*　　535
willing] lovely *S*　　　537 in her Lap infus'd] all infus'd in joy *S*　　　542 When
98: And 97　　546 Night:] Night. 97 98　　547 Bread;] Bread: 97 98　　548
Bed:] Bed. 97 98　　558 Flames] Flame 98

His broken Axeltrees, and blunted War:
And send him forth agen, with furbish'd Arms,
To wake the lazy War, with Trumpets loud Alarms.
The rest refresh the scaly Snakes, that fold 5
The Shield of *Pallas*; and renew their Gold.
Full on the Crest the *Gorgon*'s Head they place,
With Eyes that rowl in Death, and with distorted Face.
   My Sons, said *Vulcan*, set your Tasks aside,
Your Strength, and Master Skill, must now be try'd. 5
Arms, for a Heroe forge: Arms that require
Your Force, your Speed, and all your forming Fire.
He said: They set their former Work aside:
And their new Toils with eager haste divide.
A Flood of molten Silver, Brass, and Gold, 5
And deadly Steel, in the large Furnace rowl'd;
Of this, their artful Hands a Shield prepare;
Alone sufficient to sustain the War.
Sev'n Orbs within a spacious round they close;
One stirs the Fire, and one the Bellows blows. 5
The hissing Steel is in the Smithy drown'd;
The Grot with beaten Anvils groans around.
By turns their Arms advance, in equal time:
By turns their Hands descend, and Hammers chime.
They turn the glowing Mass, with crooked Tongs: 5
The fiery Work proceeds, with Rustick Songs.
   While, at the *Lemnian* God's Command, they urge
Their Labours thus, and ply th' *Eolian* Forge:
The chearful Morn salutes *Evander*'s Eyes;
And Songs of chirping Birds invite to rise. 6
He leaves his lowly Bed; his Buskins meet
Above his Ankles; Sandals sheath his Feet:
He sets his trusty Sword upon his side;
And o're his Shoulder throws a Panther's Hide.
Two Menial Dogs before their Master press'd: 6
Thus clad, and guarded thus, he seeks his Kingly Guest.
Mindful of promis'd Aid, he mends his Pace:
But meets *Æneas* in the middle Space.
Young *Pallas* did his Father's Steps attend;
And true *Achates* waited on his Friend. 6

     597 *Editor's paragraph*

They join their Hands; a secret Seat they chuse;
Th' *Arcadian* first, their former Talk renews.
Undaunted Prince, I never can believe
The *Trojan* Empire lost, while you survive.
Command th' Assistance of a faithful Friend: 615
But feeble are the Succours I can send.
Our narrow Kingdom, here the *Tyber* bounds;
That other side the *Latian* State surrounds;
Insults our Walls, and wastes our fruitful Grounds.
But mighty Nations I prepare, to join   620
Their Arms with yours, and aid your just Design.
You come, as by your better Genius sent:
And Fortune seems to favour your intent.
Not far from hence there stands a Hilly Town,
Of ancient Building, and of high Renown;   625
Torn from the *Tuscans*, by the *Lydian* Race;
Who gave the Name of *Cære*, to the Place
Once *Agyllina* call'd: It flourish'd long
In Pride of Wealth; and warlike People strong.
'Till curs'd *Mezentius*, in a fatal Hour,   630
Assum'd the Crown, with Arbitrary Pow'r.
What Words can paint those execrable Times;
The Subjects Suff'rings, and the Tyrant's Crimes!
That Blood, those Murthers, O ye Gods replace
On his own Head, and on his impious Race!   635
The living, and the Dead, at his Command
Were coupled, Face to Face, and Hand to Hand:
'Till choak'd with Stench, in loath'd Embraces ty'd,
The ling'ring Wretches pin'd away, and dy'd.
Thus plung'd in Ills, and meditating more,   640
The People's Patience tyr'd, no longer bore
The raging Monster: But with Arms beset
His House, and Vengeance and Destruction threat.
They fire his Palace: While the Flame ascends,
They force his Guards; and execute his Friends.   645
He cleaves the Crowd; and favour'd by the Night,
To *Turnus* friendly Court directs his flight.
By just Revenge the *Tuscans* set on Fire,
With Arms, their King to Punishment require:

641 tyr'd] try'd *98*   647 *Turnus*] *Turnus's 97 98*

Their num'rous Troops, now muster'd on the Strand,   650
My Counsel shall submit to your Command.
Their Navy swarms upon the Coasts: They cry
To hoist their Anchors; but the Gods deny.
An ancient Augur, skill'd in future Fate,
With these foreboding Words restrains their Hate.   655
Ye brave in Arms, ye *Lydian* Blood, the Flow'r
Of *Tuscan* Youth, and choice of all their Pow'r,
Whom just Revenge against *Mezentius* arms,
To seek your Tyrant's Death, by lawful Arms:
Know this; no Native of our Land may lead   660
This pow'rful People: Seek a Foreign Head.

   Aw'd with these Words, in Camps they still abide;
And wait with longing Looks their promis'd Guide.
Tarchon, the *Tuscan* Chief, to me has sent
Their Crown, and ev'ry Regal Ornament: 665
The People join their own with his Desire;
And All, my Conduct, as their King, require.
But the chill Blood that creeps within my Veins,
And Age, and listless Limbs unfit for Pains,
And a Soul conscious of its own Decay,   670
Have forc'd me to refuse Imperial Sway.
My *Pallas* were more fit to mount the Throne;
And shou'd, but he's a *Sabine* Mother's Son;
And half a Native: But in you combine
A Manly Vigour, and a Foreign Line.   675
Where Fate and smiling Fortune shew the Way,
Pursue the ready Path to Sov'raign Sway.
The Staff of my declining Days, my Son,
Shall make your good or ill Success his own.
In fighting Fields from you shall learn to dare: 680
And serve the hard Apprentiship of War.
Your matchless Courage, and your Conduct view;
And early shall begin t' admire and copy you.
Besides, two hundred Horse he shall command:
Tho' few, a warlike and well chosen Band.   685
These in my Name are listed: And my Son
As many more has added in his own.

   Scarce had he said; *Achates* and his Guest,

With downcast Eyes their silent Grief exprest:
Who short of Succours; and in deep Despair, 690
Shook at the dismal Prospect of the War.
But his bright Mother, from a breaking Cloud,
To chear her Issue, thunder'd thrice aloud.
Thrice, forky Lightning flash'd along the Sky;
And *Tyrrhene* Trumpets thrice were heard on high. 695
Then, gazing up, repeated Peals they hear:
And, in a Heav'n serene, refulgent Arms appear;
Red'ning the Skies, and glitt'ring all around,
The temper'd Metals clash; and yield a Silver sound.
The rest stood trembling, struck with awe divine: 700
Æneas onely conscious to the Sign;
Presag'd th' Event; and joyful view'd, above,
Th' accomplish'd Promise of the Queen of Love.
Then, to th' *Arcadian* King: This Prodigy
(Dismiss your Fear) belongs alone to me. 705
Heav'n calls me to the War: Th' expected Sign
Is giv'n of promis'd Aid, and Arms Divine.
My Goddess-Mother, whose Indulgent Care,
Foresaw the Dangers of the growing War;
This Omen gave; when Bright *Vulcanian* Arms, 710
Fated from force of Steel by *Stygian* Charms,
Suspended, shone on high: She then foreshow'd
Approaching Fights, and Fields to float in Blood.
Turnus shall dearly pay for Faith forsworn;
And Corps, and Swords, and Shields, on *Tyber* born, 715
Shall choak his Flood: Now sound the loud Alarms;
And *Latian* Troops prepare your perjur'd Arms.
   He said; and rising from his homely Throne,
The Solemn Rites of *Hercules* begun:
And on his Altars wak'd the sleeping Fires: 720
Then chearful to his Household-Gods retires.
There offers chosen Sheep: Th' *Arcadian* King
And *Trojan* Youth the same Oblations bring.
Next of his Men, and Ships, he makes review,
Draws out the best, and ablest of the Crew. 725
Down with the falling Stream the Refuse run:

To raise with joyful News his drooping Son.
Steeds are prepar'd to mount the *Trojan* Band;
Who wait their Leader to the *Tyrrhene* Land.
A sprightly Courser, fairer than the rest,   730
The King himself presents his Royal Guest.
A Lyons Hide his Back and Limbs infold;
Precious with studded work, and Paws of Gold.
Fame through the little City spreads aloud
Th' intended March, amid the fearful Crowd: 735
The Matrons beat their Breasts; dissolve in Tears;
And double their Devotion in their Fears.
The War at hand appears with more affright:
And rises ev'ry Moment to the sight.

 Then, old *Evander*, with a close embrace,   740
Strain'd his departing Friend; and Tears o're-flow his Face:
Wou'd Heav'n, said he, my strength and youth recall,
Such as I was beneath *Preneste*'s Wall;
Then when I made the foremost Foes retire,
And set whole heaps of conquer'd Shields on Fire.   745
When *Herilus* in single Fight I slew;
Whom with three lives *Feronia* did endue:
And thrice I sent him to the *Stygian* Shore;
Till the last Ebbing Soul return'd no more:
Such, if I stood renew'd, not these Alarms,   750
Nor Death, shou'd rend me from my *Pallas* arms:
Nor Proud *Mezentius*, thus unpunish'd, boast
His Rapes and Murthers on the *Tuscan* Coast.
Ye Gods! and mighty *Jove*, in pity bring
Relief, and hear a Father, and a King.   755
If Fate and you, reserve these Eyes, to see
My Son return with Peace and Victory;
If the lov'd Boy shall bless his Father's sight;
If we shall meet again with more delight;
Then draw my Life in length, let me sustain,   760
In hopes of his Embrace, the worst of Pain.
But if your hard Decrees, which O I dread,
. Have doom'd to death his undeserving head;
This, O this very Moment, let me die;
While Hopes and Fears in equal ballance lye.   765

   740 *Editor's paragraph*

While yet Possest of all his Youthful Charms,
I strain him close within these Aged Arms:
Before that fatal news my Soul shall wound!
He said, and, swooning, sunk upon the ground;
His Servants bore him off: And softly laid   770
His languish'd Limbs upon his homely Bed.
  The Horsemen march; the Gates are open'd wide;
Æneas at their head, *Achates* by his side.
Next these the *Trojan* Leaders rode along:
Last, follows in the Reer, th' *Arcadian* Throng.   775
Young *Pallas* shone conspicuous o're the rest;
Guilded his Arms, Embroider'd was his Vest.
So, from the Seas, exerts his radiant head
The Star, by whom the Lights of Heav'n are led:
Shakes from his rosie Locks the perly Dews;   780
Dispels the darkness, and the Day renews.
The trembling Wives, the Walls and Turrets crowd;
And follow, with their Eyes, the dusty Cloud:
Which Winds disperse by fits; and shew from far
The blaze of Arms, and Shields, and shining War.   785
The Troops, drawn up in beautiful Array,
O're heathy Plains pursue the ready way.
Repeated peals of showts are heard around:
The Neighing Coursers answer to the sound:
And shake with horny Hoofs the solid ground.   790
  A greenwood Shade, for long Religion known,
Stands by the Streams that wash the *Tuscan* Town:
Incompass'd round with gloomy Hills above,
Which add a holy horrour to the Grove.
The first Inhabitants, of *Grecian* Blood,   795
That sacred Forest to *Sylvanus* vow'd:
The Guardian of their Flocks, and Fields; and pay
Their due Devotions on his annual day.
Not far from hence, along the River's side,
In Tents secure, the *Tuscan* Troops abide;   800
By *Tarchon* led. Now, from a rising ground,
Æneas cast his wond'ring Eyes around;
And all the *Tyrrhene* Army had in sight,
Stretch'd on the spacious Plain from left to right.
Thether his warlike Train the *Trojan* led;   805

Refresh'd his Men, and weary'd Horses fed.
   Mean time the Mother Goddess, crown'd with Charms,
Breaks through the Clouds, and brings the fated Arms.
Within a winding Vale she finds her Son,
On the cool River's Banks, retir'd alone.   810
She shews her heav'nly Form, without disguise,
And gives her self to his desiring Eyes.
Behold, she said, perform'd, in ev'ry part
My promise made; and *Vulcan*'s labour'd Art.
Now seek, secure, the *Latian* Enemy;   815
And haughty *Turnus* to the Field defy.
She said: And having first her Son embrac'd;
The radiant Arms beneath an Oak she plac'd.
Proud of the Gift, he rowl'd his greedy sight
Around the Work, and gaz'd with vast delight.   820
He lifts, he turns, he poizes, and admires
The Crested Helm, that vomits radiant Fires:
His hands the fatal Sword, and Corslet hold:
One keen with temper'd Steel, one stiff with Gold.
Both ample, flaming both, and beamy bright: 825
So shines a Cloud, when edg'd with adverse Light.
He shakes the pointed Spear; and longs to try
The plated Cuishes, on his manly thigh;
But most admires the Shields Mysterious mould,
And *Roman* Triumphs rising on the Gold.   830
For those, emboss'd, the Heav'nly Smith had wrought,
(Not in the Rolls of future Fate untaught,)
The Wars in Order, and the Race Divine
Of Warriors, issuing from the *Julian* Line.
The Cave of *Mars* was dress'd with mossy Greens: 835
There, by the Wolf, were laid the Martial Twins.
Intrepid on her swelling Dugs they hung;
The foster Dam loll'd out her fawning Tongue:
They suck'd secure, while bending back her Head,
She lick'd their tender Limbs; and form'd them as they fed. 840
Not far from thence new *Rome* appears, with Games
Projected for the Rape of *Sabine* Dames.
The Pit resounds with Shrieks: A War succeeds,
For breach of Publick Faith, and unexampl'd Deeds.

828 thigh;] thigh, *97*: thigh. *98*

Here for Revenge the *Sabine* Troops contend: 845
The *Romans* there with Arms the Prey defend.
Weary'd with tedious War, at length they cease;
And both the Kings and Kingdoms plight the Peace.
The friendly Chiefs, before *Jove*'s Altar stand;
Both arm'd, with each a Charger in his Hand: 850
A fatted Sow, for Sacrifice is led;
With Imprecations on the perjur'd Head.
Near this, the Traytor *Metius*, stretch'd between
Four fiery Steeds, is dragg'd along the Green;
By *Tullus* doom: The Brambles drink his Blood;   855
And his torn Limbs are left, the Vulture's Food.
There, *Porsena* to *Rome* proud *Tarquin* brings;
And wou'd by Force restore the banish'd Kings.
One Tyrant, for his fellow Tyrant fights:
The *Roman* Youth assert their Native Rights.   860
Before the Town the *Tuscan* Army lies:
To win by Famine, or by Fraud surprise.
Their King, half threat'ning, half disdaining stood:
While *Cocles* broke the Bridge; and stem'd the Flood.
The Captive Maids there tempt the raging Tide: 865
Scap'd from their Chains, with *Clelia* for their Guide.
   High on a Rock Heroick *Manlius* stood;
To guard the Temple, and the Temple's God:
Then *Rome* was poor; and there you might behold
The Palace, thatch'd with Straw, now roof'd with Gold.   870
The Silver Goose before the shining Gate
There flew; and by her Cackle, sav'd the State.
She told the *Gauls* approach: Th' approaching *Gauls*,
Obscure in Night, ascend, and seize the Walls.
The Gold, dissembl'd well their yellow Hair: 875
And Golden Chains on their white Necks they wear.
Gold are their Vests: Long *Alpine* Spears they wield:
And their left Arm sustains a length of Shield.
Hard by, the leaping *Salian* Priests advance:
And naked thro' the Streets the mad *Luperci* dance;   880
In Caps of Wool: The Targets dropt from Heav'n:
Here modest Matrons in soft Litters driv'n,
To pay their Vows in solemn Pomp appear:

   880 dance;] dance: *97 98*   881 Wool:] Wool. *97 98*

And odorous Gums in their chast Hands they bear.
Far hence remov'd, the *Stygian* Seats are seen: 885
Pains of the damn'd, and punish'd *Catiline*:
Hung on a Rock the Traytor; and around,
The Furies hissing from the neather Ground.
Apart from these, the happy Souls, he draws:
And *Cato*'s holy Ghost, dispensing Laws.   890
Betwixt the Quarters, flows a Golden Sea:
But foaming Surges, there, in Silver play.
The dancing Dolphins, with their Tails, divide
The glitt'ring Waves; and cut the precious Tide.
Amid the Main, two mighty Fleets engage   895
Their Brazen Beaks; oppos'd with equal Rage.
Actium, surveys the well disputed Prize:
Leucate's wat'ry Plain, with foamy Billows fries.
Young *Cæsar*, on the Stern, in Armour bright;
Here leads the *Romans* and their Gods to fight: 900
His beamy Temples shoot their Flames afar;
And o're his Head is hung the *Julian* Star.
Agrippa seconds him, with prosp'rous Gales:
And, with propitious Gods, his Foes assails.
A Naval Crown, that binds his Manly Brows,   905
The happy Fortune of the Fight foreshows.
 Rang'd on the Line oppos'd, *Antonius* brings
Barbarian Aids, and Troops of *Eastern* Kings.
Th' *Arabians* near, and *Bactrians* from afar,
Of Tongues discordant, and a mingled War.   910
And, rich in gaudy Robes, amidst the Strife,
His ill Fate follows him; th' *Egyptian* Wife.
Moving they fight: With Oars, and forky Prows,
The Froth is gather'd; and the Water glows.
It seems, as if the *Cyclades* again   915
Were rooted up, and justled in the Main:
Or floating Mountains, floating Mountains meet:
Such is the fierce Encounter of the Fleet.
Fire-balls are thrown; and pointed Jav'lins fly:
The Fields of *Neptune* take a Purple Dye.   920
The Queen her self, amidst the loud Alarms,
With Cymbals toss'd her fainting Souldiers warms.
Fool as she was; who had not yet divin'd

Her cruel Fate; nor saw the Snakes behind.
Her Country Gods, the Monsters of the Sky,   925
Great *Neptune*, *Pallas*, and Love's Queen, defy.
The Dog *Anubis* barks, but barks in vain;
Nor longer dares oppose th' Ætherial Train.
Mars, in the middle of the shining Shield
Is grav'd, and strides along the liquid Field.   930
The *Diræ* sowse from Heav'n, with swift Descent:
And Discord, dy'd in Blood, with Garments rent,
Divides the Preace: Her Steps, *Bellona* treads,
And shakes her Iron Rod above their Heads.
This seen, *Apollo*, from his *Actian* height,   935
Pours down his Arrows: At whose winged flight
The trembling *Indians*, and *Egyptians* yield:
And soft *Sabæans* quit the wat'ry Field.
The fatal Mistress hoists her silken Sails;
And, shrinking from the Fight, invokes the Gales.   940
Aghast she looks; and heaves her Breast, for Breath:
Panting, and pale with fear of future Death.
The God had figur'd her, as driv'n along,
By Winds and Waves; and scudding thro' the Throng.
Just opposite, sad *Nilus*, opens wide   945
His Arms, and ample Bosom, to the Tide.
And spreads his Mantle o're the winding Coast:
In which he wraps his Queen, and hides the flying Hoast.
The Victor, to the Gods his Thanks express'd:
And *Rome* triumphant, with his Presence bless'd.   950
Three hundred Temples in the Town he plac'd:
With Spoils and Altars ev'ry Temple grac'd.
Three shining Nights, and three succeeding Days, ⎫
The Fields resound with Shouts; the Streets with Praise: ⎬
The Domes with Songs, the Theatres with Plays. ⎭   955
All Altars flame: Before each Altar lies,
Drench'd in his Gore, the destin'd Sacrifice.
Great *Cæsar* sits sublime upon his Throne;
Before *Apollo*'s Porch of *Parian* Stone:
Accepts the Presents vow'd for Victory;   960
And hangs the monumental Crowns on high.
Vast Crowds of vanquish'd Nations march along:
Various in Arms, in Habit, and in Tongue.

Here, *Mulciber* assigns the proper Place
For *Carians*, and th' ungirt *Numidian* Race; 965
Then ranks the *Thracians* in the second Row;
With *Scythians*, expert in the Dart and Bow.
And here the tam'd *Euphrates* humbly glides;
And there the *Rhine* submits her swelling Tides;
And proud *Araxes*, whom no Bridge cou'd bind: 970
The *Danes* unconquer'd Offspring, march behind;
And *Morini*, the last of Human Kind.

  These Figures, on the Shield divinely wrought,
By *Vulcan* labour'd, and by *Venus* brought,
With Joy and Wonder fill the Hero's thought. 975
Unknown the Names, he yet admires the Grace;
And bears aloft the Fame, and Fortune of his Race.

THE NINTH BOOK OF THE ÆNEIS

THE ARGUMENT

Turnus *takes Advantage of Æneas's Absence, fires some of his Ships, (which
are transform'd into Sea-Nymphs) and assaults his Camp. The Trojans
reduc'd to the last Extremities, send* Nisus *and* Euryalus *to recall Æneas;
which furnishes the Poet with that admirable Episode of their Friendship,
Generosity; and the conclusion of their Adventures.* 5

WHILE these Affairs in distant Places pass'd,
   The various *Iris Juno* sends with haste,
To find bold *Turnus*, who, with anxious Thought,
The secret Shade of his great Grandsire sought.
Retir'd alone she found the daring Man; 5
And op'd her rosie Lips, and thus began.
What none of all the Gods cou'd grant thy Vows;
That, *Turnus*, this auspicious Day bestows.
Æneas, gone to seek th' *Arcadian* Prince,
Has left the *Trojan* Camp without defence; 10
And, short of Succours there; employs his Pains
In Parts remote to raise the *Tuscan* Swains:
Now snatch an Hour that favours thy Designs,
Unite thy Forces, and attack their Lines.
This said, on equal Wings she pois'd her Weight, 15

969 Tides;] Tides. *97 98*

And form'd a radiant Rainbow in her flight.
  The *Daunian* Heroe lifts his Hands and Eyes;
And thus invokes the Goddess as she flies.
Iris, the Grace of Heav'n, what Pow'r Divine
Has sent thee down, thro' dusky Clouds to shine?   20
See they divide; immortal Day appears;
And glitt'ring Planets dancing in their Spheres!
With Joy, these happy Omens I obey;
And follow to the War, the God that leads the Way.
  Thus having said, as by the Brook he stood,   25
He scoop'd the Water from the Crystal Flood;
Then with his Hands the drops to Heav'n he throws,
And loads the Pow'rs above with offer'd Vows.
  Now march the bold Confed'rates thro' the Plain;
Well hors'd, well clad, a rich and shining Train: 30
Messapus leads the Van; and in the Reer,
The Sons of *Tyrrheus* in bright Arms appear.
In the Main Battel, with his flaming Crest,
The mighty *Turnus* tow'rs above the rest:
Silent they move; majestically slow,   35
Like ebbing *Nile,* or *Ganges* in his flow.
The *Trojans* view the dusty Cloud from far;
And the dark Menace of the distant War.
Caicus from the Rampire saw it rise,
Blackning the Fields, and thickning thro' the Skies.   40
Then to his Fellows thus aloud he calls,
What rowling Clouds, my Friends, approach the Walls?
Arm, arm, and man the Works; prepare your Spears,
And pointed Darts; the *Latian* Hoast appears.
  Thus warn'd, they shut their Gates; with Shouts ascend   45
The Bulwarks, and secure their Foes attend.
For their wise Gen'ral with foreseeing Care,
Had charg'd them not to tempt the doubtful War:
Nor, tho' provok'd, in open Fields advance;
But close within their Lines attend their chance.   50
Unwilling, yet they keep the strict Command;
And sourly wait in Arms the Hostile Band.
The fiery *Turnus* flew before the rest,
A Pye-ball'd Steed of *Thracian* Strain he press'd;
His Helm of massy Gold; and Crimson was his Crest.   55

With twenty Horse to second his Designs,
An unexpected Foe, he fac'd the Lines.

   Is there, he said, in Arms who bravely dare,
His Leader's Honour, and his Danger share?
Then, spurring on, his brandish'd Dart he threw,   60
In sign of War, applauding Shouts ensue.

   Amaz'd to find a dastard Race that run
Behind the Rampires, and the Battel shun,
He rides around the Camp, with rowling Eyes,
And stops at ev'ry Post; and ev'ry Passage tries.   65
So roams the nightly Wolf about the Fold,
Wet with descending Show'rs, and stiff with cold;
He howls for Hunger, and he grins for Pain;
His gnashing Teeth are exercis'd in vain:
And impotent of Anger, finds no way   70
In his distended Paws to grasp the Prey.
The Mothers listen; but the bleating Lambs
Securely swig the Dug, beneath the Dams.
Thus ranges eager *Turnus* o're the Plain,
Sharp with Desire, and furious with Disdain: 75
Surveys each Passage with a piercing Sight;
To force his Foes in equal Field to fight.
Thus, while he gazes round, at length he spies
Where, fenc'd with strong Redoubts, their Navy lies;
Close underneath the Walls: The washing Tyde   80
Secures from all approach this weaker side.
He takes the wish'd Occasion; fills his Hand
With ready Fires, and shakes a flaming Brand:
Urg'd by his Presence, ev'ry Soul is warm'd,
And ev'ry Hand with kindled Firrs is arm'd.   85
From the fir'd Pines the scatt'ring Sparkles fly;
Fat Vapours mix'd with Flames involve the Sky.
What Pow'r, O Muses, cou'd avert the Flame
Which threaten'd, in the Fleet, the *Trojan* Name!
Tell: For the Fact thro' length of Time obscure,   90
Is hard to Faith; yet shall the Fame endure.

   'Tis said, that when the Chief prepar'd his flight,
And fell'd his Timber from Mount *Ida*'s height,
The Grandam Goddess then approach'd her Son,
And with a Mother's Majesty begun.   95

Grant me, she said, the sole Request I bring,
Since conquer'd Heav'n has own'd you for its King:
On *Ida*'s Brows, for Ages past, there stood,
With Firrs and Maples fill'd, a shady Wood:
And on the Summit rose a Sacred Grove,   100
Where I was worshipp'd with Religious Love;
Those Woods, that Holy Grove, my long delight,
I gave the *Trojan* Prince, to speed his flight.
Now fill'd with Fear, on their behalf I come;
Let neither Winds o'reset, nor Waves intomb   105
The floating Forests of the Sacred Pine;
But let it be their Safety to be mine.
Then thus reply'd her awful Son; who rowls
The radiant Stars, and Heav'n and Earth controuls;
How dare you, Mother, endless Date demand,   110
For Vessels moulded by a Mortal Hand?
What then is Fate? Shall bold *Æneas* ride
Of Safety certain, on th' uncertain Tide?
Yet what I can, I grant: When, wafted o're,
The Chief is landed on the *Latian* Shore,   115
Whatever Ships escape the raging Storms,
At my Command shall change their fading Forms
To Nymphs Divine: and plow the wat'ry Way,
Like *Dotis*, and the Daughters of the Sea.
　　To seal his sacred Vow, by *Styx* he swore,   120
The Lake of liquid Pitch, the dreery Shore;
And *Phlegethon*'s innavigable Flood,
And the black Regions of his Brother God:
He said; and shook the Skies with his Imperial Nod.
　　And now at length the number'd Hours were come,   125
Prefix'd by Fate's irrevocable Doom,
When the great Mother of the Gods was free
To save her Ships, and finish *Jove*'s Decree.
First, from the Quarter of the Morn, there sprung
A Light that sign'd the Heav'ns, and shot along;   130
Then from a Cloud, fring'd round with Golden Fires,
Were Timbrels heard, and *Berecynthian* Quires:
And last a Voice, with more than Mortal Sounds,
Both Hosts in Arms oppos'd, with equal Horrour wounds.
　　O *Trojan* Race, your needless Aid forbear;   135

And know my Ships are my peculiar Care.
With greater ease the bold *Rutulian* may,
With hissing Brands, attempt to burn the Sea,
Than sindge my sacred Pines. But you my Charge,
Loos'd from your crooked Anchors lanch at large,   140
Exalted each a Nymph: Forsake the Sand,
And swim the Seas, at *Cybele*'s Command.
No sooner had the Goddess ceas'd to speak,
When lo, th' obedient Ships, their Haulsers break;
And, strange to tell, like Dolphins in the Main,   145
They plunge their Prows, and dive, and spring again:
As many beauteous Maids the Billows sweep,
As rode before tall Vessels on the Deep.

    The Foes, surpriz'd with Wonder, stood aghast,
Messapus curb'd his fiery Courser's haste;   150
Old *Tyber* roar'd; and raising up his Head,
Call'd back his Waters to their Oozy Bed.
Turnus alone, undaunted, bore the Shock;
And with these Words his trembling Troops bespoke.
These Monsters for the *Trojans* Fate are meant,   155
And are by *Jove* for black Presages sent.
He takes the Cowards last Relief away;
For fly they cannot; and, constrain'd to stay,
Must yield unfought, a base inglorious Prey.
The liquid half of all the Globe, is lost;   160
Heav'n shuts the Seas, and we secure the Coast.
Theirs is no more, than that small spot of Ground,
Which Myryads of our Martial Men surround.
Their Fates I fear not; or vain Oracles;
'Twas giv'n to *Venus*, they shou'd cross the Seas;   165
And land secure upon the *Latian* Plains:
Their promis'd Hour is pass'd, and mine remains.
'Tis in the Fate of *Turnus*, to destroy
With Sword and Fire the faithless Race of *Troy*.
Shall such Affronts as these, alone inflame   170
The *Grecian* Brothers, and the *Grecian* Name?
My Cause and theirs is one; a fatal Strife,
And final Ruin, for a ravish'd Wife.

The Ninth Book. 149 *Editor's paragraph*   163 Myryads ... Men 98: Millions...
Troops 97   165 Seas;] Seas: 97 98   166 Plains:] Plains, 97 98

Was't not enough, that, punish'd for the Crime,
They fell; but will they fall a second Time?   175
One wou'd have thought they paid enough before,
To curse the costly Sex; and durst offend no more.
Can they securely trust their feeble Wall,
A slight Partition, a thin Interval,
Betwixt their Fate and them; when *Troy*, tho' built   180
By Hands Divine, yet perish'd by their Guilt?
Lend me, for once, my Friends, your valiant Hands,
To force from out their Lines these dastard Bands.
Less than a thousand Ships will end this War;
Nor *Vulcan* needs his fated Arms prepare.   185
Let all the *Tuscans*, all th' *Arcadians* join,
Nor these, nor those shall frustrate my Design.
Let them not fear the Treasons of the Night;
The robb'd *Palladium*, the pretended flight:
Our Onset shall be made in open Light.   190
No wooden Engine shall their Town betray,
Fires they shall have around, but Fires by Day.
No *Grecian* Babes before their Camp appear,
Whom *Hector*'s Arms detain'd, to the tenth tardy Year.
Now, since the Sun is rowling to the *West*,   195
Give we the silent Night to needful Rest:
Refresh your Bodies, and your Arms prepare,
The Morn shall end the small Remains of War.

   The Post of Honour to *Messapus* falls,
To keep the Nightly Guard; to watch the Walls;   200
To pitch the Fires at Distances around,
And close the *Trojans* in their scanty Ground.
Twice seven *Rutulian* Captains ready stand;
And twice seven hundred Horse these Chiefs command:
All clad in shining Arms the Works invest;   205
Each with a radiant Helm, and waving Crest.
Stretch'd at their length, they press the grassy Ground;
They laugh, they sing, the jolly Bowls go round:
With Lights, and chearful Fires renew the Day;
And pass the wakeful Night in Feasts and Play.   210
   The *Trojans*, from above, their Foes beheld;
And with arm'd Legions all the Rampires fill'd;
Seiz'd with Affright, their Gates they first explore,

Join Works to Works with Bridges; Tow'r to Tow'r:
Thus all things needful for Defence, abound;   215
Mnestheus, and brave *Seresthus* walk the round:
Commission'd by their Absent Prince, to share
The common Danger, and divide the Care.
The Souldiers draw their Lots; and as they fall,
By turns relieve each other on the Wall.   220
   Nigh where the Foes their utmost Guards advance,
To watch the Gate, was warlike *Nisus* chance.
His Father *Hyrtacus* of Noble Blood;
His Mother was a Hunt'ress of the Wood:
And sent him to the Wars; well cou'd he bear   225
His Lance in fight, and dart the flying Spear:
But better skill'd unerring Shafts to send:
Beside him stood *Euryalus* his Friend.
Euryalus, than whom the *Trojan* Hoast
No fairer Face, or sweeter Air could boast.   230
Scarce had the Down to shade his Cheeks begun;
One was their Care, and their Delight was one.
One Common hazard in the War they shar'd;
And now were both by choice upon the Guard.
   Then *Nisus*, thus: Or do the Gods inspire   235
This warmth, or make we Gods of our Desire?
A gen'rous ardour boils within my Breast,
Eager of Action, Enemy to Rest:
This urges me to fight, and fires my Mind,
To leave a memorable Name behind.   240

219-30 *The version in* Sylvæ *opens*

> The *Trojan* Camp the common danger shar'd;
> By trojans they watch'd the Walls; and kept the Nightly Guard:
> To Warlike *Nisus* fell the Gate by Lot,
> (Whom *Hyrtacus* on Huntress *Ida* got:
> And sent to Sea *Æneas* to attend,)
> Well cou'd he dart the Spear, and shafts unerring send.   }
> Beside him stood *Euryalus*, his ever Faithful friend.
> No Youth in all the *Trojan* Host was seen
> More beautiful in arms, or of a Nobler meen;

231 had] was *S*   to shade his Cheeks] upon his Chin *S*   232 Care, and their
Delight] Friendship, their desire *S*   233 One . . . shar'd;] With minds united
in the Field they warr'd, *S*   235-6 Then . . . Desire?] *S has*

> Then *Nisus* thus:
> Or do the Gods this Warlike warmth inspire,
> Or makes Each Man a God of his desire?

237 gen'rous] Noble *S*   238 to] of *S*   239 This] That *S*   and fires
my Mind,] or undertake *S*   240 To . . . behind.] Some Deed that may my
Fame immortal make. *S*

Thou see'st the Foe secure: how faintly shine
Their scatter'd Fires! the most in Sleep supine;
Along the ground, an easie Conquest lye;
The wakeful few, the fuming Flaggon ply:
All hush'd around. Now hear what I revolve;   245
A Thought unripe; and scarcely yet resolve.
Our absent Prince both Camp and Council mourn;
By Message both wou'd hasten his return:
If they confer what I demand, on thee,
(For Fame is Recompence enough for me)   250
Methinks, beneath yon Hill, I have espy'd
A way that safely will my passage guide.
    Euryalus stood list'ning while he spoke;
With love of Praise, and noble Envy struck;
Then to his ardent Friend expos'd his Mind: ⎤   255
All this alone, and leaving me behind,   ⎟
Am I unworthy, *Nisus*, to be join'd?   ⎦
Think'st thou I can my share of Glory yield,
Or send thee unassisted to the Field?
Not so my Father taught my Childhood Arms;   260
Born in a Siege, and bred among Alarms!
Nor is my Youth unworthy of my Friend,
Nor of the Heav'n-born Heroe I attend.
The thing call'd Life, with ease I can disclaim;
And think it oversold to purchase Fame.   265
    Then *Nisus*, thus; alas! thy tender years
Wou'd minister new matter to my Fears:
So may the Gods, who view this friendly Strife,
Restore me to thy lov'd Embrace with life,
Condemn'd to pay my Vows (as sure I trust,)   270

---

243 Along . . . lye;] Dissolv'd in Ease, and drunk with Victory: *S*   244 wakeful
few,] few awake *S*   246 A . . . resolve.] Within my mind, and what my labouring thoughts resolve. *S*   247 Prince] Lord *S*   249 If they confer what I
demand] The gifts propos'd if they confer *S*   250 for] to *S*   258 I can
my share of Glory] my Share of honour I will *S*   261 among] amongst *S*   263
Nor] Or *S*   266 Then . . . years] *S has*
                    To whom his Friend;
                    I cou'd not think, alas, thy Tender years
268–71 So . . . Unjust.] *S has*
                    Nor is it just thou shoudst thy Wish obtain;
                    So *Jove* in Triumph bring me back again;
                    To those dear eyes; or if a God there be
                    To pious Friends, propitious more than he.

This thy Request is Cruel and Unjust.
But if some Chance, as many Chances are,
And doubtful Hazards in the deeds of War;
If one shou'd reach my Head, there let it fall,
And spare thy Life; I wou'd not perish all.   275
Thy bloomy Youth deserves a longer date;
Live thou to mourn thy Love's unhappy Fate:
To bear my mangled Body from the Foe;
Or buy it back, and Fun'ral Rites bestow.
Or if hard Fortune shall those Dues deny,   280
Thou canst at least an empty Tomb supply.
O let not me the Widows Tears renew;
Nor let a Mother's Curse my Name pursue;
Thy Pious Parent, who, for love of thee,
Forsook the Coasts of friendly *Sicily*,   285
Her Age, committing to the Seas and Wind,
When ev'ry weary Matron staid behind.
To this, *Euryalus*, you plead in vain,
And but protract the Cause you cannot gain:
No more delays, but haste. With that he wakes   290
The nodding Watch; each to his Office takes.
The Guard reliev'd, the gen'rous Couple went
To find the Council at the Royal Tent.

   All Creatures else forgot their daily Care;
And Sleep, the common Gift of Nature, share: 29
Except the *Trojan* Peers, who wakeful sate

272 Chance] one *S*   Chances] sure there *S*   273 And . . . War;] Of adverse
accidents in doubtful War, *S*   276 bloomy Youth deserves] Youth is worthy
of *S*   277 Live . . . Fate:] Do thou remain to mourn thy Lovers fate; *S*   280
those Dues] my Corps *S*   281 Thou . . . supply.] Those dues, with empty
Marble to supply. *S*   283 Nor let] Let not *S*   284 Parent] Mother *S* for
love of] in Love to *S*   285 Forsook the Coasts] Left the Fair Coast *S* friendly]
fruitful *S*   288 you plead] thou pleadst *S*   289 protract] delayst *S* you
cannot] thou canst not *S*   290 delays, but haste.] 'tis loss of time: *S*   292
the gen'rous Couple] in Company they *S*   294 *Editor's paragraph*   All . . .
Care;] Now every living thing lay void of care, *S*   296–303 Except . . . Spear.]
S has

       Mean time the *Trojan* Peers in Council sate
       And call'd their Chief Commanders, to debate ⎫
       The weighty business of th' indanger'd State. ⎬
       What next was to be done, who to be sent ⎭
       T' inform *Æneas* of the Foes intent.
       In midst of all the quiet Camp they held
       Nocturnal Council; each sustains a Shield
       Which his o'relabour'd Arm can hardly rear;
       And leans upon a long projected Spear.

In nightly Council for th' indanger'd State.
They vote a Message to their absent Chief;
Shew their Distress; and beg a swift Relief.
Amid the Camp a silent Seat they chose,   300
Remote from Clamour, and secure from Foes.
On their left Arms their ample Shields they bear,
The right reclin'd upon the bending Spear.
Now *Nisus* and his friend approach the Guard,
And beg Admission, eager to be heard: 305
Th' Affair important, not to be deferr'd.
Ascanius bids 'em be conducted in;
Ord'ring the more experienc'd to begin.
Then *Nisus* thus. Ye Fathers lend your Ears;
Nor judge our bold Attempt beyond our Years.   310
The Foe securely drench'd in Sleep and Wine,
Neglect their Watch; the Fires but thinly shine:
And where the Smoke, in cloudy Vapours flies,
Cov'ring the Plain, and curling to the Skies,
Betwixt two Paths, which at the Gate divide,   315
Close by the Sea, a Passage we have spy'd,
Which will our way to great *Æneas* guide.
Expect each Hour to see him safe again,
Loaded with Spoils of Foes in Battel slain.
Snatch we the lucky Minute while we may: 320
Nor can we be mistaken in the way;
For hunting in the Vale, we both have seen
The rising Turrets, and the Stream between;
And know the winding Course, with ev'ry Ford.
He ceas'd: And old *Alethes* took the Word.   325
  Our Country Gods, in whom our Trust we place,
Will yet from Ruin save the *Trojan* Race:

305 Admission] admittance *S*   307 'em] them *S*   308 Ord'ring . . . begin.]
Then thus, commanded, *Nisus* does begin. *S*   309 Then . . . Ears] Ye *Trojan*
Fathers lend attentive Ears *S*   310 bold Attempt beyond] our undertaking
by *S*   311 Foe] Foes *S*   312 Neglect their Watch; the] Their Watch neglect;
their *S*   313 cloudy] thickning *S*   314 curling to] Clouding all *S*   315–
17 Betwixt . . . guide.] *S* has
          Betwixt the spaces we have mark'd a way,
          Close by the Gate and Coasting by the Sea;
          This Passage undisturb'd, and unespy'd
          Our Steps will safely to *Æneas* guide,
318 safe] back *S*   322 both] oft *S*   323 and] with *S*   324 the] its *S*
325 ceas'd:] paus'd, *S*

While we behold such dauntless Worth appear
In dawning Youth; and Souls so void of Fear.
Then, into Tears of Joy the Father broke;   330
Each in his longing Arms by Turns he took:
Panted and paus'd; and thus again he spoke.
Ye brave young Men, what equal Gifts can we,
In recompence of such Desert, decree?
The greatest, sure, and best you can receive,   335
The Gods, and your own conscious Worth will give.
The rest our grateful Gen'ral will bestow;
And young *Ascanius* 'till his Manhood owe.
    And I, whose Welfare in my Father lies,
Ascanius adds, by the great Deities,   340
By my dear Country, by my household Gods,
By hoary *Vesta*'s Rites, and dark Abodes,
Adjure you both; (on you my Fortune stands,
That and my Faith I plight into your Hands:)
Make me but happy in his safe Return,   345
Whose wanted Presence I can only mourn;
Your common Gift shall two large Goblets be,
Of Silver, wrought with curious Imagery;
And high emboss'd, which, when old *Priam* reign'd,
My conqu'ring Sire at sack'd *Arisba* gain'd.   350
And more, two Tripods cast in antick Mould,
With two great Talents of the finest Gold:
Beside a costly Bowl, ingrav'd with Art,
Which *Dido* gave, when first she gave her Heart.
But if in conquer'd *Italy* we reign,   355
When Spoils by Lot the Victor shall obtain;
Thou saw'st the Courser by proud *Turnus* press'd,
That, *Nisus*, and his Arms, and nodding Crest,

---

328 dauntless] springing *S*   329 dawning Youth; and Souls] youth so brave,
and breasts *S*   330–2 Then . . . spoke.] *S has*
    (With this he took the hand of either Boy,
    Embrac'd them closely both, and wept for joy:)

334 In] What *S*   of] for *S*   336 and your own conscious Worth] your vertue
and your fame *S*   340 the great] all the *S*   341 my dear] our great *S*   by
my] and our *S*   346 Whose . . . mourn;] (For I No other loss but only his
can mourn,) *S*   347 Your common] *Nisus* your *S*   353–4 Beside . . . Heart.]
S has
    Besides a Boul which *Tyrian* Art did grave;
    The Present that *Sidonian Dido* gave.

356 Victor] Victors *S*   358 *Nisus*, and his] and his golden *S*   nodding] sanguine *S*

And Shield, from Chance exempt, shall be thy Share; ⎫
Twelve lab'ring Slaves, twelve Handmaids young and fair, ⎬ 360
All clad in rich Attire, and train'd with Care. ⎭
And last, a *Latian* Field with fruitful Plains;
And a large Portion of the King's Domains.
But thou, whose Years are more to mine ally'd,
No Fate my vow'd Affection shall divide   365
From thee, Heroick Youth; be wholly mine:
Take full Possession; all my Soul is thine.
One Faith, one Fame, one Fate shall both attend;
My Life's Companion, and my Bosom Friend.
My Peace shall be committed to thy Care,   370
And to thy Conduct, my Concerns in War.
    Then thus the young *Euryalus* reply'd;
Whatever Fortune, good or bad betide,
The same shall be my Age, as now my Youth;
No time shall find me wanting to my Truth.   375
This only from your Goodness let me gain;
(And this ungranted, all Rewards are vain)
Of *Priam*'s Royal Race my Mother came;
And sure the best that ever bore the Name:
Whom neither *Troy*, nor *Sicily* cou'd hold   380
From me departing, but o'respent, and old,
My Fate she follow'd; ignorant of this,
Whatever Danger, neither parting Kiss,
Nor pious Blessing taken, her I leave;
And, in this only Act of all my Life deceive.   385
By this right Hand, and conscious Night I swear,
My Soul so sad a farewel could not bear.
Be you her Comfort; fill my vacant place,
(Permit me to presume so great a Grace)
Support her Age, forsaken and distress'd,   390

---

359 Chance exempt, shall be thy] lot exempted, thou shalt *S*   360–3 Twelve
. . . Domains.] *S has*

> With these, twelve captive Dam'sels young and fair:
> Male Slaves as many; well appointed all
> With Vests and Arms, shall to thy portion fall:
> And last a fruitful Field to thee shall rest,
> The large demenes the *Latian* King possest.

366 Heroick] O wondrous *S*   wholly] ever *S*   368–9 *transposed from S*   372
young] bold *S*   376 Goodness] bounty *S*   377 ungranted] not granted *S*
386 right] your *S*   387 Soul] youth *S*   388 Comfort] Patron *S*

That hope alone will fortifie my Breast
Against the worst of Fortunes, and of Fears.
He said: The mov'd Assistants melt in Tears.
    Then thus *Ascanius*, (wonder-struck to see
That Image of his filial Piety;)   39
So great Beginnings, in so green an Age,
Exact the Faith, which I again ingage.
Thy Mother all the Dues shall justly claim
Creusa had; and only want the Name.
Whate're Event thy bold Attempt shall have,   40
'Tis Merit to have born a Son so brave.
Now by my Head, a sacred Oath, I swear,
(My Father us'd it) what returning here
Crown'd with Success, I for thy self prepare,
That, if thou fail, shall thy lov'd Mother share.   40
    He said; and weeping while he spoke the Word,
From his broad Belt he drew a shining Sword,
Magnificent with Gold. *Lycaon* made,
And in an Iv'ry Scabbard sheath'd the Blade:
This was his Gift: Great *Mnestheus* gave his Friend   41
A Lyon's Hide, his Body to defend:
And good *Alethes* furnish'd him beside,
With his own trusty Helm, of Temper try'd.
    Thus arm'd they went. The Noble *Trojans* wait
Their issuing forth, and follow to the Gate,   41
With Prayers and Vows; above the rest appears
Ascanius, manly far beyond his Years,
And Messages committed to their Care,
Which all in Winds were lost, and flitting Air.
    The Trenches first they pass'd: Then took their Way   42
Where their proud Foes in pitch'd Pavilions lay;

393 The mov'd Assistants melt in Tears.] th' Assistants shed presaging tears. *S*
394–5 Then . . . Piety;)] *S has*
            But above all, *Ascanius* mov'd to see
            That image of paternal piety.
            Then thus reply'd.—
397 the] that *S*   I again] firmly I *S*   398 Dues shall justly] priviledge shall *S*
400 bold Attempt] enterprise *S*   402 Now by] By this *S*   405 That . . .
share.] Thy Parent and thy Family shall share: *S*   410 Great] while *S*   gave
his Friend] did provide *S*   411–13 A . . . try'd.] *S has*
            For *Nisus* Arms; a grisley Lions Hide;
            And true *Alethes* chang'd with him his helm of temper try'd.
415 issuing] going *S*   Gate,] Gate. *S 97 98*   416 Vows;] Vows *S*: Vows,
97 98   417 beyond] above *S*   419 flitting] empty *S*

To many fatal, e're themselves were slain:
They found the careless Hoast dispers'd upon the Plain.
Who gorg'd, and drunk with Wine, supinely snore;
Unharnass'd Chariots stand along the Shore: 425
Amidst the Wheels and Reins, the Goblet by,
A Medly of Debauch and War they lye.
Observing *Nisus* shew'd his Friend the sight;
Behold a Conquest gain'd without a Fight.
Occasion offers, and I stand prepar'd;   430
There lies our Way; be thou upon the Guard,
And look around; while I securely go,
And hew a Passage, thro the sleeping Foe.
Softly he spoke; then striding, took his way,
With his drawn Sword, where haughty *Rhamnes* lay: 435
His Head rais'd high, on Tapestry beneath,
And heaving from his Breast, he drew his Breath:
A King and Prophet by King *Turnus* lov'd;
But Fate by Prescience cannot be remov'd.
Him, and his sleeping Slaves he slew. Then spies   440
Where *Rhemus*, with his rich Retinue lies:
His Armor-bearer first, and next he kills
His Charioteer, intrench'd betwixt the Wheels
And his lov'd Horses: Last invades their Lord;
Full on his Neck he drives the fatal Sword: 445
The gasping Head flies off; a Purple flood
Flows from the Trunk, that welters in the Blood:
Which by the spurning Heels, dispers'd around,
The Bed besprinkles, and bedews the Ground.
Lamus the bold, and *Lamryus* the strong,   450

423 They found the careless] The careless *S*   424 Who gorg'd, and] They
found, who *S*   425 along] upon *S*   426 Amidst the] Midst *S*   Reins, the]
reins, and arms, the *S*   429 Behold . . . Fight.] Then thus: behold a Conquest
without fight. *S*   430 offers, and I stand] calls the Sword to be *S*   431
There lies our Way; be] Our way lies there, stand *S*   432 around;] behind, *S*
433 And . . . Foe.] To cut an ample passage through the Foe. *S*   434 striding,]
stalking *S*   437 drew] puff'd *S*   440 Him, and his] Three *S*   slew.] soon
subdues: *S*   441 rich] proud *S*   445 drives] aims *S*   447 welters]
wallows *S*   448 around,] around *S*   449 Bed besprinkles,] bed,
besprinkles *S*   450–5 *Lamus* . . . Day.] *S has*

> Then *Lamyrus* with *Lamus* and the young
> *Serranus*, who with gaming did prolong
> The night: opprest with wine and slumber lay
> The beauteous Youth, and dreamt of lucky Play;   }
> More lucky had it been protracted till the day.

He slew; and then *Serranus* fair and young:
From Dice and Wine the Youth retir'd to Rest,
And puff'd the fumy God from out his Breast:
Ev'n then he dreamt of Drink and lucky Play;
More lucky had it lasted 'till the Day.   45

    The famish'd Lyon thus, with Hunger bold,
O'releaps the Fences of the Nightly Fold;
And tears the peaceful Flocks: With silent Awe
Trembling they lye, and pant beneath his Paw.

    Nor with less Rage *Euryalus* employs   460
The wrathful Sword, or fewer Foes destroys:
But on th' ignoble Crowd his Fury flew:
He *Fadus*, *Hebesus*, and *Rhœtus* slew.

Oppress'd with heavy Sleep the former fall,
But *Rhœtus* wakeful, and observing all: 46
Behind a spacious Jarr he slink'd for fear;
The fatal Iron found, and reach'd him there.

For as he rose, it pierc'd his naked side;
And reeking, thence return'd in Crimson dy'd.
The Wound pours out a Stream of Wine and Blood,   470
The Purple Soul comes floating in the flood.

    Now where *Messapus* Quarter'd they arrive;
The Fires were fainting there, and just alive.
The Warriour-Horses ty'd in order fed;
Nisus observ'd the Discipline, and said,   475

Our eager thirst of Blood may both betray;
And see the scatter'd Streaks of dawning day,
Foe to Nocturnal Thefts: No more, my Friend,
Here let our glutted Execution end:
A Lane through slaughter'd Bodies we have made: 480
The bold *Euryalus*, tho' loath, obey'd.

---

456 bold, *S*: bold; *97 98*   458 And . . . Awe] The peaceful Flock devours, and tears, and draws; *S*   459 Trembling] Wrapt up in silent fear, *S*   Paw] paws *S* 461 wrathful] vengeful *S*   or] nor *S*   463 He] Which *S*   464 Oppress'd . . . fall,] With *Abaris*; in sleep the rest did fall; *S*   465 wakeful] waking *S* 466 spacious] mighty *S*   slink'd] slunk *S*   467 fatal] sharp edg'd *S*   468 For] Full *S*   it pierc'd his naked] he plung'd it in his *S*   469 And reeking, thence] The cruel Sword *S*   470 pours out a] a blended *S*   471 The] Pours out; the *S*   474 Warriour-Horses] warlike Horses *S*   475 observ'd the Discipline] the discipline observ'd *S*   476 eager thirst] eagerness *S*   477 And . . . day,] Behold the doubtful glimmering of the day, *S*   478 Nocturnal] these nightly *S*

Of Arms, and Arras, and of Plate they find
A precious load; but these they leave behind.
Yet fond of gaudy Spoils the Boy wou'd stay
To make the rich Caparison his prey,   485
Which on the steed of conquer'd *Rhamnes* lay.
Nor did his Eyes less longingly behold
The Girdle-Belt, with Nails of burnish'd Gold.
This Present *Cedicus* the Rich, bestow'd
On *Remulus,* when Friendship first they vow'd: 490
And absent, join'd in hospitable tyes:
He dying, to his Heir bequeath'd the Prize:
Till by the Conqu'ring *Ardean* Troops oppress'd
He fell; and they the Glorious Gift possess'd.
These Glitt'ring Spoils (now made the Victor's gain)   495
He to his body suits; but suits in vain.
Messapus Helm he finds among the rest,
And laces on, and wears the waving Crest.
Proud of their Conquest, prouder of their Prey,
They leave the Camp; and take the ready way.   500
   But far they had not pass'd, before they spy'd
Three hundred Horse with *Volscens* for their Guide.
The Queen a Legion to King *Turnus* sent,
But the swift Horse the slower Foot prevent;
And now advancing, sought the Leader's Tent.   505

482-3 Of . . . behind.] *S has*
      Rich Arms and Arras which they scatter'd find,
      And Plate, a precious load they leave behind.
485 rich Caparison] proud Caparisons *S*   486 Which . . . lay.] Which deck'd
a Neighb'ring steed.— *S*   488 Girdle-Belt,] Girdle studded o're *S*   of
burnish'd Gold] of Gold *S*   489-90 This . . . vow'd:] *S has*
      Which *Rhamnes* wore: This present long ago
      On *Remulus* did *Cædicus* bestow,
491 tyes:] tyes; *97 98*   493 *Ardean* Troops] *Rutuli S*   495-6 These . . .
vain.] *S has*
      These gaudy spoils *Eurialus* now bears;
      And vainly on his brawny Shoulders wears:
497 finds] found *S*   rest] dead *S*   498 And . . . Crest.] Garnish'd with
plumes, and fitted to his head. *S*   499 *not in S*   500 ready way] safest
road *S*   501-5 But . . . Tent.] *S has*
      Mean time a Squadron of their foes abroad,
      Three hundred Horse with Bucklers arm'd, they spy'd,
      Whom *Volscens* by the Kings command did guide:
      To *Turnus* these were from the City sent,
      And to perform their Message sought his Tent.
504 prevent *98*: outwent *97*

They saw the Pair; for thro' the doubtful shade   ⎫
His shineing Helm *Euryalus* betray'd,   ⎬
On which the Moon with full reflexion play'd.   ⎭
'Tis not for nought, cry'd *Volscens*, from the Crow'd,
These Men go there; then rais'd his Voice aloud: 510
Stand, stand: why thus in Arms, and whither bent;
From whence, to whom, and on what Errand sent?
Silent they scud away, and haste their flight,
To Neighb'ring Woods, and trust themselves to night.
The speedy Horse all passages belay,   515
And spur their smoaking Steeds to Cross their way;
And watch each Entrance of the winding Wood;
Black was the Forest, thick with Beech it stood:
Horrid with Fern, and intricate with Thorn,
Few Paths of Humane Feet or Tracks of Beasts were worn. 520
The darkness of the Shades, his heavy Prey,
And Fear, mis-led the Younger from his way.
But *Nisus* hit the Turns with happier haste,
And thoughtless of his Friend, the Forest pass'd:
And *Alban* Plains, from *Alba*'s Name so call'd,   525
Where King *Latinus* then his Oxen stall'd.
Till turning at the length, he stood his ground,
And miss'd his Friend, and cast his Eyes around;
Ah Wretch, he cry'd, where have I left behind
Th' unhappy Youth, where shall I hope to find?   530
Or what way take! again He ventures back:
And treads the Mazes of his former track.

---

506 They . . . shade] *S has*

        Approaching near their utmost lines they draw;
        When bending tow'rds the left, their Captain saw
        The faithful pair; for through the doubtful shade

507 shineing] glitt'ring *S*   513 scud] make *S*   515–17 The . . . Wood;]
S has

        The speedy horsemen spur their Steeds to get
        'Twixt them and home; and every path beset,
        And all the windings of the well known Wood;

518 Forest, thick] Brake, and thick *S*   Beech] Oak *S*   519 Horrid with Fern]
With fern all horrid *S*   intricate with] perplexing *S*   520 Few . . . worn.]
Where tracks of Bears had scarce a passage worn. *S*   524 And . . . pass'd:]
Who now, unknowing, had the danger past, *S*   525 Plains,] Lakes *S*   528
And . . . around;] *S has*

        And vainly cast his longing eyes around
        For his lost friend!

530 Th' unhappy Youth, where shall I hope] Where shall I hope th' unhappy Youth *S*

He winds the Wood, and list'ning hears the noise
Of trampling Coursers, and the Riders voice.
The sound approach'd, and suddenly he view'd   535
The Foes inclosing, and his Friend pursu'd:
Forelay'd and taken, while he strove in vain,
The shelter of the friendly Shades to gain.
What shou'd he next attempt! what Arms employ,
What fruitless Force to free the Captive Boy?   540
Or desperate shou'd he rush and lose his Life,
With odds oppress'd, in such unequal strife?
    Resolv'd at length, his pointed Spear he shook;
And casting on the Moon a mournful look,
Guardian of Groves, and Goddess of the Night;   545
Fair Queen, he said, direct my Dart aright:
If e're my Pious Father for my sake
Did grateful Off'rings on thy Altars make;
Or I increas'd them with my Silvan toils,
And hung thy Holy Roofs, with Salvage Spoils;   550
Give me to scatter these. Then from his Ear
He poiz'd, and aim'd, and lanch'd the trembling Spear.
The deadly Weapon, hissing from the Grove,
Impetuous on the back of *Sulmo* drove:
Pierc'd his thin Armour, drank his Vital Blood,   555
And in his Body left the broken Wood.
He staggers round, his Eyeballs rowl in Death,
And with short sobs he gasps away his Breath.

533 He winds the] Thro the wild *S*   and list'ning] at last he *S*   534 Coursers]
Horses *S*   536 The] His *S*   538 shelter of the friendly Shades] Covert of
the Neighb'ring Wood *S*   540 What] With *S*   541–2 Or . . . strife?] *S has*

            Or tempt unequal numbers with the Sword;
            And die by him whom living he ador'd?

543 *Editor's paragraph*   at length,] on death *S*   pointed] dreadful *S*   544 on]
to *S*   545–6 Guardian . . . aright:] *S has*

            Fair Queen, said he, who dost in woods delight, ⎫
            Grace of the Stars, and Goddess of the Night;   ⎬
            Be present, and direct my Dart aright.   ⎭

546 Fair *98*: Fair, *97*   548 grateful Off'rings on thy Altars] on thy Altars
grateful offerings *S*   549 my Silvan] successful *S*   550 Holy Roofs,] Sacred
Roof *S*   551–6 Give . . . Wood.] *S has*

            Through the brown shadows guide my flying Spear
            To reach this Troop: Then poyzing from his ear
            The quiv'ring Weapon with full force he threw;
            Through the divided shades the deadly Javelin flew;
            On *Sulmo*'s back it splits; the double dart,
            Drove deeper onward, and transfixt his heart.

All stand amaz'd; a second Jav'lin flies,
With equal strength, and quivers through the Skies;　　560
This through thy Temples, *Tagus*, forc'd the way,
And in the Brain-pan warmly bury'd lay.
Fierce *Volscens* foams with Rage, and gazing round,
Descry'd not him who gave the Fatal Wound:
Nor knew to fix Revenge: but thou, he cries,　　565
Shalt pay for both, and at the Pris'ner flies,
With his drawn Sword. Then struck with deep Despair,
That cruel sight the Lover cou'd not bear:
But from his Covert rush'd in open view,
And sent his Voice before him as he flew.　　570
Me, me, he cry'd, turn all your Swords alone
On me; the Fact confess'd, the Fault my own.
He neither cou'd nor durst, the guiltless Youth;
Ye Moon and Stars bear Witness to the Truth!
His only Crime, (if Friendship can offend,)　　575
Is too much Love, to his unhappy Friend.
Too late he speaks; the Sword, which Fury guides,
Driv'n with full Force, had pierc'd his tender Sides.
Down fell the beauteous Youth; the yawning Wound
Gush'd out a Purple Stream, and stain'd the Ground.　　580
His snowy Neck reclines upon his Breast,
Like a fair Flow'r by the keen Share oppress'd:
Like a white Poppy sinking on the Plain,
Whose heavy Head is overcharg'd with Rain.
Despair, and Rage, and Vengeance justly vow'd,　　585
Drove *Nisus* headlong on the hostile Crowd:

---

560 With equal strength, and quivers] From his stretch'd arm, and hisses *S*　　561
This through thy Temples, *Tagus*,] The Lance through *Tagus* Temples *S*　　the]
its *S*　　562 the] his *S*　　564 not him who gave] no Author of *S*　　565
knew] where *S*　　568 cruel] fatal *S*　　571–2 Me . . . own.] *S has*

> Me, me, employ your Sword on me alone:
> The crime confess'd; the fact was all my own.

575 Crime, (if Friendship can] fault, if that be to *S*　　576 Is too much Love, to]
Was too much loving *S*　　577 Too . . . guides,] *S has*

> Too late, alas, he speaks;
> The Sword, which unrelenting fury guides

579 yawning] gaping *S*　　580 Purple] Crimson *S*　　581 snowy] nodding *S*
upon his] on his white *S*　　582 by the keen Share] in furrow'd Fields *S*　　583
Like a white Poppy sinking] By the keen Share: or Poppy *S*　　585 Despair, and
Rage, and Vengeance justly] Disdain, despair, and deadly vengeance *S*

Volscens he seeks; on him alone he bends;
Born back, and bor'd, by his surrounding Friends,
Onward he press'd: and kept him still in sight;
Then whirl'd aloft his Sword, with all his might: 590
Th' unerring Steel descended while he spoke;
Pierc'd his wide Mouth, and thro' his Weazon broke:
Dying, he slew; and stagg'ring on the Plain,
With swimming Eyes he sought his Lover slain:
Then quiet on his bleeding Bosom fell;   595
Content in Death, to be reveng'd so well.
　　O happy Friends! for if my Verse can give
Immortal Life, your Fame shall ever live:
Fix'd as the Capitol's Foundation lies;
And spread, where e're the *Roman* Eagle flies!   600
　　The conqu'ring Party, first divide the Prey,
Then their slain Leader to the Camp convey.
With Wonder, as they went, the Troops were fill'd,
To see such Numbers whom so few had kill'd.
Serranus, *Rhamnes*, and the rest they found;   ⎫
Vast Crowds the dying and the dead surround: ⎬ 605
And the yet reeking Blood o'reflows the Ground.   ⎭
All knew the Helmet which *Messapus* lost;
But mourn'd a Purchase, that so dear had cost.
Now rose the ruddy Morn from *Tithon*'s Bed;   610
And with the Dawns of Day the Skies o'respread.
Nor long the Sun his daily Course withheld,
But added Colours to the World reveal'd.
When early *Turnus* wak'ning with the Light,
All clad in Armour calls his Troops to fight.   615
His Martial Men with fierce Harangues he fir'd;
And his own Ardor, in their Souls inspir'd.
This done, to give new Terror to his Foes,
The Heads of *Nisus*, and his Friend he shows,
Rais'd high on pointed Spears: A ghastly Sight;   620

587 on] at *S*　　588 bor'd,] push'd *S*　　589 Onward he press'd:] He still press'd
on; *S*　　591-2 Th' unerring . . . broke:] *S has*

　　　Th' unerring Weapon flew; and wing'd with death,
　　　Enter'd his gaping Mouth, and stop'd his breath.

594 With swimming Eyes he sought] Sought for the Body of *S*　　　595 quiet on
his bleeding Bosom] quietly on his dear Breast he *S*　　　597 Friends] pair *S*
598 Immortal Life,] Eternity; *S*　　602 Leader *98*: General *97*

Loud peals of Shouts ensue, and barbarous Delight.
Mean time the *Trojans* run, where Danger calls,
They line their Trenches, and they man their Walls:
In Front extended to the left they stood:
Safe was the right surrounded by the Flood. 62
But casting from their Tow'rs a frightful view,
They saw the Faces, which too well they knew;
Tho' then disguis'd in Death, and smear'd all o're
With Filth obscene, and dropping putrid Gore.
Soon hasty Fame, thro' the sad City bears 63
The mournful Message to the Mother's Ears:
An icy Cold benums her Limbs: She shakes:
Her Cheeks the Blood, her Hand the Web forsakes.
She runs the Rampires round amidst the War, ⎫
Nor fears the flying Darts: She rends her Hair, ⎬ 63
And fills with loud Laments the liquid Air. ⎭
Thus then, my lov'd *Euryalus* appears;
Thus looks the Prop of my declining Years!
Was't on this Face, my famish'd Eyes I fed,
Ah how unlike the living, is the dead! 64
And cou'dst thou leave me, cruel, thus alone,
Not one kind Kiss from a departing Son!
No Look, no last adieu before he went,
In an ill-boding Hour to Slaughter sent!
Cold on the Ground, and pressing foreign Clay, 64
To *Latian* Dogs, and Fowls he lies a Prey!
Nor was I near to close his dying Eyes,
To wash his Wounds, to weep his Obsequies:
To call about his Corps his crying Friends,
Or spread the Mantle, (made for other ends,) 65(
On his dear Body, which I wove with Care,
Nor did my daily Pains, or nightly labour spare.
Where shall I find his Corps, what Earth sustains
His Trunk dismember'd, and his cold Remains?
For this, alas, I left my needful Ease, 65
Expos'd my Life to Winds, and winter Seas!
If any pity touch *Rutulian* Hearts,
Here empty all your Quivers, all your Darts:
Or if they fail, thou *Jove* conclude my Woe,
And send me Thunder-struck to Shades below! 66(

Her Shrieks and Clamours, pierce the *Trojans* Ears,
Unman their Courage, and augment their Fears:
Nor young *Ascanius* cou'd the sight sustain,
Nor old *Ilioneus* his Tears restrain:
But *Actor* and *Idæus*, jointly sent,   665
To bear the madding Mother to her Tent.
   And now the Trumpets terribly from far,
With rattling Clangor, rouze the sleepy War.
The Souldiers Shouts succeed the Brazen Sounds;
And Heav'n, from Pole to Pole, the Noise rebounds.   670
The *Volscians* bear their Shields upon their Head,
And rushing forward, form a moving Shed;
These fill the Ditch, those pull the Bulwarks down:
Some raise the Ladders, others scale the Town.
But where void Spaces on the Walls appear,   675
Or thin Defence, they pour their Forces there.
With Poles and missive Weapons from afar,
The *Trojans* keep aloof the rising War.
Taught by their ten Years Siege defensive fight;
They rowl down Ribs of Rocks, an unresisted Weight: 680
To break the Penthouse with the pond'rous Blow;
Which yet the patient *Volscians* undergo.
But cou'd not bear th' unequal Combat long;
For where the *Trojans* find the thickest Throng,
The Ruin falls: Their shatter'd Shields give way,   685
And their crush'd Heads become an easie Prey.
They shrink for Fear, abated of their Rage,
Nor longer dare in a blind Fight engage.
Contented now to gaul them from below
With Darts and Slings, and with the distant Bow.   690
   Elsewhere *Mezentius*, terrible to view,
A blazing Pine within the Trenches threw.
But brave *Messapus*, *Neptune*'s warlike Son,
Broke down the Palisades, the Trenches Won,
And loud for Ladders calls, to scale the Town.   695
   Calliope begin: Ye sacred Nine,
Inspire your Poet in his high Design;
To sing what Slaughter manly *Turnus* made:
What Souls he sent below the *Stygian* Shade.

      667 *Editor's paragraph*

What Fame the Souldiers with their Captain share,   700
And the vast Circuit of the fatal War.
For you in singing Martial Facts excel;
You best remember; and alone can tell.
    There stood a Tow'r, amazing to the sight,
Built up of Beams; and of stupendous height;   705
Art, and the nature of the Place conspir'd,
To furnish all the Strength, that War requir'd.
To level this, the bold *Italians* join;
The wary *Trojans* obviate their design:
With weighty Stones o'rewhelm their Troops below,   710
Shoot through the Loopholes, and sharp Jav'lins throw.
Turnus, the Chief, toss'd from his thund'ring Hand,
Against the wooden Walls, a flaming Brand:
It stuck, the fiery Plague: The Winds were high;
The Planks were season'd, and the Timber dry.   715
Contagion caught the Posts: It spread along,
Scorch'd, and to distance drove the scatter'd Throng.
The *Trojans* fled; the Fire pursu'd amain,
Still gath'ring fast upon the trembling Train;
Till crowding to the Corners of the Wall,   720
Down the Defence, and the Defenders fall.
The mighty flaw makes Heav'n it self resound,
The Dead, and dying *Trojans* strew the Ground.
The Tow'r that follow'd on the fallen Crew,
Whelm'd o're their Heads, and bury'd whom it slew: 725
Some stuck upon the Darts themselves had sent;
All, the same equal Ruin underwent.
    Young *Lycus* and *Helenor* only scape;
Sav'd, how they know not, from the steepy Leap.
Helenor, elder of the two; by Birth,   730
On one side Royal, one a Son of Earth,
Whom to the *Lydian* King, *Lycimnia* bare,
And sent her boasted Bastard to the War:
(A Priviledge which none but Free-men share.)
Slight were his Arms, a Sword and Silver Shield,   735
No Marks of Honour charg'd its empty Field.
Light as he fell, so light the Youth arose,
And rising found himself amidst his Foes.
Nor flight was left, nor hopes to force his Way;

Embolden'd by Despair, he stood at Bay: 740
And like a Stag, whom all the Troop surrounds
Of eager Huntsmen, and invading Hounds;
Resolv'd on Death, he dissipates his Fears,
And bounds aloft, against the pointed Spears:
So dares the Youth, secure of Death; and throws 745
His dying Body, on his thickest Foes.
  But *Lycus*, swifter of his Feet, by far,
Runs, doubles, winds and turns, amidst the War:
Springs to the Walls, and leaves his Foes behind,
And snatches at the Beam he first can find. 750
Looks up, and leaps aloft at all the stretch,
In hopes the helping Hand of some kind Friend to reach.
But *Turnus* follow'd hard his hunted Prey,
(His Spear had almost reach'd him in the way,
Short of his Reins, and scarce a Span behind,) 755
Fool, said the Chief, tho' fleeter than the Wind,
Coud'st thou presume to scape, when I pursue?
He said, and downward by the Feet he drew
The trembling Dastard: at the Tug he falls,
Vast Ruins come along, rent from the smoking Walls. 760
Thus on some silver Swan, or tim'rous Hare,
Jove's Bird comes sowsing down, from upper Air;
Her crooked Tallons truss the fearful Prey:
Then out of sight she soars, and wings her way.
So seizes the grim Wolf the tender Lamb, 765
In vain lamented by the bleating Dam.
  Then rushing onward, with a barb'rous cry,
The Troops of *Turnus* to the Combat fly.
The Ditch with Faggots fill'd, the daring Foe
Toss'd Firebrands to the steepy Turrets throw. 770
  Ilioneus, as bold *Lucetius* came
To force the Gate, and feed the kindling Flame,
Rowl'd down the Fragment of a Rock so right,
It crush'd him double underneath the weight.
Two more young *Liger* and *Asylas* slew; 775
To bend the Bow young *Liger* better knew;
Asylas best the pointed Jav'lin threw.
Brave *Cæneus* laid *Ortygius* on the Plain,
The Victor *Cæneus* was by *Turnus* slain.

By the same Hand, *Clonius* and *Itys* fall,   780
Sagar, and *Ida*, standing on the Wall.
From *Capys* Arms his Fate *Privernus* found;
Hurt by *Themilla* first; but slight the Wound;
His Shield thrown by, to mitigate the smart,
He clap'd his Hand upon the wounded part: 785
The second Shaft came swift and unespy'd,
And pierc'd his Hand, and nail'd it to his side:
Transfix'd his breathing Lungs, and beating heart;
The Soul came issuing out, and hiss'd against the Dart.

   The Son of *Arcens* shone amid the rest,   790
In glitt'ring Armour, and a Purple Vest.
Fair was his Face, his Eyes inspiring Love,
Bred by his Father in the *Martian* Grove,
Where the fat Altars of *Palicus* flame;
And sent in Arms to purchase early Fame.   795
Him, when he spy'd from far, the *Thuscan* King
Laid by the Lance, and took him to the Sling:
Thrice whirl'd the Thong around his head, and threw:
The heated Lead half melted as it flew:
It pierc'd his hollow Temples and his Brain;   800
The Youth came tumbling down, and spurn'd the Plain.

   Then Young *Ascanius*, who before this day
Was wont in Woods to shoot the salvage Prey,
First bent in Martial Strife, the twanging Bow;
And exercis'd against a Humane Foe.   805
With this bereft *Numanus* of his life,
Who *Turnus* younger Sister took to Wife.
Proud of his Realm, and of his Royal Bride,
Vaunting before his Troops, and lengthen'd with a Stride, }
In these Insulting terms, the *Trojans* he defy'd.   }   810
Twice Conquer'd Cowards, now your shame is shown,
Coop'd up a second time within your Town!
Who dare not issue forth in open Field,
But hold your Walls before you for a Shield:
Thus threat you War, thus our Alliance force!   815
What Gods, what madness hether steer'd your Course!
You shall not find the Sons of *Atreus* here,

Nor need the Frauds of sly *Ulysses* fear.
Strong from the Cradle, of a sturdy Brood,
We bear our new-born Infants to the Flood;   820
There bath'd amid the Stream, our Boys we hold,
With Winter harden'd, and inur'd to Cold.
They wake before the Day to range the Wood,
Kill e're they eat, nor tast unconquer'd Food.
No Sports, but what belong to War they know,   825
To break the stubborn Colt, to bend the Bow.
Our Youth, of Labour patient, earn their Bread;
Hardly they work, with frugal Diet fed.
From Ploughs and Harrows sent to seek Renown,
They fight in Fields, and storm the shaken Town.   830
No part of Life from Toils of War is free;
No change in Age, or diff'rence in Degree.
We plow, and till in Arms; our Oxen feel,
Instead of Goads, the Spur, and pointed Steel:
Th' inverted Lance makes Furrows in the Plain;   835
Ev'n time that changes all, yet changes us in vain:
The Body, not the Mind: Nor can controul
Th' immortal Vigour, or abate the Soul.
Our Helms defend the Young, disguise the Grey:
We live by Plunder, and delight in Prey.   840
Your Vests embroyder'd with rich Purple shine;
In Sloth you Glory, and in Dances join.
Your Vests have sweeping Sleeves: With female Pride,
Your Turbants underneath your Chins are ty'd.
Go, *Phrygians*, to your *Dindymus* agen;   845
Go, less then Women, in the Shapes of Men.
Go, mix'd with Eunuchs, in the Mother's Rites,
Where with unequal Sound the Flute invites.
Sing, dance, and howl by turns in *Ida*'s Shade;
Resign the War to Men, who know the Martial Trade.   850
    This foul Reproach, *Ascanius* cou'd not hear
With Patience, or a vow'd Revenge forbear.
At the full stretch of both his Hands, he drew,
And almost join'd the Horns of the tough Eugh.
But first, before the Throne of *Jove* he stood;   855
And thus with lifted Hands invok'd the God.
My first Attempt, great *Jupiter* succeed;

An annual Off'ring in thy Grove shall bleed:
A snow-white Steer, before thy Altar led,
Who like his Mother bears aloft his Head,   860
Buts with his threatning Brows, and bellowing stands,
And dares the Fight, and spurns the yellow Sands.
  Jove bow'd the Heav'ns, and lent a gracious Ear,
And thunder'd on the left, amidst the clear.
Sounded at once the Bow; and swiftly flies   865
The feather'd Death, and hisses thro' the Skies.
The Steel thro' both his Temples forc'd the way:
Extended on the Ground, *Numanus* lay.
Go now, vain Boaster, and true Valour scorn;
The *Phrygians* twice subdu'd, yet make this third Return.   870
Ascanius said no more: The *Trojans* shake
The Heav'ns with Shouting, and new Vigour take.
  Apollo then bestrode a Golden Cloud,
To view the feats of Arms, and fighting Crowd;
And thus the beardless Victor, he bespoke aloud.   875
Advance Illustrious Youth, increase in Fame,
And wide from East to West extend thy Name.
Offspring of Gods thy self; and *Rome* shall owe
To thee, a Race of Demigods below.
This is the Way to Heav'n: The Pow'rs Divine   880
From this beginning date the *Julian* Line.
To thee, to them, and their victorious Heirs,
The conquer'd War is due; and the vast World is theirs.
Troy is too narrow for thy Name. He said,
And plunging downward shot his radiant Head;   885
Dispell'd the breathing Air, that broke his Flight,
Shorn of his Beams, a Man to Mortal sight.
Old *Butes* Form he took, *Anchises* Squire,
Now left to rule *Ascanius*, by his Sire:
His wrinkled Visage, and his hoary Hairs,   890
His Meen, his Habit, and his Arms he wears;
And thus salutes the Boy, too forward for his Years.
Suffice it thee, thy Father's worthy Son,
The warlike Prize thou hast already won:
The God of Archers gives thy Youth a part   895
Of his own Praise; nor envies equal Art.
Now tempt the War no more. He said, and flew

Obscure in Air, and vanish'd from their view.
The *Trojans*, by his Arms, their Patron know;
And hear the twanging of his Heav'nly Bow. 900
Then duteous Force they use; and *Phœbus* Name,
To keep from Fight, the Youth too fond of Fame.
Undaunted they themselves no Danger shun:
From Wall to Wall, the Shouts and Clamours run.
They bend their Bows; they whirl their Slings around: 905
Heaps of spent Arrows fall; and strew the Ground;
And Helms, and Shields, and ratling Arms resound.
The Combate thickens, like the Storm that flies
From Westward, when the Show'ry Kids arise:
Or patt'ring Hail comes pouring on the Main, 910
When *Jupiter* descends in harden'd Rain.
Or bellowing Clouds burst with a stormy Sound,
And with an armed Winter strew the Ground.
   Pand'rus and *Bitias*, Thunder-bolts of War,
Whom *Hiera*, to bold *Alcanor* bare 915
On *Ida*'s Top, two Youths of Height and Size,
Like Firrs that on their Mother Mountain rise;
Presuming on their Force, the Gates unbar,
And of their own Accord invite the War.
With Fates averse, against their King's Command, 920
Arm'd on the right, and on the left they stand;
And flank the Passage: Shining Steel they wear,
And waving Crests, above their Heads appear.
Thus two tall Oaks, that *Padus* Banks adorn,
Lift up to Heav'n their leafy Heads unshorn; 925
And overpress'd with Nature's heavy load,
Dance to the whistling Winds, and at each other nod.
In flows a Tyde of *Latians*, when they see
The Gate set open, and the Passage free.
Bold *Quercens*, with rash *Tmarus* rushing on, 930
Equicolus, that in bright Armour shone,
And *Hæmon* first; but soon repuls'd they fly,
Or in the well-defended Pass they dye.
These with Success are fir'd, and those with Rage;
And each on equal Terms at length ingage. 935
Drawn from their Lines, and issuing on the Plain,

932 first;] first, *97 98*

The *Trojans* hand to hand the Fight maintain.
  Fierce *Turnus* in another Quarter fought,
When suddenly th' unhop'd for News was brought;
The Foes had left the fastness of their Place,   940
Prevail'd in Fight, and had his Men in Chace.
He quits th' Attack, and, to prevent their Fate,
Runs, where the Gyant Brothers guard the Gate.
The first he met, *Antiphates* the brave,
But base begotten on a *Theban* Slave,   945
Sarpedon's Son he slew: The deadly Dart
Found Passage thro' his Breast, and pierc'd his Heart.
Fix'd in the Wound th' *Italian* Cornel stood;
Warm'd in his Lungs, and in his vital Blood.
Aphidnus next, and *Erymanthus* dies,   950
And *Meropes*, and the Gygantick Size
Of *Bitias*, threat'ning with his ardent Eyes.
Not by the feeble Dart he fell oppress'd,
A Dart were lost, within that roomy Breast;
But from a knotted Lance, large, heavy, strong;   955
Which roar'd like Thunder as it whirl'd along:
Not two Bull-hides th' impetuous Force withhold;
Nor Coat of double Male, with Scales of Gold.
Down sunk the Monster-Bulk, and press'd the Ground;
His Arms and clatt'ring Shield, on the vast Body sound.   960
Not with less Ruin, than the *Bajan* Mole,
(Rais'd on the Seas the Surges to controul,)
At once comes tumbling down the rocky Wall,
Prone to the Deep the Stones disjointed fall,
Of the vast Pile; the scatter'd Ocean flies;   965
Black Sands, discolour'd Froth, and mingled Mud arise.
The frighted Billows rowl, and seek the Shores:
Then trembles *Prochyta*, then *Ischia* roars:
Typhœus thrown beneath, by *Jove*'s Command,
Astonish'd at the Flaw, that shakes the Land,   970
Soon shifts his weary side, and scarce awake,
With Wonder feels the weight press lighter on his Back.
   The Warrior God the *Latian* Troops inspir'd;
New strung their Sinews, and their Courage fir'd:
But chills the *Trojan* Hearts with cold Affright;   975

945 Slave,] Slave; 97 98

Then black Despair precipitates their Flight.
When *Pandarus* beheld his Brother kill'd,
The Town with Fear, and wild Confusion fill'd,
He turns the Hindges of the heavy Gate
With both his Hands; and adds his Shoulders to the weight. 980
Some happier Friends, within the Walls inclos'd;
The rest shut out, to certain Death expos'd.
Fool as he was, and frantick in his Care,
T' admit young *Turnus*, and include the War.
He thrust amid the Crowd, securely bold; 985
Like a fierce Tyger pent amid the Fold.
Too late his blazing Buckler they descry;
And sparkling Fires that shot from either Eye:
His mighty Members, and his ample Breast,
His ratt'ling Armour, and his Crimson Crest. 990
Far from that hated Face the *Trojans* fly;
All but the Fool who sought his Destiny.
Mad *Pandarus* steps forth, with Vengeance vow'd
For *Bitias* Death, and threatens thus aloud.
These are not *Ardea*'s Walls, nor this the Town 995
Amata proffers with *Lavinia*'s Crown:
'Tis hostile Earth you tread; of hope bereft,
No means of safe Return by flight are left.
To whom with Count'nance calm, and Soul sedate,
Thus *Turnus*: Then begin; and try thy Fate: 1000
My Message to the Ghost of *Priam* bear,
Tell him a new *Achilles* sent thee there.
A Lance of tough ground-Ash the *Trojan* threw,
Rough in the Rind, and knotted as it grew,
With his full force he whirl'd it first around; 1005
But the soft yielding Air receiv'd the wound:
Imperial *Juno* turn'd the Course before;
And fix'd the wand'ring Weapon in the door.
But hope not thou, said *Turnus*, when I strike,
To shun thy Fate, our Force is not alike: 1010
Nor thy Steel temper'd by the *Lemnian* God:
Then rising, on its utmost stretch he stood:
And aim'd from high: the full descending blow
Cleaves the broad Front, and beardless Cheeks in two:

994 *Bitias*] *Bitias*'s *97 98*   1013 high: *98*: high, *97*

Down sinks the Giant with a thund'ring sound,   101
His pond'rous Limbs oppress the trembling ground;
Blood, Brains, and Foam, gush from the gaping Wound.
Scalp, Face, and Shoulders, the keen Steel divides;
And the shar'd Visage hangs on equal sides.
The *Trojans* fly from their approaching Fate: 102
And had the Victor then secur'd the Gate,
And, to his Troops without, unclos'd the Barrs;
One lucky Day had ended all his Wars.
But boiling Youth, and blind Desire of Blood,   102
Push'd on his Fury, to pursue the Crowd:
Hamstring'd behind unhappy *Gyges* dy'd;
Then *Phalaris* is added to his side:
The pointed Jav'lins from the dead he drew,
And their Friends Arms against their Fellows threw.
Strong *Halys* stands in vain; weak *Phlegys* flies;   103
Saturnia, still at hand, new Force and Fire supplies.
Then *Halius*, *Prytanis*, *Alcander* fall;
(Ingag'd against the Foes who scal'd the Wall:)
But whom they fear'd without, they found within:
At last, tho' late, by *Linceus* he was seen.   103
He calls new Succours, and assaults the Prince,
But weak his Force, and vain is their Defence.
Turn'd to the right, his Sword the Heroe drew;
And at one blow the bold Aggressor slew.
He joints the Neck: And with a stroke so strong   104
The Helm flies off; and bears the Head along.
Next him, the Huntsman *Amycus* he kill'd,
In Darts, invenom'd, and in Poyson skill'd.
Then *Clytius* fell beneath his fatal Spear,
And *Creteus*, whom the Muses held so dear: 104
He fought with Courage, and he sung the fight:
Arms were his buis'ness, Verses his delight.
    The *Trojan* Chiefs behold, with Rage and Grief,
Their slaughter'd Friends, and hasten their Relief.
Bold *Mnestheus* rallies first the broken Train,   105
Whom brave *Seresthus*, and his Troop sustain.
To save the living, and revenge the dead;
Against one Warriour's Arms all *Troy* they led.
O, void of Sense and Courage, *Mnestheus* cry'd,

Where can you hope your Coward Heads to hide? 1055
Ah, where beyond these Rampires can you run!
One Man, and in your Camp inclos'd, you shun!
Shall then a single Sword such Slaughter boast,
And pass unpunish'd from a Num'rous Hoast?
Forsaking Honour, and renouncing Fame, 1060
Your Gods, your Country, and your King you shame.
  This just Reproach their Vertue does excite,
They stand, they joyn, they thicken to the Fight.
  Now *Turnus* doubts, and yet disdains to yield;
But with slow paces measures back the Field: 1065
And Inches to the Walls, where *Tyber*'s Tide,
Washing the Camp, defends the weaker side.
The more he loses, they advance the more;
And tread in ev'ry Step he trod before.
They showt, they bear him back, and whom by Might 1070
They cannot Conquer, they oppress with Weight.
  As compass'd with a Wood of Spears around,
The Lordly Lyon, still maintains his Ground;
Grins horrible, retires, and turns again;
Threats his distended Paws, and shakes his Mane; 1075
He loses while in vain he presses on,
Nor will his Courage let him dare to run:
So *Turnus* fares; and unresolv'd of flight,
Moves tardy back, and just recedes from fight.
Yet twice, inrag'd, the Combat he renews; 1080
Twice breaks, and twice his broken Foes pursues:
But now they swarm; and with fresh Troops supply'd,
Come rowling on, and rush from ev'ry side.
Nor *Juno*, who sustain'd his Arms before,
Dares with new strength suffice th' exhausted store. 1085
For *Jove*, with sour Commands, sent *Iris* down,
To force th' Invader from the frighted Town.
  With Labour spent, no Longer can he wield
The heavy Fauchion, or sustain the Shield:
O'rewhelm'd with Darts, which from afar they fling, 1090
The Weapons round his hollow Temples ring:
His golden Helm gives way: with stony blows
Batter'd, and flat, and beaten to his Brows.

1065 Field:] Field. *97 98*   1073 Ground; *98*: Ground. *97*

His Crest is rash'd away; his ample Shield
Is falsify'd, and round with Jav'lins fill'd.　　　　　109
　　The Foe now faint, the *Trojans* overwhelm:
And *Mnestheus* lays hard load upon his Helm.
Sick sweat succeeds, he drops at ev'ry pore,
With driving Dust his Cheeks are pasted o're.
Shorter and shorter ev'ry Gasp he takes,　　　　　110
And vain Efforts, and hurtless Blows he makes.
Arm'd as he was, at length, he leap'd from high;
Plung'd in the Flood, and made the Waters fly.
The yellow God, the welcome Burthen bore,
And wip'd the Sweat, and wash'd away the Gore:　　110
Then gently wafts him to the farther Coast;
And sends him safe to chear his anxious Hoast.

THE TENTH BOOK OF THE ÆNEIS

THE ARGUMENT

Jupiter calling a Council of the Gods, forbids them to engage in either Party. At
Æneas's *return there is a bloody Battel:* Turnus *killing* Pallas; Æneas,
Lausus *and* Mezentius. Mezentius *is describ'd as an Atheist;* Lausus *as
a pious and virtuous Youth: The different Actions and Death of these two, are
the Subject of a Noble Episode.*　　　　　5

THE Gates of Heav'n unfold; *Jove* summons all
　　The Gods to Council, in the Common Hall.
Sublimely seated, he surveys from far
The Fields, the Camp, the Fortune of the War;
And all th' inferior World: From first to last　　　　5
The Sov'raign Senate in Degrees are plac'd.
　　Then thus th' Almighty Sire began. Ye Gods,
Natives, or Denizons, of blest Abodes;
From whence these Murmurs, and this change of Mind,
This backward Fate from what was first design'd?　　10
Why this protracted War? When my Commands
Pronounc'd a Peace, and gave the *Latian* Lands.
What Fear or Hope on either part divides
Our Heav'ns, and arms our Pow'rs on diff'rent sides?

A lawful Time of War at length will come, ⎫ 15
(Nor need your haste anticipate the Doom,) ⎬
When *Carthage* shall contend the World with *Rome*: ⎭
Shall force the rigid Rocks, and *Alpine* Chains;
And like a Flood come pouring on the Plains.
Then is your time for Faction and Debate, 20
For partial Favour, and permitted Hate.
Let now your immature Dissention cease;
Sit quiet, and compose your Souls to Peace.
   Thus *Jupiter* in few unfolds the Charge:
But lovely *Venus* thus replies at large. 25
O Pow'r immense, Eternal Energy!
(For to what else Protection can we fly,)
Seest thou the proud *Rutulians*, how they dare
In Fields, unpunish'd, and insult my Care?
How lofty *Turnus* vaunts amidst his Train, 30
In shining Arms, triumphant on the Plain?
Ev'n in their Lines and Trenches they contend;
And scarce their Walls the *Trojan* Troops defend:
The Town is fill'd with Slaughter, and o'refloats,
With a red Deluge, their increasing Moats. 35
Æneas ignorant, and far from thence,
Has left a Camp expos'd, without Defence.
This endless outrage shall they still sustain?
Shall *Troy* renew'd be forc'd, and fir'd again?
A second Siege my banish'd Issue fears, 40
And a new *Diomede* in Arms appears.
One more audacious Mortal will be found;
And I thy Daughter wait another Wound.
Yet, if with Fates averse, without thy Leave,
The *Latian* Lands my Progeny receive; 45
Bear they the Pains of violated Law,
And thy Protection from their Aid withdraw.
But if the Gods their sure Success foretel,
If those of Heav'n consent with those of Hell,
To promise *Italy*; who dare debate 50
The Pow'r of *Jove*, or fix another Fate?
What shou'd I tell of Tempests on the Main,
Of *Eolus* usurping *Neptune*'s Reign?

  The Tenth Book. 17 contend *98*: contest *97*

Of *Iris* sent; with *Bachanalian* Heat,
T' inspire the Matrons, and destroy the Fleet.   55
Now *Juno* to the *Stygian* Sky descends,
Sollicites Hell for Aid, and arms the Fiends.
That new Example wanted yet above:
An Act that well became the Wife of *Jove*.
Alecto, rais'd by her, with Rage inflames   60
The peaceful Bosoms of the *Latian* Dames.
Imperial Sway no more exalts my Mind:
(Such hopes I had indeed, while Heav'n was kind)
Now let my happier Foes possess my place,
Whom *Jove* prefers before the *Trojan* Race;   } 65
And conquer they, whom you with Conquest grace.   }
Since you can spare, from all your wide Command,
No spot of Earth, no hospitable Land,
Which may my wand'ring Fugitives receive;
(Since haughty *Juno* will not give you leave)   70
Then, Father, (if I still may use that Name)
By ruin'd *Troy*, yet smoking from the Flame,
I beg you let *Ascanius*, by my Care,
Be freed from Danger, and dismiss'd the War:
Inglorious let him live, without a Crown;   } 75
The Father may be cast on Coasts unknown,   }
Strugling with Fate; but let me save the Son.   }
Mine is *Cythera*, mine the *Cyprian* Tow'rs;
In those Recesses, and those sacred Bow'rs,
Obscurely let him rest; his Right resign   80
To promis'd Empire, and his *Julian* Line.
Then *Carthage* may th' *Ausonian* Towns destroy,
Nor fear the Race of a rejected Boy.
What profits it my Son, to scape the Fire,
Arm'd with his Gods, and loaded with his Sire;   85
To pass the Perils of the Seas and Wind,
Evade the *Greeks*, and leave the War behind;
To reach th' *Italian* Shores: If after all,
Our second *Pergamus* is doom'd to fall?
Much better had he curb'd his high Desires,   90
And hover'd o're his ill extinguish'd Fires.
To *Simois* Banks the Fugitives restore,
And give them back to War, and all the Woes before.

Deep indignation swell'd *Saturnia*'s Heart:
And must I own, she said, my secret Smart? 95
What with more decence were in silence kept,
And but for this unjust Reproach had slept?
Did God, or Man, your Fav'rite Son advise,
With War unhop'd the *Latians* to surprise?
By Fate you boast, and by the Gods Decree, 100
He left his Native Land for *Italy*:
Confess the Truth; by mad *Cassandra*, more
Than Heav'n, inspir'd, he sought a foreign Shore!
Did I perswade to trust his second *Troy*,
To the raw Conduct of a beardless Boy? 105
With Walls unfinish'd, which himself forsakes,
And thro' the Waves a wand'ring Voyage takes?
When have I urg'd him meanly to demand
The *Tuscan* Aid, and arm a quiet Land?
Did I or *Iris* give this mad Advice, 110
Or made the Fool himself the fatal Choice?
You think it hard, the *Latians* shou'd destroy
With Swords your *Trojans*, and with Fires your *Troy*:
Hard and unjust indeed, for Men to draw
Their Native Air, nor take a foreign Law: 115
That *Turnus* is permitted still to live,
To whom his Birth a God and Goddess give:
But yet 'tis just and lawful for your Line,
To drive their Fields, and Force with Fraud to join.
Realms, not your own, among your Clans divide, 120
And from the Bridegroom tear the promis'd Bride:
Petition, while you publick Arms prepare;
Pretend a Peace, and yet provoke a War.
'Twas giv'n to you, your darling Son to shroud,
To draw the Dastard from the fighting Crowd; } 125
And for a Man obtend an empty Cloud.
From flaming Fleets you turn'd the Fire away,
And chang'd the Ships to Daughters of the Sea.
But 'tis my Crime, the Queen of Heav'n offends,
If she presume to save her suff'ring Friends. 130
Your Son, not knowing what his Foes decree,
You say is absent: Absent let him be.

107 takes *98*: makes *97*

Yours is *Cythera*, yours the *Cyprian* Tow'rs,
The soft Recesses, and the Sacred Bow'rs.
Why do you then these needless Arms prepare,   135
And thus provoke a People prone to War?
Did I with Fire the *Trojan* Town deface,
Or hinder from return your exil'd Race?
Was I the Cause of Mischief, or the Man,
Whose lawless Lust the fatal War began?   140
Think on whose Faith th'Adult'rous Youth rely'd;
Who promis'd, who procur'd the *Spartan* Bride?
When all th' united States of *Greece* combin'd,
To purge the World of the perfidious Kind;
Then was your time to fear the *Trojan* Fate: 145
Your Quarrels and Complaints are now too late.
    Thus *Juno*. Murmurs rise, with mix'd Applause;
Just as they favour, or dislike the Cause:
So Winds, when yet unfledg'd in Woods they lie,
In whispers first their tender Voices try: 150
Then issue on the Main with bellowing rage,
And Storms to trembling Mariners presage.
    Then thus to both reply'd th' Imperial God,
Who shakes Heav'ns Axels with his awful Nod.
(When he begins, the silent Senate stand   155
With Rev'rence, list'ning to the dread Command:
The Clouds dispel; the Winds their Breath restrain;
And the hush'd Waves lie flatted on the Main.)
    Cœlestials! Your attentive Ears incline;
Since, said the God, the *Trojans* must not join   160
In wish'd Alliance with the *Latian* Line;
Since endless jarrings, and immortal Hate,
Tend but to discompose our happy State;
The War henceforward be resign'd to Fate.
Each to his proper Fortune stand or fall,   165
Equal and unconcern'd I look on all.
Rutulians, *Trojans*, are the same to me;
And both shall draw the Lots their Fates decree.
Let these assault; if Fortune be their Friend;
And if she favours those, let those defend: 170
The Fates will find their way. The Thund'rer said;

140 fatal *98*: bloody *97*

And shook the sacred Honours of his Head;
Attesting *Styx*, th' Inviolable Flood,
And the black Regions of his Brother God.
Trembled the Poles of Heav'n; and Earth confess'd the Nod. 175
This end the Sessions had: The Senate rise,
And to his Palace wait their Sov'raign thro' the Skies.
   Mean time, intent upon their Siege, the Foes
Within their Walls the *Trojan* Hoast inclose:
They wound, they kill, they watch at ev'ry Gate: 180
Renew the Fires, and urge their happy Fate.
   Th' *Æneans* wish in vain their wanted Chief,
Hopeless of flight, more hopeless of Relief:
Thin on the Tow'rs they stand; and ev'n those few,
A feeble, fainting, and dejected Crew: 185
Yet in the face of Danger some there stood:
The two bold Brothers of *Sarpedon*'s Blood,
Asius, and *Acmon*: both th' *Assaraci*:
Young *Hæmon*, and tho' young, resolv'd to dye.
With these were *Clarus* and *Thymætes* join'd; 190
Tibris and *Castor*, both of *Lycian* Kind.
From *Acmon*'s Hands a rowling Stone there came,
So large, it half deserv'd a Mountain's Name:
Strong sinew'd was the Youth, and big of Bone,
His Brother *Mnestheus* cou'd not more have done: 195
Or the great Father of th' intrepid Son.
Some Firebrands throw, some flights of Arrows send;
And some with Darts, and some with Stones defend.
   Amid the Press appears the beauteous Boy,
The Care of *Venus*, and the Hope of *Troy*. 200
His lovely Face unarm'd, his Head was bare,
In ringlets o're his Shoulders hung his Hair.
His Forehead circled with a Diadem;
Distinguish'd from the Crowd, he shines a Gem,
Enchas'd in Gold, or Polish'd Iv'ry set, 205
Amidst the meaner foil of sable Jett.
   Nor *Ismarus* was wanting to the War,
Directing Ointed Arrows from afar;
And Death with Poyson arm'd: In *Lydia* born,
Where plenteous Harvests the fat Fields adorn: 210
Where proud *Pactolus* floats the fruitful Lands,

And leaves a rich manure of Golden Sands.
There *Capys*, Author of the *Capuan* Name:
And there was *Mnestheus* too increas'd in Fame:
Since *Turnus* from the Camp He cast with shame.   215

    Thus Mortal War was wag'd on either side,
Mean time the Heroe cuts the Nightly Tyde.
For, anxious, from *Evander* when he went,
He sought the *Tyrrhene* Camp, and *Tarchon*'s Tent;
Expos'd the Cause of coming to the Chief;   220
His Name, and Country told, and ask'd Relief:
Propos'd the Terms; his own small strength declar'd,
What Vengeance proud *Mezentius* had prepar'd:
What *Turnus*, bold and violent, design'd;
Then shew'd the slippry state of Humane-kind,   225
And fickle Fortune; warn'd him to beware:
And to his wholsom Counsel added Pray'r.
Tarchon, without delay, the Treaty signs;
And to the *Trojan* Troops the *Tuscan* joins.

    They soon set sail; nor now the Fates withstand;   230
Their Forces trusted with a Foreign Hand.
Æneas leads; upon his Stern appear,
Two Lyons carv'd, which rising *Ida* bear:
Ida, to wand'ring *Trojans* ever dear.
Under their grateful Shade *Æneas* sate,   235
Revolving Wars Events, and various Fate.
His left young *Pallas* kept, fix'd to his side,
And oft of Winds enquir'd, and of the Tyde:
Oft of the Stars, and of their wat'ry Way;
And what he suffer'd both by Land and Sea.   240

    Now sacred Sisters open all your Spring,
The *Tuscan* Leaders, and their Army sing;
Which follow'd great *Æneas* to the War:
Their Arms, their Numbers, and their Names declare.

    A thousand Youths brave *Massicus* obey,   245
Born in the *Tyger*, thro' the foaming Sea;
From *Clusium* brought, and *Cosa*, by his Care;
For Arms, light Quivers, Bows, and Shafts they bear.
Fierce *Abas* next, his Men bright Armour wore;
His Stern, *Apollo*'s Golden Statue bore.   250

247 *Clusium*] *Asium* 97 98

Six hundred *Populonea* sent along,
All skill'd in Martial Exercise, and strong.
Three hundred more for Battel *Ilva* joins,
An Isle renown'd for Steel, and unexhausted Mines.
Asylas on his Prow the third appears,   255
Who Heav'n interprets, and the wand'ring Stars:
From offer'd Entrails Prodigies expounds,
And Peals of Thunder, with presaging Sounds.
A thousand Spears in warlike Order stand,
Sent by the *Pisans* under his Command.   260
  Fair *Astur* follows in the wat'ry Field,
Proud of his manag'd Horse, and painted Shield.
Gravisca noisom from the neighb'ring Fen,
And his own *Cære* sent three hundred Men:
With those which *Minio*'s Fields, and *Pyrgi* gave;   265
All bred in Arms, unanimous and brave.
  Thou Muse the Name of *Cyniras* renew,
And brave *Cupavo* follow'd but by few:
Whose Helm confess'd the Lineage of the Man,
And bore, with Wings display'd, a silver Swan.   270
Love was the fault of his fam'd Ancestry,
Whose Forms, and Fortunes in his Ensigns fly.
For *Cycnus* lov'd unhappy *Phaeton*,
And sung his Loss in Poplar Groves, alone;
Beneath the Sister shades to sooth his Grief;   275
Heav'n heard his Song, and hasten'd his Relief:
And chang'd to snowy Plumes his hoary Hair,
And wing'd his Flight, to chant aloft in Air.
His Son *Cupavo* brush'd the briny Flood;
Upon his Stern a brawny *Centaur* stood,   280
Who heav'd a Rock, and threat'ning still to throw,
With lifted Hands, alarm'd the Seas below:
They seem'd to fear the formidable Sight,
And rowl'd their Billows on, to speed his Flight.
  Ocnus was next, who led his Native Train,   285
Of hardy Warriors, thro' the wat'ry Plain.
The Son of *Manto*, by the *Tuscan* Stream,
From whence the *Mantuan* Town derives the Name.
An ancient City, but of mix'd Descent,
Three sev'ral Tribes compose the Government: 290

Four Towns are under each; but all obey
The *Mantuan* Laws, and own the *Tuscan* Sway.

    Hate to *Mezentius*, arm'd five hundred more,
Whom *Mincius* .rom his Sire *Benacus* bore;
(*Mincius* with Wreaths of Reeds his forehead cover'd o're.)   295
These grave *Auletes* leads. A hundred sweep,
With stretching Oars at once the glassy deep:
Him, and his Martial Train, the *Triton* bears,
High on his Poop the Sea-green God appears:
Frowning he seems his crooked Shell to sound,   300
And at the Blast the Billows dance around.
A hairy Man above the Waste he shows,
A *Porpoise* Tail beneath his Belly grows;
And ends a Fish: His Breast the Waves divides,
And Froth and Foam augment the murm'ring Tides.   305
    Full thirty Ships transport the chosen Train,
For *Troy*'s Relief, and scour the briny Main.

    Now was the World forsaken by the Sun,
And *Phœbe* half her nightly Race had run.
The careful Chief, who never clos'd his Eyes,   310
Himself the Rudder holds, the Sails supplies.
A Choir of *Nereids* meet him on the Flood,
Once his own Gallies, hewn from *Ida*'s Wood:
But now as many Nymphs the Sea they sweep,
As rode before tall Vessels on the Deep.   315
They know him from afar; and, in a Ring,
Inclose the Ship that bore the *Trojan* King.
Cymodoce, whose Voice excell'd the rest,
Above the Waves advanc'd her snowy Breast,
Her right Hand stops the Stern, her left divides   320
The curling Ocean, and corrects the Tides:
She spoke for all the Choir; and thus began,
With pleasing Words to warn th' unknowing Man.
Sleeps our lov'd Lord? O Goddess-born! awake,
Spread ev'ry Sail, pursue your wat'ry Track;   325
And haste your Course. Your Navy once were we,
From *Ida*'s Height descending to the Sea:
'Till *Turnus*, as at Anchor fix'd we stood,
Presum'd to violate our holy Wood.

Then loos'd from Shore we fled his Fires prophane; 330
(Unwillingly we broke our Master's Chain)
And since have sought you thro' the *Tuscan* Main.
The mighty Mother chang'd our Forms to these,
And gave us Life Immortal in the Seas.
But young *Ascanius*, in his Camp distress'd, 335
By your insulting Foes is hardly press'd.
Th' *Arcadian* Horsemen, and *Etrurian* Hoast
Advance in order on the *Latian* Coast:
To cut their way the *Daunian* Chief designs,
Before their Troops can reach the *Trojan* Lines. 340
Thou, when the rosie Morn restores the Light,
First arm thy Souldiers for th' ensuing Fight:
Thy self the fated Sword of *Vulcan* wield,
And bear aloft th' impenetrable Shield.
To Morrow's Sun, unless my Skill be vain, 345
Shall see huge heaps of Foes in Battel slain.
Parting, she spoke; and with Immortal Force,
Push'd on the Vessel in her wat'ry Course:
(For well she knew the Way) impell'd behind,
The Ship flew forward, and outstrip'd the Wind. 350
The rest make up: Unknowing of the cause
The Chief admires their Speed, and happy Omens draws.
    Then thus he pray'd, and fix'd on Heav'n his Eyes;
Hear thou, great Mother of the Deities!
With Turrets crown'd, (on *Ida*'s holy Hill, 355
Fierce Tygers, rein'd and curb'd, obey thy Will.)
Firm thy own Omens, lead us on to fight,
And let thy *Phrygians* conquer in thy right.
    He said no more. And now renewing Day
Had chas'd the Shadows of the Night away. 360
He charg'd the Souldiers with preventing Care,
Their Flags to follow, and their Arms prepare;
Warn'd of th' ensuing Fight, and bad 'em hope the War.
    Now, from his lofty Poop, he view'd below
His Camp incompass'd, and th' inclosing Foe. 365
His blazing Shield imbrac'd, he held on high;
The Camp receive the sign, and with loud Shouts reply.
Hope arms their Courage: From their Tow'rs they throw

368 Courage *98*: Anger *97*

Their Darts with double Force, and drive the Foe.
Thus, at the signal giv'n, the Cranes arise   370
Before the stormy South, and blacken all the Skies.
    King *Turnus* wonder'd at the Fight renew'd;
'Till, looking back, the *Trojan* Fleet he view'd:
The Seas with swelling Canvass cover'd o're;
And the swift Ships descending on the Shore.   375
The *Latians* saw from far, with dazl'd Eyes,
The radiant Crest that seem'd in Flames to rise,
And dart diffusive Fires around the Field;
And the keen glitt'ring of the Golden Shield.
    Thus threatning Comets, when by Night they rise,   380
Shoot sanguine Streams, and sadden all the Skies:
So *Sirius*, flashing forth sinister Lights,
Pale humane kind with Plagues, and with dry Famine frights.
Yet *Turnus*, with undaunted Mind is bent
To man the Shores, and hinder their Descent: 385
And thus awakes the Courage of his Friends.
What you so long have wish'd, kind Fortune sends:
In ardent Arms to meet th' invading Foe:
You find, and find him at Advantage now.
Yours is the Day, you need but only dare: 390
Your Swords will make you Masters of the War.
Your Sires, your Sons, your Houses, and your Lands,
And dearest Wifes, are all within your Hands.
Be mindful of the Race from whence you came;
And emulate in Arms your Fathers Fame.   395
Now take the Time, while stagg'ring yet they stand
With Feet unfirm; and prepossess the Strand:
Fortune befriends the bold. Nor more he said,
But ballanc'd whom to leave, and whom to lead:
Then these elects, the Landing to prevent;   400
And those he leaves to keep the City pent.
   Mean time the *Trojan* sends his Troops ashore:
Some are by Boats expos'd, by Bridges more.
With lab'ring Oars they bear along the Strand,
Where the Tide languishes, and leap a-land.   405
Tarchon observes the Coast with careful Eyes,
And where no Foord he finds, no Water fryes,

388 ardent *98*: equal *97*

Nor Billows with unequal Murmurs roar;
But smoothly slide along, and swell the Shoar;
That Course he steer'd, and thus he gave command.   410
Here ply your Oars, and at all hazard land:
Force on the Vessel that her Keel may wound
This hated Soil, and furrow hostile Ground.
Let me securely land, I ask no more,
Then sink my Ships, or shatter on the Shore.   415
  This fiery Speech inflames his fearful Friends,
They tug at ev'ry Oar; and ev'ry Stretcher bends:
They run their Ships aground, the Vessels knock,
(Thus forc'd ashore) and tremble with the shock.
Tarchon's alone was lost, that stranded stood,   420
Stuck on a Bank, and beaten by the Flood.
She breaks her Back, the loosen'd Sides give way,
And plunge the *Tuscan* Souldiers in the Sea.
Their broken Oars, and floating Planks withstand
Their Passage, while they labour to the Land;   425
And ebbing Tides bear back upon th' uncertain Sand.
  Now *Turnus* leads his Troops, without delay,
Advancing to the Margin of the Sea.
The Trumpets sound: *Æneas* first assail'd
The Clowns new rais'd and raw; and soon prevail'd.   430
Great *Theron* fell, an Omen of the Fight:
Great *Theron* large of Limbs, of Gyant height.
He first in open Field defy'd the Prince,
But Armour scal'd with Gold was no Defence
Against the fated Sword, which open'd wide   435
His plated Shield, and pierc'd his naked side.
  Next, *Lycas* fell; who, not like others born,
Was from his wretched Mother rip'd and torn:
Sacred, O *Phœbus*! from his Birth to thee,
For his beginning Life from biting Steel was free.   440
Not far from him was *Gyas* laid along,
Of monst'rous Bulk; with *Cisseus* fierce and strong:
Vain Bulk and Strength; for when the Chief assail'd,
Nor Valour, nor *Herculean* Arms avail'd;
Nor their fam'd Father, wont in War to go   445
With great *Alcides*, while he toil'd below.

    410 command. *98*: command, *97*

The noisie *Pharos* next receiv'd his Death,
Æneas writh'd his Dart, and stopp'd his bawling Breath.
Then wretched *Cydon* had receiv'd his Doom,
Who courted *Clytius* in his beardless Bloom,   450
And sought with lust obscene polluted Joys:
The *Trojan* Sword had cur'd his love of Boys,
Had not his sev'n bold Brethren stop'd the Course
Of the fierce Champion, with united Force.
Sev'n Darts were thrown at once, and some rebound   455
From his bright Shield, some on his Helmet sound:
The rest had reach'd him, but his Mother's Care
Prevented those, and turn'd aside in Air.

The Prince then call'd *Achates*, to supply
The Spears, that knew the way to Victory.   460
Those fatal Weapons, which inur'd to Blood,
In *Grecian* Bodies under *Ilium* stood:
Not one of those my Hand shall toss in vain
Against our Foes, on this contended Plain.
He said: Then seiz'd a mighty Spear, and threw;   465
Which, wing'd with Fate, thro' *Mæon*'s Buckler flew:
Pierc'd all the brazen Plates, and reach'd his Heart:
He stagger'd with intolerable Smart.
Alcanor saw; and reach'd, but reach'd in vain,
His helping Hand, his Brother to sustain.   470
A second Spear, which kept the former Course,
From the same Hand, and sent with equal Force,
His right Arm pierc'd, and holding on, bereft
His use of both, and pinion'd down his left.
Then *Numitor*, from his dead Brother drew   475
Th' ill-omend Spear, and at the *Trojan* threw:
Preventing Fate directs the Lance awry,
Which glancing, only mark'd *Achates* Thigh.

In Pride of Youth the *Sabine Clausus* came,
And from afar, at *Driops* took his Aim.   480
The Spear flew hissing thro' the middle Space,
And pierc'd his Throat, directed at his Face:
It stop'd at once the Passage of his Wind,
And the free Soul to flitting Air resign'd:
His Forehead was the first that struck the Ground;   485
Life-blood, and Life rush'd mingl'd thro' the Wound.

He slew three Brothers of the *Borean* Race,
And three, whom *Ismarus*, their Native Place,
Had sent to War, but all the Sons of *Thrace*.
Halesus next, the bold *Aurunci* leads;   490
The Son of *Neptune* to his Aid succeeds,
Conspicuous on his Horse: On either Hand
These fight to keep, and those to win the Land.
With mutual Blood th' *Ausonian* Soil is dy'd,
While on its Borders each their Claim decide.   495
    As wint'ry Winds contending in the Sky,
With equal force of Lungs their Titles try,
They rage, they roar; the doubtful rack of Heav'n
Stands without Motion, and the Tyde undriv'n:
Each bent to conquer, neither side to yield;   500
They long suspend the Fortune of the Field.
Both Armies thus perform what Courage can:
Foot set to Foot, and mingled Man to Man.
    But in another part, th' *Arcadian* Horse,
With ill Success ingage the *Latin* Force.   505
For where th' impetuous Torrent rushing down,
Huge craggy Stones, and rooted Trees had thrown:
They left their Coursers, and unus'd to Fight
On Foot, were scatter'd in a shameful flight.
Pallas, who with Disdain and Grief, had view'd   510
His Foes pursuing, and his Friends pursu'd;
Us'd Threatnings mix'd with Pray'rs, his last Ressource;
With these to move their Minds, with those to fire their Force.
Which way, Companions! Whether wou'd you run?
By you your selves, and mighty Battels won;   515
By my great Sire, by his establish'd Name,
And early promise of my Future Fame;
By my Youth emulous of equal Right,
To share his Honours, shun ignoble Flight.
Trust not your Feet, your Hands must hew your way   520
Thro' yon black Body, and that thick Array:
'Tis thro' that forward Path that we must come:
There lies our Way, and that our Passage home.

       503 mingled *98*: crowded *97*

Nor Pow'rs above, nor Destinies below,
Oppress our Arms; with equal Strength we go; 52.
With Mortal Hands to meet a Mortal Foe.
See on what Foot we stand: A scanty Shore;
The Sea behind, our Enemies before:
No Passage left, unless we swim the Main;
Or forcing these, the *Trojan* Trenches gain. 53◦
This said, he strode with eager haste along,
And bore amidst the thickest of the Throng.
Lagus, the first he met, with Fate to Foe,
Had heav'd a Stone of mighty Weight to throw:
Stooping, the Spear descended on his Chine, 53
Just where the Bone distinguish'd either Loin:
It stuck so fast, so deeply bury'd lay,
That scarce the Victor forc'd the Steel away.
　Hisbon came on, but while he mov'd too slow
To wish'd Revenge, the Prince prevents his Blow: 54◦
For warding his at once, at once he press'd;
And plung'd the fatal Weapon in his Breast.
Then leud *Anchemolus* he laid in Dust,
Who stain'd his Stepdam's Bed with impious Lust.
And after him the *Daucian* Twins were slain, 54↊
Laris and *Thimbrus,* on the *Latian* Plain:
So wond'rous like in Feature, Shape, and Size,
As caus'd an Error in their Parents Eyes.
Grateful Mistake! but soon the Sword decides
The nice Distinction, and their Fate divides. 55◦
For *Thimbrus* Head was lop'd: and *Laris* Hand
Dismember'd, sought its Owner on the Strand:
The trembling Fingers yet the Fauchion strain,
And threaten still th' intended Stroke in vain.
　Now, to renew the Charge, th' *Arcadians* came: 55↊
Sight of such Acts, and sense of honest Shame,
And Grief, with Anger mix'd, their Minds inflame.
Then, with a casual Blow was *Rhœteus* slain,
Who chanc'd, as *Pallas* threw, to cross the Plain:
The flying Spear was after *Ilus* sent, 56◦
But *Rhœteus* happen'd on a Death unmeant:
From *Teuthras,* and from *Tyres* while he fled,

The Lance, athwart his Body, laid him dead:
Rowl'd from his Chariot with a Mortal Wound,
And intercepted Fate, he spurn'd the Ground.   565
   As, when in Summer, welcome Winds arise,
The watchful Shepherd to the Forest flies,
And fires the midmost Plants; Contagion spreads,
And catching Flames infect the neighb'ring Heads;
Around the Forest flies the furious Blast,   570
And all the leafie Nation sinks at last;
And *Vulcan* rides in Triumph o're the Wast;
The Pastor pleas'd with his dire Victory,
Beholds the satiate Flames in Sheets ascend the Sky:
So *Pallas* Troops their scatter'd Strength unite;   575
And pouring on their Foes, their Prince delight.
   Halesus came, fierce with desire of Blood,
(But first collected in his Arms he stood)
Advancing then, he ply'd the Spear so well,
Ladon, *Demodocus*, and *Pheres* fell: 580
Around his Head he toss'd his glitt'ring Brand,
And from *Strimonius* hew'd his better Hand,
Held up to guard his Throat: Then hurl'd a Stone
At *Thoas* ample Front, and pierc'd the Bone:
It struck beneath the space of either Eye,   585
And Blood, and mingled Brains, together fly.
Deep skill'd in future Fates, *Halesus* Sire,
Did with the Youth to lonely Groves retire:
But when the Father's Mortal Race was run,
Dire Destiny laid hold upon the Son,   590
And haul'd him to the War: to find beneath
Th' *Evandrian* Spear, a memorable Death.
   Pallas th' Encounter seeks, but e're he throws,
To *Tuscan Tyber* thus address'd his Vows:
O sacred Stream direct my flying Dart;   595
And give to pass the proud *Halesus* Heart:
His Arms and Spoils thy holy Oak shall bear:
Pleas'd with the Bribe, the God receiv'd his Pray'r.
For while his Shield protects a Friend distress'd,
The Dart came driving on, and pierc'd his Breast.   600
   But *Lausus*, no small portion of the War,

Permits not Panick Fear to reign too far,
Caus'd by the Death of so renown'd a Knight;
But by his own Example chears the Fight.
Fierce *Abas* first he slew, *Abas*, the stay   605
Of *Trojan* Hopes, and hind'rance of the Day.
The *Phrygian* Troops escap'd the *Greeks* in vain,
They, and their mix'd Allies, now load the Plain.

  To the rude shock of War both Armies came,
Their Leaders equal, and their Strength the same.   610
The Rear so press'd the Front, they cou'd not wield
Their angry Weapons, to dispute the Field.
Here *Pallas* urges on, and *Lausus* there,
Of equal Youth and Beauty both appear,
But both by Fate forbid to breath their Native Air.   615
Their Congress in the Field great *Jove* withstands,
Both doom'd to fall, but fall by greater Hands.

  Mean time *Juturna* warns the *Daunian* Chief
Of *Lausus* Danger, urging swift Relief.
With his driv'n Chariot he divides the Crowd,   620
And making to his Friends, thus calls aloud:
Let none presume his needless Aid to join;
Retire, and clear the Field, the Fight is mine:
To this right Hand is *Pallas* only due:
Oh were his Father here my just Revenge to view!   625
From the forbidden Space his Men retir'd;
Pallas, their Awe, and his stern Words admir'd:
Survey'd him o're and o're with wond'ring sight,
Struck with his haughty Meen, and tow'ring Height.
Then to the King; your empty Vaunts forbear: 630
Success I hope, and Fate I cannot fear.
Alive or dead, I shall deserve a Name:
Jove is impartial, and to both the same.
He said, and to the void advanc'd his Pace;
Pale Horror sate on each *Arcadian* Face.   635
Then *Turnus*, from his Chariot leaping light,
Address'd himself on Foot to single Fight.
And, as a Lyon, when he spies from far
A Bull, that seems to meditate the War,
Bending his Neck, and spurning back the Sand;   640

639 War,] War; *97 98*   640 Sand;] Sand, *97 98*

Runs roaring downward from his hilly Stand:
Imagine eager *Turnus* not more slow,
To rush from high on his unequal Foe.
    Young *Pallas*, when he saw the Chief advance
Within due distance of his flying Lance;   645
Prepares to charge him first: Resolv'd to try
If Fortune wou'd his want of Force supply.
And thus to Heav'n and *Hercules* address'd.
Alcides, once on Earth *Evander*'s Guest,
His Son adjures you by those Holy Rites,   650
That hospitable Board, those Genial Nights;
Assist my great Attempt to gain this Prize,
And let proud *Turnus* view, with dying Eyes,
His ravish'd Spoils. 'Twas heard, the vain Request;
Alcides mourn'd: And stifled Sighs within his Breast.   655
Then *Jove*, to sooth his Sorrow, thus began:
Short bounds of Life are set to Mortal Man,
'Tis Vertues work alone to stretch the narrow Span.
So many Sons of Gods in bloody Fight,
Around the Walls of *Troy*, have lost the Light: 660
My own *Sarpedon* fell beneath his Foe,
Nor I, his mighty Sire, cou'd ward the Blow.
Ev'n *Turnus* shortly shall resign his Breath;
And stands already on the Verge of Death.
This said, the God permits the fatal Fight,   665
But from the *Latian* Fields averts his sight.
    Now with full Force his Spear young *Pallas* threw;
And having thrown, his shining Fauchion drew:
The Steel just graz'd along the Shoulder Joint,
And mark'd it slightly with the glancing Point.   670
Fierce *Turnus* first to nearer distance drew,
And poiz'd his pointed Spear before he threw:
Then, as the winged Weapon whiz'd along;
See now, said he, whose Arm is better strung.
The Spear kept on the fatal Course, unstay'd   675
By Plates of Ir'n, which o're the Shield were laid:
Thro' folded Brass, and tough Bull-hides it pass'd,
His Corslet pierc'd, and reach'd his Heart at last.
In vain the Youth tugs at the broken Wood,
The Soul comes issuing with the vital Blood: 680

He falls; his Arms upon his Body sound;
And with his bloody Teeth he bites the Ground.
    Turnus bestrode the Corps: *Arcadians* hear,
Said he; my Message to your Master bear:
Such as the Sire deserv'd, the Son I send: 685
It costs him dear to be the *Phrygians* Friend.
The lifeless Body, tell him, I bestow
Unask'd, to rest his wand'ring Ghost below.
He said, and trampled down with all the Force
Of his left Foot, and spurn'd the wretched Corse: 690
Then snatch'd the shining Belt, with Gold inlaid;
The Belt *Eurytion*'s artful Hands had made:
Where fifty fatal Brides, express'd to sight,
All, in the compass of one mournful Night,
Depriv'd their Bridegrooms of returning Light.   695
    In an ill Hour insulting *Turnus* tore
Those Golden Spoils, and in a worse he wore.
O Mortals! blind in Fate, who never know
To bear high Fortune, or endure the low!
The Time shall come, when *Turnus*, but in vain,   700
Shall wish untouch'd the Trophies of the slain:
Shall wish the fatal Belt were far away;
And curse the dire Remembrance of the Day.
    The sad *Arcadians* from th' unhappy Field,
Bear back the breathless Body on a Shield.   705
O Grace and Grief of War! at once restor'd
With Praises to thy Sire, at once deplor'd.
One Day first sent thee to the fighting Field,
Beheld whole heaps of Foes in Battel kill'd;
One Day beheld thee dead, and born upon thy Shield.   710
This dismal News, not from uncertain Fame,
But sad Spectators, to the Heroe came:
His Friends upon the brink of Ruin stand,
Unless reliev'd by his victorious Hand.
He whirls his Sword around, without delay,   715
And hews through adverse Foes an ample Way;
To find fierce *Turnus*, of his Conquest proud:
Evander, *Pallas*, all that Friendship ow'd
To large Deserts, are present to his Eyes;

His plighted Hand, and hospitable Ties. 720
   Four Sons of *Sulmo*, four whom *Ufens* bred,
He took in fight, and living Victims led,
To please the Ghost of *Pallas*; and expire
In Sacrifice, before his Fun'ral Fire.
At *Magus* next he threw: He stoop'd below 725
The flying Spear, and shun'd the promis'd Blow.
Then creeping, clasp'd the Hero's Knees, and pray'd:
By young *Iulus*, by thy Father's Shade,
O spare my Life, and send me back to see
My longing Sire, and tender Progeny. 730
A lofty House I have, and Wealth untold,
In Silver Ingots, and in Bars of Gold:
All these, and Sums besides, which see no Day,
The Ransom of this one poor Life shall pay.
If I survive, will *Troy* the less prevail? 735
A single Soul's too light to turn the Scale.
He said. The Heroe sternly thus reply'd:
Thy Barrs, and Ingots, and the Sums beside,
Leave for thy Childrens Lot. Thy *Turnus* broke
All Rules of War, by one relentless Stroke 740
When *Pallas* fell: So deems, nor deems alone,
My Father's Shadow, but my living Son.
Thus having said, of kind Remorse bereft,
He seiz'd his Helm, and drag'd him with his left:
Then with his right Hand, while his Neck he wreath'd, 745
Up to the hilts his shining Fauchion sheath'd.
   Apollo's Priest, *Emonides*, was near,
His holy Fillets on his Front appear;
Glitt'ring in Arms he shone amidst the Crowd;
Much of his God, more of his Purple proud: 750
Him the fierce *Trojan* follow'd thro' the Field;
The holy Coward fell: And forc'd to yield,
The Prince stood o're the Priest; and at one Blow,
Sent him an Off'ring to the Shades below.
His Arms *Seresthus* on his Shoulders bears, 755
Design'd a Trophee to the God of Wars.
   Vulcanian Cæculus renews the Fight;
And *Umbro* born upon the Mountains Height:

735 will *97 (errata)*: shall *97 (text)*

The Champion chears his Troops t' encounter those:
And seeks Revenge himself on other Foes.   76c
At *Anxur's* Shield he drove, and at the Blow,
Both Shield and Arm to Ground together go.
Anxur had boasted much of magick Charms,
And thought he wore impenetrable Arms;
So made by mutter'd Spells: And from the Spheres,   76§
Had Life secur'd, in vain, for length of Years.
Then *Tarquitus* the Field in Triumph trod;
A Nymph his Mother, and his Sire a God.
Exulting in bright Arms he braves the Prince;
With his protended Lance He makes defence: 77c
Bears back his feeble Foe; then pressing on,
Arrests his better Hand, and drags him down.
Stands o're the prostrate Wretch, and as he lay,
Vain Tales inventing, and prepar'd to pray:
Mows off his Head, the Trunk a Moment stood,   77§
Then sunk, and rowl'd along the Sand in Blood.
  The vengeful Victor thus upbraids the slain;
Lye there, proud Man unpity'd, on the Plain:
Lye there, inglorious, and without a Tomb,
Far from thy Mother, and thy Native Home: 78c
Expos'd to salvage Beasts, and Birds of Prey;
Or thrown for Food to Monsters of the Sea.
  On *Lycas* and *Antæus* next he ran,
Two Chiefs of *Turnus*, and who led his Van.
They fled for Fear; with these he chas'd along,   78§
Camers the yellow Lock'd, and *Numa* strong,
Both great in Arms, and both were fair, and young:
Camers, was Son to *Volscens* lately slain;
In Wealth surpassing all the *Latian* Train,
And in *Amycla* fix'd his silent, easy Reign.   79c
  And as *Ægeon*, when with Heav'n he strove,
Stood opposite in Arms to mighty *Jove*;
Mov'd all his hundred Hands, provok'd the War,
Defy'd the forky Lightning from afar:
At fifty Mouths his flaming Breath expires,   79§
And Flash for Flash returns, and Fires for Fires:
In his right Hand as many Swords he wields,

778 Man unpity'd,] Man, unpity'd *98*

And takes the Thunder on as many Shields:
With Strength like his the *Trojan* Heroe stood,
And soon the Fields with falling Corps were strowd, } 800
When once his Fauchion found the Taste of Blood.

　　With Fury scarce to be conceiv'd, he flew
Against *Niphæus*, whom four Coursers drew.
They, when they see the fiery Chief advance,
And pushing at their Chests his pointed Lance; 805
Wheel'd with so swift a Motion, mad with Fear,
They threw their Master headlong from the Chair:
They stare, they start, nor stop their Course before
They bear the bounding Chariot to the Shore.

　　Now *Lucagus*, and *Liger* scour the Plains, } 810
With two white Steeds, but *Liger* holds the Reins,
And *Lucagus* the lofty Seat maintains.
Bold Brethren both, the former wav'd in Air }
His flaming Sword; *Æneas* couch'd his Spear,
Unus'd to Threats, and more unus'd to Fear. } 815
Then *Liger* thus. Thy Confidence is vain
To scape from hence, as from the *Trojan* Plain:
Nor these the Steeds which *Diomede* bestrode,
Nor this the Chariot where *Achilles* rode:
Nor *Venus* Veil is here, nor *Neptune*'s Shield: 820
Thy fatal Hour is come; and this the Field.
Thus *Liger* vainly vaunts: The *Trojan* Peer
Return'd his answer with his flying Spear.
As *Lucagus* to lash his Horses bends,
Prone to the Wheels, and his left Foot protends; 825
Prepar'd for Fight: the fatal Dart arrives,
And thro' the borders of his Buckler drives.
Pass'd through, and pierc'd his Groin; the deadly Wound,
Cast from his Chariot, rowl'd him on the Ground.
Whom thus the Chief upbraids with scornful spight: 830
Blame not the slowness of your Steeds in flight;
Vain Shadows did not force their swift Retreat:
But you your self forsake your empty Seat.
He said, and seiz'd at once the loosen'd Rein,
(For *Liger* lay already on the Plain, 835

820 *Venus*] *Venus*'s *97 98*　　825 protends;] protends: *97 98*　　826 Fight:]
Fight, *97 98*　　828 through, and . . . Groin;] through; and . . . Groin, *97 98*

By the same Shock) then, stretching out his Hands,
The Recreant thus his wretched Life demands.
Now by thy self, O more than Mortal Man!
By her and him from whom thy Breath began,
Who form'd thee thus Divine, I beg thee spare   840
This forfeit Life, and hear thy Suppliant's Pray'r.
Thus much he spoke, and more he wou'd have said,
But the stern Heroe turn'd aside his Head,
And cut him short. I hear another Man,
You talk'd not thus before the Fight began;   845
Now take your turn: And, as a Brother shou'd,
Attend your Brother to the *Stygian* Flood:
Then thro' his Breast his fatal Sword he sent,
And the Soul issu'd at the gaping Vent.

As Storms the Skies, and Torrents tear the Ground,   850
Thus rag'd the Prince, and scatter'd Deaths around:
At length *Ascanius*, and the *Trojan* Train,
Broke from the Camp, so long besieg'd in vain.
Mean time the King of Gods and Mortal Man,
Held Conference with his Queen, and thus began: 855
My Sister Goddess, and well pleasing Wife,
Still think you *Venus* Aid supports the Strife;
Sustains her *Trojans*: Or themselves alone,
With inborn Valour force their Fortune on?
How fierce in Fight, with Courage undecay'd;   860
Judge if such Warriors want immortal Aid.
To whom the Goddess, with the charming Eyes,
Soft in her Tone submissively replies.

Why, O my Sov'raign Lord, whose Frown I fear,
And cannot, unconcern'd, your Anger bear;   865
Why urge you thus my Grief? When if I still,
(As once I was) were Mistress of your Will:
From your Almighty Pow'r, your pleasing Wife
Might gain the Grace of lengthning *Turnus* Life:
Securely snatch him from the fatal Fight,   870
And give him to his aged Father's sight.
Now let him perish, since you hold it good,
And glut the *Trojans* with his pious Blood.

Yet from our Lineage he derives his Name,
And in the fourth degree, from God *Pilumnus* came: 875
Yet he devoutly pays you Rites Divine,
And offers daily Incense at your Shrine.

Then shortly thus the Sov'raign God reply'd;
Since in my Pow'r and Goodness you confide;
If for a little Space, a lengthen'd Span,   880
You beg Reprieve for this expiring Man:
I grant you leave to take your *Turnus* hence,
From Instant Fate, and can so far dispense.
But if some secret Meaning lies beneath,
To save the short-liv'd Youth from destin'd Death: 885
Or if a farther Thought you entertain,
To change the Fates; you feed your hopes in vain.

To whom the Goddess thus, with weeping Eyes,
And what if that Request your Tongue denies,
Your Heart shou'd grant; and not a short Reprieve,   890
But length of certain Life to *Turnus* give.
Now speedy Death attends the guiltless Youth,
If my presaging Soul divines with Truth.
Which, O! I wish might err thro' causeless Fears,
And you, (for you have Pow'r) prolong his Years.   895

Thus having said, involv'd in Clouds, she flies,
And drives a Storm before her thro' the Skies.
Swift she descends, alighting on the Plain,
Where the fierce Foes a dubious Fight maintain.
Of Air condens'd, a Spectre soon she made,   900
And what *Æneas* was, such seem'd the Shade.
Adorn'd with *Dardan* Arms, the Phantom bore
His Head aloft, a Plumy Crest he wore:
This Hand appear'd a shining Sword to wield,
And that sustain'd an imitated Shield: 905
With manly Meen He stalk'd along the Ground;
Nor wanted Voice bely'd, nor vaunting Sound.
(Thus haunting Ghosts appear to waking Sight,
Or dreadful Visions in our Dreams by Night.)
The Spectre seems the *Daunian* Chief to dare,   910
And flourishes his empty Sword in Air:
At this advancing *Turnus* hurl'd his Spear;
The Phantom wheel'd, and seem'd to fly for Fear.

Deluded *Turnus* thought the *Trojan* fled,
And with vain hopes his haughty Fancy fed.   915
Whether, O Coward, (thus he calls aloud,
Nor found he spoke to Wind, and chas'd a Cloud;)
Why thus forsake your Bride? Receive from me
The fated Land you sought so long by Sea.
He said, and brandishing at once his Blade,   920
With eager Pace pursu'd the flying Shade.
By chance a Ship was fasten'd to the Shore,
Which from old *Clusium* King *Osinius* bore:
The Plank was ready laid for safe ascent;
For shelter there the trembling Shadow bent: } 925
And skip'd, and sculk'd, and under Hatches went.
Exulting *Turnus*, with regardless haste,
Ascends the Plank, and to the Gally pass'd:
Scarce had he reach'd the Prow, *Saturnia*'s Hand
The Haulsers cuts, and shoots the Ship from Land.   930
With Wind in Poop, the Vessel plows the Sea,
And measures back with speed her former Way.
Mean time *Æneas* seeks his absent Foe,
And sends his slaughter'd Troops to Shades below.

    The guileful Phantom now forsook the shrowd,   935
And flew sublime, and vanish'd in a Cloud.
Too late young *Turnus* the Delusion found,
Far on the Sea, still making from the Ground.
Then thankless for a Life redeem'd by Shame;
With sense of Honour stung, and forfeit Fame: 940
Fearful besides of what in Fight had pass'd,
His Hands, and hagger'd Eyes to Heav'n he cast.
O *Jove*! he cry'd, for what Offence have I
Deserv'd to bear this endless Infamy:
Whence am I forc'd, and whether am I born,   945
How, and with what Reproach shall I return?
Shall ever I behold the *Latian* Plain,
Or see *Laurentum*'s lofty Tow'rs again?
What will they say of their deserting Chief?
The War was mine, I fly from their Relief: 950
I led to Slaughter, and in Slaughter leave;
And ev'n from hence their dying Groans receive.

    924 Plank was *97* (errata): Planks were *97* (*text*)

Here over-match'd in Fight, in heaps they lye,
There scatter'd o're the Fields ignobly fly.
Gape wide, O Earth! and draw me down alive, }955
Or, oh ye pitying Winds, a Wretch relieve;
On Sands or Shelves the splitting Vessel drive:
Or set me Shipwrack'd on some desart Shore,
Where no *Rutulian* Eyes may see me more:
Unknown to Friends, or Foes, or conscious Fame, 960
Lest she should follow, and my flight proclaim.
　Thus *Turnus* rav'd, and various Fates revolv'd,
The Choice was doubtful, but the Death resolv'd.
And now the Sword, and now the Sea took place:
That to revenge, and this to purge Disgrace. 965
Sometimes he thought to swim the stormy Main,
By stretch of Arms the distant Shore to gain:
Thrice he the Sword assay'd, and thrice the Flood;
But *Juno* mov'd with Pity both withstood:
And thrice repress'd his Rage: strong Gales supply'd, 970
And push'd the Vessel o're the swelling Tide.
At length she lands him on his Native Shores,
And to his Father's longing Arms restores.
　Mean time, by *Jove*'s Impulse, *Mezentius* arm'd:
Succeeding *Turnus*; with his ardour warm'd 975
His fainting Friends, reproach'd their shameful flight,
Repell'd the Victors, and renew'd the Fight.
Against their King the *Tuscan* Troops conspire,
Such is their Hate, and such their fierce desire
Of wish'd Revenge: On him, and him alone, 980
All Hands employ'd, and all their Darts are thrown.
He, like a solid Rock by Seas inclos'd,
To raging Winds and roaring Waves oppos'd;
From his proud Summit looking down, disdains
Their empty Menace, and unmov'd remains. 985
　Beneath his Feet fell haughty *Hebrus* dead,
Then *Latagus*; and *Palmus* as he fled:
At *Latagus* a weighty Stone he flung,
His Face was flatted, and his Helmet rung.
But *Palmus* from behind receives his Wound, 990
Hamstring'd he falls, and grovels on the Ground:
His Crest and Armor from his Body torn,

Thy Shoulders, *Lausus*, and thy Head adorn.
Evas and *Mymas*, both of *Troy*, he slew,
Mymas his Birth from fair *Theano* drew: 995
Born on that fatal Night, when, big with Fire,
The Queen produc'd young *Paris* to his Sire.
But *Paris* in the *Phrygian* Fields was slain,
Unthinking *Mymas* on the *Latian* Plain.

And as a salvage Boar on Mountains bred,   1000
With forest Mast, and fatning Marshes fed;
When once he sees himself in Toils inclos'd,
By Huntsmen and their eager Hounds oppos'd:
He whets his Tusks, and turns, and dares the War:
Th' Invaders dart their Jav'lins from afar;   1005
All keep aloof, and safely shout around,
But none presumes to give a nearer Wound:
He frets and froaths, erects his bristled Hide,
And shakes a Grove of Lances from his Side:
Not otherwise the Troops, with Hate inspir'd,   1010
And just Revenge, against the Tyrant fir'd;
Their Darts with Clamour at a distance drive:
And only keep the languish'd War alive.

From *Coritus* came *Acron* to the Fight,
Who left his Spouse betroath'd, and unconsummate Night.   1015
Mezentius sees him thro' the Squadrons ride,
Proud of the Purple Favours of his Bride.
Then, as a hungry Lyon, who beholds
A Gamesom Goat, who frisks about the Folds;
Or beamy stag that grazes on the Plain: 1020
He runs, he roars, he shakes his rising Mane;
He grins, and opens wide his greedy Jaws,
The Prey lyes panting underneath his Paws:
He fills his famish'd Maw, his Mouth runs o're
With unchew'd Morsels, while he churns the Gore: 1025
So proud *Mezentius* rushes on his Foes,
And first unhappy *Acron* overthrows:
Stretch'd at his length, he spurns the swarthy Ground,
The Lance besmear'd with Blood, lies broken in the wound.

Then with Disdain the haughty Victor view'd   1030

1007 Wound:] Wound. *97 98*

Orodes flying, nor the Wretch pursu'd:
Nor thought the Dastard's Back deserv'd a Wound,
But running gain'd th' Advantage of the Ground.
Then turning short, he met him Face to Face,
To give his Victory the better grace.   1035
Orodes falls, in equal Fight oppress'd:
Mezentius fix'd his Foot upon his Breast,
And rested Lance: And thus aloud he cries,
Lo here the Champion of my Rebels lies.
The Fields around with *Io Pæan* ring,   1040
And peals of Shouts applaud the conqu'ring King.
At this the vanquish'd, with his dying Breath,
Thus faintly spoke, and prophesy'd in Death:
Nor thou, proud Man, unpunish'd shalt remain;
Like Death attends thee on this fatal Plain.   1045
Then, sourly smiling, thus the King reply'd,
For what belongs to me let *Jove* provide:
But dye thou first, whatever Chance ensue:
He said, and from the Wound the Weapon drew:
A hov'ring Mist came swimming o're his sight,   1050
And seal'd his Eyes in everlasting Night.
    By *Cædicus*, *Alcathous* was slain,
Sacrator laid *Hydaspes* on the Plain:
Orses the strong to greater Strength must yield;
He, with *Parthenius*, were by *Rapo* kill'd.   1055
Then brave *Messapus Ericetes* slew,
Who from *Lycaon*'s Blood his Lineage drew.
But from his headstrong Horse his Fate he found,
Who threw his Master as he made a bound,
The Chief alighting, stuck him to the Ground.   1060
Then *Clonius* hand to hand, on Foot assails,
The *Trojan* sinks, and *Neptune*'s Son prevails.
    Agis the *Lycian* stepping forth with Pride,
To single Fight the boldest Foe defy'd.
Whom *Tuscan Valerus* by Force o'recame,   1065
And not bely'd his mighty Father's Fame.
Salius to Death the great *Antronius* sent,
But the same Fate the Victor underwent:
Slain by *Nealces* Hand, well skill'd to throw
The flying Dart, and draw the far-deceiving Bow.   1070

Thus equal Deaths are dealt with equal Chance;
By turns they quit their Ground, by turns advance:
Victors, and vanquish'd, in the various Field,
Nor wholly overcome, nor wholly yield.
The Gods from Heav'n survey the fatal Strife,   1075
And mourn the Miseries of Human Life.
Above the rest two Goddesses appear
Concern'd for each: Here *Venus*, *Juno* there:
Amidst the Crowd Infernal *Atè* shakes
Her Scourge aloft, and Crest of hissing Snakes.   1080

Once more the proud *Mezentius*, with Disdain,
Brandish'd his Spear, and rush'd into the Plain:
Where tow'ring in the midmost Ranks he stood,
Like tall *Orion* stalking o're the Flood:
When with his brawny Breast he cuts the Waves,   1085
His Shoulders scarce the topmost Billow laves.
Or like a Mountain Ash, whose Roots are spread,
Deep fix'd in Earth; in Clouds he hides his Head.

The *Trojan* Prince beheld him from afar,
And dauntless undertook the doubtful War.   1090
Collected in his Strength, and like a Rock,
Poiz'd on his Base, *Mezentius* stood the Shock.
He stood, and measuring first with careful Eyes,
The space his Spear cou'd reach, aloud he cries:
My strong right Hand, and Sword, assist my Stroke,   1095
(Those only Gods *Mezentius* will invoke)
His Armour from the *Trojan* Pyrate torn,
By my triumphant *Lausus* shall be worn.
He said, and with his utmost force he threw
The massy Spear, which, hissing as it flew,   1100
Reach'd the Cœlestial Shield that stop'd the course;
But glancing thence, the yet unbroken Force
Took a new bent obliquely, and betwixt
The Side and Bowels fam'd *Anthores* fix'd.

1071–1313 *See Commentary*   1071 with] and *S*   1075 fatal] doubtful *S*   1080
Crest of hissing] hissing Crest of *S*   1081 the proud *Mezentius*, with] *Mezentius*,
with a proud *S*   1084 tall] vast *S*   1088 Earth; *S*: Earth, 97 98   1088
In S there follows Thus arm'd, he took the field:—   1090 And . . . War.] With
joyful eyes, and undertook the war. *S*   1091 his Strength] himself *S*   1092
Shock.] shock *S*   1093 He . . . Eyes,] Of his great Foe: then measuring with
his eyes *S*   1098 By . . . worn.] Shall by my *Lausus* be in triumph worn. *S*
1099 with his utmost] straight with all his *S*   1101 Shield] Shield; *S*

Anthores had from *Argos* travell'd far,   1105
Alcides Friend, and Brother of the War:
'Till tir'd with Toils, fair *Italy* he chose,
And in *Evander*'s Palace sought Repose:
Now falling by another's Wound, his Eyes
He casts to Heav'n, on *Argos* thinks, and dyes.   1110
    The pious *Trojan* then his Jav'lin sent,
The Shield gave way: Thro' treble Plates it went
Of solid Brass, of Linnen trebly rowl'd,
And three Bull-hides which round the Buckler fold.
All these it pass'd, resistless in the Course,   1115
Transpierc'd his Thigh, and spent its dying Force.
The gaping Wound gush'd out a Crimson Flood;
The *Trojan*, glad with sight of hostile Blood,
His Fauchion drew, to closer Fight address'd,
And with new Force his fainting Foe oppress'd.   1120
    His Father's Peril *Lausus* view'd with Grief,
He sigh'd, he wept, he ran to his Relief.
And here, Heroick Youth, 'tis here I must
To thy immortal Memory be just;
And sing an Act so noble and so new,   1125
Posterity will scarce believe 'tis true.
Pain'd with his Wound, and useless for the Fight,
The Father sought to save himself by Flight:
Incumber'd, slow he drag'd the Spear along,
Which pierc'd his thigh, and in his Buckler hung.   1130
The pious Youth, resolv'd on Death, below
The lifted Sword, springs forth to face the Foe;
Protects his Parent, and prevents the Blow.
Shouts of Applause ran ringing thro' the Field,
To see the Son the vanquish'd Father shield: 1135
All fir'd with gen'rous Indignation strive;
And with a storm of Darts, to distance drive
The *Trojan* Chief; who held at Bay from far,
On his *Vulcanian* Orb sustain'd the War.
    As when thick Hail comes ratling in the Wind,   1140
The Plowman, Passenger, and lab'ring Hind,

1114 fold *S*: rowl'd *97 98*   1115 resistless in the] with unresisted *S*   1121
Peril] danger *S*   1123 Heroick] O wond'rous *S*   1126 will] shall S   'tis] it *S*
1131 on Death, below] to undergo *S*   1132 forth] out *S*   the] his *S*   1133
Parent] Father *S*   1136 gen'rous Indignation] Noble Emulation *S*

For shelter to the neighb'ring Covert fly;
Or hous'd, or safe in hollow Caverns lye:
But that o'reblown, when Heav'n above 'em smiles,
Return to Travel, and renew their Toils: 1145
Æneas thus o'rewhelm'd on ev'ry side,
The storm of Darts, undaunted, did abide;
And thus to *Lausus* loud with friendly threat'ning cry'd.
Why wilt thou rush to certain Death, and Rage
In rash Attempts, beyond thy tender Age: 1150
Betray'd by pious Love? Nor thus forborn
The Youth desists, but with insulting Scorn
Provokes the ling'ring Prince: Whose Patience tyr'd,
Gave Place, and all his Breast with Fury fir'd.
For now the Fates prepar'd their sharpen'd Sheers;   1155
And lifted high the flaming Sword appears:
Which full descending, with a frightful sway,
Thro Shield and Corslet forc'd th' impetuous Way,
And bury'd deep in his fair Bosom lay.
The purple Streams thro' the thin Armour strove,   1160
And drench'd th' imbroider'd Coat his Mother wove:
And Life at length forsook his heaving Heart,
Loath from so sweet a Mansion to depart.

But when, with Blood, and Paleness all o'respread,
The pious Prince beheld young *Lausus* dead;   1165
He griev'd, he wept, the sight an Image brought
Of his own filial Love; a sadly pleasing Thought.
Then stretch'd his Hand to hold him up, and said,
Poor hapless Youth! what Praises can be paid
To Love so great, to such transcendent Store   1170
Of early Worth, and sure Presage of more?
Accept what e're *Æneas* can afford,
Untouch'd thy Arms, untaken be thy Sword:
And all that pleas'd thee living still remain
Inviolate, and sacred to the slain.   1175

1146 o'rewhelm'd] o'rewhelm'd; *S*   1149 Death, and Rage] death? and rage *S*
1152 Scorn] scorn: *S*   1155 sharpen'd *98*: cruel *S 97*   1156 flaming] con-
quering *S*   1157 frightful] fearful *S*   1158 Corslet] Cuirasse *S*   1160
purple] springing *S*   1161 th' imbroider'd] the golden *S*   his Mother] his
careful Mother *S*   1164 o'respread] bespread *S*   1168 hold] raise *S*

Thy Body on thy Parents I bestow,
To rest thy Soul, at least if Shadows know,
Or have a sense of human Things below.
There to thy fellow Ghosts with Glory tell,
'Twas by the great *Æneas* hand I fell.   1180
With this his distant Friends he beckons near,
Provokes their Duty, and prevents their Fear:
Himself assists to lift him from the Ground,
With clotted Locks, and Blood that well'd from out the Wound.

   Mean time his Father, now no Father, stood,   1185
And wash'd his Wounds by *Tyber*'s yellow Flood:
Oppress'd with Anguish, panting, and o'respent,
His fainting Limbs against an Oak he leant.
A Bough his Brazen Helmet did sustain,
His heavier Arms lay scatter'd on the Plain.   1190
A chosen Train of Youth around him stand,
His drooping Head was rested on his hand:
His grisly Beard his pensive Bosom sought,
And all on *Lausus* ran his restless thought.

Careful, concern'd his Danger to prevent,   1195
He much enquir'd, and many a Message sent
To warn him from the Field: Alas! in vain,
Behold his mournful Followers bear him slain:
O're his broad Shield still gush'd the yawning Wound,
And drew a bloody Trail along the Ground.   1200

   Far off he heard their Cries, far off divin'd
The dire Event, with a foreboding Mind.
With Dust he sprinkled first his hoary Head,
Then both his lifted hands to Heav'n he spread;
Last, the dear Corps embracing, thus he said.   1205
What Joys, alas! cou'd this frail Being give,
That I have been so covetous to live?
To see my Son, and such a Son, resign
His Life a Ransom for preserving mine?
And am I then preserv'd, and art thou lost?   1210

1177 rest thy Soul,] please thy Ghost; *S*   1178 sense] tast *S*   1181 his
distant Friends he beckons] he bids his distant Friends draw *S*   1183 lift]
raise *S*   1184 With clotted Locks, and] His Locks deform'd with *S*   the] his *S*
1185 his] the *S*   1188 an Oak] a tree *S*   1191 A chosen Train of Youth]
Of Youth a chosen Troop *S*   1192 His drooping Head was] His head hung
down, and *S*   1196 He much] Much he *S*   1198 slain:] slain *S*   1199
O're his broad Shield] On their broad shields; *S*   yawning] gaping *S*

How much too dear has that Redemption cost!
'Tis now my bitter Banishment I feel;
This is a Wound too deep for time to heal.
My Guilt thy growing Virtues did defame;
My Blackness blotted thy unblemish'd Name.   121:
Chas'd from a Throne, abandon'd, and exil'd
For foul Misdeeds, were Punishments too mild:
I ow'd my People these, and from their hate,
With less Resentment cou'd have born my Fate.
And yet I live, and yet sustain the sight   122(
Of hated Men, and of more hated Light:
But will not long. With that he rais'd from Ground
His fainting Limbs, that stagger'd with his Wound.
Yet with a Mind resolv'd, and unappal'd
With Pains or Perils, for his Courser call'd: 122:

Well mouth'd, well manag'd, whom himself did dress,
With daily Care, and mounted with Success;
His Aid in Arms, his Ornament in Peace.

   Soothing his Courage with a gentle Stroke,
The Steed seem'd sensible, while thus he spoke.   123(
O *Rhæbus* we have liv'd too long for me,
(If Life and Long were Terms that cou'd agree)
This Day thou either shalt bring back the Head,
And bloody Trophees of the *Trojan* dead:
This Day thou either shalt revenge my Woe   123:
For murther'd *Lausus*, on his cruel Foe;
Or if inexorable Fate deny
Our Conquest, with thy conquer'd Master dye:
For after such a Lord, I rest secure,
Thou wilt no foreign Reins, or *Trojan* Load endure.   124(
He said: And straight th' officious Courser kneels
To take his wonted Weight. His Hands he fills
With pointed Jav'lins: On his Head he lac'd
His glitt'ring Helm, which terribly was grac'd
With waving Horse-hair, nodding from afar;   124:
Then spurr'd his thund'ring Steed amidst the War.
Love, Anguish, Wrath, and Grief, to Madness wrought,

1219 Resentment] injustice *S*   1220 sustain] support *S*   1221 hated Men]
hateful Men *S*   1230 Steed] Horse *S*   1232 Life and Long *98*: long and
Life *S*: Life and long *97*   1245 waving] crested *S*

Despair, and secret Shame, and conscious thought
Of inborn Worth, his lab'ring Soul oppress'd,
Rowl'd in his Eyes, and rag'd within his Breast.   1250
Then loud he call'd *Æneas* thrice by Name,
The loud repeated Voice to glad *Æneas* came.
Great *Jove*, he said, and the far-shooting God,
Inspire thy Mind to make thy Challenge good.
He spoke no more, but hasten'd, void of Fear,   1255
And threaten'd with his long protended Spear.

    To whom *Mezentius* thus. Thy Vaunts are vain,
My *Lausus* lies extended on the Plain:
He's lost! thy Conquest is already won,
The wretched Sire is murther'd in the Son.   1260
Nor Fate I fear, but all the Gods defy,
Forbear thy Threats, my Bus'ness is to dye;
But first receive this parting Legacy.
He said: And straight a whirling Dart he sent:
Another after, and another went.   1265
Round in a spacious Ring he rides the Field,
And vainly plies th' impenetrable Shield:
Thrice rode he round, and thrice *Æneas* wheel'd.
Turn'd as he turn'd; the Golden Orb withstood
The Strokes, and bore about an Iron Wood.   1270
Impatient of Delay, and weary grown,
Still to defend, and to defend alone:
To wrench the Darts which in his Buckler light,
Urg'd, and o're-labour'd in unequal Fight:
At length resolv'd, he throws with all his Force,   1275
Full at the Temples of the Warrior Horse.
Just where the Stroke was aim'd, th' unerring Spear
Made way, and stood transfix'd thro' either Ear.
Seiz'd with unwonted Pain, surpriz'd with Fright,
The wounded Steed curvets; and, rais'd upright,   1280

1253 he said] said he *S*   1255 spoke] said *S*   void of Fear] to appear *S*
1260 The . . . Son.] This was my only way to be undone. *S*   1275 length] last *S*
1276 Warrior] warlike *S*   1277 Just where the Stroke was aim'd,] Betwixt
the Temples pass'd *S*   1278 Made way, and] And piercing *S*   thro' either] from
ear to *S*   1279 unwonted] the suddain *S*   1280–6 The . . . overlaid.] *S has*

    The Courser bounds aloft and stands upright:
    He beats his Hoofs a while in aire; then prest
    With anguish, Floundering falls the gen'rous beast
    And his cast rider, with his weight opprest.

Lights on his Feet before: His Hoofs behind
Spring up in Air aloft, and lash the Wind.
Down comes the Rider headlong from his height,
His Horse came after with unweildy weight:
And flound'ring forward, pitching on his Head,   1285
His Lord's incumber'd Shoulder overlaid.
   From either Hoast the mingl'd Shouts, and Cries,
Of *Trojans* and *Rutulians* rend the Skies.
Æneas hast'ning, wav'd his fatal Sword
High o're his head, with this reproachful Word.   1290
Now, where are now thy Vaunts, the fierce Disdain
Of proud *Mezentius*, and the lofty Strain?
   Strugling, and wildly staring on the Skies,
With scarce recover'd Sight, he thus replies.
Why these insulting Words, this waste of Breath,   1295
To Souls undaunted, and secure of Death?
'Tis no Dishonour for the Brave to dye,
Nor came I here with hope of Victory:
Nor ask I Life, nor fought with that design,
As I had us'd my Fortune, use thou thine.   1300
My dying Son contracted no such Band;
The Gift is hateful from his Murd'rer's hand.
For this, this only Favour let me sue,
(If Pity can to conquer'd Foes be due)
Refuse it not: But let my Body have,   1305
The last Retreat of Human Kind, a Grave.
Too well I know th' insulting People's Hate;
Protect me from their Vengeance after Fate:
This Refuge for my poor Remains provide,
And lay my much lov'd *Lausus* by my side: 1310
He said, and to the Sword his Throat apply'd.
The Crimson Stream distain'd his Arms around,
And the disdainful Soul came rushing thro' the Wound.

1294 Sight] breath *S*   1295 Words] threats *S*   1299–1300 Nor . . . thine.]
S has

     But, with a glorious Fate, to end my pain;
     When *Lausus* fell, I was already slain:
     Nor ask I life,

See Commentary   1302 The Gift is hateful] Nor wou'd I take it *S*   1304 can
to conquer'd Foes] to a conquer'd foe *S*   1305 it not] not that *S*   1307
th' insulting] my injur'd *S*   1311 the Sword his Throat *97 (errata) S:* his
Throat the Sword *97 (text)*

THE ELEVENTH BOOK OF THE ÆNEIS

THE ARGUMENT

Æneas erects a Trophy of the Spoils of Mezentius*; grants a Truce for burying
the dead; and sends home the Body of* Pallas *with great Solemnity.* Latinus
calls a Council to propose offers of Peace to Æneas*, which occasions great
Animosity betwixt* Turnus *and* Drances*: In the mean time there is a sharp
Engagement of the Horse; wherein* Camilla *signalizes her self; is kill'd: And* 5
the Latine *Troops are entirely defeated.*

SCARCE had the rosie Morning rais'd her Head
  Above the Waves, and left her wat'ry Bed;
The Pious Chief, whom double Cares attend
For his unbury'd Souldiers, and his Friend,
Yet first to Heav'n perform'd a Victor's Vows;   5
He bar'd an ancient Oak of all her Boughs:
Then on a rising Ground the Trunk he plac'd;
Which with the Spoils of his dead Foe he grac'd.
The Coat of Arms by proud *Mezentius* worn,
Now on a naked Snag in Triumph born,   10
Was hung on high; and glitter'd from afar:
A Trophy sacred to the God of War.
Above his Arms, fix'd on the leafless Wood,
Appear'd his Plumy Crest, besmeard with Blood;
His brazen Buckler on the left was seen;   15
Trunchions of shiver'd Lances hung between:
And on the right was plac'd his Corslet, bor'd;
And to the Neck was ty'd his unavailing Sword.
A Crowd of Chiefs inclose the Godlike Man:
Who thus, conspicuous in the midst, began.   20
    Our Toils, my Friends, are crown'd with sure Success:
The greater Part perform'd, atchieve the less.
Now follow chearful to the trembling Town;
Press but an Entrance, and presume it won.
Fear is no more: For fierce *Mezentius* lies,   25
As the first Fruits of War, a Sacrifice.
Turnus shall fall extended on the Plain;
And in this Omen is already slain.

The Eleventh Book. 4 Friend,] Friend: *97 98*   14 besmeard with *98:* distilling *97*
917.19 III   A a

Prepar'd in Arms pursue your happy Chance;
That none unwarn'd may plead his Ignorance: 30
And I, at Heav'n's appointed Hour, may find
Your warlike Ensigns waving in the Wind.
Mean time the Rites and Fun'ral Pomps prepare,
Due to your dead Companions of the War:
The last Respect the living can bestow,   35
To shield their Shadows from Contempt below.
That conquer'd Earth be theirs for which they fought;
And which for us with their own blood they bought.
But first the Corps of our unhappy Friend,
To the sad City of *Evander* send: 40
Who not inglorious in his Ages bloom
Was hurry'd hence by too severe a Doom.
    Thus, weeping while he spoke, he took his Way,
Where, new in Death, lamented *Pallas* lay:
Acœtes watch'd the Corps; whose Youth deserv'd   45
The Father's Trust, and now the Son he serv'd
With equal Faith, but less auspicious Care:
Th' Attendants of the slain, his Sorrow share.
A Troop of *Trojans* mix'd with these appear,
And mourning Matrons with dishevell'd Hair.   50
Soon as the Prince appears, they raise a Cry;
All beat their Breasts, and Echoes rend the Sky.
They rear his drooping Forehead from the Ground;
But when *Æneas* view'd the grisly Wound
Which *Pallas* in his Manly Bosom bore,   55
And the fair Flesh distain'd with Purple Gore:
First, melting into Tears, the pious Man
Deplor'd so sad a sight, then thus began.
    Unhappy Youth! When Fortune gave the rest
Of my full Wishes, she refus'd the best!   60
She came; but brought not thee along; to bless
My longing Eyes, and share in my Success:
She grudg'd thy safe Return the Triumphs due
To prosp'rous Valour, in the publick View.
Not thus I promis'd, when thy Father lent   65
Thy needless Succour with a sad Consent;
Embrac'd me parting for th' *Etrurian* Land,

66 needless *98*: needful *97*

And sent me to possess a large Command.
He warn'd, and from his own Experience told,
Our Foes were warlike, disciplin'd, and bold: 70
And now perhaps, in hopes of thy return,
Rich Odours on his loaded Altars burn;
While we, with vain officious Pomp, prepare
To send him back his Portion of the War;
A bloody breathless Body: which can owe   75
No farther Debt, but to the Pow'rs below.
The wretched Father, e're his Race is run,
Shall view the Fun'ral Honours of his Son.
These are my Triumphs of the *Latian* War;
Fruits of my plighted Faith, and boasted Care.   80
And yet, unhappy Sire, thou shalt not see
A Son, whose Death disgrac'd his Ancestry:
Thou shalt not blush, old Man, however griev'd:
Thy *Pallas* no dishonest Wound receiv'd.
He dy'd no Death to make thee wish, too late,   85
Thou hadst not liv'd to see his shameful Fate:
But what a Champion has th' *Ausonian* Coast,
And what a Friend hast thou, *Ascanius,* lost!
   Thus having mourn'd, he gave the Word around,
To raise the breathless Body from the Ground;   90
And chose a thousand Horse, the flow'r of all
His warlike Troops, to wait the Funeral:
To bear him back, and share *Evander*'s Grief;
(A well becoming, but a weak Relief.)
Of Oaken Twigs they twist an easie Bier;   95
Then on their Shoulders the sad Burden rear.
The Body on this Rural Herse is born,
Strewd Leaves and Funeral Greens the Bier adorn.
All pale he lies, and looks a lovely Flow'r,
New cropt by Virgin Hands, to dress the Bow'r;   100
Unfaded yet, but yet unfed below,
No more to Mother Earth or the green Stem shall owe.
Then two fair Vests, of wond'rous Work and Cost,
Of Purple woven, and with Gold emboss'd,
For Ornament the *Trojan* Heroe brought,   105
Which with her Hands *Sidonian Dido* wrought.

              90 breathless *98*: lifeless *97*

One Vest array'd the Corps, and one they spread
O're his clos'd Eyes, and wrap'd around his Head:
That when the yellow Hair in Flame shou'd fall,
The catching Fire might burn the Golden Caul.   110
Besides, the Spoils of Foes in Battel slain,
When he descended on the *Latian* Plain:
Arms, Trappings, Horses, by the Herse are led
In long Array, (th' Atchievments of the Dead.)
Then, pinion'd with their hands behind, appear   115
Th' unhappy Captives, marching in the Rear:
Appointed Off'rings in the Victor's Name,
To sprinkle with their Blood, the Fun'ral Flame.
Inferior Trophees by the Chiefs are born;
Gantlets and Helms, their loaded hands adorn: 120
And fair Inscriptions fix'd, and Titles read,
Of *Latian* Leaders conquer'd by the Dead.
　　Acœtes on his Pupil's Corps attends,
With feeble Steps; supported by his Friends:
Pausing at ev'ry Pace; in Sorrow drown'd,   125
Betwixt their Arms he sinks upon the Ground.
Where grov'ling, while he lies in deep Despair,
He beats his Breast, and rends his hoary Hair.
The Champion's Chariot next is seen to rowl,
Besmear'd with hostile blood, and honourably foul.   130
To close the Pomp, *Æthon*, the Steed of State,
Is led, the Fun'rals of his Lord to wait.
Stripp'd of his Trappings, with a sullen Pace
He walks, and the big Tears run rolling down his Face.
The Lance of *Pallas*, and the Crimson Crest,   135
Are born behind; the Victor seiz'd the rest.
The March begins: The Trumpets hoarsly sound,
The Pikes and Lances trail along the Ground.
Thus while the *Trojan* and *Arcadian* Horse,
To *Pallantean* Tow'rs direct their Course,   140
In long Procession rank'd; the pious Chief
Stop'd in the Rear, and gave a vent to Grief.
The publick Care, he said, which War attends
Diverts our present Woes, at least suspends:
Peace with the *Manes* of great *Pallas* dwell;   145

120 loaded *97 (errata)*: heads and *97 (text)*

Hail holy Relicks, and a last farewel!
He said no more, but inly though he mourn'd,
Restrain'd his Tears, and to the Camp return'd.
    Now Suppliants, from *Laurentum* sent, demand
A Truce, with Olive Branches in their hand. 150
Obtest his Clemency, and from the Plain
Beg leave to draw the Bodies of their slain.
They plead, that none those common Rites deny
To conquer'd Foes, that in fair Battel dye.
All cause of Hate was ended in their Death; 155
Nor cou'd he War with Bodies void of Breath.
A King, they hop'd, wou'd hear a King's Request:
Whose Son he once was call'd, and once his Guest.
    Their Suit, which was too just to be deny'd,
The Heroe grants, and farther thus reply'd: 160
O *Latian* Princes, how severe a Fate
In causeless Quarrels has involv'd your State!
And arm'd against an unoffending Man,
Who sought your Friendship e're the War began!
You beg a Truce, which I wou'd gladly give, 165
Not only for the slain, but those who live.
I came not hether but by Heav'n's Command,
And sent by Fate to share the *Latian* Land.
Nor wage I Wars unjust; your King deny'd
My proffer'd Friendship, and my promis'd Bride. 170
Left me for *Turnus*; *Turnus* then should try
His Cause in Arms, to Conquer or to dye.
My Right and his are in dispute: The slain
Fell without fault, our Quarrel to maintain.
In equal Arms let us alone contend; 175
And let him vanquish, whom his Fates befriend.
This is the way, so tell him, to possess
The Royal Virgin, and restore the Peace.
Bear this my Message back; with ample leave
That your slain Friends may Fun'ral Rites receive. 180
    Thus having said, th' Embassadors amaz'd,
Stood mute a while, and on each other gaz'd:
Drances, their Chief, who harbour'd in his Breast
Long hate to *Turnus*, as his Foe profess'd,
Broke silence first, and to the Godlike Man, 185

With graceful action bowing, thus began.

   Auspicious Prince, in Arms a mighty Name,
But yet whose Actions far transcend your Fame;
Wou'd I your Justice or your Force express,
Thought can but equal; and all Words are less: 190
Your Answer we shall thankfully relate,
And Favours granted to the *Latian* State:
If wish'd Success our Labour shall attend,
Think Peace concluded, and the King your Friend:
Let *Turnus* leave the Realm to your Command;   195
And seek Alliance in some other Land:
Build you the City which your Fates assign;
We shall be proud in the great Work to join.

   Thus *Drances*; and his Words so well perswade
The rest impower'd, that soon a Truce is made.   200
Twelve days the term allow'd: And during those,
Latians and *Trojans*, now no longer Foes,
Mix'd in the Woods, for Fun'ral Piles prepare,
To fell the Timber, and forget the War.
Loud Axes thro' the groaning Groves resound: 205
Oak, Mountain Ash, and Poplar, spread the Ground:
Firrs fall from high: And some the Trunks receive,
In Loaden Wains, with Wedges some they cleave.

   And now the Fatal News, by Fame is blown
Thro' the short Circuit of th' *Arcadian* Town,   210
Of *Pallas* slain: By Fame, which just before
His Triumphs on distended Pinions bore.
Rushing from out the Gate, the People stand,
Each with a Fun'ral Flambeau in his hand:
Wildly they stare, distracted with amaze: 215
The Fields are lighten'd with a fiery blaze,
That cast a sullen Splendor on their Friends,
(The marching Troop which their dead Prince attends.)
Both Parties meet: They raise a doleful Cry:
The Matrons from the Walls with shrieks reply;   } 220
And their mix'd mourning rends the vaulted Sky.
The Town is fill'd with Tumult and with Tears;
Till the loud Clamours reach *Evander*'s Ears:
Forgetful of his State, he runs along,

209 *Editor's paragraph*

With a disorder'd pace, and cleaves the Throng: 225
Falls on the Corps, and groaning there he lies,
With silent Grief that speaks but at his Eyes:
Short Sighs and Sobs succeed; 'till Sorrow breaks
A Passage, and at once he weeps and speaks.

   O *Pallas*! thou hast fail'd thy plighted Word! 230
To fight with Caution, not to tempt the Sword:
I warn'd thee, but in vain; for well I knew
What Perils youthful Ardour wou'd pursue:
That boiling Blood wou'd carry thee too far;
Young as thou wert in Dangers, raw to War! 235
O curst Essay of Arms, disast'rous Doom,
Prelude of bloody Fields, and Fights to come!
Hard Elements of unauspicious War,
Vain Vows to Heav'n, and unavailing Care!
Thrice happy thou, dear Partner of my Bed, 240
Whose holy Soul the Stroke of Fortune fled:
Præscious of Ills, and leaving me behind,
To drink the Dregs of Life by Fate assign'd.
Beyond the Goal of Nature I have gon;
My *Pallas* late set out, but reach'd too soon. 245
If, for my League against th' *Ausonian* State,
Amidst their Weapons I had found my Fate,
(Deserv'd from them,) then I had been return'd
A breathless Victor, and my Son had mourn'd.
Yet will I not my *Trojan* Friend upbraid, 250
Nor grudge th' Alliance I so gladly made.
'Twas not his Fault my *Pallas* fell so young,
But my own Crime for having liv'd too long.
Yet, since the Gods had destin'd him to dye,
At least he led the way to Victory: 255
First for his Friends he won the fatal Shore,
And sent whole Herds of slaughter'd Foes before:
A Death too great, too glorious to deplore.
Nor will I add new Honours to thy Grave;
Content with those the *Trojan* Heroe gave. 260
That Funeral Pomp thy *Phrygian* Friends design'd;
In which the *Tuscan* Chiefs, and Army join'd:
Great Spoils, and Trophees gain'd by thee, they bear:
Then let thy own Atchievments be thy share.

Even thou, O *Turnus*, hadst a Trophy stood,   265
Whose mighty Trunk had better grac'd the Wood,
If *Pallas* had arriv'd, with equal length
Of Years, to match thy Bulk with equal Strength.
But why, unhappy Man, dost thou detain
These Troops, to view the Tears thou shedst in vain!   270
Go, Friends, this Message to your Lord relate;
Tell him, that if I bear my bitter Fate,
And after *Pallas* Death, live ling'ring on,
'Tis to behold his Vengeance for my Son.
I stay for *Turnus*; whose devoted Head   275
Is owing to the living and the dead:
My Son and I expect it from his Hand;
'Tis all that he can give, or we demand.
Joy is no more: But I would gladly go,
To greet my *Pallas* with such News below.   280
   The Morn had now dispell'd the Shades of Night;
Restoring Toils, when she restor'd the Light:
The *Trojan* King, and *Tuscan* Chief, command
To raise the Piles, along the winding Strand:
Their Friends convey the dead to Fun'ral Fires;   ⎫   285
Black smould'ring Smoke from the green Wood expires;   ⎬
The Light of Heav'n is choak'd, and the new Day retires. ⎭
Then thrice around the kindled Piles they go:
(For ancient Custom had ordain'd it so)
Thrice Horse and Foot about the Fires are led,   290
And thrice with loud Laments they hail the dead.
Tears trickling down their Breasts bedew the Ground;
And Drums and Trumpets mix their mournful Sound.
Amid the Blaze, their pious Brethren throw
The Spoils, in Battel taken from the Foe: 295
Helms, Bitts emboss'd, and Swords of shining Steel,
One casts a Target, one a Chariot Wheel:
Some to their Fellows their own Arms restore;
The Fauchions which in luckless Fight they bore:
Their Bucklers pierc'd, their Darts bestow'd in vain,   300
And shiver'd Lances gather'd from the Plain.
Whole Herds of offer'd Bulls about the Fire,
And bristled Boars, and wooly Sheep expire.
Around the Piles a careful Troop attends,

To watch the wasting Flames, and weep their burning Friends: 305
Ling'ring along the Shore, 'till dewy Night
New decks the Face of Heav'n with starry Light.
   The conquer'd *Latians*, with like Pious Care,
Piles without number for their Dead prepare;
Part, in the Places where they fell, are laid; 310
And part are to the neighb'ring Fields convey'd.
The Corps of Kings, and Captains of Renown,
Born off in State, are bury'd in the Town:
The rest, unhonour'd, and without a Name,
Are cast a common heap to feed the Flame. 315
Trojans and *Latians* vie with like desires: ⎫
To make the Field of Battel shine with Fires: ⎬
And the promiscuous Blaze to Heav'n aspires. ⎭
   Now had the Morning thrice renew'd the Light,
And thrice dispell'd the Shadows of the Night; 320
When those who round the wasted Fires remain,
Perform the last sad Office to the slain:
They rake the yet warm Ashes, from below;
These, and the Bones unburn'd, in Earth bestow:
These Relicks with their Country Rites they grace; 325
And raise a mount of Turf to mark the place.
   But in the Palace of the King, appears
A Scene more solemn, and a Pomp of Tears.
Maids, Matrons, Widows, mix their common Moans:
Orphans their Sires, and Sires lament their Sons. 330
All in that universal Sorrow share,
And curse the Cause of this unhappy War.
A broken League, a Bride unjustly sought,
A Crown usurp'd, which with their Blood is bought!
These are the Crimes, with which they load the Name 335
Of *Turnus*, and on him alone exclaim.
Let him, who lords it o're th' *Ausonian* Land,
Engage the *Trojan* Heroe hand to hand:
His is the Gain, our Lot is but to serve:
'Tis just, the sway he seeks, he shoud deserve. 340
This *Drances* aggravates; and adds, with spight,
His Foe expects, and dares him to the Fight.
Nor *Turnus* wants a Party to support

   305 Friends:] Friends. *97 98*   306 Night] Night, *97 98*

His Cause and Credit, in the *Latian* Court.
His former Acts secure his present Fame;   345
And the Queen shades him with her mighty Name.
   While thus their factious Minds with Fury burn;
The Legats from th' *Ætolian* Prince return:
Sad News they bring, that after all the Cost,
And Care employ'd, their Embassy is lost: 350
That *Diomede* refus'd his Aid in War;
Unmov'd with Presents, and as deaf to Pray'r.
Some new Alliance must elswhere be sought;
Or Peace with *Troy* on hard Conditions bought.
   Latinus, sunk in Sorrow, finds too late,   355
A Foreign Son is pointed out by Fate:
And till *Æneas* shall *Lavinia* wed,
The wrath of Heav'n is hov'ring o're his Head.
The Gods, he saw, espous'd the juster side,
When late their Titles in the Field were try'd: } 360
Witness the fresh Laments, and Fun'ral Tears undry'd.
   Thus, full of anxious Thought, he summons all
The *Latian* Senate to the Council Hall:
The Princes come, commanded by their Head,
And crowd the Paths that to the Palace lead.   365
Supream in Pow'r, and reverenc'd for his Years,
He takes the Throne, and in the midst appears:
Majestically sad, he sits in State,
And bids his Envoys their Success relate.
   When *Venulus* began, the murmuring Sound   370
Was hush'd, and sacred Silence reign'd around.
We have, said he, perform'd your high Command;
And pass'd with Peril a long Tract of Land:
We reach'd the Place desir'd, with Wonder fill'd,
The *Grecian* Tents, and rising Tow'rs beheld.   375
Great *Diomede* has compass'd round with Walls
The City, which *Argyripa* he calls;
From his own *Argos* nam'd: We touch'd, with Joy,
The Royal Hand that raz'd unhappy *Troy*.
When introduc'd, our Presents first we bring,   380
Then crave an instant Audience from the King:
His Leave obtain'd, our Native Soil we name;
And tell th' important Cause for which we came.

Attentively he heard us, while we spoke;
Then, with soft Accents, and a pleasing Look,   385
Made this return. *Ausonian* Race, of old
Renown'd for Peace, and for an Age of Gold,
What Madness has your alter'd Minds possess'd,
To change for War hereditary Rest?
Sollicite Arms unknown, and tempt the Sword,   390
(A needless Ill your Ancestors abhorr'd?)
We; (for my self I speak, and all the Name
Of *Grecians*, who to *Troy*'s Destruction came;)
Omitting those who were in Battel slain,
Or born by rowling *Simois* to the Main: 395
Not one but suffer'd, and too dearly bought
The Prize of Honour which in Arms he sought.
Some doom'd to Death, and some in Exile driv'n,
Out-casts, abandon'd by the Care of Heav'n:
So worn, so wretched, so despis'd a Crew,   400
As ev'n old *Priam* might with Pity view.
Witness the Vessels by *Minerva* toss'd
In Storms, the vengeful *Capharæan* Coast;
Th' *Eubæan* Rocks! The Prince, whose Brother led
Our Armies to revenge his injur'd Bed,   405
In *Egypt* lost; *Ulysses*, with his Men,
Have seen *Charybdis*, and the *Cyclops* Den:
Why shou'd I name *Idomeneus*, in vain
Restor'd to Scepters, and expell'd again?
Or young *Achilles* by his Rival slain?   410
Ev'n he, the King of Men, the foremost Name
Of all the *Greeks*, and most renown'd by Fame,
The proud Revenger of another's Wife,
Yet by his own Adult'ress lost his Life:
Fell at his Threshold, and the Spoils of *Troy*,   415
The foul Polluters of his Bed enjoy.
The Gods have envy'd me the sweets of Life,
My much lov'd Country, and my more lov'd Wife:
Banish'd from both, I mourn; while in the Sky
Transform'd to Birds, my lost Companions fly: 420
Hov'ring about the Coasts they make their Moan;
And cuff the Cliffs with Pinions not their own.
What squalid Spectres, in the dead of Night,

Break my short Sleep, and skim before my sight!
I might have promis'd to my self those Harms,   425
Mad as I was, when I with Mortal Arms
Presum'd against Immortal Pow'rs to move;
And violate with Wounds the Queen of Love.
Such Arms, this Hand shall never more employ;
No Hate remains with me to ruin'd *Troy*.   430
I war not with its Dust; nor am I glad
To think of past Events, or good or bad.
Your Presents I return: What e're you bring
To buy my Friendship, send the *Trojan* King.
We met in fight, I know him to my Cost;   435
With what a whirling force his Lance he toss'd:
Heav'ns what a spring was in his Arm, to throw:
How high he held his Shield, and rose at ev'ry blow!
Had *Troy* produc'd two more, his Match in Might,
They would have chang'd the Fortune of the Fight: 440
Th' Invasion of the *Greeks* had been return'd:
Our Empire wasted, and our Cities burn'd.
The long Defence the *Trojan* People made,
The War protracted, and the Siege delay'd,
Were due to *Hector*'s and this Heroe's hand: 445
Both brave alike, and equal in Command;
Æneas, not inferior in the Field,
In pious reverence to the Gods, excell'd.
Make peace, ye *Latians*, and avoid with Care
Th' impending Dangers of a fatal War.   450
He said no more; but with this cold Excuse,
Refus'd th' Alliance, and advis'd a Truce.
   Thus *Venulus* concluded his Report.
A Jarring Murmur fill'd the factious Court:
As when a Torrent rowls with rapid force,   455
And dashes o're the Stones that stop the Course;
The Flood, constrain'd within a scanty space,
Roars horrible along th' uneasie race:
White foam in gath'ring Eddies floats around:
The rocky Shores rebellow to the sound.   460
   The Murmur ceas'd: Then from his lofty Throne
The King invok'd the Gods, and thus begun.
I wish, ye *Latins*, what we now debate

Had been resolv'd before it was too late:
Much better had it been for you and me,   465
Unforc'd by this our last Necessity,
To have been earlier wise; than now to call
A Council, when the Foe surrounds the Wall.
O Citizens! we wage unequal War,
With men, not only Heav'n's peculiar Care,   470
But Heav'n's own Race: Unconquer'd in the Field,
Or Conquer'd, yet unknowing how to yield.
What Hopes you had in *Diomede*, lay down:
Our Hopes must center on our selves alone.
Yet those how feeble, and, indeed, how vain,   475
You see too well; nor need my Words explain.
Vanquish'd without ressource; laid flat by Fate,
Factions within, a Foe without the Gate;
Not but I grant, that all perform'd their parts,
With manly Force, and with undaunted Hearts: 480
With our united Strength the War we wag'd;
With equal Numbers, equal Arms engag'd:
You see th' Event—Now hear what I propose,
To save our Friends, and satisfie our Foes:
A Tract of Land the *Latins* have possess'd   485
Along the *Tyber*, stretching to the West,
Which now *Rutulians* and *Auruncans* till:
And their mix'd Cattle graze the fruitful Hill;
Those Mountains fill'd with Firs, that lower Land,
If you consent, the *Trojan* shall Command.   490
Call'd into part of what is ours; and there,
On terms agreed, the common Country share.
There let 'em build, and settle if they please;
Unless they chuse once more to cross the Seas,
In search of Seats remote from *Italy*;   495
And from unwelcome Inmates set us free.
Then twice ten Gallies let us build with Speed,
Or twice as many more, if more they need;
Materials are at hand: A well-grown Wood
Runs equal with the Margin of the Flood: 500
Let them the Number, and the Form assign;
The Care and Cost of all the Stores be mine.
To treat the Peace, a hundred Senators

Shall be commission'd hence with ample Pow'rs;
With Olive crown'd: The Presents they shall bear,　　505
A Purple Robe, a Royal Iv'ry Chair;
And all the marks of Sway that *Latian* Monarchs wear;
And Sums of Gold. Among your selves debate
This great Affair, and save the sinking State.

　　Then *Drances* took the word; who grudg'd, long since,　510
The rising Glories of the *Daunian* Prince.
Factious and rich, bold at the Council Board,
But cautious in the Field, he shun'd the Sword;
A closs Caballer, and Tongue-valiant Lord.
Noble his Mother was, and near the Throne,　　515
But what his Father's Parentage, unknown.
He rose, and took th' Advantage of the Times,
To load young *Turnus* with invidious Crimes.

　　Such Truths, O King, said he, your Words contain,
As strike the Sence, and all Replies are vain.　　520
Nor are your Loyal Subjects now to seek
What common Needs require; but fear to speak.
Let him give leave of Speech, that haughty Man,
Whose Pride this unauspicious War began:
For whose Ambition (let me dare to say,　　525
Fear set apart, tho' Death is in my Way)
The Plains of *Latium* run with Blood arround;
So many Valiant Heroes bite the Ground:
Dejected Grief in ev'ry Face appears;
A Town in Mourning, and a Land in Tears.　　530
While he th' undoubted Author of our Harms,
The Man who menaces the Gods with Arms,
Yet, after all his Boasts, forsook the Fight,
And sought his safety in ignoble Flight.

　　Now, best of Kings, since you propose to send　535
Such bounteous Presents to your *Trojan* Friend;
Add yet a greater at our joint Request,
One which he values more than all the rest;
Give him the fair *Lavinia* for his Bride:
With that Alliance let the League be ty'd:　　540
And for the bleeding Land a lasting Peace provide.
Let Insolence no longer awe the Throne,
But with a Father's Right bestow your own.

For this Maligner of the general Good,
If still we fear his Force, he must be woo'd: 545
His haughty Godhead we with Pray'rs implore,
Your Scepter to release, and our just Rights restore.
O cursed Cause of all our Ills, must we
Wage Wars unjust, and fall in Fight for thee!
What right hast thou to rule the *Latian* State,   550
And send us out to meet our certain Fate?
'Tis a destructive War; from *Turnus* Hand
Our Peace and publick safety we demand.
Let the fair Bride to the brave Chief remain;
If not, the Peace without the Pledge is vain.   555
Turnus, I know you think me not your Friend,
Nor will I much with your Belief contend:
I beg your Greatness not to give the Law
In others Realms, but, beaten, to withdraw.
Pity your own, or pity our Estate;   560
Nor twist our Fortunes with your sinking Fate.
Your Interest is the War shou'd never cease;
But we have felt enough, to wish the Peace:
A Land exhausted to the last remains,
Depopulated Towns, and driven Plains.   565
Yet, if desire of Fame, and thirst of Pow'r,
A Beauteous Princess, with a Crown in Dow'r,
So fire your Mind, in Arms assert your Right;
And meet your Foe, who dares you to the Fight.
Mankind, it seems, is made for you alone;   570
We, but the Slaves who mount you to the Throne:
A base ignoble Crowd, without a Name,
Unwept, unworthy of the Fun'ral Flame:
By Duty bound to forfeit each his Life,
That *Turnus* may possess a Royal Wife.   575
Permit not, Mighty Man, so mean a Crew
Shou'd share such Triumphs; and detain from you
The Post of Honour, your undoubted Due:
Rather alone your matchless Force employ;
To merit, what alone you must enjoy.   580
    These Words, so full of Malice, mix'd with Art,
Inflam'd with Rage the youthful Hero's Heart.

559 others] other *98*   578 undoubted *98*: unquestion'd *97*

Then groaning from the bottom of his Breast,
He heav'd for Wind, and thus his Wrath express'd.
You, *Drances*, never want a Stream of Words,   585
Then, when the Publick Need requires our Swords.
First in the Council-hall to steer the State;
And ever foremost in a Tongue debate:
While our strong Walls secure us from the Foe,
E're yet with Blood our Ditches overflow: 590
But let the potent Orator declaim,
And with the brand of Coward blot my Name;
Free Leave is giv'n him, when his fatal Hand
Has cover'd with more Corps the sanguine Strand;
And high as mine his tow'ring Trophees stand.   595
If any Doubt remains who dares the most,
Let us decide it at the *Trojans* cost:
And issue both abrest, where Honour calls;
Foes are not far to seek without the Walls.
Unless his noisie Tongue can only fight;   600
And Feet were giv'n him but to speed his Flight.
I beaten from the Field? I forc'd away?
Who, but so known a Dastard, dares to say?
Had he but ev'n beheld the Fight, his Eyes
Had witness'd for me what his Tongue denies: 605
What heaps of *Trojans* by this Hand were slain,
And how the bloody *Tyber* swell'd the Main.
All saw, but he, th' *Arcadian* Troops retire,
In scatter'd Squadrons, and their Prince expire.
The Gyant Brothers, in their Camp, have found   610
I was not forc'd with ease to quit my Ground.
Not such the *Trojans* try'd me, when inclos'd,
I singly their united Arms oppos'd:
First forc'd an Entrance thro' their thick Array;
Then, glutted with their Slaughter, freed my Way.   615
'Tis a destructive War? So let it be,
But to the *Phrygian* Pirate, and to thee.
Mean time proceed to fill the People's Ears
With false Reports, their Minds with panick Fears:
Extol the Strength of a twice conquer'd Race,   620
Our Foes encourage, and our Friends debase.

588 in *98*: at *97*   debate:] debate. *97 98*

Believe thy Fables, and the *Trojan* Town
Triumphant stands, the *Grecians* are o'rethrown:
Suppliant at *Hector*'s Feet *Achilles* lyes;
And *Diomede* from fierce *Æneas* flies.   625
Say rapid *Aufidus* with awful Dread
Runs backward from the Sea, and hides his Head,
When the great *Trojan* on his Bank appears:
For that's as true as thy dissembl'd Fears
Of my Revenge: Dismiss that Vanity,   630
Thou, *Drances*, art below a Death from me.
Let that vile Soul in that vile Body rest;
The Lodging is well worthy of the Guest.

   Now, Royal Father, to the present state
Of our Affairs, and of this high Debate;   635
If in your Arms thus early you diffide,
And think your Fortune is already try'd;
If one Defeat has brought us down so low;
As never more in Fields to meet the Foe;
Then I conclude for Peace: 'Tis time to treat,   640
And lye like Vassals at the Victor's Feet.
But oh, if any ancient Blood remains,
One drop of all our Fathers in our Veins;
That Man would I prefer before the rest,
Who dar'd his Death with an undaunted Breast;   645
Who comely fell, by no dishonest Wound,
To shun that Sight; and dying gnaw'd the Ground.
But if we still have fresh Recruits in store,
If our Confederates can afford us more;
If the contended Field we bravely fought;   650
And not a bloodless Victory was bought:
Their Losses equall'd ours, and for their slain,
With equal Fires they fill'd the shining Plain;
Why thus unforc'd shou'd we so tamely yield;
And e're the Trumpet sounds, resign the Field?   655
Good unexpected, Evils unforeseen,
Appear by Turns, as Fortune shifts the Scene:
Some, rais'd aloft, come tumbling down amain;
Then fall so hard, they bound and rise again.
If *Diomede* refuse his Aid to lend,   660

The great *Messapus* yet remains our Friend:
Tolumnius, who foretels Events, is ours;
Th' *Italian* Chiefs, and Princes, joyn their Pow'rs:
Nor least in Number, nor in Name the last,
Your own brave Subjects have your Cause embrac'd.   665
Above the rest, the *Volscian Amazon*
Contains an Army in her self alone:
And heads a Squadron, terrible to sight,
With glitt'ring Shields, in Brazen Armour bright.
Yet if the Foe a single Fight demand,   670
And I alone the Publick Peace withstand;
If you consent, he shall not be refus'd,
Nor find a Hand to Victory unus'd.
This new *Achilles*, let him take the Field,
With fated Armour, and *Vulcanian* Shield;   675
For you, my Royal Father, and my Fame,
I, *Turnus*, not the least of all my Name,
Devote my Soul. He calls me hand to hand,
And I alone will answer his Demand.
Drances shall rest secure, and neither share   680
The Danger, nor divide the Prize of War.
    While they debate; nor these nor those will yield;
Æneas draws his Forces to the Field:
And moves his Camp. The Scouts, with flying Speed
Return, and thro' the frighted City spread   685
Th' unpleasing News, the *Trojans* are descry'd,
In Battel marching by the River side;
And bending to the Town. They take th' Allarm,
Some tremble, some are bold, all in Confusion arm.
Th' impetuous Youth press forward to the Field;   690
They clash the Sword, and clatter on the Shield:
The fearful Matrons raise a screaming Cry;
Old feeble Men with fainter Groans reply:
A jarring Sound results, and mingles in the Sky.
Like that of Swans remurm'ring to the Floods;   695
Or Birds of diff'ring kinds in hollow Woods.
Turnus th' occasion takes, and cries aloud,
Talk on, ye quaint Haranguers of the Crowd:
Declaim in praise of Peace, when Danger calls;
And the fierce Foes in Arms approach the Walls.   700

He said, and turning short, with speedy Pace,
Casts back a scornful Glance, and quits the Place.
   Thou, *Volusus*, the *Volscian* Troops command
To mount; and lead thy self our *Ardean* Band.
Messapus, and *Catillus*, post your Force   705
Along the Fields, to charge the *Trojan* Horse.
Some guard the Passes, others man the Wall;
Drawn up in Arms, the rest attend my Call.
   They swarm from ev'ry Quarter of the Town;
And with disorder'd haste the Rampires crown.   710
Good old *Latinus*, when he saw, too late,
The gath'ring Storm, just breaking on the State,
Dismiss'd the Council, 'till a fitter time.
And own'd his easie Temper as his Crime:
Who, forc'd against his reason, had comply'd   715
To break the Treaty for the promis'd Bride.
   Some help to sink new Trenches, others aid
To ram the Stones, or raise the Palisade.
Hoarse Trumpets sound th' Alarm: Around the Walls
Runs a distracted Crew, whom their last Labour calls. 720
A sad Procession in the Streets is seen,
Of Matrons that attend the Mother Queen:
High in her Chair she sits, and at her side,
With downcast Eyes appears the fatal Bride.
They mount the Cliff, where *Pallas* Temple stands; 725
Pray'rs in their Mouths, and Presents in their Hands:
With Censers, first they fume the sacred Shrine;
Then in this common Supplication joyn.
O Patroness of Arms, unspotted Maid,
Propitious hear, and lend thy *Latins* Aid: 730
Break short the Pirat's Lance; pronounce his Fate,
And lay the *Phrygian* low before the Gate.
   Now *Turnus* arms for Fight: His Back and Breast,
Well temper'd Steel, and scaly Brass invest:
The Cuishes, which his brawny Thighs infold,   735
Are mingled Metal damask'd o're with Gold.
His faithful Fauchion sits upon his side;
Nor Casque, nor Crest, his manly Features hide:
But bare to view, amid surrounding Friends,

     725 *Pallas*] *Pallas*'s *97 98*   733 *Editor's paragraph*

With Godlike Grace, he from the Tow'r descends.   740
Exulting in his Strength, he seems to dare
His absent Rival, and to promise War.

   Freed from his Keepers, thus with broken Reins,
The wanton Courser prances o're the Plains:
Or in the Pride of Youth o'releaps the Mounds;   745
And snuffs the Females in forbidden Grounds.
Or seeks his wat'ring in the well known Flood,
To quench his Thirst, and cool his fiery Blood:
He swims luxuriant, in the liquid Plain,
And o're his Shoulder flows his waving Mane: 750
He neighs, he snorts, he bears his Head on high;
Before his ample Chest the frothy Waters fly.

   Soon as the Prince appears without the Gate,
The *Volscians*, with their Virgin Leader, wait
His last Commands. Then with a graceful Meen,   755
Lights from her lofty Steed, the Warrior Queen:
Her Squadron imitates, and each descends;
Whose common Sute *Camilla* thus commends.

   If Sence of Honour, if a Soul secure
Of inborn Worth, that can all Tests endure,   760
Can promise ought; or on it self rely,
Greatly to dare, to conquer or to dye:
Then, I alone, sustain'd by these, will meet
The *Tyrrhene* Troops, and promise their Defeat.
Ours be the Danger, ours the sole Renown;   765
You, Gen'ral, stay behind, and guard the Town.

   Turnus a while stood mute, with glad Surprize,
And on the fierce Virago fix'd his Eyes:
Then thus return'd: O Grace of *Italy*,
With what becoming Thanks can I reply!   770
Not only Words lye lab'ring in my Breast;
But Thought it self is by thy Praise opprest.
Yet rob me not of all, but let me join
My Toils, my Hazard, and my Fame, with thine.
The *Trojan*, (not in Stratagem unskill'd,)   775
Sends his light Horse before to scour the Field:
Himself, thro' steep Ascents, and thorny Brakes,
A larger Compass to the City takes.

       776 Horse *98*: Foot *97*

This news my Scouts confirm: And I prepare
To foil his Cunning, and his Force to dare.   780
With chosen Foot his Passage to forelay;
And place an Ambush in the winding way.
Thou, with thy *Volscians*, face the *Tuscan* Horse:
The brave *Messapus* shall thy Troops inforce;
With those of *Tibur*; and the *Latian* Band: 785
Subjected all to thy Supream Command.
    This said, he warns *Messapus* to the War:
Then ev'ry Chief exhorts, with equal Care.
All thus encourag'd, his own Troops he joins,
And hastes to prosecute his deep Designs.   790
    Inclos'd with Hills, a winding Valley lies,
By Nature form'd for Fraud, and fitted for Surprize:
A narrow Track, by Human Steps untrode,
Leads, thro' perplexing Thorns, to this obscure abode.
High o're the Vale a steepy Mountain stands;   795
Whence the surveying Sight the neather Ground commands.
The top is level: an offensive Seat
Of War; and from the War a safe Retreat.
For, on the right, and left, is room to press
The Foes at hand, or from afar distress: 800
To drive 'em headlong downward; and to pour
On their descending backs, a stony show'r.
Thither young *Turnus* took the well known way;
Possess'd the Pass, and in blind Ambush lay.
    Mean time, *Latonian Phœbe* from the Skies,   805
Beheld th' approaching War with hateful Eies.
And call'd the light-foot *Opis*, to her aid,
Her most belov'd, and ever trusty Maid.
Then with a sigh began: *Camilla* goes
To meet her Death, amidst her Fatal Foes.   810
The Nymph I lov'd of all my Mortal Train;
Invested with *Diana*'s Arms, in vain.
Nor is my kindness for the Virgin, new,
'Twas born with Her, and with her Years it grew:
Her Father *Metabus*, when forc'd away   815
From old *Privernum*, for Tyrannick sway;
Snatch'd up, and sav'd from his prevailing Foes,
This tender Babe, Companion of his Woes.

Casmilla was her Mother; but he drown'd
One hissing Letter in a softer sound,   820
And call'd *Camilla*. Thro the Woods, he flies;
Wrap'd in his Robe the Royal Infant lies.
His Foes in sight, he mends his weary pace;
With shouts and clamours they pursue the Chace.
The Banks of *Amasene* at length he gains;   825
The raging Flood his farther flight restrains:
Rais'd o're the Borders with unusual Rains.
Prepar'd to Plunge into the Stream, He fears:
Not for himself, but for the Charge he bears.
Anxious he stops a while; and thinks in haste;   830
Then, desp'rate in Distress, resolves at last.
A knotty Lance of well-boil'd Oak he bore;
The middle part with Cork he cover'd o're:
He clos'd the Child within the hollow Space;
With Twigs of bending Osier bound the Case.   835
Then pois'd the Spear, heavy with Human Weight;
And thus invok'd my Favour for the Freight.
Accept, great Goddess of the Woods, he said,
Sent by her Sire, this dedicated Maid:
Thro' Air she flies a Suppliant to thy Shrine;   840
And the first Weapons that she knows, are thine.
He said; and with full Force the Spear he threw:
Above the sounding Waves *Camilla* flew.
Then, press'd by Foes, he stemm'd the stormy Tyde;
And gain'd, by stress of Arms, the farther Side.   845
His fasten'd Spear he pull'd from out the Ground;
And, Victor of his Vows, his Infant Nymph unbound.
Nor after that, in Towns which Walls inclose,
Wou'd trust his hunted Life amidst his Foes.
But rough, in open Air he chose to lye: 850
Earth was his Couch, his Cov'ring was the Sky.
On Hills unshorn, or in a desart Den,
He shunn'd the dire Society of Men.
A Shepherd's solitary Life he led:
His Daughter with the Milk of Mares he fed;   855
The Dugs of Bears, and ev'ry Salvage Beast,
He drew, and thro' her Lips the Liquor press'd.

819 drown'd] drown'd, *97 98*

The little *Amazon* cou'd scarcely go,
He loads her with a Quiver and a Bow:
And, that she might her stagg'ring Steps command,   860
He with a slender Jav'lin fills her Hand:
Her flowing Hair no golden Fillet bound;
Nor swept her trayling Robe the dusty Ground.
Instead of these, a Tyger's Hide o'respread
Her Back and Shoulders, fasten'd to her Head.   865
The flying Dart she first attempts to fling;
And round her tender Temples toss'd the Sling:
Then, as her Strength with Years increas'd, began
To pierce aloft in Air the soaring Swan:
And from the Clouds to fetch the Heron and the Crane. } 870
The *Tuscan* Matrons with each other vy'd,
To bless their Rival Sons with such a Bride:
But she disdains their Love; to share with me
The Silvan Shades, and vow'd Virginity.
And, oh! I wish, contented with my Cares   875
Of Salvage Spoils, she had not sought the Wars:
Then had she been of my Cœlestial Train;
And shun'd the Fate that dooms her to be slain.
But, since opposing Heav'n's Decree, she goes
To find her Death among forbidden Foes;   880
Haste with these Arms, and take thy steepy flight,
Where, with the Gods averse, the *Latins* fight:
This Bow to thee, this Quiver, I bequeath,
This chosen Arrow to revenge her Death.
By what e're Hand *Camilla* shall be slain,   885
Or of the *Trojan*, or *Italian* Train,
Let him not pass unpunish'd from the Plain.
Then, in a hollow Cloud, my self will Aid,
To bear the breathless Body of my Maid:
Unspoil'd shall be her Arms, and unprofan'd   890
Her holy Limbs with any Human Hand:
And in a Marble Tomb laid in her Native Land.
   She said: The faithful Nymph descends from high
With rapid flight, and cuts the sounding Sky;
Black Clouds and stormy Winds around her Body fly. } 895
   By this, the *Trojan* and the *Tuscan* Horse,
Drawn up in Squadrons, with united Force,

Approach the Walls; the sprightly Coursers bound;
Press forward on their Bitts, and shift their Ground:
Shields, Arms, and Spears, flash horribly from far;   900
And the Fields glitter with a waving War.
Oppos'd to these, come on with furious Force,
Messapus, *Coras*, and the *Latian* Horse;
These in the Body plac'd; on either hand
Sustain'd, and clos'd by fair *Camilla*'s Band.   905
Advancing in a Line, they couch their Spears;
And less and less the middle Space appears.
Thick Smoak obscures the Field: And scarce are seen
The neighing Coursers, and the shouting Men.
In distance of their Darts they stop their Course;   910
Then Man to Man they rush, and Horse to Horse.
The face of Heav'n their flying Jav'lins hide;
And Deaths unseen are dealt on either side.
Tyrrhenus, and *Aconteus*, void of Fear,
By metled Coursers born in full Carreer,   915
Meet first oppos'd: and, with a mighty Shock,
Their Horses Heads against each other knock.
Far from his Steed is fierce *Aconteus* cast;   ⎫
As with an Engin's force, or Lightning's blast: ⎬
He rowls along in Blood, and breathes his last.   ⎭   920
The *Latin* Squadrons take a sudden fright;
And sling their Shields behind, to save their Backs in flight.
Spurring at speed to their own Walls they drew;
Close in the rear the *Tuscan* Troops pursue:
And urge their flight. *Asylas* leads the Chase;   925
'Till seiz'd with Shame they wheel about and face:
Receive their Foes, and raise a threat'ning Cry:
The *Tuscans* take their turn to fear and fly.
   So swelling Surges, with a thund'ring Roar,
Driv'n on each others Backs, insult the Shoar;   930
Bound o're the Rocks, incroach upon the Land;
And far upon the Beach eject the Sand.
Then backward with a Swing, they take their Way;
Repuls'd from upper Ground, and seek their Mother Sea:
With equal hurry quit th' invaded Shore;   935
And swallow back the Sand, and Stones they spew'd before.

Twice were the *Tuscans* Masters of the Field,
Twice by the *Latins*, in their turn repell'd.
Asham'd at length, to the third Charge they ran,
Both Hoasts resolv'd, and mingled Man to Man: 940
Now dying Groans are heard, the Fields are strow'd
With falling Bodies, and are drunk with Blood:
Arms, Horses, Men, on heaps together lye:
Confus'd the Fight, and more confus'd the Cry.
Orsilochus, who durst not press too near 945
Strong *Remulus*, at distance drove his Spear;
And stuck the Steel beneath his Horses Ear:
The fiery Steed, impatient of the Wound,
Curvets, and springing upward with a Bound,
His helpless Lord cast backward on the Ground. 950
Catillus pierc'd *Iolas* first; then drew
His reeking Lance, and at *Herminius* threw:
The mighty Champion of the *Tuscan* Crew.
His Neck and Throat unarm'd, his Head was bare,
But shaded with a length of yellow Hair: 955
Secure, he fought, expos'd on ev'ry part,
A spacious mark for Swords, and for the flying Dart:
Across the Shoulders came the feather'd Wound;
Transfix'd, he fell, and doubled to the Ground.
   The Sands with streaming Blood are sanguine dy'd; 960
And Death with Honour, sought on either side.
   Resistless through the War, *Camilla* rode;
In Danger unappall'd, and pleas'd with Blood.
One side was bare for her exerted Brest;
One Shoulder with her painted Quiver press'd. 965
Now from afar her Fatal Jav'lins play;
Now with her Axe's edge she hews her Way:
Diana's Arms upon her Shoulder sound;
And when, too closely press'd, she quits the Ground;
From her bent Bow she sends a backward Wound. 970
Her Maids, in Martial Pomp, on either side,
Larina, *Tulla*, fierce *Tarpeia* ride;
Italians all: in Peace, their Queen's delight:
In War the bold Companions of the Fight.

939 ran, *98:* ran *97*   957 the flying Dart *98:* the Dart *97*   958 feather'd
98: flying *97*

So march'd the *Thracian Amazons* of old,   975
When *Thermodon* with bloody Billows rowl'd:
Such Troops as these in shining Arms were seen;
When *Theseus* met in Fight their Maiden Queen.
Such to the Field *Penthisilea* led,
From the fierce Virgin when the *Grecians* fled: 980
With such, return'd Triumphant from the War;
Her Maids with Cries attend the lofty Carr:
They clash with manly force their Moony Shields;
With Female Showts resound the *Phrygian* Fields.

Who formost, and who last, Heroick Maid,   985
On the cold Earth were by thy Courage laid?
Thy Spear, of Mountain Ash, *Eumenius* first,
With fury driv'n, from side to side transpierc'd:
A purple Stream came spowting from the Wound;
Bath'd in his Blood he lies, and bites the Ground.   990
Lyris and *Pagasus* at once she slew;
The former, as the slacken'd Reins he drew,
Of his faint steed: the latter, as he stretch'd
His Arm to prop his Friend, the Jav'lin reach'd.
By the same Weapon, sent from the same Hand,   995
Both fall together, and both spurn the Sand.
Amastrus next is added to the slain:
The rest in Rout she follows o're the Plain.
Tereus, Harpalicus, Demophöon,
And *Chromys*, at full Speed her Fury shun.   1000
Of all her deadly Darts, not one she lost;
Each was attended with a *Trojan* Ghost.
Young *Ornithus* bestrode a Hunter Steed,
Swift for the Chase, and of *Apulian* Breed:
Him, from afar, she spy'd in Arms unknown;   1005
O're his broad Back an Oxes hide was thrown:
His Helm a Wolf, whose gaping Jaws were spread,
A cov'ring for his Cheeks, and grinn'd around his Head.
He clench'd within his Hand an Iron Prong;
And tow'rd above the rest, conspicuous in the Throng.   1010
Him soon she singled from the flying Train,
And slew with ease: Then thus insults the slain.
Vain Hunter didst thou think thro' Woods to chase
The Salvage Herd, a vile and trembling Race:

Here cease thy Vaunts, and own my Victory;   1015
A Woman-Warrior was too strong for thee.
Yet if the Ghosts demand the Conqu'ror's Name,
Confessing great *Camilla*, save thy Shame.
Then *Butes*, and *Orsilochus*, she slew:
The bulkiest Bodies of the *Trojan* Crew.   1020
But *Butes* Breast to Breast: the Spear descends
Above the Gorget, where his Helmet ends;
And o're the Shield which his left Side defends.
Orsilochus and she, their Coursers ply;
He seems to follow, and she seems to fly.   1025
But in a narrower Ring she makes the Race;
And then he flies, and she pursues the Chase.
Gath'ring at length on her deluded Foe,
She swings her Axe, and rises to the Blow:
Full on the Helm behind, with such a sway   1030
The Weapon falls, the riven Steel gives way:
He groans, he roars, he sues in vain for Grace;
Brains, mingled with his Blood, besmear his Face.
Astonish'd *Aunus* just arrives by Chance,
To see his Fall, nor farther dares advance: 1035
But fixing on the horrid Maid his Eye,
He stares, and shakes, and finds it vain to fly.
Yet like a true *Ligurian*, born to cheat,
(At least while Fortune favour'd his Deceit)
Cries out aloud, what Courage have you shown,   1040
Who trust your Coursers Strength, and not your own?
Forego the vantage of your Horse, alight,
And then on equal Terms begin the Fight:
It shall be seen, weak Woman, what you can,
When Foot to Foot, you combat with a Man.   1045
He said: She glows with Anger and Disdain,
Dismounts with speed to dare him on the Plain;
And leaves her Horse at large among her Train.
With her drawn Sword defies him to the Field;
And marching, lifts aloft her maiden Shield: 1050
The Youth, who thought his Cunning did succeed,
Reins round his Horse, and urges all his Speed.
Adds the remembrance of the Spur, and hides
The goring Rowels in his bleeding Sides.

Vain Fool, and Coward, cries the lofty Maid,   1055
Caught in the Train, which thou thy self hast laid!
On others practise thy *Ligurian* Arts;
Thin Stratagems, and Tricks of little Hearts
Are lost on me. Nor shalt thou safe retire,
With vaunting Lyes to thy fallacious Sire.   1060
At this, so fast her flying Feet she sped,
That soon she strain'd beyond his Horse's Head:
Then turning short, at once she seiz'd the Rein,
And laid the Boaster grov'ling on the Plain.
Not with more ease the Falcon from above,   1065
Trusses, in middle Air, the trembling Dove:
Then Plumes the Prey, in her strong Pounces bound:
The Feathers foul with Blood come tumbling to the ground.
    Now mighty *Jove*, from his superior height,
With his broad Eye surveys th' unequal Fight.   1070
He fires the Breast of *Tarchon* with Disdain;
And sends him to redeem th' abandon'd Plain.
Betwixt the broken Ranks the *Tuscan* rides,
And these encourages, and those he chides:
Recalls each Leader, by his Name, from flight;   1075
Renews their Ardour; and restores the Fight.
What Panick Fear has seiz'd your Souls, O shame,
O Brand perpetual of th' *Etrurian* Name;
Cowards incurable, a Woman's Hand
Drives, breaks, and scatters your ignoble Band!   1080
Now cast away the Sword, and quit the Shield:
What use of Weapons which you dare not wield?
Not thus you fly your Female Foes, by Night,
Nor shun the Feast, when the full Bowls invite:
When to fat Off'rings the glad *Augur* calls;   1085
And the shrill Horn-pipe sounds to *Bacchanals*.
These are your study'd Cares; your lewd Delight;
Swift to debauch; but slow to Manly Fight.
Thus having said, he spurs amid the Foes;
Not managing the Life he meant to lose.   1090
The first he found he seiz'd, with headlong haste,
In his strong Gripe; and clasp'd around the Waste:
'Twas *Venulus*; whom from his Horse he tore,

And, (laid athwart his own,) in Triumph bore.
Loud Shouts ensue: The *Latins* turn their Eyes,   1095
And view th' unusual sight with vast Surprize.
The fiery *Tarchon*, flying o're the Plains,
Press'd in his Arms the pond'rous Prey sustains:
Then, with his shorten'd Spear, explores around
His jointed Arms, to fix a deadly Wound.   1100
Nor less the Captive struggles for his Life;
He writhes his Body to prolong the Strife:
And, fencing for his naked Throat, exerts
His utmost Vigour, and the point averts.
  So stoops the yellow Eagle from on high,   1105
And bears a speckled Serpent thro' the Sky;
Fast'ning his crooked Tallons on the Prey:
The Pris'ner hisses thro' the liquid Way,
Resists the Royal Hawk, and tho' opprest,
She fights in Volumes, and erects her Crest: 1110
Turn'd to her Foe, she stiffens ev'ry Scale;
And shoots her forky Tongue, and whisks her threat'ning Tail.
Against the Victour all Defence is weak;
Th' imperial Bird still plies her with his Beak:
He tears her Bowels, and her Breast he gores;   1115
Then claps his Pinions, and securely soars.
  Thus, thro' the midst of circling Enemies,
Strong *Tarchon* snatch'd and bore away his Prize:
The *Tyrrhene* Troops, that shrunk before, now press
The *Latins*, and presume the like Success.   1120
  Then, *Aruns* doom'd to Death, his Arts assay'd
To murther, unespy'd, the *Volscian* Maid,
This way, and that his winding Course he bends;
And wheresoe're she turns, her Steps attends.
When she retires victorious from the Chase,   1125
He wheels about with Care, and shifts his place:
When rushing on, she seeks her Foes in Fight,
He keeps aloof, but keeps her still in sight:
He threats, and trembles, trying ev'ry Way
Unseen to kill, and safely to betray.   1130
  Chloreus, the Priest of *Cybelè*, from far,
Glitt'ring in *Phrygian* Arms amidst the War,
Was by the Virgin view'd: The Steed he press'd

Was proud with Trappings; and his brawny Chest
With Scales of guilded Brass was cover'd o're: 1135
A Robe of *Tyrian* Dye the Rider wore.
With deadly Wounds he gaul'd the distant Foe;
Gnossian his Shafts, and *Lycian* was his Bow:
A Golden Helm his Front, and head surrounds;
A guilded Quiver from his Shoulder sounds.   1140
Gold, weav'd with Linen, on his Thighs he wore:
With Flowers of Needlework distinguish'd o're:
With Golden Buckles bound, and gather'd up before.
Him, the fierce Maid beheld with ardent Eyes;
Fond and Ambitious of so Rich a Prize: 1145
Or that the Temple might his Trophees hold,
Or else to shine her self in *Trojan* Gold:
Blind in her haste, she chases him alone,
And seeks his Life, regardless of her own.
This lucky Moment the slye Traytor chose: 1150
Then, starting from his Ambush up he rose,
And threw, but first to Heav'n address'd his Vows.
O Patron of *Soractes* high Abodes,
Phœbus the Ruling Pow'r among the Gods;
Whom first we serve; whole Woods of unctuous Pine   1155
Are fell'd for thee, and to thy Glory shine;
By thee protected, with our naked Soles,
Thro' Flames unsing'd we march, and tread the kindled Coals:
Give me, propitious Pow'r, to wash away
The Stains of this dishonourable Day: 1160
Nor Spoils, nor Triumph, from the Fact I claim;
But with my future Actions trust my Fame.
Let me, by stealth, this Female Plague o'recome;
And from the Field, return inglorious home.
　　Apollo heard, and granting half his Pray'r,   1165
Shuffled in Winds the rest, and toss'd in empty Air.
He gives the Death desir'd; his safe return,
By Southern Tempests to the Seas is born.
　　Now, when the Jav'lin whizz'd along the Skies,
Both Armies on *Camilla* turn'd their Eyes,   1170
Directed by the Sound: Of either Host,
Th' unhappy Virgin, tho' concern'd the most,

1155 serve;] serve, 97 98　　　1163 stealth,] stealth; 97 98

Was only deaf; so greedy was she bent
On Golden Spoils, and on her Prey intent:
Till in her Pap the winged Weapon stood   1175
Infix'd; and deeply drunk the purple Blood.
Her sad Attendants hasten to sustain
Their dying Lady drooping on the Plain.
Far from their sight the trembling *Aruns* flies,
With beating Heart, and Fear confus'd with Joys;   1180
Nor dares he farther to pursue his Blow;
Or ev'n to bear the sight of his expiring Foe.
  As when the Wolf has torn a Bullocks Hide,
At unawares, or ranch'd a Shepherd's Side:
Conscious of his audacious deed, he flies,   1185
And claps his quiv'ring Tail between his Thighs:
So, speeding once, the Wretch no more attends;
But spurring forward herds among his Friends.
  She wrench'd the Jav'lin with her dying Hands;
But wedg'd within her Breast the Weapon stands: 1190
The Wood she draws, the steely Point remains,
She staggers in her Seat, with agonizing Pains:
A gath'ring Mist o'reclouds her chearful Eyes;
And from her Cheeks the rosie Colour flies.
Then, turns to her, whom, of her Female Train,   1195
She trusted most, and thus she speaks with Pain.
Acca, 'tis past! He swims before my sight,
Inexorable Death; and claims his right.
Bear my last Words to *Turnus*, fly with speed,
And bid him timely to my Charge succeed: 1200
Repel the *Trojans*, and the Town relieve:
Farewel; and in this Kiss my parting Breath receive.
She said; and sliding, sunk upon the Plain;
Dying, her open'd Hand forsakes the Rein;
Short, and more short, she pants: By slow degrees   1205
Her Mind the Passage from her Body frees.
She drops her Sword, she nods her plumy Crest;
Her drooping Head declining on her Breast:
In the last Sigh her strugling Soul expires;
And murm'ring with Disdain, to *Stygian* Sounds retires.   1210
  A Shout, that struck the Golden Stars, ensu'd:

1184 a *98*: the *97*   1189 *Editor's paragraph*

Despair and Rage, the languish'd Fight renew'd.
The *Trojan* Troops, and *Tuscans* in a Line,
Advance to charge; the mix'd *Arcadians* join.
But *Cynthia's* Maid, high seated, from afar   1215
Surveys the Field, and fortune of the War:
Unmov'd a while, 'till prostrate on the Plain,
Welt'ring in Blood, she sees *Camilla* slain;
And round her Corps, of Friends and Foes a fighting Train.
Then, from the bottom of her Breast, she drew   1220
A mournful Sigh, and these sad Words ensue:
Too dear a Fine, ah much lamented Maid,
For warring with the *Trojans*, thou hast paid!
Nor ought avail'd, in this unhappy Strife,
Diana's sacred Arms, to save thy Life.   1225
Yet unreveng'd thy Goddess will not leave
Her Vot'rys Death, nor with vain Sorrow grieve.
Branded the Wretch, and be his Name abhorr'd;
But after Ages shall thy Praise record.
Th' inglorious Coward soon shall press the Plain;   1230
Thus vows thy Queen, and thus the Fates ordain.
   High o're the Field, there stood a hilly Mound;
Sacred the Place, and spread with Oaks around;
Where, in a Marble Tomb, *Dercennus* lay,
A King that once in *Latium* bore the Sway.   1235
The beauteous *Opis* thither bent her flight,
To mark the Traytor *Aruns*, from the height.
Him, in refulgent Arms she soon espy'd,
Swoln with success, and loudly thus she cry'd.
Thy backward steps, vain boaster, are too late;   1240
Turn, like a Man at length, and meet thy Fate.
Charg'd with my Message to *Camilla* go;
And say I sent thee to the Shades below;
An Honour undeserv'd from *Cynthia's* Bow.
   She said: and from her Quiver chose with speed   1245
The winged Shaft, predestin'd for the Deed:
Then, to the stubborn Eugh her strength apply'd;
Till the far distant Horns approach'd on either side.
The Bow-string touch'd her Breast, so strong she drew;
Whizzing in Air the fatal Arrow flew.   1250
At once the twanging Bow, and sounding Dart

The Traytor heard, and felt the point within his heart.
Him, beating with his heels, in pangs of death,
His flying Friends to foreign Fields bequeath.
The Conqu'ring Damsel, with expanded Wings,   1255
The welcome Message to her Mistress brings.
    Their Leader lost, the *Volscians* quit the Field;
And, unsustain'd, the Chiefs of *Turnus* yield.
The frighted Souldiers, when their Captains fly,
More on their speed than on their Strength rely.   1260
Confus'd in flight, they bear each other down:
And spur their Horses headlong to the Town.
Driv'n by their Foes, and to their Fears resign'd,
Not once they turn; but take their Wounds behind.
These drop the Shield, and those the Lance forego;   1265
Or on their Shoulders bear the slacken'd Bow.
The Hoofs of Horses with a ratling sound,
Beat short, and thick, and shake the rotten ground.
Black clouds of dust, come rowling in the Sky,
And o're the darken'd Walls, and Rampires fly.   1270
The trembling Matrons, from their lofty Stands,
Rend Heav'n with Female Shrieks; and wring their Hands.
All pressing on, Pursuers and pursu'd,
Are crush'd in Crowds, a mingled Multitude.
Some happy few escape: the Throng too late   1275
Rush on for Entrance, till they choak the Gate.
Ev'n in the sight of home, the wretched Sire
Looks on, and sees his helpless Son expire.
Then, in a fright, the folding Gates they close:
But leave their Friends excluded with their Foes.   1280
The vanquish'd cry; the Victors loudly shout;
Tis Terror all within; and Slaughter all without.
Blind in their Fear, they bounce against the wall,
Or to the Moats pursu'd, precipitate their fall.
    The *Latian* Virgins, valiant with despair,   1285
Arm'd on the Tow'rs the Common Danger share:
So much of Zeal their Country's Cause inspir'd;
So much *Camilla*'s great Example fir'd.
Poles, sharpen'd in the flames, from high they throw;
With imitated Darts to gaul the Foe.   1290

1284 the *98*: their *97*

Their Lives, for Godlike freedom they bequeath;
And crowd each other to be first in death.
Mean time, to *Turnus*, ambush'd in the shade,
With heavy tydings, came th' Unhappy Maid.
The *Volscians* overthrown, *Camilla* kill'd,   1295
The Foes entirely Masters of the Field,
Like a resistless Flood, come rowling on:
The cry goes off the Plain, and thickens to the Town.
  Inflam'd with Rage, (for so the Furies fire
The *Daunian's* Breast, and so the Fates require,)   1300
He leaves the hilly Pass, the Woods in vain
Possess'd, and downward issues on the Plain:
Scarce was he gone, when to the Streights, now freed
From secret Foes, the *Trojan* Troops succeed.
Thro' the black Forest, and the ferny Brake,   1305
Unknowingly secure, their Way they take.
From the rough Mountains to the Plain descend;
And there, in Order drawn, their Line extend.
Both Armies, now, in open Fields are seen:
Nor far the distance of the Space between.   1310
Both to the City bend: *Æneas* sees,
Thro' smoaking Fields, his hast'ning Enemies.
And *Turnus* views the *Trojans* in Array,
And hears th' approaching Horses proudly neigh.
Soon had their Hoasts in bloody Battel join'd;   1315
But westward to the Sea the Sun declin'd.
Intrench'd before the Town, both Armies lye:
While Night with sable Wings involves the Sky.

THE TWELFTH BOOK OF THE ÆNEIS

THE ARGUMENT

*Turnus challenges Æneas to a single Combat: Articles are agreed on, but
broken by the* Rutuli, *who wound Æneas: He is miraculously cur'd by*
Venus, *forces* Turnus *to a Duel, and concludes the Poem with his Death.*

WHEN *Turnus* saw the *Latins* leave the Field;
Their Armies broken, and their Courage quell'd;

1318 involves *98*: o'respreads *97*

Himself become the Mark of publick Spight,
His Honour question'd for the promis'd Fight:
The more he was with Vulgar hate oppress'd;   5
The more his Fury boil'd within his Breast:
He rowz'd his Vigour for the last Debate;
And rais'd his haughty Soul, to meet his Fate.
   As when the Swains the *Lybian* Lion chase,
He makes a sour Retreat, nor mends his Pace;   10
But if the pointed Jav'lin pierce his Side,
The lordly Beast returns with double Pride:
He wrenches out the Steel, he roars for Pain;
His sides he lashes, and erects his Mane.
So *Turnus* fares; his Eye-balls flash with Fire,   15
Through his wide Nostrils Clouds of Smoke expire.
   Trembling with Rage, around the Court he ran;
At length approach'd the King, and thus began.
No more excuses or Delays: I stand
In Arms prepar'd to Combat, hand to hand,   20
This base Deserter of his Native Land.
The *Trojan*, by his Word, is bound to take
The same Conditions which himself did make.
Renew the Truce, the solemn Rites prepare;
And to my single Virtue trust the War.   25
The *Latians* unconcern'd shall see the Fight;
This Arm unaided shall assert your Right:
Then, if my prostrate Body press the Plain,
To him the Crown, and beauteous Bride remain.
   To whom the King sedately thus reply'd;   30
Brave Youth, the more your Valour has been try'd,
The more becomes it us, with due Respect
To weigh the chance of War, which you neglect.
You want not Wealth, or a successive Throne,
Or Cities, which your Arms have made your own;   35
My Towns and Treasures are at your Command;
And stor'd with blooming Beauties is my Land:
Laurentum more than one *Lavinia* sees,
Unmarry'd, fair, of Noble Families.
Now let me speak; and you with Patience hear,   40
Things which perhaps may grate a Lover's Ear:

The Twelfth Book. 16 Through *98*: And *97*

But sound Advice, proceeding from a heart,
Sincerely yours, and free from fraudful Art.
   The Gods, by Signs, have manifestly shown,
No Prince, *Italian* born, shou'd heir my Throne: 45
Oft have our Augurs, in Prediction skill'd,
And oft our Priests, a Foreign Son reveal'd.
Yet, won by Worth, that cannot be withstood,
Brib'd by my Kindness to my kindred Blood,
Urg'd by my Wife, who wou'd not be deny'd;   50
I promis'd my *Lavinia* for your Bride:
Her from her plighted Lord by force I took;
All tyes of Treaties, and of Honour broke:
On your Account I wag'd an impious War,
With what Success 'tis needless to declare;   } 55
I, and my Subjects feel; and you have had your Share.
Twice vanquish'd, while in bloody Fields we strive,
Scarce in our Walls, we keep our Hopes alive:
The rowling Flood runs warm with human Gore;
The Bones of *Latians*, blanch the neighb'ring Shore: 60
Why put I not an end to this Debate,
Still unresolv'd, and still a Slave to Fate?
If *Turnus* Death a lasting Peace can give,
Why shou'd I not procure it, whilst you live.
Shou'd I to doubtful Arms your Youth betray,   65
What wou'd my Kinsmen, the *Rutulians*, say?
And shou'd you fall in Fight, (which Heav'n defend) }
How curse the Cause, which hasten'd to his end,
The Daughter's Lover, and the Father's Friend?   }
Weigh in your Mind, the various Chance of War,   70
Pity your Parent's Age; and ease his Care.
   Such balmy Words he pour'd, but all in vain;
The proffer'd Med'cine but provok'd the Pain.
The wrathful Youth disdaining the Relief,
With intermitting Sobs, thus vents his Grief.   75
The care, O best of Fathers, which you take
For my Concerns, at my Desire, forsake.
Permit me not to languish out my Days;
But make the best exchange of Life for Praise.
This Arm, this Lance, can well dispute the Prize;   80

And the Blood follows, where the Weapon flies:
His Goddess Mother is not near, to shrowd
The flying Coward, with an empty Cloud.
   But now the Queen, who fear'd for *Turnus* Life,
And loath'd the hard Conditions of the Strife,   85
Held him by Force; and, dying in his Death,
In these sad Accents gave her Sorrow breath.
O *Turnus* I adjure thee by these Tears;
And what e're price *Amata's* Honour bears
Within thy Breast, since thou art all my hope,   90
My sickly Mind's repose, my sinking Age's Prop;
Since on the safety of thy Life alone,
Depends *Latinus*, and the *Latian* Throne:
Refuse me not this one, this only Pray'r;
To wave the Combat, and pursue the War.   95
Whatever chance attends this fatal Strife,
Think it includes in thine *Amata's* Life.
I cannot live a Slave; or see my Throne
Usurp'd by Strangers, or a *Trojan* Son.
   At this, a Flood of Tears *Lavinia* shed;   100
A crimson Blush her beauteous Face o'respread;
Varying her Cheeks by Turns, with white and red.
The driving Colours, never at a stay,
Run here and there; and flush, and fade away.
Delightful change! Thus *Indian* Iv'ry shows,   105
Which with the bord'ring Paint of Purple glows;
Or Lillies damask'd by the neighb'ring Rose.
The Lover gaz'd, and burning with desire,
The more he look'd, the more he fed the Fire:
Revenge, and jealous Rage, and secret Spight;   110
Rowl in his Breast, and rowze him to the Fight.
   Then fixing on the Queen his ardent Eyes,
Firm to his first intent, he thus replies.
O Mother, do not by your Tears prepare
Such boding Omens, and prejudge the War.   115
Resolv'd on Fight, I am no longer free
To shun my Death, if Heav'n my Death decree.
   Then turning to the Herald, thus pursues;
Go, greet the *Trojan* with ungrateful News,
Denounce from me, that when to Morrow's Light   120

Shall guild the Heav'ns, he need not urge the Fight:
The *Trojan* and *Rutulian* Troops, no more
Shall dye, with mutual Blood, the *Latian* Shore:
Our single Swords the Quarrel shall decide,
And to the Victor be the beauteous Bride.   125
    He said, and striding on, with speedy Pace,
He sought his Coursers of the *Thracian* Race.
At his Approach, they toss their Heads on high;
And proudly neighing, promise Victory.
The Sires of these *Orythia* sent from far,   130
To grace *Pilumnus*, when he went to War.
The drifts of *Thracian* Snows were scarce so white,
Nor Northern Winds in fleetness match'd their Flight.
Officious Grooms stand ready by his Side;   ⎫
And some with Combs their flowing Manes divide,   ⎬ 135
And others stroke their Chests, and gently sooth their Pride.   ⎭
    He sheath'd his Limbs in Arms; a temper'd Mass
Of golden Metal those, and Mountain Brass.
Then to his Head his glitt'ring Helm he ty'd;
And girt his faithful Fauchion to his side.   140
In his *Ætnean* Forge, the God of Fire
That Fauchion labour'd for the Hero's Sire:
Immortal Keenness on the Blade bestow'd,
And plung'd it hissing in the *Stygian* Flood.
Prop'd on a Pillar, which the Ceiling bore,   145
Was plac'd the Lance *Auruncan Actor* wore;
Which with such Force he brandish'd in his Hand,
The tough Ash trembled like an Osyer Wand.
Then cry'd, O pond'rous Spoil of *Actor* slain,
And never yet by *Turnus* toss'd in vain,   150
Fail not this Day thy wonted Force: But go,
Sent by this Hand, to pierce the *Trojan* Foe:
Give me to tear his Corslet from his Breast,
And from that Eunuch Head, to rend the Crest:
Drag'd in the Dust, his frizled Hair to soil;   155
Hot from the vexing Ir'n, and smear'd with fragrant Oyl.
    Thus while he raves, from his wide Nostrils flies
A fiery Steam, and Sparkles from his Eyes.
So fares the Bull in his lov'd Female's sight;

Proudly he bellows, and preludes the fight: 160
He tries his goring Horns against a Tree;
And meditates his absent Enemy:
He pushes at the Winds, he digs the Strand
With his black Hoofs, and spurns the yellow Sand.
    Nor less the *Trojan*, in his *Lemnian* Arms,   165
To future Fight his Manly Courage warms:
He whets his Fury, and with Joy prepares,
To terminate at once the ling'ring Wars.
To chear his Cheifs, and tender Son, relates
What Heav'n had promis'd, and expounds the Fates.   170
Then to the *Latian* King he sends, to cease
The Rage of Arms, and ratifie the Peace.
    The Morn ensuing from the Mountain's height,
Had scarcely spread the Skies with rosie Light;
Th' Etherial Coursers bounding from the Sea,   175
From out their flaming Nostrils breath'd the Day:
When now the *Trojan* and *Rutulian* Guard,
In friendly Labour join'd, the List prepar'd.
Beneath the Walls, they measure out the Space;
Then sacred Altars rear, on sods of Grass;   } 180
Where, with Religious Rites, their common Gods they place.
In purest white, the Priests their Heads attire,
And living Waters bear, and holy Fire:
And o're their Linnen Hoods, and shaded Hair,
Long twisted Wreaths of sacred Vervain wear.   185
    In Order issuing from the Town, appears
The *Latin* Legion, arm'd with pointed Spears;
And from the Fields, advancing on a Line,
The *Trojan* and the *Tuscan* Forces join:
Their various Arms afford a pleasing Sight;   190
A peaceful Train they seem, in Peace prepar'd for Fight.
    Betwixt the Ranks the proud Commanders ride,
Glitt'ring with Gold, and Vests in Purple dy'd.
Here *Mnestheus* Author of the *Memmian* Line,
And there *Messapus* born of Seed Divine.   195
The Sign is giv'n, and round the listed Space,
Each Man in order fills his proper Place.
Reclining on their ample Shields, they stand;

And fix their pointed Lances in the Sand.
Now, studious of the sight, a num'rous Throng   200
Of either Sex promiscuous, old and young,
Swarm from the Town: By those who rest behind,
The Gates and Walls, and Houses tops are lin'd.
    Mean time the Queen of Heav'n beheld the sight,
With Eyes unpleas'd, from Mount *Albano's* height: 205
(Since call'd *Albano*, by succeeding Fame,
But then an empty Hill, without a Name.)
She thence survey'd the Field, the *Trojan* Pow'rs,
The *Latian* Squadrons, and *Laurentine* Tow'rs.
Then thus the Goddess of the Skies bespake,   210
With Sighs and Tears, the Goddess of the Lake;
King *Turnus* Sister, once a lovely Maid,
E're to the Lust of lawless *Jove* betray'd:
Compress'd by Force, but by the grateful God,
Now made the *Nais* of the neighb'ring Flood.   215
    O Nymph, the Pride of living Lakes, said she,
O most renown'd, and most belov'd by me,
Long hast thou known, nor need I to record
The wanton sallies of my wand'ring Lord:
Of ev'ry *Latian* fair, whom *Jove* mis-led,   220
To mount by Stealth my violated Bed,
To thee alone I grudg'd not his Embrace;
But gave a part of Heav'n, and an unenvy'd Place.
Now learn from me, thy near approaching Grief,
Nor think my Wishes want to thy Relief.   225
While fortune favour'd, nor Heav'n's King deny'd,
To lend my Succour to the *Latian* side,
I sav'd thy Brother, and the sinking State:
But now he struggles with unequal Fate;
And goes with Gods averse, o'rematch'd in Might,   230
To meet inevitable Death in Fight:
Nor must I break the Truce, nor can sustain the sight.
Thou, if thou dar'st, thy present Aid supply;
It well becomes a Sister's Care to try.
    At this the lovely Nymph, with Grief oppress'd,   235
Thrice tore her Hair, and beat her comely Breast.
To whom *Saturnia* thus; thy Tears are late;
Haste, snatch him, if he can be snatch'd from Fate:

New Tumults kindle, violate the Truce;
Who knows what changeful Fortune may produce?   240
'Tis not a Crime t' attempt what I decree,
Or if it were, discharge the Crime on me.
She said, and, sailing on the winged Wind,
Left the sad Nymph suspended in her Mind.
    And now in Pomp the peaceful Kings appear: 245
Four Steeds the Chariot of *Latinus* bear:
Twelve golden Beams around his Temples play,
To mark his Lineage from the God of Day.
Two snowy Coursers *Turnus* Chariot yoke,
And in his Hand two Massy Spears he shook: 250
Then issu'd from the Camp, in Arms Divine,
Æneas, Author of the *Roman* Line:
And by his side *Ascanius* took his Place,
The second Hope of *Rome*'s Immortal Race.
Adorn'd in white, a rev'rend Priest appears;   255
And Off'rings to the flaming Altars bears;
A Porket, and a Lamb, that never suffer'd Shears.
Then, to the rising Sun he turns his Eyes,
And strews the Beasts, design'd for Sacrifice,
With Salt, and Meal: With like officious Care   260
He marks their Foreheads, and he clips their Hair.
Betwixt their Horns the Purple Wine he sheds,
With the same gen'rous Juice the Flame he feeds.
Æneas then unsheath'd his shining Sword,
And thus with pious Pray'rs the Gods ador'd.   265
    All-seeing Sun, and thou *Ausonian* Soil,
For which I have sustain'd so long a Toil,
Thou King of Heav'n, and thou the Queen of Air,
(Propitious now, and reconcil'd by Pray'r,)
Thou God of War, whose unresisted Sway   270
The Labours and Events of Arms obey;
Ye living Fountains, and ye running Floods,
All Pow'rs of Ocean, all Etherial Gods,
Hear, and bear Record: if I fall in Field,
Or Recreant in the Fight, to *Turnus* yield,   275
My *Trojans* shall encrease *Evander*'s Town;
Ascanius shall renounce th' *Ausonian* Crown:

All Claims, all Questions of Debate shall cease;
Nor he, nor they, with Force infringe the Peace.
But if my juster Arms prevail in Fight,   280
As sure they shall, if I divine aright,
My *Trojans* shall not o're th' *Italians* Reign;
Both equal, both unconquer'd shall remain:
Join'd in their Laws, their Lands, and their Abodes;
I ask but Altars for my weary Gods: 285
The Care of those Religious Rites be mine;
The Crown to King *Latinus* I resign:
His be the Sov'raign Sway. Nor will I share
His Pow'r in Peace, or his Command in War.
For me, my Friends another Town shall frame,   290
And bless the rising Tow'rs, with fair *Lavinia's* Name.
    Thus he. Then with erected Eyes and Hands,
The *Latian* King before his Altar stands.
By the same Heav'n, said he, and Earth, and Main,
And all the Pow'rs, that all the three contain;   295
By Hell below, and by that upper God,
Whose Thunder signs the Peace, who seals it with his Nod;
So let *Latona's* double Offspring hear,
And double fronted *Janus*, what I swear;
I touch the sacred Altars, touch the Flames,   300
And all those Pow'rs attest, and all their Names:
Whatever Chance befall on either Side,
No term of time this Union shall divide:
No Force, no Fortune, shall my Vows unbind,
Or shake the stedfast Tenour of my Mind: 305
Not tho' the circling Seas shou'd break their Bound,
O'reflow the Shores, or sap the solid Ground;
Not tho' the Lamps of Heav'n their Spheres forsake,
Hurl'd down, and hissing in the neather Lake:
Ev'n as this Royal Scepter, (for he bore   310
A Scepter in his Hand) shall never more
Shoot out in Branches, or renew the Birth;
(An Orphan now, cut from the Mother Earth
By the keen Axe, dishonour'd of its Hair,
And cas'd in Brass, for *Latian* Kings to bear.)   315
    When thus in publick view the Peace was ty'd,
With solemn Vows, and sworn on either side,

All dues perform'd which holy Rites require;
The Victim Beasts are slain before the Fire:
The trembling Entrails from their Bodies torn,
And to the fatten'd Flames in Chargers born.
    Already the *Rutulians* deem their Man
O'rematch'd in Arms, before the Fight began.
First rising Fears are whisper'd thro' the Crowd;
Then, gath'ring sound, they murmur more aloud.
Now side to side, they measure with their Eyes
The Champions bulk, their Sinews, and their Sise:
The nearer they approach, the more is known
Th' apparent Disadvantage of their own.
Turnus himself, appears in publick sight,
Conscious of Fate, desponding of the Fight.
Slowly he moves; and at his Altar stands
With eyes dejected, and with trembling hands:
And while he mutters undistinguish'd Pray'rs,
A livid deadness in his Cheeks appears.
    With anxious Pleasure when *Juturna* view'd
Th' increasing Fright of the mad Multitude,
When their short Sighs, and thickning Sobs she heard,
And found their ready Minds for Change prepar'd;
Dissembling her immortal Form, she took
Camertus Meen, his Habit, and his Look;
A Chief of ancient Blood: in Arms well known
Was his great Sire, and he, his greater Son.
His Shape assum'd, amid the Ranks she ran,
And humouring their first Motions, thus began.
    For shame, *Rutulians*, can you bear the sight,
Of one expos'd for all, in single Fight?
Can we, before the Face of Heav'n, confess
Our Courage colder, or our Numbers less?
View all the *Trojan* Hoast, th' *Arcadian* Band,
And *Tuscan* Army; count 'em as they stand;
Undaunted to the Battel, if we goe,
Scarce ev'ry second Man will share a Foe.
Turnus, 'tis true, in this unequal Strife
Shall lose, with Honour, his devoted Life:
Or change it rather for immortal Fame,

320

325

330

335

340

345

350

355

322 deem *98*: deem'd *97*   351 stand;] stand, *97 98*

Succeeding to the Gods, from whence he came:
But you, a servile, and inglorious Band,
For Foreign Lords shall sow your Native Land:
Those fruitful Fields, your fighting Fathers gain'd,   360
Which have so long their lazy Sons sustain'd.
　　With Words like these, she carry'd her Design;
A rising Murmur runs along the Line.
Then ev'n the City Troops, and *Latians*, tir'd
With tedious War, seem with new Souls inspir'd: 365
Their Champion's Fate with Pity they lament;
And of the League, so lately sworn, repent.
　　Nor fails the Goddess to foment the Rage
With lying Wonders, and a false Presage:
But adds a Sign, which, present to their Eyes,   370
Inspires new Courage, and a glad Surprize.
For, sudden, in the fiery Tracts above,
Appears in Pomp th' Imperial Bird of *Jove*:
A plump of Fowl he spies, that swim the Lakes;
And o're their Heads his sounding Pinions shakes.   375
Then stooping on the fairest of the Train,
In his strong Tallons truss'd a silver Swan.
Th' *Italians* wonder at th' unusual sight;
But while he lags, and labours in his flight,
Behold the Dastard Fowl return anew;   380
And with united force the Foe pursue:
Clam'rous around the Royal Hawk they fly;
And thick'ning in a Cloud, o'reshade the Sky.
They cuff, they scratch, they cross his airy Course;
Nor can th' incumber'd Bird sustain their Force: 385
But vex'd, not vanquish'd, drops the pond'rous Prey;
And, lighten'd of his Burthen, wings his Way.
　　Th' *Ausonian* Bands with Shouts salute the sight:
Eager of Action, and demand the Fight.
Then King *Tolumnius*, vers'd in Augur's Arts,   390
Cries out, and thus his boasted Skill imparts.
At length 'tis granted, what I long desir'd;
This, this is what my frequent Vows requir'd.
Ye Gods, I take your Omen, and obey;
Advance, my Friends, and charge, I lead the Way.   395
These are the Foreign Foes, whose impious Band,

Like that rapacious Bird, infest our Land:
But soon, like him, they shall be forc'd to Sea
By Strength united, and forego the Prey:
Your timely Succour to your Country bring; 400
Haste to the Rescue; and redeem your King.
   He said: And pressing onward, thro' the Crew,
Poiz'd in his lifted Arm, his Lance he threw.
The winged Weapon, whistling in the Wind,
Came driving on; nor miss'd the Mark design'd. 405
At once the Cornel rattled in the Skies;
At once tumultuous Shouts, and Clamours rise.
Nine Brothers in a goodly Band there stood,
Born of *Arcadian* mix'd with *Tuscan* Blood:
Gylippus Sons: The fatal Jav'lin flew, 410
Aim'd at the midmost of the friendly Crew.
A Passage thro' the jointed Arms it found,
Just where the Belt was to the Body bound;
And struck the gentle Youth, extended on the Ground.
Then fir'd with pious Rage, the gen'rous Train 415
Run madly forward, to revenge the slain.
And some with eager haste their Jav'lins throw;
And some, with Sword in hand, assault the Foe.
   The wish'd Insult the *Latine* Troops embrace;
And meet their Ardour in the middle Space. 420
The *Trojans*, *Tuscans*, and *Arcadian* Line,
With equal Courage obviate their Design.
Peace leaves the violated Fields; and Hate
Both Armies urges to their mutual Fate.
With impious Haste their Altars are o'return'd, 425
The Sacrifice half broil'd, and half unburn'd.
Thick Storms of Steel from either Army fly,
And Clouds of clashing Darts obscure the Sky:
Brands from the Fire, are missive Weapons made;
With Chargers, Bowls, and all the Priestly Trade. 430
Latinus frighted, hastens from the Fray,
And bears his unregarded Gods away.
These on their Horses vault, those yoke the Car;
The rest with Swords on high, run headlong to the War.
   Messapus, eager to confound the Peace, 435
Spurr'd his hot Courser thro' the fighting Preace,

At King *Aulestes*; by his Purple known
A *Tuscan* Prince, and by his Regal Crown:
And with a Shock encount'ring, bore him down.
Backward he fell; and as his Fate design'd,   440
The Ruins of an Altar were behind:
There pitching on his Shoulders, and his Head,
Amid the scatt'ring Fires he lay supinely spread.
The beamy Spear, descending from above,
His Cuirass pierc'd, and thro' his Body drove.   445
Then, with a scornful Smile, the Victor cries;
The Gods have found a fitter Sacrifice.
Greedy of Spoils, th' *Italians* strip the dead
Of his rich Armour; and uncrown his Head.

    Priest *Chorinæus* arm'd his better Hand,   450
From his own Altar, with a blazing Brand:
And, as *Ebusus* with a thund'ring Pace
Advanc'd to Battel, dash'd it on his Face:
His bristly Beard shines out with sudden Fires,
The crackling Crop a noisom scent expires.   455
Following the blow, he seiz'd his curling Crown
With his left Hand; his other cast him down.
The prostrate Body with his Knees he press'd;
And plung'd his holy Ponyard in his Breast.

    While *Podalirius*, with his Sword, pursu'd   460
The Shepherd *Alsus* thro' the flying Crowd,
Swiftly he turns; and aims a deadly blow,
Full on the Front of his unwary Foe.
The broad Axe enters, with a crashing Sound,
And cleaves the Chin, with one continu'd Wound: 465
Warm Blood, and mingled Brains, besmear his Arms around.
An Iron Sleep his stupid Eyes oppress'd,
And seal'd their heavy Lids in endless rest.
But good *Æneas* rush'd amid the Bands,
Bare was his Head, and naked were his Hands,   470
In sign of Truce: Then thus he cries aloud,
What sudden Rage, what new Desire of Blood
Inflames your alter'd Minds? O *Trojans* cease
From impious Arms, nor violate the Peace.
By Human Sanctions, and by Laws Divine,   475
The Terms are all agreed, the War is mine.

Dismiss your Fears, and let the Fight ensue;
This Hand alone shall right the Gods and you:
Our injur'd Altars, and their broken Vow,
To this avenging Sword the faithless *Turnus* owe.　　480
　　Thus while he spoke, unmindful of Defence,
A winged Arrow struck the Pious Prince.
But whether from some Human Hand it came,
Or Hostile God, is left unknown by Fame:
No Human Hand, or Hostile God was found,　　485
To boast the Triumph of so base a Wound.
　　When *Turnus* saw the *Trojan* quit the Plain,
His Chiefs dismay'd, his Troops a fainting Train:
Th' unhoped Event his heighten'd Soul inspires,
At once his Arms and Coursers he requires.　　490
Then, with a leap, his lofty Chariot gains,
And with a ready hand assumes the Reins.
He drives impetuous, and where e're he goes,
He leaves behind a Lane of slaughter'd Foes.
These his Lance reaches, over those he rowls　　495
His rapid Car, and crushes out their Souls:
In vain the vanquish'd fly; the Victor sends
The dead Mens Weapons at their living Friends.
　　Thus on the Banks of *Hebrus* freezing Flood
The God of Battels in his angry Mood,　　500
Clashing his Sword against his brazen Shield,
Lets loose the Reins, and scours along the Field:
Before the Wind his fiery Coursers fly,
Groans the sad Earth, resounds the ratling Sky.
Wrath, Terror, Treason, Tumult, and Despair,　　505
Dire Faces, and deform'd, surround the Car;
Friends of the God, and Followers of the War.
　　With Fury not unlike, nor less Disdain,
Exulting *Turnus* flies along the Plain:
His smoaking Horses, at their utmost Speed,　　510
He lashes on; and urges o're the dead.
Their Fetlocks run with Blood; and when they bound,
The Gore, and gath'ring Dust, are dash'd around.
Thamyris and *Pholus*, Masters of the War,
He kill'd at hand, but *Sthenelus* afar:　　515

500 Battels] Battel's *97 98*

From far the Sons of *Imbracus* he slew,
Glaucus, and *Lades*, of the *Lycian* Crew:
Both taught to fight on Foot, in Battel join'd;
Or mount the Courser that outstrips the Wind.
Mean time *Eumedes*, vaunting in the Field,   520
New fir'd the *Trojans*, and their Foes repell'd.
This Son of *Dolon* bore his Grandsire's Name;
But emulated more his Father's Fame.
His guileful Father, sent a nightly Spy,
The *Grecian* Camp and Order to descry: 525
Hard Enterprise, and well he might require
Achilles Carr, and Horses for his hire:
But, met upon the Scout, th' *Etolian* Prince
In Death bestow'd a juster Recompence.
Fierce *Turnus* view'd the *Trojan* from afar;   530
And lanch'd his Jav'lin from his lofty Carr:
Then lightly leaping down pursu'd the Blow,
And, pressing with his Foot, his prostrate Foe,
Wrench'd from his feeble hold the shining Sword;
And plung'd it in the Bosom of its Lord.   535
Possess, said he, the fruit of all thy Pains,
And measure, at thy length, our *Latian* Plains.
Thus are my Foes rewarded by my hand,
Thus may they build their Town, and thus enjoy the Land.
Then *Dares*, *Butes*, *Sybaris* he slew,   540
Whom o're his Neck his flound'ring Courser threw.
As when loud *Boreas* with his blust'ring Train,
Stoops from above, incumbent on the Main;
Where e're he flies, he drives the Rack before;
And rowls the Billows on th' *Ægean* Shore: 545
So where resistless *Turnus* takes his Course,
The scatter'd Squadrons bend before his force:
His Crest of Horses Hair is blown behind,
By adverse Air; and rustles in the Wind.
This, haughty *Phegeus* saw with high Disdain,   }   550
And as the Chariot rowl'd along the Plain,   }
Light from the Ground he leapt, and seiz'd the Rein.   }
Thus hung in Air, he still retain'd his hold;
The Coursers frighted, and their Course control'd.
The Lance of *Turnus* reach'd him as he hung,   555

And pierc'd his plated Arms; but pass'd along,
And only raz'd the Skin: he turn'd, and held
Against his threat'ning Foe his ample Shield:
Then call'd for Aid: but while he cry'd in vain,
The Chariot bore him backward on the Plain.   560
He lies revers'd; the Victor King descends,
And strikes so justly where his Helmet ends,
He lops the Head. The *Latian* Fields are drunk
With streams that issue from the bleeding Trunk.

While he triumphs, and while the *Trojans* yield,   565
The wounded Prince is forc'd to leave the Field:
Strong *Mnestheus,* and *Achates* often try'd,
And young *Ascanius,* weeping by his side,
Conduct him to his Tent: Scarce can he rear
His Limbs from Earth, supported on his Spear.   570
Resolv'd in Mind, regardless of the Smart,
He tugs with both his Hands, and breaks the Dart.
The Steel remains. No readier way he found
To draw the Weapon, than t' inlarge the Wound.
Eager of Fight, impatient of delay,   575
He begs; and his unwilling Friends obey.

Iäpis was at hand to prove his Art,
Whose blooming Youth so fir'd *Apollo*'s Heart,
That for his Love he proffer'd to bestow
His tuneful Harp, and his unerring Bow.   580
The pious Youth, more studious how to save
His aged Sire, now sinking to the Grave,
Preferr'd the pow'r of Plants, and silent Praise
Of healing Arts, before *Phœbeian* Bays.

Prop'd on his Lance the pensive Heroe stood,   585
And heard, and saw unmov'd, the mourning Crowd.
The fam'd Physician tucks his Robes around,
With ready Hands, and hastens to the Wound.
With gentle Touches he performs his part,
This way and that, solliciting the Dart,   } 590
And exercises all his Heav'nly Art.
All softning Simples, known of Sov'raign Use,
He presses out, and pours their noble Juice;
These first infus'd, to lenifie the Pain,
He tugs with Pincers, but he tugs in vain.   595

Then, to the Patron of his Art he pray'd;
The Patron of his Art refus'd his Aid.
    Mean time the War approaches to the Tents;
Th' Allarm grows hotter, and the Noise augments:
The driving Dust proclaims the Danger near,   600
And first their Friends, and then their Foes appear;
Their Friends retreat, their Foes pursue the Rear.
The Camp is fill'd with Terror and Affright,
The hissing Shafts within the Trench alight:
An undistinguish'd Noise ascends the Sky;   605
The Shouts of those who kill, and Groans of those who dye.
    But now the Goddess Mother, mov'd with Grief,
And pierc'd with Pity, hastens her Relief.
A Branch of healing *Dittany* she brought;
Which in the *Cretan* Fields with Care she sought: 610
Rough is the Stem, which woolly Leafs surround;
The Leafs with Flow'rs, the Flow'rs with Purple crown'd:
Well known to wounded Goats; a sure Relief
To draw the pointed Steel, and ease the Grief.
This *Venus* brings, in Clouds involv'd; and brews   615
Th' extracted Liquor with *Ambrosian* Dews,
And od'rous *Panacee*: Unseen she stands,
Temp'ring the mixture with her Heav'nly Hands:
And pours it in a Bowl, already crown'd
With Juice of medc'nal herbs prepar'd to bathe the Wound. 620
The Leech, unknowing of superior Art,
Which aids the Cure, with this foments the part;
And in a Moment ceas'd the raging smart.
Stanch'd is the Blood, and in the bottom stands:
The Steel, but scarcely touch'd with tender Hands,   625
Moves up, and follows of its own Accord;
And Health and Vigour are at once restor'd.
Iäpis first perceiv'd the closing Wound;
And first the Footsteps of a God he found.
Arms, Arms, he cries, the Sword and Shield prepare,   630
And send the willing Chief, renew'd to War.
This is no Mortal Work, no Cure of mine,
Nor Art's effect, but done by Hands Divine:
Some God our General to the Battel sends;
Some God preserves his Life for greater Ends.   635

The Heroe arms in haste: His hands infold
His Thighs with Cuisses of refulgent Gold:
Inflam'd to fight, and rushing to the Field,
That Hand sustaining the Cœlestial Shield,
This gripes the Lance; and with such Vigour shakes,   640
That to the Rest the beamy Weapon quakes.
Then, with a close Embrace he strain'd his Son;
And kissing thro' his Helmet, thus begun.
My Son, from my Example learn the War,
In Camps to suffer, and in Fields to dare: 645
But happier Chance than mine attend thy Care.
This Day my hand thy tender Age shall shield,
And crown with Honours of the conquer'd Field:
Thou, when thy riper Years shall send thee forth,
To toils of War, be mindful of my Worth: 650
Assert thy birthright; and in Arms be known,
For *Hector*'s Nephew, and *Æneas* Son.
    He said, and, striding, issu'd on the Plain;
Anteus, and *Mnestheus*, and a num'rous Train
Attend his Steps: The rest their Weapons take,   655
And crowding to the Field, the Camp forsake.
A cloud of blinding Dust is rais'd around;
Labours beneath their Feet the trembling ground.
    Now *Turnus*, posted on a Hill, from far
Beheld the progress of the moving War: 660
With him the *Latins* view'd the cover'd Plains;
And the chill Blood ran backward in their Veins.
Juturna saw th' advancing Troops appear;
And heard the hostile Sound, and fled for Fear.
Æneas leads; and draws a sweeping Train,   665
Clos'd in their Ranks, and pouring on the Plain.
As when a Whirlwind rushing to the Shore,
From the mid Ocean, drives the Waves before:
The painful Hind, with heavy Heart foresees,
The flatted Fields, and slaughter of the Trees;   670
With like impetuous Rage the Prince appears,
Before his doubled Front; nor less Destruction bears.
And now both Armies shock, in open Field;
Osyris is by strong *Thymbræus* kill'd.

    652 *Æneas*] *Æneas*'s *97 98*   671 like] less *98*

Archetius, Ufens, Epulon, are slain;   675
(All fam'd in Arms, and of the *Latian* Train;)
By *Gyas, Mnestheus,* and *Achates* Hand:
The fatal Augur falls, by whose command
The Truce was broken, and whose Lance embru'd
With *Trojan* Blood, th' unhappy Fight renew'd.   680
Loud Shouts and Clamours rend the liquid Sky;
And o're the Field the frighted *Latins* fly.
The Prince disdains the Dastards to pursue,
Nor moves to meet in Arms the fighting few:
Turnus alone, amid the dusky Plain,   685
He seeks, and to the Combat calls in vain.
Juturna heard, and seiz'd with Mortal Fear,
Forc'd from the Beam her Brother's Charioteer;
Assumes his Shape, his Armour, and his Meen;
And like *Metiscus,* in his Seat is seen.   690
   As the black Swallow near the Palace plies;
O're empty Courts, and under Arches flies;
Now hawks aloft, now skims along the Flood,
To furnish her loquacious Nest with Food:
So drives the rapid Goddess o're the Plains;   695
The smoaking Horses run with loosen'd Reins.
She steers a various Course among the Foes;
Now here, now there, her conqu'ring Brother shows:
Now with a straight, now with a wheeling flight,
She turns, and bends, but shuns the single Fight.   700
Æneas, fir'd with Fury, breaks the Crowd,
And seeks his Foe, and calls by name aloud:
He runs within a narrower Ring, and tries
To stop the Chariot, but the Chariot flies.
If he but gain a glimps, *Juturna* fears,   705
And far away the *Daunian* Heroe bears.
   What shou'd he do! nor Arts nor Arms avail;
And various Cares in vain his Mind assail.
The great *Messapus* thund'ring thro' the Field,
In his left hand two pointed Jav'lins held;   710
Encountring on the Prince, one Dart he drew,
And with unerring aim, and utmost Vigour threw.
Æneas saw it come, and stooping low
Beneath his Buckler, shunn'd the threatning blow.

The Weapon hiss'd above his Head, and tore   715
The waving Plume, which on his Helm he wore.
Forc'd by this hostile Act, and fir'd with spight,
That flying *Turnus* still declin'd the Fight;
The Prince, whose Piety had long repell'd
His inborn ardour, now invades the Field: 720
Invokes the Pow'rs of violated Peace,
Their Rites, and injur'd Altars to redress:
Then, to his Rage abandoning the Rein,
With Blood and slaughter'd Bodies fills the Plain.

    What God can tell, what Numbers can display   725
The various Labours of that fatal Day!
What Chiefs, and Champions fell on either side,
In Combat slain, or by what Deaths they dy'd?
Whom *Turnus*, whom the *Trojan* Heroe kill'd:
Who shar'd the Fame, and fortune of the Field?   730
Jove, cou'dst thou view, and not avert thy sight,
Two jarring Nations join'd in cruel fight,
Whom Leagues of lasting Love so shortly shall unite!

    Æneas first *Rutulian Sucro* found,
Whose Valour made the *Trojans* quit their Ground: 735
Betwixt his Ribs the Jav'lin drove so just,
It reach'd his Heart, nor needs a second Thrust.
Now *Turnus*, at two blows, two Brethren slew;
First from his Horse fierce *Amycus* he threw;
Then leaping on the Ground, on Foot assail'd   740
Diores, and in equal Fight prevail'd.
Their lifeless Trunks he leaves upon the place;
Their Heads distilling Gore, his Chariot grace.

    Three cold on Earth the *Trojan* Heroe threw;
Whom without respite at one Charge he slew.   745
Cethegus, Tanais, Talus, fell oppress'd,
And sad *Onythes*, added to the rest;
Of *Theban* Blood, whom *Peridia* bore.

    Turnus, two Brothers from the *Lycian* Shore,
And from *Apollo*'s Fane to Battel sent,   750
O'rethrew, nor *Phœbus* cou'd their Fate prevent.
Peaceful *Menætes* after these he kill'd,
Who long had shunn'd the Dangers of the Field:

          746 *Talus*] *Tagus* 97 98

On *Lerna*'s Lake a silent Life he led,
And with his Nets and Angle earn'd his Bread.   755
Nor pompous Cares, nor Palaces he knew,
But wisely from th' infectious World withdrew.
Poor was his House; his Father's painful Hand
Discharg'd his Rent, and plough'd another's Land.
    As Flames among the lofty Woods are thrown,   760
On diff'rent sides, and both by Winds are blown,
The Laurels crackle in the sputt'ring Fire;
The frighted Silvans from their Shades retire:
Or as two neighb'ring Torrents fall from high,
Rapid they run; the foamy Waters fry: 765
They rowl to Sea with unresisted Force,
And down the Rocks precipitate their Course:
Not with less rage the Rival Heroes take
Their diff'rent Ways; nor less Destruction make.
With Spears afar, with Swords at hand they strike;   770
And zeal of Slaughter fires their Souls alike.
Like them, their dauntless Men maintain the Field,
And Hearts are pierc'd unknowing how to yield:
They blow for blow return, and wound for wound;
And heaps of Bodies raise the level Ground.   775
    Murranus, boasting of his Blood, that springs
From a long Royal Race of *Latian* Kings,
Is by the *Trojan* from his Chariot thrown,
Crush'd with the weight of an unweildy Stone:
Betwixt the Wheels he fell; the Wheels that bore   780
His living Load, his dying Body tore.
His starting Steeds, to shun the glitt'ring Sword,
Paw down his trampled Limbs, forgetful of their Lord.
    Fierce *Hillus* threaten'd high; and face to face
Affronted *Turnus* in the middle space: 785
The Prince encounter'd him in full Carreer,
And at his Temples aim'd the deadly Spear:
So fatally the flying Weapon sped,
That thro' his Brazen Helm it pierc'd his Head.
Nor *Cretheus* cou'dst thou scape from *Turnus* hand,   790
In vain the strongest of th' *Arcadian* Band:

787 the *98*: his *97*   790 *Cretheus*] *Cisseus 97 98. See Commentary*

Nor to *Cupentus* cou'd his Gods afford
Availing Aid against th' *Ænean* Sword;
Which to his naked Heart pursu'd the Course:
Nor could his plated Shield sustain the Force.   795
   Iölas fell, whom not the *Grecian* Pow'rs,
Nor great Subvertor of the *Trojan* Tow'rs,
Were doom'd to kill, while Heav'n prolong'd his Date:
But who can pass the Bounds prefix'd by Fate?
In high *Lyrnessus*, and in *Troy*, he held   800
Two Palaces, and was from each expell'd:
Of all the mighty Man, the last Remains
A little spot of Foreign Earth contains.
   And now both Hosts their broken Troops unite,
In equal Ranks, and mix in mortal Fight.   805
Seresthus, and undaunted *Mnestheus* join
The *Trojan*, *Tuscan*, and *Arcadian* Line:
Sea-born *Messapus*, with *Atinas*, heads
The *Latin* Squadrons, and to Battel leads.
They strike, they push, they throng the scanty space; ⎫ 810
Resolv'd on Death, impatient of Disgrace;   ⎬
And where one falls, another fills his Place.   ⎭
   The *Cyprian* Goddess now inspires her Son
To leave th' unfinish'd Fight, and storm the Town.
For while he rowls his Eyes around the Plain,   815
In quest of *Turnus*, whom he seeks in vain,
He views th' ungarded City from afar,
In careless quiet, and secure of War:
Occasion offers, and excites his Mind,
To dare beyond the Task he first design'd.   820
Resolv'd, he calls his Chiefs: they leave the Fight;
Attended thus, he takes a neighb'ring Height:
The crowding Troops about their Gen'ral stand,
All under Arms, and wait his high Command.
Then thus the lofty Prince: Hear and obey,   825
Ye *Trojan* Bands, without the least delay.
Jove is with us, and what I have decreed
Requires our utmost Vigour, and our Speed.
Your instant Arms against the Town prepare;
The source of Mischief, and the Seat of War.   830

792 afford] afford, *97 98*   793 Sword;] Sword: *97 98*

This Day the _Latian_ Tow'rs, that mate the Sky,
Shall level with the Plain in Ashes lye:
The People shall be Slaves; unless in time
They kneel for Pardon, and repent their Crime.
Twice have our Foes been vanquish'd on the Plain;   835
Then shall I wait till _Turnus_ will be slain?
Your Force against the perjur'd City bend:
There it began, and there the War shall end.
The Peace profan'd our rightful Arms requires:
Cleanse the polluted Place with purging Fires.   840
    He finish'd; and one Soul inspiring all,
Form'd in a Wedge, the Foot approach the Wall.
Without the Town, an unprovided Train
Of gaping, gazing Citizens are slain.
Some Firebrands, others scaling Ladders bear;   845
And those they toss aloft, and these they rear:
The Flames now lanch'd, the feather'd Arrows fly,
And Clouds of missive Arms obscure the Sky.
Advancing to the Front, the Heroe stands,
And stretching out to Heav'n his Pious Hands;   850
Attests the Gods, asserts his Innocence,
Upbraids with breach of Faith th' _Ausonian_ Prince:
Declares the Royal Honour doubly stain'd,
And twice the Rites of holy Peace profan'd.
    Dissenting Clamours in the Town arise;   855
Each will be heard, and all at once advise.
One part for Peace, and one for War contends:
Some wou'd exclude their Foes, and some admit their Friends.
The helpless King is hurry'd in the Throng;
And what e're Tide prevails, is born along.   860
    Thus when the Swain, within a hollow Rock,
Invades the Bees, with suffocating Smoke,
They run around, or labour on their Wings,
Disus'd to flight; and shoot their sleepy Stings:
To shun the bitter Fumes in vain they try;   865
Black Vapours, issuing from the Vent, involve the Sky.
    But Fate, and envious Fortune, now prepare
To plunge the _Latins_ in the last despair.
The Queen, who saw the Foes invade the Town;
And brands on tops of burning Houses thrown: 870

Cast round her Eyes, distracted with her Fear;
No Troops of *Turnus* in the Field appear.
Once more she stares abroad, but still in vain:
And then concludes the Royal Youth is slain.
Mad with her Anguish, impotent to bear   875
The mighty Grief, she loaths the vital Air.
She calls her self the Cause of all this Ill,
And owns the dire Effects of her ungovern'd Will:
She raves against the Gods, she beats her Breast,
She tears with both her hands her Purple Vest.   880
Then round a Beam a running Noose she ty'd;
And, fasten'd by the Neck, obscenely dy'd.

   Soon as the fatal News by Fame was blown,
And to her Dames, and to her Daughter known;
The sad *Lavinia* rends her yellow Hair,   885
And rosie Cheeks; the rest her Sorrow share:
With Shrieks the Palace rings, and Madness of Despair.
The spreading Rumor fills the Publick Place;
Confusion, Fear, Distraction, and Disgrace,
And silent shame, are seen in ev'ry Face.   890
Latinus tears his Garments as he goes,
Both for his publick, and his private Woes:
With Filth his venerable Beard besmears,
And sordid Dust deforms his Silver Hairs.
And much he blames the softness of his Mind,   895
Obnoxious to the Charms of Womankind,
And soon seduc'd to change, what he so well design'd:
To break the solemn League so long desir'd,
Nor finish what his Fates, and those of *Troy* requir'd,

   Now *Turnus* rowls aloof o're empty Plains,   900
And here and there some stragling Foes he gleans.
His flying Coursers please him less and less,
Asham'd of easie Fight, and cheap Success.
Thus half contented, anxious in his Mind,
The distant Cries come driving in the Wind: 905
Shouts from the Walls, but Shouts in Murmurs drown'd;
A jarring mixture, and a boding sound.
Alas, said he, what mean these dismal Cries,
What doleful Clamours from the Town arise?
Confus'd he stops, and backward pulls the Reins: 910

She, who the Driver's Office now sustains,
Replies; Neglect, my Lord, these new Alarms;
Here fight, and urge the Fortune of your Arms:
There want not others to defend the Wall:
If by your Rival's Hand th' *Italians* fall,   915
So shall your fatal Sword his Friends oppress,
In Honour equal, equal in Success.
   To this, the Prince; O Sister, (for I knew
The Peace infring'd, proceeded first from you,)
I knew you, when you mingled first in Fight,   920
And now in vain you wou'd deceive my Sight:
Why, Goddess, this unprofitable Care?
Who sent you down from Heav'n, involv'd in Air,
Your share of Mortal Sorrows to sustain,
And see your Brother bleeding on the Plain?   925
For, to what Pow'r can *Turnus* have recourse,
Or how resist his Fates prevailing force!
These Eyes beheld *Murranus* bite the Ground,
Mighty the Man, and mighty was the Wound.
I heard my dearest Friend, with dying Breath,   930
My Name invoking to revenge his Death:
Brave *Ufens* fell with Honour on the Place;
To shun the shameful sight of my disgrace.
On Earth supine, a Manly Corps he lies;
His Vest and Armour are the Victor's Prize.   935
Then, shall I see *Laurentum* in a flame,
Which only wanted to compleat my shame?
How will the *Latins* hoot their Champion's flight;
How *Drances* will insult, and point them to the sight!
Is Death so hard to bear? Ye Gods below,   940
(Since those above so small Compassion show,)
Receive a Soul unsully'd yet with shame,
Which not belies my great Forefather's Name.
   He said: And while he spoke, with flying speed,
Came *Sages* urging on his foamy Steed;   945
Fix'd on his wounded Face a Shaft he bore,
And seeking *Turnus* sent his Voice before:
Turnus, on you, on you alone depends
Our last Relief; compassionate your Friends.

939 insult *98*: be pleas'd *97*

Like Lightning, fierce *Æneas*, rowling on,   950
With Arms invests, with Flames invades the Town:
The Brands are toss'd on high; the Winds conspire
To drive along the Deluge of the Fire:
All Eyes are fix'd on you; your Foes rejoice;
Ev'n the King staggers, and suspends his Choice: 955
Doubts to deliver, or defend the Town;
Whom to reject, or whom to call his Son.
The Queen, on whom your utmost hopes were plac'd,
Her self suborning Death, has breath'd her last.
'Tis true, *Messapus*, fearless of his Fate,   960
With fierce *Atinas* Aid, defends the Gate:
On ev'ry side surrounded by the Foe;
The more they kill, the greater Numbers grow;
An Iron Harvest mounts, and still remains to mow.
You, far aloof from your forsaken Bands,   965
Your rowling Chariot drive o're empty Sands.
   Stupid he sate, his Eyes on Earth declin'd,
And various Cares revolving in his Mind:
Rage boiling from the bottom of his Breast,
And Sorrow mix'd with Shame, his Soul oppress'd: 970
And conscious Worth lay lab'ring in his Thought;
And Love by Jealousie to Madness wrought.
By slow degrees his Reason drove away
The Mists of Passion, and resum'd her Sway.
Then, rising on his Car, he turn'd his Look;   975
And saw the Town involv'd in Fire and Smoke.
A wooden Tow'r with Flames already blaz'd,
Which his own Hands on Beams and Rafters rais'd:
And Bridges laid above to join the Space;
And Wheels below to rowl from place to place.   980
Sister, the Fates have vanquish'd: Let us go
The way which Heav'n and my hard Fortune show.
The Fight is fix'd: Nor shall the branded Name
Of a base Coward blot your Brother's Fame.
Death is my choice; but suffer me to try   985
My Force, and vent my Rage before I dye.
He said, and leaping down without delay,
Thro Crowds of scatter'd Foes he free'd his way.
Striding he pass'd, impetuous as the Wind,

And left the grieving Goddess far behind.　　　　　990
As when a Fragment, from a Mountain torn
By raging Tempests, or by Torrents born,
Or sapp'd by time, or loosen'd from the Roots,
Prone thro' the Void the Rocky Ruine shoots,
Rowling from Crag to Crag, from Steep to Steep;　　　995
Down sink, at once the Shepherds and their Sheep,
Involv'd alike, they rush to neather Ground,
Stun'd with the *shock* they fall, and stun'd from *Earth* rebound:
So *Turnus*, hasting headlong to the Town,
Should'ring and shoving, bore the Squadrons down.　　　1000
Still pressing onward, to the Walls he drew,
Where Shafts, and Spears, and Darts promiscuous flew;
And sanguine Streams the slipp'ry Ground embrew.
First stretching out his Arm, in sign of Peace,
He cries aloud, to make the Combat cease:　　　1005
Rutulians hold, and *Latin* Troops retire;
The Fight is mine, and me the Gods require.
Tis just that I shou'd vindicate alone
The broken Truce, or for the Breach atone.
This Day shall free from Wars th' *Ausonian* State;　　　1010
Or finish my Misfortunes in my Fate.
　　Both Armies from their bloody Work desist:
And bearing backward, form a spacious List.
The *Trojan* Heroe who receiv'd from Fame
The welcome Sound, and heard the Champion's Name,　　　1015
Soon leaves the taken Works, and mounted Walls,
Greedy of War, where greater Glory calls.
He springs to Fight, exulting in his Force;
His jointed Armour rattles in the Course.
Like *Eryx*, or like *Athos*, great he shows,　　　1020
Or Father *Apennine*, when white with Snows,
His Head Divine, obscure in Clouds he hides:
And shakes the sounding Forest on his sides.
　　The Nations over-aw'd, surcease the Fight,
Immoveable their Bodies, fix'd their sight:　　　1025
Ev'n Death stands still; nor from above they throw
Their Darts, nor drive their batt'ring Rams below.
In silent Order either Army stands;
And drop their Swords, unknowing, from their Hands.

Th' *Ausonian* King beholds, with wond'ring sight,   1030
Two mighty Champions match'd in single Fight:
Born under Climes remote; and brought by Fate,
With Swords to try their Titles to the State.
  Now in clos'd Field, each other from afar
They view; and rushing on, begin the War.   1035
They launch their Spears, then hand to hand they meet;
The trembling Soil resounds beneath their Feet:
Their Bucklers clash; thick blows descend from high,
And flakes of Fire from their hard Helmets fly.
Courage conspires with Chance; and both ingage   1040
With equal Fortune yet, and mutual Rage.
  As when two Bulls for their fair Female fight,
In *Sila*'s Shades, or on *Taburnus* height;
With Horns adverse they meet: the Keeper flies;
Mute stands the Herd, the Heifars rowl their Eyes;   1045
And wait th' Event; which Victor they shall bear,
And who shall be the Lord, to rule the lusty Year:
With rage of Love the jealous Rivals burn,
And Push for Push, and Wound for Wound return:
Their Dewlaps gor'd, their sides are lav'd in Blood;   1050
Loud Cries and roaring Sounds rebellow thro' the Wood:
Such was the Combat in the listed Ground;
So clash their Swords and so their Shields resound.
  Jove sets the Beam; in either Scale he lays
The Champions Fate, and each exactly weighs.   1055
On this side Life, and lucky Chance ascends:
Loaded with Death, that other Scale descends.
Rais'd on the Stretch, young *Turnus* aims a blow,
Full on the Helm of his unguarded Foe:
Shrill Shouts and Clamours ring on either side;   1060
As Hopes and Fears their panting Hearts divide.
But all in pieces flies the Traytor Sword,
And, in the middle Stroke deserts his Lord.
Now 'tis but Death, or Flight: disarm'd he flies,
When in his Hand, an unknown Hilt he spies.   1065
Fame says that *Turnus*, when his Steeds he join'd,
Hurrying to War, disorder'd in his Mind,
Snatch'd the first Weapon, which his haste cou'd find.

1041 Fortune yet, and *98*: Fortune, and with *97*

'Twas not the fated Sword his Father bore;
But that his Charioteer *Metiscus* wore.   1070
This, while the *Trojans* fled, the Toughness held;
But vain against the great *Vulcanian* Shield,
The mortal-temper'd Steel deceiv'd his Hand:
The shiver'd fragments shone amid the Sand.
    Surpris'd with fear, he fled along the Field;   1075
And now forthright, and now in Orbits wheel'd.
For here the *Trojan* Troops the List surround;
And there the Pass is clos'd with Pools and marshy Ground.
Æneas hastens, tho' with heavier Pace,
His Wound so newly knit, retards the Chase: 1080
And oft his trembling Knees their Aid refuse,
Yet pressing foot by foot his Foe pursues.
    Thus, when a fearful Stag is clos'd around
With Crimson Toils, or in a River found;
High on the Bank the deep-mouth'd Hound appears;   1085
Still opening, following still, where e're he steers:
The persecuted Creature, to, and fro,
Turns here and there, to scape his *Umbrian* Foe:
Steep is th' Ascent; and if he gains the Land,
The Purple Death is pitch'd along the Strand: 1090
His eager Foe determin'd to the Chace,
Stretch'd at his length gains Ground at ev'ry Pace:
Now to his beamy Head he makes his way,
And now he holds, or thinks he holds his Prey:
Just at the pinch the Stag springs out with fear,   1095
He bites the Wind, and fills his sounding Jaws with Air.
The Rocks, the Lakes, the Meadows ring with Cries;
The mortal Tumult mounts, and thunders in the Skies.
    Thus flies the *Daunian* Prince: and, flying, blames
His tardy Troops; and calling by their Names,   1100
Demands his trusty Sword. The *Trojan* threats
The Realm with Ruin, and their ancient Seats
To lay in Ashes, if they dare supply
With Arms or Aid, his vanquish'd Enemy:
Thus menacing, he still pursues the Course,   1105
With Vigour, tho' diminish'd of his Force.
Ten times, already, round the listed place,
One Chief had fled, and t'other giv'n the Chace:

No trivial Prize is play'd; for on the Life
Or Death of *Turnus*, now depends the Strife.   1110
   Within the space, an Olive Tree had stood,
A sacred Shade, a venerable Wood,
For Vows to *Faunus* paid, the *Latins* Guardian God.
Here hung the Vests, and Tablets were ingrav'd,
Of sinking Mariners, from Shipwrack sav'd.   1115
With heedless Hands the *Trojans* fell'd the Tree,
To make the Ground inclos'd for Combat free.
Deep in the Root, whether by Fate, or Chance,
Or erring haste, the *Trojan* drove his Lance:
Then stoop'd, and tug'd with Force immense to free   1120
Th' incumber'd Spear from the tenacious Tree:
That whom his fainting Limbs pursu'd in vain,
His flying Weapon might from far attain.
   Confus'd with Fear, bereft of Human Aid,
Then *Turnus* to the Gods, and first to *Faunus* pray'd.   1125
O *Faunus* pity, and thou Mother Earth,
Where I thy foster Son receiv'd my Birth,
Hold fast the Steel; if my Religious Hand
Your Plant has honour'd, which your Foes profan'd;
Propitious hear my pious Pray'r! He said,   1130
Nor with successless Vows invok'd their Aid.
Th' incumbent Heroe, wrench'd, and pull'd, and strain'd;
But still the stubborn Earth the Steel detain'd.
Juturna took her time; and while in vain
He strove, assum'd *Metiscus* Form again: 1135
And, in that imitated Shape, restor'd
To the despairing Prince, his *Daunian* Sword.
The Queen of Love, who, with Disdain and Grief,
Saw the bold Nymph afford this prompt Relief;
T' assert her Off-spring, with a greater Deed,   1140
From the tough Root the ling'ring Weapon freed.
   Once more erect, the Rival Chiefs advance;
One trusts the Sword, and one the pointed Lance:
And both resolv'd alike, to try their fatal Chance.
   Mean time Imperial *Jove* to *Juno* spoke,   1145
Who from a shining Cloud beheld the shock;
What new Arrest, O Queen of Heav'n, is sent
To stop the Fates now lab'ring in th' Event.

What farther hopes are left thee to pursue?
Divine *Æneas*, (and thou know'st it too,)
Fore-doom'd to these Cœlestial Seats is due.   } 1150
What more Attempts for *Turnus* can be made,
That thus thou ling'rest in this lonely Shade!
Is it becoming of the due Respect,
And awful Honour of a God Elect,   1155
A Wound unworthy of our State to feel;
Patient of Human Hands, and earthly Steel?
Or seems it Just, the Sister shou'd restore,
A second Sword, when one was lost before;
And arm a conquer'd Wretch, against his Conqueror?   } 1160
For what without thy knowledge and avow,
Nay more, thy Dictate, durst *Juturna* do?
At last, in deference to my Love, forbear
To lodge within thy Soul this anxious Care:
Reclin'd upon my Breast, thy Grief unload;   1165
Who shou'd relieve the Goddess, but the God?
Now, all things to their utmost Issue tend;
Push'd by the Fates to their appointed End:
While leave was giv'n thee, and a lawful Hour
For Vengeance, Wrath, and unresisted Pow'r: 1170
Toss'd on the Seas thou cou'd'st thy Foes distress,
And driv'n ashore, with Hostile Arms oppress:
Deform the Royal House; and from the side
Of the Just Bridegroom, tear the plighted Bride:
      Now cease at my Command. The Thund'rer said: 1175
And with dejected Eyes this Answer *Juno* made.
Because your dread Decree too well I knew;
From *Turnus*, and from Earth unwilling I withdrew.
Else shou'd you not behold me here alone,
Involv'd in empty Clouds, my Friends bemoan: 1180
But girt with vengeful Flames, in open sight,
Engag'd against my Foes in Mortal Fight.
'Tis true *Juturna* mingled in the Strife
By my Command, to save her Brother's Life;
At least to try: But by the *Stygian* Lake,   1185
(The most Religious Oath the Gods can take,)
With this restriction, not to bend the Bow,

Or toss the Spear, or trembling Dart to throw.
And now resign'd to your Superior Might,
And tir'd with fruitless Toils, I loath the Fight.   1190
This let me beg, (and this no Fates withstand)
Both for my self, and for your Fathers Land,
That when the Nuptial Bed shall bind the Peace;
(Which I, since you ordain, consent to bless,)
The Laws of either Nation be the same;   1195
But let the *Latins* still retain their Name:
Speak the same Language which they spoke before;
Wear the same Habits, which their Grandsires wore:
Call them not *Trojans*: Perish the Renown,
And Name of *Troy*, with that detested Town.   1200
Latium be *Latium* still; let *Alba* reign,
And *Rome*'s immortal Majesty remain.

   Then thus the Founder of Mankind replies:
(Unruffled was his Front, serene his Eyes,)
Can *Saturn*'s Issue, and Heav'ns other Heir,   1205
Such endless Anger in her Bosom bear?
Be Mistress, and your full Desires obtain:
But quench the Choler you foment in vain.
From ancient Blood th' *Ausonian* People sprung,
Shall keep their Name, their Habit, and their Tongue.   1210
The *Trojans* to their Customs shall be ty'd,
I will, my self, their common Rites provide;
The Natives shall command, the Foreigners subside.
All shall be *Latium*; *Troy* without a Name:
And her lost Sons forget from whence they came.   1215
From Blood so mix'd, a pious Race shall flow,
Equal to Gods, excelling all below.
No Nation more Respect to you shall pay,
Or greater Off'rings on your Altars lay.
Juno consents, well pleas'd that her Desires   1220
Had found Success, and from the Cloud retires.

   The Peace thus made, the Thund'rer next prepares
To force the wat'ry Goddess from the Wars.
Deep in the dismal Regions, void of Light,
Three Daughters at a Birth were born to Night: 1225

These their brown Mother, brooding on her Care,
Indu'd with windy Wings to flit in Air:
With Serpents girt alike; and crown'd with hissing Hair.
In Heav'n the *Diræ* call'd, and still at hand,
Before the Throne of angry *Jove* they stand.   1230
His Ministers of Wrath; and ready still
The Minds of Mortal Men with Fears to fill:
When e're the moody Sire, to wreak his Hate
On Realms, or Towns deserving of their Fate,
Hurls down Diseases, Death, and deadly Care,   1235
And terrifies the guilty World with War.
One Sister Plague of these from Heav'n he sent,
To fright *Juturna* with a dire Portent.
The Pest comes whirling down: by far more slow
Springs the swift Arrow from the *Parthian* Bow,   1240
Or *Cydon* Eugh; when traversing the Skies,
And drench'd in pois'nous Juice, the sure Destruction flies.
With such a sudden, and unseen a flight,
Shot thro' the Clouds the Daughter of the Night.
Soon as the Field inclos'd she had in view,   1245
And from afar her destin'd Quarry knew:
Contracted, to the boding Bird she turns,
Which haunts the ruin'd Piles, and hallow'd Urns;
And beats about the Tombs with nightly Wings;
Where Songs obscene on Sepulchres she sings.   1250
Thus lessen'd in her Form, with frightful Cries,
The Fury round unhappy *Turnus* flies,
Flaps on his Shield, and flutters o're his Eyes.

   A lazy Chilness crept along his Blood,
Choak'd was his Voice, his Hair with Horror stood.   1255
Juturna from afar beheld her fly,
And knew th' ill Omen, by her screaming Cry,
And stridour of her Wings. Amaz'd with Fear,
Her beauteous Breast she beat, and rent her flowing Hair.
Ah me, she cries, in this unequal Strife,   1260
What can thy Sister more to save thy Life!
Weak as I am, can I, alas, contend
In Arms, with that inexorable Fiend!
Now, now, I quit the Field! forbear to fright

My tender Soul, ye baleful Birds of Night!   1265
The lashing of your Wings I know too well:
The sounding Flight, and Fun'ral Screams of Hell!
These are the Gifts you bring from haughty *Jove*,
The worthy Recompence of ravish'd Love!
Did he for this exempt my Life from Fate?   1270
O hard Conditions of Immortal State!
Tho' born to Death, not priviledg'd to dye,
But forc'd to bear impos'd Eternity!
Take back your envious Bribes, and let me go
Companion to my Brother's Ghost below!   1275
The Joys are vanish'd: Nothing now remains,
Of Life Immortal, but Immortal Pains.
What Earth will open her devouring Womb,
To rest a weary Goddess in the Tomb!
She drew a length of Sighs; nor more she said;   1280
But in her Azure Mantle wrap'd her Head:
Then plung'd into her Stream, with deep Despair,
And her last Sobs came bubling up in Air.

    Now stern *Æneas* waves his weighty Spear
Against his Foe, and thus upbraids his Fear,   1285
What farther Subterfuge can *Turnus* find;
What empty Hopes are harbour'd in his Mind?
'Tis not thy Swiftness can secure thy Flight:
Not with their Feet, but Hands, the Valiant fight.
Vary thy Shape in thousand Forms, and dare   1290
What Skill and Courage can attempt in War:
Wish for the Wings of Winds, to mount the Sky; ⎫
Or hid, within the hollow Earth to lye.   ⎬
The Champion shook his Head; and made this short reply. ⎭
No threats of thine, my manly Mind can move: 1295
Tis Hostile Heav'n I dread; and Partial *Jove*.
He, said no more: but with a Sigh, repress'd
The mighty Sorrow, in his swelling Breast.
Then, as he rowld his troubled Eyes around,   ⎫
An Antique Stone he saw: the Common Bound   ⎬   1300
Of Neighb'ring Fields; and Barrier of the Ground: ⎭
So vast, that Twelve strong Men of modern Days,
Th' enormous weight from Earth cou'd hardly raise.
He heav'd it at a Lift: and poiz'd on high,

Ran stagg'ring on, against his Enemy.   1305
But so disorder'd, that he scarcely knew
His Way: or what unwieldy weight he threw.
His knocking Knees are bent beneath the Load:
And shiv'ring Cold congeals his vital Blood.
The Stone drops from his arms: and falling short,   1310
For want of Vigour, mocks his vain Effort.
And as, when heavy Sleep has clos'd the sight,
The sickly Fancy labours in the Night:
We seem to run; and destitute of Force
Our sinking Limbs forsake us in the Course: 1315
In vain we heave for Breath; in vain we cry:
The Nerves unbrac'd, their usual Strength deny;
And, on the Tongue the falt'ring Accents dye:
So *Turnus* far'd: what ever means he try'd,
All force of Arms, and points of Art employ'd,   1320
The Fury flew athwart; and made th' Endeavour void.

   A thousand various Thoughts his Soul confound:
He star'd about; nor Aid nor Issue found:
His own Men stop the Pass; and his own Walls surround.
Once more he pauses; and looks out again: 1325
And seeks the Goddess Charioteer in vain.
Trembling he views the Thund'ring Chief advance:
And brandishing aloft the deadly Lance:
Amaz'd he cow'rs beneath his conqu'ring Foe,
Forgets to ward; and waits the coming Blow.   1330
Astonish'd while he stands, and fix'd with Fear,
Aim'd at his Shield he sees th' impending Spear.

   The Heroe measur'd first, with narrow view,
The destin'd Mark: And rising as he threw,
With its full swing the fatal Weapon flew.   1335
Not with less Rage the rattling Thunder falls;
Or Stones from batt'ring Engins break the Walls:
Swift as a Whirlwind, from an Arm so strong,
The Lance drove on; and bore the Death along.
Nought cou'd his sev'n-fold Shield the Prince avail,   1340
Nor ought beneath his Arms the Coat of Mail;
It pierc'd thro' all; and with a grizly Wound,
Transfix'd his Thigh, and doubled him to Ground.

1319 try'd, *98*: try'd *97*

With Groans the *Latins* rend the vaulted Sky:
Woods, Hills, and Valleys, to the Voice reply.   1345
  Now low on Earth the lofty Chief is laid;
With Eyes cast upward, and with Arms display'd;
And Recreant thus to the proud Victor pray'd.
I know my Death deserv'd, nor hope to live:
Use what the Gods, and thy good Fortune give.   1350
  Yet think; oh think, if Mercy may be shown,
(Thou hadst a Father once; and hast a Son:)
Pity my Sire, now sinking to the Grave;
And for *Anchises* sake, old *Daunus* save!
Or, if thy vow'd Revenge pursue my Death;   1355
Give to my Friends my Body void of Breath!
The *Latian* Chiefs have seen me beg my Life;
Thine is the Conquest, thine the Royal Wife:
Against a yielded Man, 'tis mean ignoble Strife.
  In deep Suspence the *Trojan* seem'd to stand;   1360
And just prepar'd to strike repress'd his Hand.
He rowl'd his Eyes, and ev'ry Moment felt
His manly Soul with more Compassion melt.
When, casting down a casual Glance, he spy'd
The Golden Belt that glitter'd on his side: 1365
The fatal Spoils which haughty *Turnus* tore
From dying *Pallas*, and in Triumph wore.
Then rowz'd anew to Wrath, he loudly cries,
(Flames, while he spoke, came flashing from his Eyes:)
Traytor, dost thou, dost thou to Grace pretend,   1370
Clad, as thou art, in Trophees of my Friend?
To his sad Soul a grateful Off'ring go;
'Tis *Pallas*, *Pallas* gives this deadly Blow.
He rais'd his Arm aloft; and at the Word,
Deep in his Bosom drove the shining Sword.   1375
The streaming Blood distain'd his Arms around:
And the disdainful Soul came rushing thro' the Wound.

POSTSCRIPT TO THE READER

WHAT *Virgil* wrote in the vigour of his Age, in Plenty and at Ease, I have undertaken to *Translate* in my Declining Years: strugling with Wants, oppress'd with Sickness, curb'd in my Genius, lyable to be misconstrued in all I write; and my Judges, if they are not very equitable, already prejudic'd against me, by the *Lying Character* which 5 has been given them of my Morals. Yet steady to my Principles, and not dispirited with my Afflictions, I have, by the Blessing of God on my Endeavours, overcome all difficulties; and, in some measure, acquitted my self of the Debt which I ow'd the Publick, when I undertook this Work. In the first place therefore, I thankfully acknowledge to the 10 Almighty Power, the Assistance he has given me in the beginning, the Prosecution, and *Conclusion* of my present Studies, which are more happily perform'd than I could have promis'd to my self, when I labour'd under such Discouragements. For, what I have done, Imperfect as it is, for want of Health and leisure to Correct it, will be judg'd in after Ages, 15 and possibly in the present, to be no dishonour to my Native Country; whose Language and Poetry wou'd be more esteem'd abroad, if they were better understood. Somewhat (give me leave to say) I have added to both of them in the choice of *Words*, and Harmony of Numbers which were wanting, especially the last, in all our Poets, even in those 20 who being endu'd with Genius, yet have not Cultivated their Mother-Tongue with sufficient Care; or relying on the Beauty of their Thoughts, have judg'd the Ornament of Words, and sweetness of Sound unnecessary. One is for raking in *Chaucer* (our *English Ennius*) for antiquated Words, which are never to be reviv'd, but when Sound or Significancy 25 is wanting in the present Language. But many of his deserve not this Redemption, any more than the Crouds of Men who daily die, or are slain for Six-pence in a Battel, merit to be restor'd to Life, if a Wish cou'd revive them. Others have no Ear for Verse, nor choice of Words; nor distinction of Thoughts; but mingle Farthings with their Gold to 30 make up the Sum. Here is a Field of Satire open'd to me: But since the Revolution, I have wholly renounc'd that Talent. For who wou'd give Physick to the Great when he is uncall'd? To do his Patient no good, and indanger himself for his Prescription? Neither am I ignorant, but I may justly be Condemn'd for many of those Faults, of which I have too 35 liberally Arraign'd others.

Cynthius Aurem vellit, & admonuit.

'Tis enough for me, if the Government will let me pass unquestion'd. In the mean time, I am oblig'd in gratitude, to return my Thanks to many of them, who have not only distinguish'd me from others of the 40 same Party, by a particular exception of Grace, but without considering the Man, have been Bountiful to the Poet: Have encourag'd *Virgil* to speak such *English*, as I could teach him, and rewarded his Interpreter, for the pains he has taken in bringing him over into *Britain*, by defraying the Charges of his Voyage. Even *Cerberus*, when he had receiv'd the 45 Sop, permitted *Æneas* to pass freely to *Elysium*. Had it been offer'd me, and I had refus'd it, yet still some gratitude is due to such who were willing to oblige me. But how much more to those from whom I have receiv'd the Favours which they have offer'd to one of a different Perswasion. Amongst whom I cannot omit naming the Earls of *Darby* 50 and of *Peterborough*. To the first of these, I have not the Honour to be known; and therefore his liberality was as much unexpected, as it was undeserv'd. The present Earl of *Peterborough* has been pleas'd long since to accept the tenders of my Service: His Favours are so frequent to me, that I receive them almost by prescription. No difference of Interests 55 or Opinion have been able to withdraw his Protection from me: And I might justly be condemn'd for the most unthankful of Mankind, if I did not always preserve for him a most profound Respect and inviolable Gratitude. I must also add, that if the last *Æneid* shine amongst its Fellows, 'tis owing to the Commands of Sir *William Trumball*, one of the 60 Principal Secretaries of State, who recommended it, as his Favourite, to my Care: and for his sake particularly I have made it mine. For who wou'd confess weariness, when he enjoin'd a fresh Labour? I cou'd not but invoke the assistance of a Muse, for this last Office.

> *Extremum hunc Arethusa:————* 65
> *————Neget quis Carmina Gallo?*

Neither am I to forget the Noble Present which was made me by *Gilbert Dolben* Esq; the worthy Son of the late Arch-Bishop of *York*: who, when I began this Work, enrich'd me with all the several Editions of *Virgil*, and all the Commentaries of those Editions in *Latine*. Amongst 70 which, I cou'd not but prefer the *Dolphins*; as the last, the shortest, and the most Judicious. *Fabrini* I had also sent me from *Italy*; but either he understands *Virgil* very imperfectly, or I have no knowledge of my Author.

Being Invited by that worthy Gentleman, Sir *William Bowyer*, to 75

Denham-Court, I Translated the first *Georgic* at his House, and the greatest part of the last *Æneid*. A more friendly Entertainment no Man ever
found. No wonder therefore if both those Versions surpass the rest, and
own the satisfaction I receiv'd in his Converse, with whom I had the
honour to be bred in *Cambridge*, and in the same College. The Seventh 80
Æneid was made English at *Burleigh*, the Magnificent Abode of the
Earl of *Exeter*: In a Village belonging to his Family I was born, and
under his Roof I endeavour'd to make that *Æneid* appear in English
with as much lustre as I cou'd: though my Author has not given the
finishing strokes either to it, or to the Eleventh, as I perhaps cou'd 85
prove in both, if I durst presume to Criticise my Master.

By a Letter from *Will. Walsh* of *Abberley* Esq; (who has so long
honour'd me with his Friendship, and who, without flattery, is the
best Critick of our Nation,) I have been inform'd that his Grace the
Duke of *Shrewsbury* has procur'd a Printed Copy of the *Pastorals*, *Georgics*, 90
and six first *Æneids*, from my Bookseller, and has read them in the
Country, together with my Friend. This Noble Person having been
pleas'd to give them a Commendation, which I presume not to insert;
has made me vain enough to boast of so great a favour, and to think I
have succeeded beyond my hopes; the Character of his Excellent Judg- 95
ment, the acuteness of his Wit, and his general Knowledge of good
Letters, being known as well to all the World, as the sweetness of his
disposition, his Humanity, his easiness of access, and desire of obliging
those who stand in need of his protection, are known to all who have
approach'd him; and to me in particular, who have formerly had the 100
honour of his Conversation. Whoever has given the World the Translation of part of the third *Georgic*, which he calls *The Power of Love*, has
put me to sufficient pains to make my own not inferiour to his: As my
Lord *Roscommon's* *Silenus* had formerly given me the same trouble. The
most Ingenious Mr. *Addison* of *Oxford* has also been as troublesome to 105
me as the other two, and on the same account. After his Bees, my latter
Swarm is scarcely worth the hiving. Mr. *Cowley's* praise of a Countrey
Life is Excellent; but 'tis rather an imitation of *Virgil*, than a Version.
That I have recover'd in some measure the health which I had lost by
too much application to this Work, is owing, next to God's Mercy, to 110
the Skill and Care of Dr. *Guibbons*, and Dr. *Hobbs*, the two Ornaments
of their Profession; whom I can only pay by this Acknowledgment.
The whole Faculty has always been ready to oblige me: and the only
one of them who endeavour'd to defame me, had it not in his power. I
desire pardon from my Readers for saying so much in relation to my 115

self, which concerns not them: and with my acknowledgments to all
my Subscribers, have only to add, that the few Notes which follow, are
par maniere d'acquit, because I had oblig'd my self by Articles, to do
somewhat of that kind. These scattering Observations are rather
guesses at my Author's meaning in some passages, than proofs that so   120
he meant. The Unlearn'd may have recourse to any Poetical Dictionary
in *English*, for the Names of Persons, Places, or Fables, which the Learned
need not: But that little which I say, is either new or necessary. And
the first of these qualifications never fails to invite a Reader, if not to
please him.   125

Alexander's Feast;
OR THE POWER OF MUSIQUE.
AN ODE,
In HONOUR of St. CECILIA's Day

I

'TWAS at the Royal Feast, for *Persia* won,
    By *Philip*'s Warlike Son:
  Aloft in awful State
  The God-like Heroe sate
    On his Imperial Throne: 5
His valiant Peers were plac'd around;
Their Brows with Roses and with Myrtles bound.
(So shou'd Desert in Arms be Crown'd:)
The Lovely *Thais* by his side,
Sate like a blooming *Eastern* Bride   10
In Flow'r of Youth and Beauty's Pride.
  Happy, happy, happy Pair!
  None but the Brave
  None but the Brave
  None but the Brave deserves the Fair.   15

CHORUS

Happy, happy, happy Pair!
None but the Brave
None but the Brave
None but the Brave deserves the Fair.

II

Timotheus plac'd on high   20
  Amid the tuneful Quire,
  With flying Fingers touch'd the Lyre:
The trembling Notes ascend the Sky,
    And Heav'nly Joys inspire.

Alexander's Feast. Text from the first edition, 1697, collated with Fables Ancient and Modern, *1700*

The Song began from *Jove*; 25
Who left his blissful Seats above,
(Such is the Pow'r of mighty Love.)
A Dragon's fiery Form bely'd the God:
Sublime on Radiant Spires He rode,
    When He to fair *Olympia* press'd: 30
    And while He sought her snowy Breast:
Then, round her slender Waste he curl'd,
And stamp'd an Image of himself, a Sov'raign of the World.
The list'ning Crowd admire the lofty Sound,
A present Deity, they shout around: 35
A present Deity the vaulted Roofs rebound.
        With ravish'd Ears
        The Monarch hears,
        Assumes the God,
        Affects to nod, 40
    And seems to shake the Spheres.

CHORUS

*   With ravish'd Ears*
*   The Monarch hears,*
*   Assumes the God,*
*   Affects to Nod,* 45
*   And seems to shake the Spheres.*

III

The Praise of *Bacchus* then, the sweet Musician sung;
    Of *Bacchus* ever Fair, and ever Young:
        The jolly God in Triumph comes;
        Sound the Trumpets; beat the Drums: 50
        Flush'd with a purple Grace
        He shews his honest Face,
Now give the Hautboys breath; He comes, He comes.
    Bacchus ever Fair and Young,
        Drinking Joys did first ordain: 55
    Bacchus Blessings are a Treasure;
    Drinking is the Soldiers Pleasure;
        Rich the Treasure,
        Sweet the Pleasure;
        Sweet is Pleasure after Pain. 60

CHORUS

Bacchus Blessings are a Treasure;
Drinking is the Soldier's Pleasure;
 Rich the Treasure,
 Sweet the Pleasure;
Sweet is Pleasure after Pain.   65

IV

 Sooth'd with the Sound the King grew vain;
  Fought all his Battails o'er again;
And thrice He routed all his Foes; and thrice He slew the slain.
   The Master saw the Madness rise;
   His glowing Cheeks, his ardent Eyes; 70
  And while He Heav'n and Earth defy'd,
  Chang'd his hand, and check'd his Pride.
    He chose a Mournful Muse
    Soft Pity to infuse:
   He sung *Darius* Great and Good, 75
    By too severe a Fate,
   Fallen, fallen, fallen, fallen,
    Fallen from his high Estate
    And weltring in his Blood:
 Deserted at his utmost Need, 80
 By those his former Bounty fed:
 On the bare Earth expos'd He lyes,
 With not a Friend to close his Eyes.

 With down-cast Looks the joyless Victor sate,
  Revolveing in his alter'd Soul 85
   The various Turns of Chance below;
  And, now and then, a Sigh he stole;
  And Tears began to flow.

CHORUS

Revolveing in his alter'd Soul
 The various Turns of Chance below; 90
And, now and then, a Sigh he stole;
 And Tears began to flow.

61 *Treasure; 1700: Treasure,* 97

V

The Mighty Master smil'd to see
That Love was in the next Degree:
'Twas but a Kindred-Sound to move;   95
For Pity melts the Mind to Love.
    Softly sweet, in *Lydian* Measures,
    Soon He sooth'd his Soul to Pleasures.
    War, he sung, is Toil and Trouble;
    Honour but an empty Bubble.   100
        Never ending, still beginning,
    Fighting still, and still destroying,
        If the World be worth thy Winning,
    Think, O think, it worth Enjoying.
        Lovely *Thais* sits beside thee,   105
        Take the Good the Gods provide thee.

The Many rend the Skies, with loud Applause;
So Love was Crown'd, but Musique won the Cause.
    The Prince, unable to conceal his Pain,
        Gaz'd on the Fair   110
        Who caus'd his Care,
        And sigh'd and look'd, sigh'd and look'd,
    Sigh'd and look'd, and sigh'd again:
At length, with Love and Wine at once oppress'd,
The vanquish'd Victor sunk upon her Breast.   115

CHORUS

    The Prince, unable to conceal his Pain,
        Gaz'd on the Fair
        Who caus'd his Care,
    And sigh'd and look'd, sigh'd and look'd,
    Sigh'd and look'd, and sigh'd again: 120
At length, with Love and Wine at once oppress'd,
The vanquish'd Victor sunk upon her Breast.

VI

Now strike the Golden Lyre again:
A lowder yet, and yet a lowder Strain.

Break his Bands of Sleep asunder, 125
And rouze him, like a rattling Peal of Thunder.
Hark, hark, the horrid Sound
Has rais'd up his Head,
As awak'd from the Dead,
And amaz'd, he stares around. 130
Revenge, Revenge, *Timotheus* cries,
See the Furies arise!
See the Snakes that they rear,
How they hiss in their Hair,
And the Sparkles that flash from their Eyes! 135
Behold a ghastly Band,
Each a Torch in his Hand!
Those are *Grecian* Ghosts, that in Battail were slayn,
And unbury'd remain
Inglorious on the Plain. 140
Give the Vengeance due
To the Valiant Crew.
Behold how they toss their Torches on high,
How they point to the *Persian* Abodes,
And glitt'ring Temples of their Hostile Gods! 145
The Princes applaud, with a furious Joy;
And the King seyz'd a Flambeau, with Zeal to destroy;
Thais led the Way,
To light him to his Prey,
And, like another *Hellen*, fir'd another *Troy*. 150

CHORUS

And the King seyz'd a Flambeau, with Zeal to destroy;
Thais *led the Way,*
To light him to his Prey,
And, like another Hellen, *fir'd another* Troy.

VII

Thus, long ago 155
'Ere heaving Bellows learn'd to blow,
While Organs yet were mute;
Timotheus, to his breathing Flute,
And sounding Lyre,

Cou'd swell the Soul to rage, or kindle soft Desire.   160
   At last Divine *Cecilia* came,
   Inventress of the Vocal Frame;
The sweet Enthusiast, from her Sacred Store,
   Enlarg'd the former narrow Bounds,
   And added Length to solemn Sounds,   165
With Nature's Mother-Wit, and Arts unknown before.
   Let old *Timotheus* yield the Prize,
   Or both divide the Crown;
   He rais'd a Mortal to the Skies;
   She drew an Angel down.   170

Grand CHORUS

At last Divine Cecilia *came,*
Inventress of the Vocal Frame;
The sweet Enthusiast, from her Sacred Store,
Enlarg'd the former narrow Bounds,
And added Length to solemn Sounds,   175
With Nature's Mother-Wit, and Arts unknown before.
Let old Timotheus *yield the Prize,*
Or both divide the Crown;
He rais'd a Mortal to the Skies;
She drew an Angel down.   180

To Mr. *GRANVILLE*, on his Excellent Tragedy, call'd *HEROICK LOVE*

AUSPICIOUS Poet, wert thou not my Friend,
  How could I envy, what I must commend!
But since 'tis Natures Law in Love and Wit
That Youth shou'd Reign, and with'ring Age submit,
With less regret, those Lawrels I resign,   5
Which dying on my Brows, revive on thine.
With better Grace an Ancient Chief may yield
The long contended Honours of the Field,
Than venture all his Fortune at a Cast,
And Fight, like *Hannibal*, to lose at last.   10

To Mr. Granville. Text from Heroick Love: A Tragedy, *1698*

Young Princes Obstinate to win the Prize,
Thô Yearly beaten, Yearly yet they rise:
Old Monarchs though Successful, still in Doubt,
Catch at a Peace; and wisely turn Devout.
Thine be the Lawrel then; thy blooming Age   15
Can best, if any can, support the Stage:
Which so declines, that shortly we may see,
Players and Plays reduc'd to second Infancy.
Sharp to the World, but thoughtless of Renown,
They Plot not on the Stage, but on the Town,   20
And in Despair their Empty Pit to fill,
Set up some Foreign Monster in a Bill:
Thus they jog on; still tricking, never thriving;
And Murd'ring Plays, which they miscal Reviving.
Our Sense is Nonsense, through their Pipes convey'd;   25
Scarce can a Poet know the Play He made;
'Tis so disguis'd in Death: Nor thinks 'tis He
That suffers in the Mangled Tragedy.
Thus *Itys* first was kill'd, and after dress'd
For his own Sire the Chief Invited Guest.   30
I say not this of thy successful Scenes;
Where thine was all the Glory, theirs the Gains;
With length of Time, much Judgment, and more Toil,
Not ill they Acted, what they cou'd not spoil:
Their Setting-Sun still shoots a Glim'ring Ray,   35
Like Ancient *Rome*, Majestick in decay:
And better gleanings, their worn Soil can boast,
Then the Crab-Vintage of the Neighb'ring Coast.
This difference, yet the judging World will see;
Thou Copiest *Homer*, and they Copy thee.   40

To my Friend, the *AUTHOR*
[PETER MOTTEUX]

'TIS hard, my Friend, to write in such an Age,
    As damns not only Poets, but the Stage.
That sacred Art, by Heav'n it self infus'd,

To Peter Motteux. Text from Motteux's Beauty in Distress. A Tragedy, *1698*

Which *Moses*, *David*, *Salomon* have us'd,
Is now to be no more: The Muses Foes 5
Wou'd sink their Maker's Praises into Prose.
Were they content to prune the lavish Vine
Of straggling Branches, and improve the Wine,
Who but a mad Man wou'd his Faults defend?
All wou'd submit; for all but Fools will mend. 10
But, when to common sense they give the Lie,
And turn distorted Words to Blasphemy,
They give the Scandal; and the Wise discern,
Their Glosses teach an Age too apt to learn.
What I have loosly, or profanely writ, 15
Let them to Fires (their due desert) commit.
Nor, when accus'd by me, let *them* complain:
Their Faults and not their Function I arraign.
Rebellion, worse than Witchcraft, they pursu'd:
The Pulpit preach'd the Crime; the People ru'd. 20
The Stage was silenc'd: for the Saints wou'd see
In fields perform'd their plotted Tragedy.
But let us first reform: and then so live,
That we may teach our Teachers to forgive.
Our Desk be plac'd below their lofty Chairs, 25
Ours be the Practice, as the Precept theirs.
The moral part at least we may divide,
Humility reward, and punish Pride:
Ambition, Int'rest, Avarice accuse:
These are the Province of the Tragic Muse. 30
These hast thou chosen; and the public Voice
Has equal'd thy performance, with thy choice.
Time, Action, Place, are so preserv'd by thee
That ev'n *Corneille*, might with envy see
Th' Alliance of his tripled Unity. 35
Thy Incidents, perhaps, too thick are sown;
But too much Plenty is thy fault alone:
At least but two, can that good Crime commit;
Thou in Design, and *Wycherley* in Wit.
Let thy own *Gauls* condemn thee if they dare; 40
Contented to be thinly regular.
Born there, but not for them, our fruitful Soil
With more Increase rewards thy happy Toil.

Their Tongue infeebled, is refin'd so much,
That, like pure Gold, it bends at ev'ry touch: 45
Our sturdy *Teuton*, yet will Art obey,
More fit for manly thought, and strengthen'd with Allay.
But whence art thou inspir'd, and Thou alone
To flourish in an Idiom, not thine own?
It moves our wonder, that a foreign Guest   50
Shou'd over-match the most, and match the best.
In underpraising, thy Deserts I wrong:
Here, find the first deficience of our Tongue:
Words, once my stock, are wanting to commend
So Great a Poet, and so Good a Friend.   55

PRINTED IN
GREAT BRITAIN
AT THE
UNIVERSITY PRESS
OXFORD
BY
CHARLES BATEY
PRINTER
TO THE
UNIVERSITY